SEXUAL HEALING

Reference Edition

REVISED AND EXPANDED

A Biblical Guide to Finding Freedom from Every Major Area of Sexual Sin and Brokenness

LAURUS BOOKS

OTHER EFFECTIVE TOOLS AVAILABLE BY
MASTERING LIFE MINISTRIES

- *Articles/Radio/Conference Podcasts/Videos*
  - www.MasteringLife.org

- *Documentaries*
  - www.SuchWereSomeOfYou.org
  - www.HowDoYouLikeMeNow.org
  - www.TranZformed.org
  - www.BrokenAndPouredOut.org

- *Online Store*
  - http://purepassion.us/shop/store

- *Pure Passion Apps/Streaming Channels*
  - iPhone and Android
  - AmazonFire TV, Apple TV, Google TV, iTunes, Roku (U.S. and Europe)

- *Pure Passion TV*
  - www.PurePassion.us

- *Social Media*
  - www.facebook.com/purepassiontv
  - www.twitter.com/purepassiontv
  - www.cross.tv/profile/175377?go=videos
  - www.YouTube.com/user/davidkylefoster

MASTERING LIFE MINISTRIES is a Christian organization whose mission is to equip the saints for the ministry of the church through seminars, lectures, courses, radio, television, film, and other forms of media.

We specialize in areas of modern life where people have been trapped by issues that tap into the emotional fabric of life—issues such as sexual sin and brokenness, anger management, cults and religions, etc.

We attempt to show that through intimacy with God the Father, the traumas of life, the allures of the world, and the deviances of the heart can all be overcome in the light of the glorious truth about our God and His Son, Jesus Christ.

SEXUAL HEALING

Reference Edition
REVISED AND EXPANDED

A Biblical Guide to Finding Freedom from Every Major Area of Sexual Sin and Brokenness

Equipping the Saints to do the Ministry of the Church

by a Servant of Jesus Christ

COMMENTS FROM SOME WHO

A much needed source of guidance for handling the multiplicity issues that make up sexual bondage and brokenness. This book is truly unique and one that I highly recommend.
Nancy Alcorn, Mercy Multiplied

God miraculously saved David from a sexually depraved lifestyle and equipped him to be a voice of hope for those who are trapped in the bondage of sexual immorality.
Dr. Neil T. Anderson, Freedom in Christ Ministries

I love the way this book lays out biblical, foundational principles that are essential to finding freedom from every kind of sin and brokenness. Dr. Foster's book is a vital resource for a world drowning in sexual sin and brokenness.
Mike Bickle, International House of Prayer

There is a lifetime of wisdom in this book that has the breadth needed to apply to your life.
Andrew Comiskey, Desert Stream Ministries

A major tour de force—an incredible achievement ... Thorough, frank, scripturally sound, practical, a beacon of hope ... Simply masterful ... Must be read by pastors, church leaders, and ministers of healing ... I will be unconditionally recommending it to all our leaders and ministry teams.
Peter Horrobin, Founder, Ellel Ministries

From the pen of one who has been there and who understands the pain, the hunger, the longing, the tears. I would love to see this book in the hands of every therapist, researcher, parent, pastor, as well as the sexually broken person.
Clay McLean, Director of McLean Ministries

Highly recommended!
Dr. Jerry Newcombe, D. James Kennedy Ministries

People who need help, direction and encouragement will benefit immensely from this masterpiece!
Larry Tomczak, The Awareness Group

I am delighted to recommend this book for its outstanding insights and forthright "no compromise" approach to such a difficult subject.
Jill Southern, Ellel Ministries, SE Asia and China

HAVE FOUND THIS BOOK HELPFUL

This textbook belongs in the library of every Christian counselor and deliverance minister out there! David masterfully explains the major sexual sins and addictions, examines their root causes, and offers suggested paths to freedom.
Doris Wagner, Global Spheres

Dr. Foster's book is a critical resource for helping pastors, counselors, ministry leaders, and support groups. This major reference work is unique not only for "equipping the saints" for ministry, but also as a tool for leading the broken into the presence of God so they can pursue and receive His transforming power.
Christopher West, Theology of the Body Institute

Recommendations from the First Edition

David Foster's book is important. I pray that it will be widely read. Its contribution is unique.
The late Dr. John White, Christian author and psychiatrist

I am impressed with the very solid, spiritual basis from which you work; and I can imagine that God has used your teaching material in a significant way.
Dr. Timothy Warner, Trinity Evangelical Divinity School

David's teaching on sexual healing received high praise from many quarters. I recommend both David and his teaching materials to you without hesitation.
Davide DeCarvalho, Youth With A Mission

I am most impressed by your book on sexuality. I can certainly recommend it for use by those who are struggling with their sexuality.
Dr. Archibald Hart, Fuller Theological Seminary

I am very much impressed with both its excellent quality and David Foster's own personal testimony, which speaks so eloquently of the glory of a loving and merciful God. Its sound, biblical base certainly qualifies it as an excellent resource, and I have recommended it for use in Prison Fellowship.
Linda Andrews, Prison Fellowship USA

I give my unqualified recommendation of David Foster. His book should be in the library of every pastor and counselor. The church desperately needs this specialized ministry.
Arthelene Rippy, Christian Television Network

All scripture quotations, unless otherwise indicated, are taken from the Holy Bible, New International Version, NIV. Copyright © 1973, 1978, 1984 by International Bible Society. Used by permission of Zondervan Publishing House. All rights reserved.

Scripture quotations marked NASB are from the New American Standard Bible. Copyright © 1960, 1962, 1963, 1968, 1971, 1972, 1973, 1975, 1977 by the Lockman Foundation. Used by permission.

Scripture quotations marked "author" are translations by the author.

First published in the United States of America 1995 by:
MASTERING LIFE MINISTRIES
P.O. Box 1802, Mount Juliet, TN 37121

This Edition Copyright © 2018 DAVID KYLE FOSTER

All rights reserved. In accordance with the U.S. Copyright Act of 1976, the scanning, uploading, and electronic sharing of any part of this book without the permission of the publisher is unlawful piracy and theft of the author's intellectual property. If you would like to use material from the book (other than for review purposes), prior written permission must be obtained by contacting the publisher at: laurus@thelauruscompany.com.

Paperback Book: ISBN: 978-1-943523-20-7

Questions, comments or invitations for speaking engagements:
> *MASTERING LIFE MINISTRIES*
> P.O. Box 1802
> Mount Juliet, TN 37121
> Internet: www.MasteringLife.org

Published by Laurus Books

LAURUS BOOKS
a division of
THE LAURUS COMPANY, INC.
www.TheLaurusCompany.com

This book is available in paperback from TheLaurusCompany.com, Amazon.com, ChristianBooks.com, BarnesAndNoble.com, and most other retailers around the world. Available to retailers at Spring Arbor. Also available in formats for electronic readers from their respective stores.

Table of Contents

DEDICATION	9
FROM THE AUTHOR – CHRIST IN ME	11

PART ONE: LAYING THE FOUNDATIONS

Foreword – 1st Edition	17
Foreword – Reference Edition	19
How to Use This Book	21
Introduction	23
Foundations for Healing Sexual Brokenness	26
Study Section—Foundations—Truth Therapy	33
Exercises—Foundations	43
Living by Grace Rather Than Performance Orientation	45
Study Section—Grace vs. Performance Orientation	57
Exercises—Grace vs. Performance Orientation	67
The Divine Intent for Sexuality	69
Study Section—The Divine Intent for Sexuality	77
Exercises—Divine Intent	85
God, My Father	87
Study Section—God, My Father	95
Exercises—God, My Father	101
Root Sources for Improper Sexual Development	103
Study Section—Root Sources	115
Exercises—Root Sources	121

PART TWO: SPECIFIC DYSFUNCTIONS

The Causes of Sexual Identity Confusion	125
Study Section—Sexual Identity Confusion: Causes	143
The Healing of Sexual Identity Confusion	175
Study Section—Sexual Identity Confusion: Healing	199
Exercises—Sexual Identity Confusion	217
Child Sex Abuse: The Predator	219
Child Sex Abuse: The Survivor	233
Study Section—Child Sex Abuse	245
Exercises—Child Sex Abuse	263
Sexual Addiction	265
Study Section—Sexual Addiction	281
Exercises—Sexual Addiction	303
Pornography	305
Study Section—Pornography	315
Exercises—Pornography	325
Masturbation	327
Study Section—Masturbation	343
Exercises—Masturbation	355

Voyeurism and Exhibitionism 357
    Study Section—Voyeurism and Exhibitionism 365
    Exercises—Voyeurism and Exhibitionism 371
Transgender Confusion 373
    Exercises—Transgender Confusion 385

PART THREE: COMPREHENSIVE HEALING
Why People Remain in Sexual Sin and Bondage 389
    Study Section—Why People Remain in Bondage 401
    Exercises—Why People Remain in Bondage 409
Failure and Self-Condemnation 411
    Study Section—Failure and Self-Condemnation 415
    Exercises—Failure and Self-Condemnation 421
A Comprehensive Game Plan for Sexual Healing 423
    Study Section—Comprehensive Game Plan 445
    Exercises—Comprehensive Game Plan 463
    Study Section—You As Minister 465
    Exercises—You As Minister 471
Miscellaneous Issues 473

PART FOUR: APPENDICES
Appendix I   Recommended Reading List 487
Appendix II A Brief Worship Guide 493
Appendix III Resource Directory 495

ABOUT THE AUTHOR 499

I DEDICATE THIS BOOK ENTIRELY
TO THE GLORY OF JESUS CHRIST,
MY LOVING HEAVENLY FATHER,
AND THE PRECIOUS HOLY SPIRIT.

From the Author –
Christ in Me

When I was very young, perhaps eight or nine, I began a lifelong habit of compulsive masturbation, though I didn't recognize what it was at the time. I was going through a great deal of stress, including a suicide attempt at the age of nine or ten. This soon led to a problem with pornography, which eventually became so much of an obsession that I began taking pornographic pictures of myself and others. Eventually, I even rented my home out to pornographic film crews just so I could watch. I came very close to participating, but feared damage to my film career. Ironically, I did a nude scene in the first legitimate film that I was in. Shortly thereafter, I began modeling nude for art classes and frequenting nude beaches, exhibiting all of the classic symptoms and behaviors of a full blown voyeur/exhibitionist.

My homosexual involvement began out of curiosity over what sex would be like with a male, soon after losing my virginity to a girl my age. The sexual relationship with the girl was fine, but there was something missing and I set out to find what it was.

I was young and looked even younger, and discovered while hitchhiking, that I was the idealized catch of pedophiles everywhere. I was constantly besieged with desperate pleas by them to let them touch me in intimate ways. It was the only way I knew to satisfy my acute need to be wanted. It was also the only way I knew to exert power and influence over others. In Hollywood, the worship and admiration of some of the world's most wealthy, powerful and famous men was an elixir far too sweet for me to pass up and I lived a double life as a heterosexual actor and male prostitute. The idea that I was a frustrated heterosexual thrilled the men who picked me up, and it allowed me to abstain from doing sexual things to them. Otherwise, I would probably have died from AIDS long ago.

By my middle twenties, I was a full-blown sex addict, having as many as four or five sexual encounters per night. Many times I would end an evening of prostitution by picking someone up at the local disco. I also put personal ads in the local sex newspaper in order to attract a never-ending supply of predators. I even put ads in the paper seeking to be kept by rich women. Some evenings, in the early morning hours, I would be driven to run nude through the Hollywood Hills, hiding in the bushes if someone happened by. It was something I was unable to stop myself from doing. It was very bizarre. There simply was nothing I could do to satisfy the physical, emotional and demonic cravings that ruled my life.

After ten years of this, Jesus Christ moved into my life. After discovering that He loved even me, I fell madly in love with Him. It was a discovery that still fires my soul deep within.

When I finally walked into Hollywood Presbyterian Church and asked to see one of the pastors, I knew that I was about to begin a long, long road to recovery from many compulsions and addictions. But what surprised me the most was being told that I didn't have to overcome anything—that Jesus would do it all for me. All I had to do was develop an intimate relationship with Him, sincerely desire that He change me, and then do whatever He asked me to do.

In that first session with Pastor Jack Loo, I was instantly delivered from the *compulsion* to act out my sexual desires because I learned that it was God's power that would do it, not my own. Ever since that day (some thirty-eight years at the time of this writing), I have not once had sexual relations with another person. Overnight, something that I could not help but do was overpowered by God Almighty.

I certainly have had temptations to sin the old sins, but the uncontrollable compulsion to give in has been quenched by the power of God's Holy Spirit. And that is God's promise to you, too, if you are serious about making Jesus the *Lord* of your life.

As for reorientation to heterosexuality, that has taken many years because of the ten years of involvement in homosexual encounters. God has taken me through a slowly evolving process of healing and recovery. From time to time, He points out an environmental factor that contributes to my problem and gives me the power to choose to remove it from my life. Every few months, He reveals another source of my emotional dysfunction and encourages me to ask Him to heal it. Then He does! Sometimes, He shows me an area of willful sin, or someone I need to forgive. But He does it at the pace that I can handle—not all at once. During the years following my first meeting with Pastor Loo, I have seen a resurgence of heterosexual desire. He has shown me how I picked up an aberrant view of the opposite sex, and has instructed me on His perfect intent for sexuality. I have on many occasions felt His power enter me to heal and to rebuild.

There have been temptations all along the way, and the potential is always there to reinflame those old passions, but as long as I am faithful to God, He continues to supply me with all the power I need not to respond to the tempter.

In my relationship with the Father, He has provided me with the bonding that I missed as a child. He has provided me with the unconditional love and acceptance that I so desperately sought in sexual relationships. He has shown Himself faithful as the supplier of all my needs, so that there no longer remains a bondage to pornography or masturbation or illicit sexual relationships. Whenever I feel those old feelings, He is there to quench their power, if I cry out to Him to do so.

He has delivered me from the demonic strongholds that made my sins so uncontrollably compulsive. As far as I can tell, He delivered me from at least 12 demons. In my early days as a new Christian, He gave me the presence of mind and the faith to cast them out, one by one, in the name of Jesus, and after just a few short weeks, they were completely gone.

Even when I fell briefly back into sin—once by looking at a porno magazine in an airport; and repeatedly for a while through compulsive masturbation—God remained faithful to me, not to condemn me for failing, but to be there when I was through, to forgive me and show me how to better resist the next time. Because of His loving, grace-filled approach in healing me, there hasn't been a recurrence of either of those sins for many years now (at the time of this writing, 38 years of sobriety from pornography and 10 years of sobriety from masturbation). The thought of going back to them is now ludicrous to me. Praise His holy name! And as long as I abide in Him, God's power will be there to keep me from falling for the rest of my life, and for all eternity. For whom the Son of Man sets free is free indeed (cf. John 8:36)!

God has healed me from the inside out, so that I no longer want to, or need to, commit sexual sin in order to assuage some inner emotional or psychological need. He has also given me the grace to survive these many years of celibacy—for someone as sexually active as I was, a life sentence. I had a lot to be healed from, however, and when I asked Him at one point to remove the fire from my sexual urges, He did so. It is heaven!

I'm telling you as one who *knows,* God will heal you, too. Pursue Him with all your heart; ask for what you need; ask persistently and fervently; respond to His direction; and be healed.

PART ONE:
LAYING THE FOUNDATIONS

Foreword - First Edition

We live in an exceptional age. Technology has turned the world into a village, yet a nuclear cloud threatens to bloom mushroom-like over our heads. Political events quicken their pace. Doomsday prophets, as they have always done, predict the end of the age. Yet, never has an age provided more grounds for their threats. After all, the world has to end sometime. Why not soon?

There are signs that the Church might be getting ready for the end times. New powers are poured out on her. New judgment threatens. Hidden evils are coming to light. Sins long secret are made naked before the public. There is also a much greater awareness of God's power to deliver, a new turning to God from sin.

Years ago I used to insist that there were worse sins than sexual sins. And so there are. It is what sexual sins do to you that makes them bad. They lead to lies. Lies you tell others. Worse still, lies you tell yourself until you believe those lies. Then is born pride—the worse sin of all—the sin that makes Satan satanic.

The most terrible sexual sins are those sins we commit against children and young people. They, too, are coming to light. Soon it will no longer be possible to hide them. As prophetic powers are restored to the church, shame and deceit will have no corner to skulk in.

In my role as a psychiatrist I have known about these things and their appalling extent among Christians. I have tried to cry out, but few people would listen. "You are just like all the psychiatrists—hung up on sex!" they told me. On the contrary, I was concerned with exploiters and their victims. Molesters and their quarries represent Satan's triumphs. I knew that a grieving God was waiting to cleanse His church from the plunderings of Satan. The time for God to do so has now come. A new flood of literature begins to pour from the presses, both secular and Christian, crying out against the evils of sexual exploitation.

That is why David Foster's book is important. It gives us an accurate picture not only of what it feels like to be a victim of sexual abuse, but of the resulting lifestyle of the abused. More important still, it is a book that sings with the joy of a man who has been delivered. It is a book that awakens us to an awareness of what is going on, and what God is waiting to do to correct the damage.

I pray that this book will be widely read as it takes its place among other books on the subject. Its contribution is unique.

The Late Dr. JOHN WHITE

Foreword - Reference Edition

It's one thing to identify a problem. It's another thing entirely to provide a solution to the problem. That's why it's so important for ministry leaders to function like good doctors, not only diagnosing the sickness but also prescribing the cure. And that is exactly what David Kyle Foster has done in this comprehensive book. He himself has "been there and done it," spending years deeply bound by sexual sin and perversion, only to experience healing, liberty, deliverance, and freedom in Jesus. He is living proof that the cure really works!

David first lays a strong spiritual foundation before tackling specific issues. This, alone, can be transformative, and I'm so glad he started right here. How is your relationship with God? Are you affirmed as a child of the Father? Do you know the power of His grace? How does a healthy sexuality compare to an unhealthy one? In all things, we are pointed back to the cross, the source of our healing and our repentance, and we are encouraged to lean on the Holy Spirit, who will guide us into all the truth—and that includes the truth about ourselves.

With these foundations laid, David then tackles the major issues of sexual brokenness and sin, from pornography to masturbation and from homosexuality to gender identity confusion. And with every chapter in the book, there is a study section, giving clear definitions and helpful overviews, followed by specific exercises. This book is practical!

Finally, David looks at the key reasons people do not walk in lasting freedom. He wants to see you make it. He wants you to succeed. He is cheering you on and giving you steps to take. You don't have to fall back, and you don't have to be enslaved. In fact, David believes, if you can learn to walk in freedom, you can help set others free, too.

I would encourage you to read the whole book in order, taking time to digest each chapter. But if your foundations are strong and you want to focus on one particular area, you can do that as well, going back later to read from the first page to the last.

May the same grace and truth that transformed David and countless millions of others transform you as well.

MICHAEL L. BROWN, PH.D., author of
A Queer Thing Happened to America and
Can You Be Gay and Christian?

How to Use This Book

This book is written to help you knowledgeably pray for counsel, or in other ways minister to someone you know who is trapped in sexual sin and brokenness. This book is written as if speaking to the person who needs help, so that by its example, you may learn how to help your friend. This design has the added benefit of allowing you to give this same book to the person who needs help for their own personal study.

This book contains first hand knowledge from someone who was as sexually bound as a person can get, and who God has miraculously forgiven, delivered and put in ministry in the very area where he was the most broken. I (David Kyle Foster) am that person, and in this book, I share with you what God taught me (directly and through others) as He healed and delivered me from every sexual bondage in this book. It contains both testimonial witness and knowledge. Often when people read about the awesome power and grace of God in healing one as depraved as I was, they are then inspired to believe that God will do the same for them.

This book is designed to provide not only informational reading, but to facilitate group and private study as well. Many chapters contain both a reading section and study section. Some provide one or the other. The study sections allow for quick reference for the friend counselor, as well as providing a framework for personal devotion and meditation for the hurting friend. Each study section concludes with a series of exercises that give practical guidance for the broken person who is wondering where to begin. I still use them today to wash and renew my mind during personal devotion time.

The back of this book contains suggestions for further reading (recommending the very books that God used in my life to set me free), as well as additional Christian-based counseling resources.

This manual is designed to give you one resource to turn to after you have turned to the Lord and asked for guidance. It is for both you the counselor friend, and you the friend who needs counsel. May God richly bless you with the Spirit of wisdom and revelation and may He lavishly pour out upon you His awesome power to make and to keep you holy. That is your inheritance in Christ. Take it!

Introduction

I was sitting quietly, waiting for the afternoon session of the conference to begin. The sounds of the waiting crowd made a wonderfully diffuse background for my thoughts. The morning session had been helpful, but nothing I hadn't heard before, and so I eagerly awaited the next topic—Sex and Shame. "Maybe there'll be something new for me to grab hold of," I thought. I wondered if they were going to tell it like it really is—practically, specifically, bluntly, instead of keeping it vague and theoretical like I had been hearing.

It had been a long time since I had been to an "Inner Healing" conference. I had kept away from them for a while until they had learned to eliminate guided imagery techniques—too much danger in getting messed up with demonic things that way. But I knew that God healed the inner man, and I wanted more of that.

"David!" The voice sounded familiar. "Was someone shouting at me?" I wondered.

"David!" There it was again. A nudge finally pulled me out of my thought trance. It was the pastor's wife.

"Oh, hi. Sorry. What can I do for you?" I asked.

"It's your testimony, the one you gave Bill to read."

"Yes. "

"Well, I was reading it, and the Holy Spirit suddenly came on me, and I think we should pray about it."

"Pray what?" I replied.

"I don't know. I just think we ought to pray. As I was reading it, the Holy Spirit just filled me for some reason."

I had never been confronted in such a strange way before, but what the heck, it was the pastor's wife. So, we prayed, and within seconds, the Holy Spirit started erupting from within me like a geyser—like a spring of living water.

"The Holy Spirit is doing something to me, too," I said.

"What does it mean?" she asked.

"I don't know either," I replied.

Then she looked me in the eye and said, "Do you think that perhaps

God wants you to share your sexual past with the group?"

I was stunned. How did she know about it? I had been very careful to be vague about the sexual part, in the paper I had given her husband, just in case it fell into the wrong hands. No one but a very few private counselors knew about my past. My best friends didn't know. My family didn't know. My pastor didn't even know! And she wanted me to just get up and tell the whole world? Was she crazy?!

Those were my thoughts, but not my words. It was clear that the Holy Spirit was orchestrating something here. Her suggestion did seem plausible, and I had promised the Lord that if He ever gave me a clear sign that He wanted me to tell it, I would. Before I had time to think further, I heard myself saying, "Okay."

Egad! Now I *was* crazy! "Oh, well, it's now or never," I concluded. And so I did. The scheduled speaker relinquished her time, and I suddenly became the center of attention for the entire seminar crowd. I had been ambushed by God! He knew I would only have the nerve to say yes if given no time to really think about it.

Boy, was I scared. But I also felt the power and presence of God inside, gently urging me on. It was my Father calling, and I loved Him, so I could not say no.

And so I began the story of my sexual past. God had told me that my life was a parable for others, and now I was telling the world the worst of it, on tape, no less!

In the course of my youth, I succeeded in enslaving myself to almost every sexual behavior known to man. I was a sex addict, compulsive and out of control. My inner motto was, "I'll try anything once," and with few exceptions, I did just that.

Bondage after bondage took hold during those years, so that when I was finally filled with God's Spirit and forgiveness at the age of 29, I was riddled with sexual, psychological, and emotional scars. I was an emotional corpse.

Beyond my private sexual life (crazy as it was), seven years spent on the streets of Hollywood as a male prostitute exposed me to absolutely everything, and I careened through life smashing into one perversion after the other, mercifully escaping only the most depraved activities.

Compulsive masturbation began before puberty. That led to encouraging inappropriate touching by other kids; next, pornography; then heterosexual promiscuity; homosexual activities, including abuse by pedophiles; exhibitionism; voyeurism; prostitution; group sex; satyriasis; the core problem being sexual addiction. By the time I reached 29, I considered myself insane, though technically I wasn't. I was taking absurd risks and doing things I did not even want to do. It was as if some force had captured me and was making me do its will.

If I was to ever return to the slightest semblance of normalcy, there had to be a God in heaven to carry it off. I was way beyond human help.

The wonderful end to the story is that I found that God, and He did restore me to normalcy, and more. He restored my innocence. Though I still have a mind that can remember what went before, God has given me the spirit of a child who has never known corruption or pain. Today, I even blush again.

This book is designed to encourage you to seek and find that same God—the one true God and Father of Jesus Christ—who is waiting to restore you. You are not too far gone. There is no such condition with God. His forgiveness extends to every inch of this universe and to every person in it who will come to Him like a child, humbly and contrite in spirit.

By the time I had finished sharing my story with the seminar crowd, there were few dry eyes. And when the leader asked if there was anyone who wanted to come forward for healing, over half of the crowd came forth. The power of the Holy Spirit not only drew them to the front, He began manifesting His presence with power, and many received God's healing touch that day.

I received a miraculous healing as well. By the time I had said my final sentence, God had begun shooting streams of power through my chest. I could feel His pleasure as He told me in His own way how happy He was over what I had done. It was wonderful to feel the pleasure of God and to know that I had caused it. It was a moment I will never forget.

In the process of exposing the sins that had remained hidden in the dark places of my soul, God's marvelous light was able to flood those murky regions, and I was profoundly freed from the hold that they had over me. You see, in keeping my real self hidden, I had never been able to be myself. I had been walking through life, as it were, with a mask on, and had prevented God's healing light from reaching the dark places.

I am not suggesting that you declare your sins to the world in the public way that I have. It was clearly a call from God for me to do so. But I am suggesting that until you find someone in the body of Christ with whom you can reveal your true self, God's full healing power will not be able to operate.

Once you have found that confidant, you are ready to begin the incredible journey of restoration and so receive God's healing for the scars of your sexual past. This book is designed not to give you steps that will get you healed, but to keep you on the right track for receiving God's plan for your individual healing. He will reveal to you precisely what you need to do to be healed. I can tell you how to stand under the light, but it is the Light who does the rest.

The one true God and Father of Jesus Christ is waiting to restore you. You are not too far gone. There is no such condition with God. His forgiveness extends to every inch of this universe and to every person in it who will come to Him, humble and contrite. He will heal you if you want Him to. He will forgive you if you ask Him to. No exceptions. That is how wonderful He is!

No matter what your sexual problem, God can heal it. In the following pages, I have addressed the more common sexual dysfunctions and what God has taught me on how to be healed from them. This is not an intellectual, theoretical exercise on what should work, but a real-life, practical testimonial of what does work. And to that extent, it is also a book of praise to the one and only Son of God, the Lord Jesus Christ, who alone can restore you to sexual health again.

It is important that you read every chapter in this book, even those that address problems that you do not have. There are principles in each that apply to more than just the sexual dysfunction being discussed in the chapter. For example, the chapter on "Sexual Identity Confusion" includes a prototype plan for healing any kind of profound sexual compulsion. Its principles can be used, with minor alterations, for problems with masturbation, pornography, sexual addiction, and more. At the very least, it will equip you to counsel someone you may know now or may meet in the future who suffers from that problem.

Once that kind of servant's heart has begun to rule your life, you will have uncovered one of the benchmark signs that God has been doing profound work in your inner man—the very place where He needs to work in order to heal you from your sexual problem.

This book is designed to provide scriptural truths about God's call to holiness, not only for individuals, but also for group study. After you have turned to the Lord and asked for guidance through His Word and in prayer, you can turn to this manual to help you remember the truth. It is for both you, the counselor friend, and you, the friend who needs counsel. May God richly bless you with the Spirit of wisdom and revelation, and may He lavishly pour out upon you His awesome power to make and to keep you holy. That is your inheritance in Christ.

Foundations for Healing Sexual Brokenness

As you begin your quest for sexual healing, it is important not to forget who does the healing (God does), and where the ability to achieve results comes from (it comes from God). The persistence of my capacity to believe that I am the source or the cause of goodness and positive achievement in my life always amazes me. Jesus could not have been more relevant to this issue when He said, "apart from Me you can do *nothing!"*

The principle of God's prevenient grace (coupled with our helplessness) saturates the entire Bible. We learn from Jesus in John 6:44: *"No one can come to (Christ) unless the Father draws him,"* and in John 6:65: *"no one can come to (Christ) unless it has been granted him from the Father"* (NASB). Jesus taught that *the fact that we believe in Him at all is "the work of God"* (John 6:29), that *we are,* in essence, *a gift from the Father to Christ* (John 6:37, 39).

Although we understand that we are saved not by our works, but by faith, we often miss the point that even our faith has been given us by the Father. "It is the gift of God" (Eph. 2:8). "We are His workmanship" (Eph. 2:10, NASB). "He called us according to His own purpose" (2 Tim. 1:9, NASB). "By His doing you are in Christ Jesus" (1 Cor. 1:30). *"It is God who is at work in you, both to will and to work for His good pleasure"* (Phil. 2:13, NASB). Do not think more highly of yourself than you ought to think, for *"God has allotted to each man a measure of faith"* (Rom. 12:3, NASB). It is "God who works all things in all persons" (1 Cor. 12:6, NASB).

The apostle Paul made it clear that *"by the grace of God I am what I am"* and that it was "not I, but the grace of God with me" that labored (1 Cor. 15:10, NASB). And again, in Hebrews 13:21, he said that it was Jesus Christ who equipped us to do His will and who "works in us that which is pleasing in His sight."

It was according to the will and purposes of Christ that we were predestined to be adopted as sons (Eph. 1:5, 11), and that it is Christ "who works all things after the counsel of His will" (Eph. 1:11, NASB), so that we will "be to the praise of His glory" (Eph. 1:12).

From Start to Finish—Christ Alone

The point that I'm trying to make is that if God had not lifted the veil from our eyes and given us the faith to believe, we could never have come to salvation, and that the same principle—that God is the author, equipper and inspirer of all right action—applies to everything of value that we will ever do, every healing that we will ever obtain, and everything that we will ever become. It is for that reason that it can be rightly said that all glory and honor belongs to God and God alone. When we cast our crowns before Him in that final day, it will not merely be a gesture of honor; it will be the only right thing to do!

Therefore, it is incumbent upon us, as we pursue sexual healing, to reject the tendency toward self-effort and self-striving (the idea that we are somehow responsible for healing ourselves or for initiating our own affirmative actions), so that God can bring about real fruit, and so He can work permanent and effective change into our lives.

When we try to heal ourselves (even using God's tools), or worse yet, when we try to create our own tools for healing (even those based on biblical models), we stand in the way of God's healing. For if we succeed in some measure to heal ourselves, God cannot receive the glory. This is a critical point to understand because it is the very purpose of creation to bring glory to the One who died for us.

Additionally, any healing wrought in such a deficient fashion will, by virtue of the fact that the construction was done by us rather than God, be faulty, and will eventually collapse (if not sooner, certainly at the last day when God burns everything that has not been wrought by Him). Similarly, if we use our own materials (e.g., the wisdom of man), the result will be significantly substandard.

If God alone is capable of doing these things, where does that leave us? Are we to simply do nothing and wait for Him to bring these things about? Of course not. We need to turn our attention to Him, actively recognizing that He is our source for every good thing. We must learn, habitually and with all dependence, to fix our gaze upon Him. As westerners, it kind of rubs us the wrong way to submit to the concept of complete dependence on God, or on anyone for that matter. It is un-American. It is weak, and it conflicts with our strong independent spirits. It requires a level of humility that we never even dreamed existed, much less considered a virtue. In a society such as our own that is ruled by the philosophy of humanism (there is nothing greater than man), humility is indeed a weakness. However, once we have discovered that there is a Creator God Who is far greater than man, humility then becomes wisdom.

After turning a dependent heart toward the Lord, we must, with all diligence, ask Him to accomplish good things in us. Then we need to step out of the way to let Him do it.

It might be good to ask yourself, "Where am I stuck?" Perhaps you don't even *want* to seek after God with all your heart. The Bible is very clear that it is those who diligently seek Him who receive a response from Him (Heb. 11:6; Jer. 29:13). For you, I would recommend beginning where you are; ask God to give you the desire that you lack. You know that it is God who works in us the desire to do His will, so ask Him to do just that.

This is more important than we may realize because if we pray for things simply because we know that we are "supposed" to pray for them, but we don't really want them deep down in our heart, or don't really expect that God will give them to us, then we will never get anywhere.

For many of us, a simple prayer of "HELP!" is what is needed. Do it; it works!

All of us can benefit from a closer and more intimate relationship with the Lord. So, why not pray that God will begin to reveal those things about Himself that will uniquely inspire you to go further with Him. A prayer for more faith is never wrong, or one for God to pour into your heart the love that the Father has for the Son. That's a firecracker prayer!

Be persistent! Don't stop praying for these things until you get them! It is when you want things with all your heart that the Father is pleased to give them to you, especially the things of high virtue.

The "Pearls Before Swine" Principle

God's actions are always purposeful. They expect a response. If you are not willing to comply with the requirements that accompany the help that you seek, don't expect that God will answer your prayer. For example, don't expect God to give you the supernatural grace to overcome compulsive masturbation if, when He imparts the necessary grace, you are unwilling to stop pursuing that behavior.

I call this the "pearls before swine" principle. In Matthew 7:6, Jesus suggested that we not give what is precious to those who do not yet regard it as precious. God will not impart to us the power to be holy until we have come to appreciate the value of such a gift. His Son bled and died for the grace that we seek, and so the Father treats it as a pearl of great price and will not toss it to those who will only trample it underfoot. Instead, He waits until we have learned to value it enough to hold on to it and to permanently integrate it into our lives once it has been given.

You will always be left with the choice of whether to stop a sinful behavior or not, even after the grace has been given to stop. That is when you may discover that, although you thought you were serious about wanting the purity of Christ in place of the sinful habit, you really didn't want complete victory after all.

Until you are ready to respond in faith to God's offer of aid, your fervent prayer should be for a greater revelation of Who Christ is and a more complete desire to be like Him. Then, the next time the grace is given, you will gladly cling to it as the precious treasure that it is.

Thus, it is in the context of seeking God and responding to Him with all your heart—by His empowerment—that the admonition to "let God do it" makes sense. Only in that atmosphere of hunger, dependency, and willingness to obey will God impart His holiness, reveal His perfect will, and entrust to you the power to overcome the evil one in your life. Then and only then can you be an effective channel of His blessing to others who are in the process of seeking to become more like Him, but who may be at a weak moment in their journey.

These are principles that undergird everything that is said in this book. They must be buried deep into your heart so that they become a natural part of you. Even that can only be achieved by God Himself, which brings us full circle to the fundamental principle for all Christian growth and healing—that we must fix our hope and our attention on God and, diligently and with all our heart, beseech Him to bring these things about in our lives.

The "Prime Directive"

In the "Star Trek" films and television series, the crew of the starship Enterprise along with the entire Federation of Planets was governed by what they called "The Prime Directive," which was that they should not interfere with another civilization in such a way as to change its history.

God Almighty has an even greater "prime directive," which is that the purpose of life, its fulfillment and joy, and the source of all desire and power to do the will of God can be found in one place alone—in an intimate love relationship with Him. In coming to know Him, we come to love Him, learn to trust Him, and are motivated to obey Him. The answer to every dilemma and every need of man is found in simple, childlike love and intimacy with God Himself. In His arms, all our doubts and fears, wants and needs, hopes and joys find their resolution and fulfillment.

Thus, unless we pursue this "prime directive" in our lives, nothing else that we seek, whether it is healing, deliverance, freedom, identity, or purpose, will be satisfied. Nowhere else will we find the passion and the power for life. In no one else will we find meaning and fulfillment.

Do you want to be set free from bondage? Pursue intimacy with God Himself. He will show you the rest, and in partnership with your free will, He will transform you into the image of His beloved Son.

Foundational Principles

Let's review these foundational principles:
1. We are incapable of doing anything of "eternal" value on our own, including having faith, getting saved, getting healed, gaining wisdom, obtaining righteousness, loving God or man, performing good works, helping others, etc.
2. Our self-sufficient attempts to do such things block God from being able to accomplish them in and through us.
3. We are wholly dependent on God to plant in us the desire, motivation and equipping to accomplish any good thing.
4. We need to ask for what we do not have and positively respond to the grace that God gives to us.
5. Our goal is to live wholly for the glory of Jesus Christ.
6. The beginning and the end of everything that we need to do can be summed up as "the pursuit of a relationship with the God Who saved us and Who heals us and Who has a future for us."

Let me caution you: *this* is the "prescription" for your healing. It applies no matter what your individual sexual problem may be. The remainder of this book is merely "descriptive" of what God usually does to the "outside" of people in the process of bringing them to sexual health on the inside. It will give you an idea of what you may expect to hear God telling you, and encourage you as you see the same things happening in your life.

Always keep in mind that although your healing will probably parallel many of these patterns, you must still earnestly seek God for the plan that is perfect for you, one that His infinite wisdom already knows will work, and one that He will back-up with His supernatural power. That requires time spent developing an intimate relationship with Him, learning to hear His voice, obeying it, and learning to allow His power to conquer your problem for you.

If you are like most people, you will do *anything* to avoid developing an intimate relationship with God. You will follow 50 steps and 40 principles for 70 years, walk on glass—*anything*—to keep from doing the hard work of relationship. But if you skip this "prime directive," if you choose to pretend that it is just spiritual talk that does not have any practical basis in life, then you will fail to realize freedom and transformation in the way and to the degree that God has designed for you to have. And you will miss the very purpose of your life!

So once again: your healing cannot be permanently achieved simply by striving to duplicate the patterns found in the following chapters of this book; it can only effectively be achieved by first taking the steps outlined in this first chapter and then following the directions that God gives you for the outworking of your individual situation. For when God prescribes a course of action, He also sends His Spirit to back up your obedient response, making it effective.

Let me illustrate this point for you. A pornography addict who has been healed by the power of God will no longer frequent such news racks. That is what His healing looks like behaviorally—on the outside. If a second porn addict decides that the way to achieve the same healing is to mimic the behavior of the person who has been healed (by simply avoiding porn racks), he will fail. If he is strong-willed enough, he may deceive himself into thinking that he has succeeded because, for a time, he may indeed avoid pornography. But it will only be a matter of time before he will return to it because, first, the root of his behavior has not been dealt with, and second, without having developed an intimate relationship with God, he has no ongoing source of power to motivate him to continue to resist sin.

This is where secular therapy falls short. It teaches people how to maintain their "sobriety" but never connects them to the source whereby the desire and the power to stay free is replenished. There may be a tip of the hat to "God as you perceive Him," but if that god isn't the Triune God (Father, Son, and Holy Spirit), then it is no god, or worse yet, it is a demonic power. Therefore, failure is inevitable, whether it be a return to the bondage or a final, eternal separation from the one true God.

Permanent healing cannot take place through our own will-power or good intentions. It requires the power of God to work in us both to reveal and to heal the scar or bondage that legitimizes the sin for us in our subconscious, which is the real cause for the problem.

A truly healed person has been compelled by the love of God nurtured in his heart through an intimate relationship with the Lord and has been empowered to resist temptation by the Holy Spirit. The inner emotional source for the need to commit sin (and perhaps the demonic stronghold) has been supernaturally removed by God. As Jude 24 hints, he is "kept from falling" by God Himself.

Let me say it one more time—the following chapters simply describe what it looks like, much of the time, when someone is in the process of being healed by God. They are *not* prescriptive! You cannot follow them and achieve healing. That would be to fall back into the trap of self-effort. They only serve to provide you with a broad outline of what you may expect to hear directly from the Holy Spirit as you employ the principles found in this first chapter, which *is* prescriptive.

Study Section
Foundations—Truth Therapy

"*Sanctify* them by the truth; your word is truth" (John 17:17).

A. THE NATURE AND ACTIVITY OF GOD

1. God is Holy and Pure (Lev. 19:2; Ps. 99:9; Is. 6:3; Rev. 15:4).

   "The core of all sin is the belief that God is not good."
   (Oswald Chambers)

2. God is Almighty (1 Chron. 29:12; Job 42:2; Ps. 62:11; 115:3).

3. The Power of His Holiness is Absolute (Rom. 1:4; Phil. 3:21).

4. God is Lowly. He has a Servant's Heart (Phil. 2:7).

   Jesus described Himself as "meek and lowly" (KJV), or "gentle and humble in heart" (NASB) (Matthew 11:29). He is the Lamb of God, who kneels to wash our feet (cf. John 13:3-5). He is that way even now.

5. God is Love (1 John 4:16).

6. God is Wisdom (Is. 11:2; Col. 2:2-3; Eph. 1:17).

   "But to those who are the called, both Jews and Greeks, Christ the power of God and the wisdom of God" (1 Corinthians 1:24, NASB).

   "But the wisdom from above is first pure, then peaceable, gentle, reasonable, full of mercy and good fruits, unwavering, without hypocrisy" (James 3:17, NASB).

7. God is Perfect.

"For I proclaim the name of the Lord; Ascribe greatness to our God! The Rock! *His work is perfect, For all His ways are just; A God of faithfulness and without injustice, Righteous and upright is He*" (Deuteronomy 32:3-4, NASB).

"As for God, *His way is blameless*; The word of the Lord is tested; He is a shield to all who take refuge in Him" (2 Samuel 22:31, NASB).

"For the word of the Lord is upright; And all His work is done in faithfulness. He loves righteousness and justice; The earth is full of the lovingkindness of the Lord" (Psalms 33:4-5, NASB).

"Now I Nebuchadnezzar praise, exalt, and honor the King of heaven, for *all His works are true and His ways just*, and He is able to humble those who walk in pride" (Daniel 4:37, NASB).

8. God is Present.

(to Joshua) "And behold, I am with you, and will keep you wherever you go, and will bring you back to this land; for I will not leave you until I have done what I have promised you" (Genesis 28:15, NASB).

(To Moses) He said, "My presence shall go with you, and I will give you rest" (Exodus 33:14, NASB).

"But now, thus says the Lord, your Creator, O Jacob, And He who formed you, O Israel, 'Do not fear, for I have redeemed you; I have called you by name; you are Mine! *When you pass through the waters, I will be with you*; And through the rivers, they will not overflow you. When you walk through the fire, you will not be scorched, Nor will the flame burn you. For I am the Lord your God, The Holy One of Israel, your Savior; I have given Egypt as your ransom, Cush and Seba in your place. Since you are precious in My sight, Since you are honored and I love you, I will give other men in your place and other peoples in exchange for your life. *Do not fear, for I am with you*; I will bring your offspring from the east, And gather you from the west. I will say to the north, "Give them up!" And to the south, "Do not hold them back." Bring My sons from afar, And My daughters from the ends of the earth, Everyone who is called by My name, And whom I have created for My glory, Whom I have formed, even whom I have made. Bring out the people who are blind, even though they have eyes, And the deaf, even though they have ears'" (Isaiah 43:1-8, NASB).

"'Behold, the virgin shall be with child, and shall bear a Son, and they shall call His name Immanuel,'" which translated means, 'God with us'" (Matthew 1:23, NASB).

"Go therefore and make disciples of all the nations, baptizing them in the name of the Father and the Son and the Holy Spirit, teaching them to observe all that I commanded you; and *lo, I am with you always, even to the end of the age*" (Matthew 28:19-20, NASB).

9. God Draws us to Christ.

    We have been targeted for love.

    "No one can come to Me, unless the Father who sent Me draws him…No one can come to Me unless the Father has enabled him" (John 6:44, 65).

10. God Determines our Steps.

    "In his heart a man plans his course, but the Lord determines his steps" (Proverbs 16:9).

    "A man's steps are directed by the Lord" (Proverbs 20:24).

    "Trust in the Lord with all your heart and lean not on your own understanding; in all your ways acknowledge Him, and He will make your paths straight" (Proverbs 3:5-6).

    "I know, O Lord, that a man's life is not his own; it is not for man to direct his steps" (Jeremiah 10:23).

    "Your word is a lamp to my feet and a light for my path" (Psalms 119:105).

    "The Lord delights in the way of the man whose steps He has made firm; though he stumble he will not fall, for the Lord upholds him with His hand" (Psalms 37:23-24).

    "The Lord will guide you always; He will satisfy your needs in a sun-scorched land and will strengthen your frame. You will be like a well-watered garden, like a spring whose waters never fail" (Isaiah 58:11).

    "Whether you turn to the right or to the left, your ears will hear a voice behind you, saying, 'This is the way; walk in it'" (Isaiah 30:21).

When you couple these promises with the caveat that God directs in ways that are wholly consistent with His Word, you have incredible certainties to live by, for God *never* contradicts His declared will.

11. *God Works* in us *To Will* and *To Do*.

    He fights for us, so there is no place for self-striving or self-glory.

    "It is God who works in you to will and to act according to His good purpose" (Philippians 2:13).

    "There are different kinds of working, but the same God works all of them in all men" (1 Corinthians 12:6).

B. The Nature and Activity of Man

1. We are Strangers in this World.

    "All these died in faith, without receiving the promises, but having seen them and having welcomed them from a distance, and having confessed that *they were strangers and exiles on the earth*. For those who say such things make it clear that they are seeking a country of their own. And indeed if they had been thinking of that country from which they went out, they would have had opportunity to return. But as it is, they desire a better country, that is a heavenly one. Therefore God is not ashamed to be called their God; for He has prepared a city for them" (Hebrews 11:13-16, NASB).

    "Beloved, I urge you as *aliens and strangers* to abstain from fleshly lusts, which wage war against the soul" (1 Peter 2:11, NASB).

2. We are Citizens of the Kingdom of God.

    "So then you are no longer strangers and aliens, but *you are fellow citizens with the saints, and are of God's household*" (Ephesians 2:19, NASB).

    "For *our citizenship is in heaven*, from which also we eagerly wait for a Savior, the Lord Jesus Christ" (Phil. 3:20, NASB).

3. We are Soldiers in God's Army.

   "Suffer hardship with me, as a good soldier of Christ Jesus" (2 Timothy 2:3, NASB).

   "Put on the full armor of God, that you may be able to stand firm against the schemes of the devil. For our struggle is not against flesh and blood, but against the rulers, against the powers, against the world forces of this darkness, against the spiritual forces of wickedness in the heavenly places. Therefore, take up the full armor of God, that you may be able to resist in the evil day, and having done everything, to stand firm" (Ephesians 6:11-13, NASB).

4. We are a Gift of the Father to Christ.

   "All that the Father gives Me will come to Me, and whoever comes to Me I will never drive away" (John 6:37).

   "And this is the will of Him who sent Me, that I shall lose none of all that He has given Me, but raise them up at the last day" (John 6:39).

5. God Gives the Grace—We Make the Choice.

   After God gives the grace to stop a sinful behavior, we are still left with a daily "choice" of whether to use the grace or not.

   Why do we live in bondage?
   1) We do not believe in and act on the *power* of God's holiness.
   2) We do not *really* want to be free.

   In other words:
   1) We don't believe God can or wants to heal us.
   2) We don't really want absolute purity and freedom.

   Your healing will start when you want it to start, and stop when you want it to stop.

6. We Have a Purpose in Life.

   a. That we will "Be to the Praise of His Glory…"

      "The purpose of His will, in order that we…might be for the praise of His glory" (Ephesians 1:11-12).

b. ... with specific "works" planned ahead of us to carry out.

> "For we are God's workmanship, created in Christ Jesus to do good works, which God prepared in advance for us to do" (Ephesians 2:10).

> "For I know the plans I have for you," declares the Lord, "plans to prosper you and not to harm you, plans to give you hope and a future" (Jeremiah 29:11).

7. "Fixing Our Eyes Upon Jesus" Opens us up to the Power and Grace that is Necessary for Loving and Obeying Him.

    As we look at/to Him, we are transformed into His likeness, with all of the accompanying spiritual fruit.

    "Fix your thoughts on Jesus, the Apostle and High Priest whom we confess. He is faithful"(Hebrews 3:1).

    "Let us fix our eyes on Jesus, the Author and Perfecter of our faith...Consider Him...so that you will not grow weary and lose heart" (Hebrews 12:2-3).

    "And we all, with unveiled faces, beholding dimly the glory of the Lord, are being transformed into His likeness, with ever-increasing glory" (2 Cor. 3:18, author).

    Another rendering is—

    "As we behold the glory of the Lord, we are transformed into His likeness."

    In his book, *Passion for Jesus* (p. 109), Mike Bickle says:

    > "While we are discovering His beauty and delighting ourselves in Him, the Lord is sealing our spirits. We will never again be content with a life of compromise that neglects spiritual intimacy."

8. The Proper Motivation for Our Actions is "Love."

    And one of the scribes came and heard them arguing, and recognizing that He had answered them well, asked Him, "What commandment is the foremost of all?" Jesus answered, "The foremost is, 'Hear, O Israel! The Lord our God is one Lord; and you shall love the lord your God with all your heart, and with all your soul, and with all your mind, and with all your strength'" (Mark 12:28-30, NASB).

"Jesus answered and said to him, 'If anyone loves Me, he will keep My word; and My Father will love him, and We will come to him, and make Our abode with him'" (John 14:23, NASB).

"Beloved, let us love one another, for love is from God; and everyone who loves is born of God and knows God. The one who does not love does not know God, for God is love" (1 John 4:7-8, NASB).

"And we have come to know and have believed the love which God has for us. God is love, and the one who abides in love abides in God, and God abides in him…We love, because He first loved us. If someone says, 'I love God,' and hates his brother, he is a liar; for the one who does not love his brother whom he has seen, cannot love God whom he has not seen" (1 John 4:16, 19-20, NASB).

"For this is the love of God, that we keep His commandments; and His commandments are not burdensome. For whatever is born of God overcomes the world; and this is the victory that has overcome the world—our faith" (1 John 5:3-4, NASB).

C. THE INTENDED INTERRELATIONSHIP BETWEEN GOD AND MAN

1. Man Should Set His Heart Toward the Father, and Against Sin.

   Example: setting a sail into the wind on a sailboat

2. *Diligently* Seek God With All of Our Heart.

   "Anyone who comes to Him *must believe* that He exists and that He rewards those who *earnestly seek Him*" (Hebrews 11:6).

   "'You will seek Me and find Me *when you seek Me with all your heart*. I will be found by you,' declares the Lord" (Jeremiah 29:13-14).

   "I will walk in freedom, for I have *desperately sought out* Your precepts" (Psalms 119:45, author).

3. Habitually, and With All Dependence, Fix Our Gaze Upon Jesus (2 Cor. 3:18; Heb 3:1; 12:2-3).

   "Apart from Me you can do nothing" (John 15:5, NASB).

4. Inquire of the Lord, and Receive into Ourselves God's Attributes, His Power, and His Plan for Healing and Victory in Our Lives (1

Chron. 15:13; Jer. 29:11; Joshua 9:14; Ex. 23:29).

"The people who know their God will firmly resist him (the devil)" (Dan. 11:32).

"Not by might nor by power, but by My Spirit, says the Lord of hosts" (Zech. 4:6, NASB).

5. Reject the Temptations of Self-will, Self-effort and Self-striving. They Lead to Self-righteousness.

6. Clearly Establish in Our Minds That God is the Source for Everything. That way, He also receives the glory for everything.

"It is God who arms me with strength and makes my way perfect" (Psalms 18:32).

"Whoever speaks, let him speak, as it were, the utterances of God; whoever serves, let him do so as by the strength which God supplies; *so that in all things God may be glorified through Jesus Christ, to whom belongs the glory and dominion forever and ever.* Amen" (1 Peter 4:11, NASB).

7. Make a Conscious Effort, That When Things Go Wrong, Assume the Best About God, Rather Than the Worst.

8. Practical, Heartfelt, Real Prayers for "Help!"

"Help us, O God our Savior, for the glory of Your name "(Ps. 79:9).

9. Pray For a Passion to Seek and to Know God.

"You do not have because you do not ask God. When you ask, you do not receive, because you ask with wrong motives" (James 4:2c-3a).

10. Pray for a Faith that Will Not Fail.

11. Pray for a More Intimate Walk and Revelation of Him.

    Intimacy...

    a. ...generates a growing awareness of His glory, presence, power, love, acceptance, etc....resulting in increased faith, hope, confidence and joy. This has practical effects on our day to day walk and life.

    b. ...readjusts our perspective on day to day living and

life, transforming our *world*-view into a *kingdom*-view.

   c. …opens our spiritual eyes and ears to see and hear God's direction.

   d. …is where we gain wisdom.

   e. …is where we receive the continual filling of the Spirit and power.

   f. …fixes and establishes the God-man relationship as the primary relationship of our lives, as it should be. This brings certainty and confidence in God and His promises.

   g. …transforms us into His likeness. Christ is formed in us.

   h. …persuades us to trust and rely on Him, resulting in empowerment, healing and usefulness for the Kingdom we never could have had otherwise.

   i. …results in the humility of knowing just how little we know and how dependent we are on God.

12. Pray for a Desire to be Like Him.

13. Pray to be Given the Love that the Father has for the Son.

    "(Father) I have made You known to them, and will continue to make You known in order that the love You have for Me may be in them and that I Myself may be in them" (John 17:26).

    "Jesus replied: 'Love the Lord your God with all your heart and with all your soul and with all your mind. This is the first and greatest commandment'" (Matthew 22:37-38).

    "Place me like a seal over your heart, like a seal on your arm; for love is as strong as death, its jealousy unyielding as the grave. It burns like blazing fire, like a mighty flame. Many waters cannot quench love; rivers cannot wash it away. If one were to give all the wealth of his house for love, it would be utterly scorned" (Song of Songs 8:6-7).

14. Be Persistent!

    "God…acts on behalf of those who wait for Him" (Isaiah 64:4).

15. Guard Against Fooling Ourselves into Thinking that We Want God's Delivering Help and Purity When We Really Don't. This is a very common self-deception.

    "Renew a *steadfast* spirit within me…grant me a *willing* spirit, to sustain me" (Psalms 51:10, 12).

16. Seek the Masculine, *Divine Will of God*, Which is the *Power to Do Rightly* (Read Leanne Payne's, *Crisis in Masculinity*, pp. 90-95 on this).

17. Decide to Believe in God's Grace, and Live Out of It, Rather Than a Life of Performing to Earn God's Favor.

Exercises—Foundations

1. Use this study section as a devotional for the next week or so. Go at the pace the Holy Spirit sets, meditating on the truths you find and dialoguing with God about the questions you have.

2. As you meditate on the various qualities of the Lord during this devotional exercise, ask the Lord to reveal these individual truths or attributes to you in a new and deeper way than ever before. Wait on Him and anticipate a response.

3. As you come to an attribute of God or some awesome truth about Him, stop and praise Him for that attribute or truth. Ask Him to build the same trait or activate the same truth into your own life and personality.

4. Ask the Lord to reveal the hidden lies concerning spiritual reality that you may still hold on to. Repeatedly wash them away by an act of your will—speaking forth what the Bible says is true rather than what your old belief system has maintained.

5. Ask the Holy Spirit to identify for you the areas where you have chosen to believe your feelings about yourself (or the opinions of others) rather than what the Bible says is true about you. Ask God to forgive you for your unbelief and to work deep within you to replace the old lies with a heartfelt belief in the truth. Read Neil Anderson's, *Victory Over the Darkness*.

6. Talk to the Lord about God's call for Christians to be soldiers in His army. Ask Him to give you peace, understanding and direction about what that means for you.

7. Meditate on the fact that you are a gift, a present, from the Father to the Son.

8. Talk to God about the practical side of using His grace in the choices you face from day to day. How do you live in grace and yet make responsible choices each day? Where does His grace end and your responsibility begin? Is there such a dichotomy?

9. Ask God to reveal more about the purpose for your life.

10. Practice fixing your eyes (and thoughts) on Jesus and record the results in a spiritual journal.

11. Ask God to reveal to you if there are any areas in your life where you have deceived yourself into thinking you want His way when you really still love the sin more.

12. Make a permanent decision of the will—a commitment with God that with the power that He will give you, you will walk in holiness and purity the rest of your days. If you make this commitment, He will honor it by providing the means. That is guaranteed.

Living by Grace Rather Than Performance Orientation

Besides sin, the primary problem with the way people think and operate is performance orientation. Everyone has this problem to one degree or another because it is regarded as a virtuous way of living that fits very nicely into the good old American work ethic. From day one, we are programmed for performance orientation as we learn to work for good grades by performing in school, for plaques and trophies by athletic performance, and for raises and promotions by performing at work. Performance orientation is everywhere, and it does help motivate us to do our best. The problem, however, is that people carry that performance mode into their love relationships, and they try to earn the love of God and others.

What's the Matter with Performing for God?

First, we will fail. Any attempt by man to meet God's standards of perfection is doomed to failure, simply because we are not perfect. "There is no one righteous," the Bible says, "not even one; there is no one who understands . . . no one who does good, not even one" (Rom. 3:10b,12).

So if I try to prove myself worthy before God by being a good and faithful servant, I will eventually demonstrate just the opposite and I will end up feeling condemned. Performance orientation is a snare designed by Satan to keep us so filled with feelings of defeat that we will not go to God for fear of His wrath or disappointment.

Jesus said, "Apart from me, you can do nothing" (John 15:5c). Nothing? Talk about failure! Fortunately Jesus added the "apart from Me" clause, which hints at the way to overcome our fallen condition: our efforts, when united with His, will produce results. He says, "With man this is impossible, but with God all things are possible" (Matt. 19:26). In fact, He likes to lead us into impossible situations so that we will all the more quickly learn the necessity of partnering with Him in our day-to-day lives.

Performing for God's love creates a form of religion that Jesus rejects—a worldly version of loving and serving God. This is a significant problem, one to which the world itself, in its foolishness, is blind (see 1 Cor. 1:18-31). In the world, we're expected to earn what we receive; nothing is free. If something is offered "for free," we're suspicious of it. We didn't earn it, so what's the catch?

Or let's say we are friends and you decide to express your love for me by fixing me a fancy dinner. You cook all day to prepare the feast. You eagerly bring out your finest china and silver. After I eat your marvelous meal, I stand up, hand you a twenty-dollar bill, say "thanks" and walk out the door. What would you think? You'd be hurt, wouldn't you? You'd be insulted. You didn't do that for my money. How dare I think so! You were trying to express your unconditional love for me and I respond by trying to pay you for it?

Similarly, when we're trying to earn God's love and acceptance by performing for Him, we are in a very real sense trying to pay Him back for the Cross. We're uncomfortable with the idea that we didn't do anything to earn God's forgiveness. And the more aware we are of how sinful we are, the more we realize that we don't deserve what God is freely offering. Then pride and self-centeredness make us try to perform to pay Him back.

Even some who initially accept Christ's free gift of salvation turn around and try to pay Him back with good works. In other words, their motivation for obeying and serving Him is not love so much as it is an attempt to return the favor or pay the debt that they feel they've incurred by accepting His offer of salvation.

Others launch off on a campaign to prove themselves worthy, out of fear that God's love is conditional and thus must be maintained. In a sense, it's as if they're traveling back to the Cross 2,000 years ago, walking up to Jesus and trying to slip Him a twenty-dollar bill. Are they trying to tip Him for dying on the Cross?

Let's examine our hearts, with God's help, to see if our so-called love and service for Him is performance-based. We can never pay Him back for the blood of His Son.

Performing for God's love is tantamount to living by sight rather than by faith. It's unbelief! The assurance of His love for us will never come from any performance of righteousness on our part. It will only come as we gaze with the eyes of faith on the Cross, which is God's awesome demonstration of love for mankind.

God has asked us to be "certain of what we do not see" (Heb. 11:1). The world bases reality on what it feels, thinks, and experiences. But the kingdom of God is very different. It calls on us to look through a glass darkly—to take obedient actions without knowing why or what the outcome will be, but only that the God who asks is trustworthy. True faith is demonstrated in principled action.

It is hard to believe in unlimited, unconditional, unearned, unsolicited love and forgiveness. If I were God, I wouldn't do it that way. Since I'm prone to cast God in my image, this makes it truly inconceivable that He could still love me in the face of my ongoing failure to love Him. It's also difficult to believe that Jesus' death on the Cross cancels sin, so we tend to find ways to atone for it ourselves. We bathe in thoughts and feelings of condemnation as though we were in some way helping to balance the scales of justice. Refusing to take ourselves off the hook plays so nicely into the world's version of religion. Oh, we'll confess our sins all right, but many of us will refuse to truly embrace the forgiveness that God offers.

Mike Bickle has often said that God "offends the mind to reveal the heart." It's such a true statement. Did Jesus really *need* to put mud on that man's eyes to heal his blindness (see John 9:6-7)? Of course not. He had the power to raise people from the dead! Another time, Jesus told His followers that they had to eat His flesh and drink His blood, and the Bible says that many who were following Him left Him and never returned (see John 6:48-66). Why would He say that? He lost half of His people! The passage explains it by noting: "Jesus had known from the beginning which of them did not believe" (v. 64b). He was, it seems, getting rid of the hangers-on—pruning away those who weren't truly behind Him—offending their minds to reveal their hearts.

God is concerned about what we *really* believe. He's not moved by empty words. He's not fooled by pretense and show. If something untrue is going on in our hearts, He will offend our minds so that we can see our self-deception and be challenge to change. That's what He's doing to the world with His offer of unconditional grace, with His dying on the Cross. He's offending the spirit of performance, independence and self-righteousness with an offer built on grace, dependence and His singular righteousness. And many hearts turn away, never to return, because the offer requires the surrender of pride and self-sufficiency.

The world teaches us that the purpose of life is realized through position, power, prestige and material goods. This lie has found its way into the very heart of Christendom. The worship of position, power, prestige and material goods is rampant in the Body of Christ. And the core of the problem is our performance orientation. We do not know how to live in humble response to grace.

He says, "Do not conform any longer to the pattern of this world, but be transformed by the renewing of your mind" (Rom. 12:2a). "Do not love the world, or anything in the world [referring to the world's system]. If anyone loves the world, the love of the Father is not in him" (1 John 2:15).

The Bible also talks about "reckoning" ourselves dead to sin (see Rom. 6:11a) and considering ourselves "aliens and strangers in the world" (1 Pet. 2:11a). In fact, in that same verse in Peter, a clear connection is made between considering ourselves aliens and strangers to the world and the ability to abstain from sinful desires.

Let me illustrate the connection: One day when I was in prayer, the Lord asked me to stop all lying. I had been a masterful liar before giving my life to Christ, but I had already given up all but the little "lies of convenience" that we use from time to time—lies that make life smoother; such as when mom comes home from the beauty parlor and asks, "How do you like my hair?" and you just tell her it's wonderful, no matter how bad it looks, simply to make life easier and avoid offense. But God was very clear—I was to stop *all* lying. I was to be a man of truth.

So I made the commitment, and to my amazement, discovered that every time I came upon one of those uncomfortable situations where "lies of convenience" had been so helpful, God always gave me something really wise to say that was true but that also protected the feelings of the other person.

What surprised me even more was to see how directly connected my lying had been to a struggle that I had with sexual temptation. In order to maintain my immoral lifestyle, I had to hide my activities under a shroud of lies and secrecy. When God led me into a commitment to truth, the enabling foundation for that sin was removed, which forced me to more seriously commit to a life of sexual purity. When the lies went, so did the power of a firmly entrenched and seemingly unconnected stronghold of sin.

In the same way, although performance orientation can seem so unconnected to the more pressing issues of sin, it *is a key foundation for the strongholds of most sin* because performance orientation is a fundamental departure from God's ways. It is a direct attack against the Cross, which is the power source for holiness. It is a gateway sin, or a key root of sin that feeds most of the sins that man commits. It is what generates the need or desire to sin, the justification for sin, the frustration that poisons our faith in the goodness and promises of God. When the motivation of performing for God's love and acceptance is eradicated, other sins begin to falter as well.

If you are performing for Him, you are not having an intimate relationship with Him. Putting it another way, if you are not abiding in the Vine and receiving His life-giving love and affirmation, you are probably striving to earn the same. If you are not experiencing His affirming, healing presence on a regular basis, you are probably walking in performance orientation. Why? To paraphrase Augustine, our hearts are restless until they find themselves in Him. If we can't find Him one way, we will try to win Him the other way.

The result of living that way is massive insecurity. Just look at the world. They're running here and running there, killing themselves with work, striving for this, trying to achieve that, experiencing this, encountering that, finding themselves, losing themselves, toning up, dialing down, going within, letting it all out, and self-helping themselves to death, trying to find peace by focusing on self, trying to find God by focusing on their own reason and trying to find love by proving themselves worthy.

Has anyone noticed that none of that is working? A large portion of the

American church performs for God because we are flat-out afraid of intimacy. The many good works that we do keep us sufficiently busy to create an excuse for not taking the time to develop an interior life with Him. We are frantically running about serving God because deep inside we are afraid of getting too close to Him, afraid that He will reject us, and we're trying to waylay such a judgment by building up a war chest of worthiness through holy deeds. We refuse to believe that Christ has made a way through our unworthiness, so that we can feel safe and at peace in the arms of the Father. Satan knows that the deepest desire of God's heart is to have an intimate relationship with His people, so he robs God of that pleasure by instilling this performance diversion into our thinking. He will even help get someone to the mission field if it will keep them so busy trying to earn God's favor that they never really develop a love relationship with Him.

Others simply prefer the world to God. They are sufficiently talented and thus sufficiently rewarded by the world system for their admirable performance that God never seems all that necessary. The world provides them with the psychological highs that they need in order to feel affirmed, loved and important. Over time, they devise sophisticated, psychological justifications for the hollow and temporary nature of the world's version of love and affirmation. Though there is a sad acknowledgment that something is missing, they draw comfort by saying things to themselves like: "That's all there is, after all, and I have been fortunate to have experienced more of life's blessings than most," or "Life is a matter of just making the best of things and I'm satisfied that I've done that."

Instead, they should acknowledge their emptiness, take a running leap into the Father's arms and exclaim, "Worthy or not, here I come!" That's exactly what God wants them to do.

How to Fix It

Although the possible causes and reasons for being performance-oriented are many, and the damage wrought by it is extensive, the cure is singular. The cure is the grace that comes through Jesus Christ (see John 1:14,17). Let's take a look at the Scripture that lays it out most clearly, Titus 2:11-14:

> *The grace of God that brings salvation has appeared to all men. It teaches us to say "No" to ungodliness and worldly passions, and to live self-controlled, upright and godly lives in this present age, while we wait for the blessed hope—the glorious appearing of our great God and Savior, Jesus Christ, who gave himself for us to redeem us from all wickedness and to purify for himself a people that are His very own, eager to do what is good.*

Verse 11 tells us "grace . . . has appeared to *all* men." It doesn't discriminate. It has appeared to all men and it brings salvation. Grace saves, it forgives, and it is offered to everyone. So you're wrong to consider yourself a special case outside of the grace of God. It reaches to the deepest, darkest places of the globe and rescues anyone who wants to be rescued.

Verse 12 tells us grace "teaches us to say 'No' to ungodliness and worldly passions." How does being given the grace of forgiveness when I sin persuade me not to sin? I should think it would do just the opposite. In Romans 6:1-2a, Paul broached that very question. "What shall we say, then? Shall we go on sinning so that grace may increase?" His reply, *megenoito*, one of the strongest Greek words, means "Never!" or even, "God forbid." The person who says, "if I'm going to get forgiven every time I sin, then why not sin all the time?" doesn't know God very well and consequently doesn't love Him very deeply. Love for God is what makes the difference in how we respond to grace.

Titus 3:4-5a reveals "when the kindness and love of God our Savior appeared, he saved us, not because of the righteous things we had done, but because of his mercy." In other words, I don't have to perform righteousness in order to be loved by God. That removes an incredible burden from my shoulders—a burden that I was incapable of carrying anyway.

I don't have to generate holiness in order for God to love or accept me. He has done that for me. God comes into my life and performs righteousness for me. It is Christ in me performing the righteousness, provided I yield to Him and, as one Scripture puts it, "hunger and thirst for righteousness" (Matt. 5:6).

It is very clear in Scripture that the battles that God leads us into are ones that He intends to fight for us, if we will ask Him to do so. Look at the example of the battle of Jericho (see Josh. 6) or the battle between David and Goliath (see 1 Sam. 17:47). Behind the simple actions that He asked His people to perform, God was fighting the battle for them. So the Scripture says, "the battle is the Lord's."

Similarly, when faced with a battle with temptation or a trial, if I acknowledge my weakness and refuse to fight the battle myself and instead turn to God, saying, "Father, send Your power to destroy this temptation for me, destroy this evil," He honors my "declaration of dependence" and destroys the enemy for me as soon as its redemptive purpose is completed. That's how it's supposed to work. "I no longer live, but Christ lives in me" (Gal. 2:20a).

In His Arms of Love

Once we are "in Christ," God's love and acceptance of us will never again be based on our behavior. We have been made a member of Christ's body, so love and acceptance are guaranteed. God accepts us because we have united ourselves with His Son.

If you are trapped in performance thinking, that idea is likely to be most unwelcome. For you, the motivation to do good has been an assumed need to earn God's love and acceptance. If that reason is taken away, there is nothing left to motivate you to do good. A most horrifying revelation!

The fact remains: Your acceptance by God is based on Christ's work for you, not your own righteousness. That means that even if I went out tonight and committed adultery, God's love for me would not waiver. His acceptance of me would not change. I would certainly have to face consequences for my sinful actions, some of which might be quite serious, but God's love would not change because it is not, nor has it ever been, based on my performance. This eliminates the power of condemnation, which is Satan's greatest trick, and it is why the Bible says categorically that there is "no condemnation for those who are in Christ Jesus" (Rom. 8:1).

Have you ever fallen into the arms of the one you most deeply loved—the one with whom you most wanted to spend the rest of your life? Just being in that person's arms brings peace. Fear and striving vanish. You're safe now. You're loved. And you never want that moment to end. That's what it's like to be in the arms of God.

All you need to do after failing Him is return to His arms of love for cleansing and forgiveness. It is in those arms that your heart is so warmed that the impulse to rebel fades away.

Satan is trying to keep you from running back into God's arms by making you think that God doesn't like you anymore, that God doesn't approve of you anymore, that God wants you to stand in the corner and think about what you've done before He'll consider your pleas for mercy. Satan is trying to give you this false image of God because he knows that if you return to the Father's loving arms, God's love and grace will persuade you even more to be faithful the next time you are tempted.

The apostle Paul wrote that the grace of God makes us *eager* to do what is good (see Titus 2:14). How does grace make us eager to do good? In short, by causing us to fall in love with Him at deeper and deeper levels. Grace works slowly, but it works powerfully to bring about that transformation of the heart, so that we develop a desire to obey God in response to His unconditional grace, love and favor. Satan's only defense against grace is the lies that he tells us so that we won't believe in such love and grace. For if we believe that God loves us no matter what and run to His arms even when we've failed Him, Satan has lost us. God's arms change hearts. It's an inside-out job.

God is the father in the story of the prodigal son (see Luke 15:11-32), who stands with loving arms outstretched, at the start, the middle and the end of your sin and rebellion saying: "Just come back to Me." He'll stand there through 10,000 sins if He has to.

I will never forget the day that God's grace finally succeeded in undermining my rebellious heart. I was committing a certain sin for perhaps the ten thousandth time that day, when to my surprise, God spoke to me. For a moment there was a disconnect, because my concept of how things worked was that when you were sinning, God went outside to wait until you were finished, and if you were lucky, He might come back in. But I had *no* concept of God actually staying in the room while you sinned. So when He spoke to me in the middle of my sin, I thought it quite ludicrous.

He said, "David, if you will turn to Me right now, I will love you, and forgive you, and embrace you." Well, that idea seemed even more ludicrous than the first, so I cast the thought aside and continued in my sin.

The second I finished my sin, God spoke to me again and said, "David, if you will turn to Me right now, I will love you, and forgive you, and embrace you."

At that, I realized that it had been God the first time, and that in spite of casting the Lord of Glory aside in favor of a pitiful little sin, He stood resolute before me, entreating me to choose Him instead, and offering to forgive and cleanse me even if I didn't. The awesome grace and humility of it all astounded my mind and gripped my heart, and the wall of rebellion within me came crashing down.

I said to God, "Lord, if that's what you are really like, then I *want* to follow You!"

No longer did I have to defend myself against a God who was out to get me, or spoil my fun, or manipulate me for His own selfish purposes, or crucify me for failing Him one more time. No, I was faced with a God who simply loved me and wanted to embrace me in all my sin—and that was a God that I could not rebel against. After the ten thousandth and first application, God's grace had finally undermined my rebellious heart and had won my obedience. In that moment, I went from obeying God because I was *supposed to*, to obeying Him because I *wanted to*. And that, my friends, is all the difference in the world.

One day, that grace will finally have its way in you. You'll realize that God is not someone you have to protect yourself from. He is not the adversary. His commandments are not designed to restrict or control you, but rather, to protect and guide you to the highest order of fulfillment possible. He is the only One who loves you perfectly and completely.

Grace takes longer to work than law. But grace is permanent. It doesn't just keep your behavior in tow. It transforms your heart, so that you go from following God because you're supposed to, to following Him because you want to, fully and completely, from your heart. God creates oak trees and oak trees take a while to grow. But when they are grown, they are not so easily knocked down by hurricanes. That's the genius of God's way. His ingenuity is in the way He uses what seems foolish—letting people get away with sin—to convince them not to sin. In the Book of Ezekiel (36:24-27) and the Book of Jeremiah (31:33) God said He was going to write His law on our hearts. What does that mean? It means that He is going to create in us a pure and natural desire to keep the law. And He uses grace to do it.

Yes, He knows that you will take advantage of His grace—we all do. But He knows that in the long run, grace will have its effect in our hearts. Mercy *will* triumph over judgment (see Jas. 2:13).

This grace is not cheap; it cost Jesus everything. Nor does God strew it about cavalierly. He gives it only to those who understand the value of it and who want it with all of their heart. If you want it with all of your heart, if you want your heart transformed supernaturally from the inside out so that the law becomes truly a delight to you, then this chapter was commissioned by the Lord for your sake. Receive His Son, Jesus, as your Lord and your Savior. Believe in His unconditional offer of pardon and grace for your sins, and begin the transformation this very day. Say to God, "Worthy or not, here I come!"

For those of you who have already given your life to God but who now realize that you are seriously trapped in performance orientation, and want out, you may be wondering what you can do to extricate yourself from such a hellish bondage. Here are a few thoughts.

Your first instinct will be to try to perform your way out. This has been your natural modus operandi. Consequently, you must set a close watch on your mind and heart against any such inclination. Ask the Holy Spirit to flag any actions that spring from a "works righteousness" mode.

In truth, the Holy Spirit is really the One who will guide you in how to make the change. Simply and repeatedly go before Him and say, "God, this is what I want and I will do whatever it takes to be conformed to Your image." Go before Him with persistent, fervor and passion, until He blesses you with the transformation you seek (see Gen. 32:26).

Get rooted and grounded in love. Performance orientation is attached to fear because of the expectation of punishment. However, we read in 1 John 4:18, "There is no fear in love. But perfect love drives out fear, because fear has to do with punishment" (emphasis added).

Practice believing the great and precious promises of Scripture—not just intellectually, but from your heart. As Romans 6:11 suggests, "Reckon yourself dead to sin and alive to Jesus Christ." Consider as fact the statement in Galatians 2:20, "I have been crucified with Christ and I no longer live, but Christ lives in me. The life I live in the body, I live by faith in the Son of God, who loved me and gave himself for me."

Every time you catch yourself performing for God—trying to earn His favor— simply stop what you're doing and say, "I'm not going to do it this way. I am loved by God regardless of my behavior. I will love Him and serve Him for that reason alone!" You'll probably have to do this a thousand times a day for a while until it starts becoming a natural way of thinking. This is not an easy turnaround. It takes significant time and attention. It takes complete dependence on God working in you to bring it about, but it is worth every second that you put into it.

The Bible suggests that we need to forcefully take the kingdom of God (see Luke 16:16), yet that we are to rejoice in our weakness so that the power of God may rest on us (see 2 Cor. 12:9-10). So in a seeming paradox, we are to take ground for the Kingdom aggressively—by resting in God's power to do it through us. This is very different from a straightforward "performance" model.

We need to deliberately and habitually discipline ourselves to choose the right "tree" each time we are faced with an impulse to do the right thing. The Tree of the Knowledge of Good and Evil from which Adam and Eve ate represents independence from God, self-effort, and self-righteousness. They chose to make their own way, to use their own wisdom. The Tree of Life represents relationship with God, where we choose to be dependent on His wisdom and direction at all times The last Adam (Jesus) came to teach us to operate only from the wisdom of God.

In short, we need to learn how to guard our heart and mind with God's peace and God's rest (see Phil. 4:6-9). Where do you get that peace? It comes from the "prime directive"—being in His presence, being in His arms. We also need to deliberately and aggressively set our mind on things above and then put into practice what we hear from God.

Learn how to live by faith rather than by feelings. Our culture teaches us to live by our feelings. This approach began to take hold in the 1960s. "If it feels good, do it" sums it up. We learned that our feelings accurately reflected a truth that was relative and equally valid to any other, and that to do otherwise was unhealthy, unnatural and hypocritical.

Americans today have been raised with these assumptions and are no longer consciously aware of how entrenched this philosophy has become. Even Christians uncritically allow thoughts and feelings that emerge from their personal, subjective experience to overrule the fixed source of objective truth found in Scripture.

But our feelings are notoriously unreliable. Once I was lecturing, and a lady abruptly stood up and marched out of the room. I kept on teaching, but I began wondering why she had left. Clearly I had offended her with some insensitive comment, but I could not recall what it might have been. Even as I continued to lecture, I remonstrated to myself, "David, you are so insensitive, you don't even know what you said that was so insensitive. You are a menace! Get out of the pulpit before you destroy someone's life. You don't belong in the ministry." Five minutes later, the woman returned to her seat. She had gone to the ladies' room.

When the lady abruptly left, my thoughts and feelings began interpreting the event to my heart and mind—falsely—yet I didn't even consider the fact that they might be lying to me. I simply believed them and responded to what they were telling me. At that point in my life, the philosophy of this age—that personal thoughts and feelings are reliable sources of truth—was so ingrained in me that I was unaware of a problem.

To combat this state of affairs, we need to immerse ourselves in the presence of God and allow Him to correct our thinking. We need to fix our thoughts and our eyes on Jesus (see Heb. 3:1; 12:2), allowing the Word of Christ dwell in us richly (see Col. 3:16). We need to become partakers of truth and partners in truth with God.

We need to enter into a lifestyle of worship, rather than only using it as a means to please our senses or to get what we want from God. When we are immersed in performance and goal achievement, not only do we tend to manipulate and use people, we do the same to God without even realizing it. However, true-hearted worship is vital to growing in Christlikeness because it is the hearth in which we are transformed into His image (see 2 Cor. 3:18). It is also a key component of spiritual warfare, and it is a discipline that helps shift the focus from self to God.

Putting the Horse in Front of the Cart

Our culture is so steeped in the worship of self, with an attached "performance paradigm" by which we glorify certain selves over others, that entire magazines, television shows and academic curriculums are based on this worship. It is the only accepted form of public worship that is not restricted.

One consequence is found in how a self-centered man responds to the divine message. The message, "Repent!" is an affront. The idea of unconditional love is an insult to pride. For those in our culture who have failed to succeed in the performance mode, namely, addicts, criminals, etc., the message, "Repent!" only pours gasoline on the coals of their self-hatred because they see success and favor only in terms of achieving standards that they know they can never meet. Without the knowledge of God's grace, they are simply driven deeper and deeper into self-hatred (which is derived from self-centeredness).

The modern church often delivers the "Repent!" part of Jesus' message without first laying down the grace message. We tell people how wretched they are, a message that worked wonderfully in revivals of previous centuries, without discerning the times, without taking into account how that particular message will be taken by people who are steeped in worship or hatred of themselves.

God has called us to be ministers of this gospel. Considering the dynamics of this present world system, grace needs to be front and center in our lives and in our ministry. It is not enough to proclaim man a sinner. We must also offer him God's grace, so that when he falls, it will be into God's arms rather than condemnation. And as we have already seen, over the long-term, rather than causing him to want to sin even more, God's grace will actually persuade him to sin even less.

As people whom God has called to minister to others, we must ask ourselves, "Do I understand and live in grace?" because we will never be able to communicate grace until we have learned to live from it ourselves.

Here's a test. When someone looks into your eyes and confesses a sin that seems utterly detestable or horrible to you, what is the look in your eyes that they see? Is it love and compassion? Is it complete acceptance of them as persons in spite of their grievous actions?

They must see the eyes of a person who fully believes that if it wasn't for the grace of God, they might have done the same thing. And when they see humility, when they see unconditional love and compassion in response to the confession of their deepest and darkest sin, they will be seeing Jesus, and their hearts will be won back to Him in that moment. And they will listen and receive ministry and find the transformation that they've been hoping for.

Study Section—
Living by Grace rather than Performance Orientation

A. The Problem with Performing for God

1. *We can't do it!* Any attempt is doomed to failure.

    "There is no one righteous, not even one, there is no one who understands…there is no one who does good, not even one" (Romans 3:10-12).

    "I know that nothing good lives in me, that is, in my flesh. For I have the desire to do what is good, but I cannot carry it out" (Romans 7:18).

    "Apart from Me, you can do nothing" (John 15:5, NASB).

    "With man this is impossible, but with God all things are possible" (Matt. 19:26).

2. *It's religion!* It is the way the world does things, and the world's value system is corrupt.

    "Religion is a picture of God painted by the devil."
    —Mario Murillo

    a. In the world, you are expected to earn your keep.

       "Hardening of the oughteries."
       —Dudley Hall, from *Grace Works*

       "It wasn't service for which we were created. It was and is fellowship." —from *Grace Works*

    b. In the world, nothing in life is free.

- It's hard to accept a gift without having something to give in return.
- If I hand you $50, you are uncomfortable and suspicious because you didn't earn it.
- Turn the tables. If after you make dinner for me, I hand you $20, you become offended and hurt because it was a gift.

c. In the world, worth and value are based on performance.
- grades
- salaries
- positions
- awards

d. In the world, love is an earned commodity.

"Give me what I want in this relationship, and I will love you."

<u>love = sex</u>

<u>love = romantic feelings</u>

e. The Old Testament pictures Israel as God's unfaithful spouse.

f. God's definition of love = commitment and sacrifice.

"This is how we know what love is: Jesus Christ laid down His life for us" (1 John 3:16).

<u>Love = sacrifice</u>

"This is love...that God sent His Son as an atoning sacrifice for our sins" (1 John 4:10).

<u>Love = sacrifice</u>

"… love not with words, but with actions and in truth" (1 John 3:18).

<u>Love = actions</u>

"God is love" (1 John 4:16b, NASB).

<u>Love = God Himself</u>

3. It is the way of the world—Unbelief—Living by sight, not by faith.

   "We live by faith, not by sight" (2 Corinthians 5:7).

   "Faith is being sure of what we hope for and certain of what we do not see" (Hebrews 11:1).

   "Without faith, it is impossible to please God, because anyone who comes to Him must believe that He exists and that He rewards those who earnestly seek Him" (Hebrews 11:6).

   a. We live in unbelief of the unseen promises of God. It is hard to believe in unlimited, unpaid for, unsolicited, unconditional love and forgiveness. We wouldn't!

   b. It is hard to believe that Jesus' death on the Cross cancels all of our sin—past, present and future. It is foolishness!

   "For the message of the Cross is foolishness to those who are perishing" (1 Corinthians 1:18).

   "Has not God made foolish the wisdom of the world" (1 Corinthians 1:20, NASB)?

   "God chose the foolish things of the world to shame the wise" (1 Corinthians 1:27).

   c. "God offends the mind to reveal the heart" (Mike Bickle—e.g., mud on eyes; "eat My flesh and drink My blood").

   d. We live by faith in what the world tells us and shows us. Reality for us is what we have experienced rather than what God says is true. Evil appears to be in control, triumphing over good, more powerful than good. Sometimes it seems as if God doesn't care about us.

   e. It appears that the purpose of life is realized through position, power, prestige, material goods.

   f. About all of this, God says:

   "Do not conform any longer to the pattern of this world, but be transformed by the renewing of your mind" (Romans 12:2).

   "May I never boast, except in the Cross of our Lord

Jesus Christ, through which the world has been crucified to me, and I to the world" (Galatians 6:14).

"Do not love the world or anything in the world (system). If anyone loves the world, the love of the Father is not in him" (1 John 2:15).

"I am a stranger on earth" (Psalm 119:19).

"I urge you, as aliens and strangers in the world, to abstain from sinful desires, which war against your soul" (1 Peter 2:11).

"They (people of faith) admitted that they were aliens and strangers on earth. People who say such things show that they are looking for a country of their own… longing for a better country—a heavenly one. Therefore, God is not ashamed to be called their God, for He has prepared a city for them" (Hebrews 11:13, 14, 16).

4. Performing for God belies a lack of an intimate relationship with Him.
   a. Not abiding in the vine and receiving His life-giving love and affirmation.
   b. Not experiencing His affirming, healing presence.
   c. The result is mass insecurity!
      - We seek what we need from the world instead of from God.
      - We trust in what we see, not the unseen things that God calls us to trust.
      - We trust in what we feel rather than what God says.
      - Rewards for performance deceive us by providing the psychological high that we need in order to temporarily fill those unaffirmed voids.
   d. We trust in our own worldly values rather than God's truth.
   e. We trust in what we understand rather than in the evidence for God being trustworthy (e.g., the Cross).

      "Trust in the Lord with all your heart and lean not on your own understanding" (Proverbs 3:5).

B. The Cure to the Trap of Performing for God (Titus 2:11-14)

1. Grace Has Appeared To All Men (v. 11).

    a. Grace Saves

    b. Grace Forgives

    c. Grace Does Not Discriminate
       - You are not a "special case."

2. Grace Teaches Us To Say "No" To Ungodliness (v. 12a).

    a. By eliminating the need to perform righteousness.
       - ref. 3:7: "having been justified by His grace."
       - God performs through us what He requires of us.

    b. The battle is the Lord's.
       - David and Goliath (1 Samuel 17:47).
       - Jehoshaphat's praise and worship team defeat Moab and Ammon in 2 Chronicles 20:15.

    c. By accepting us based on Christ's substitutionary work.
       - My acceptance will never again be based on my behavior.

    d. By eliminating the power of guilt and condemnation, Satan's biggest trick.
       - The unending wheel of unbelief in the forgiveness of God.
       - We too often create God in our image, not as He really is.

    "There is now *no* condemnation for those who are in Christ Jesus" (Romans 8:1).

    e. By changing our will, our inner desire, and motivating us from the inside out.
       - We are transformed by His unconditional love. It breaks our heart.
       - We are attracted by His purity, rather than withdrawing or cringing away from it.

3. It is not cheap grace.

   a. Christ suffered horribly to gain this for us (v. 14a).

   b. Grace does not mean absence of discipline.

   "Those whom I love, I rebuke and discipline" (Rev. 3:19).

   "My son, do not make light of the Lord's discipline, and do not lose heart when He rebukes you, because the Lord disciplines those He loves, and He punishes everyone He accepts as a son" (Hebrews 12:5-6).
   - God's discipline draws you closer to Him—you feel cherished and protected by it.
   - God's discipline seems to follow "defiance with knowledge" rather than "weakness from hurt or habit."

   c. Grace does not mean the absence of *consequences*. Sin has its own affect on the sinner.

   "I will give you into the hands of your lovers and it is they who will inflict the punishment" (Ezek. 16:39).

   "To respond to God's love with an answering love is to enter a life of peace and joy, but to reject it is to shut oneself up with unhappiness, in a variety of forms."
   —Leon Morris, from *Testaments of Love*
   - Consequences to sin are:
     —Physical Consequences (e.g., AIDS, disease)
     —rebellious children,
     —lost opportunities,
     —lost rewards

   We reap what we sow through a natural process as a result of leaving the protective commands of God, not as a result of God personally "getting back" at us.

   "Do not be deceived: God cannot be mocked. A man reaps what he sows. The one who sows to please his flesh, from that flesh will reap destruction; the one who sows to please the Spirit, from the Spirit will reap eternal life" (Galatians 6:7-8).

   "Now this is eternal life: that they may know You, the only true God, and Jesus Christ whom you have sent" (John 17:3).

4. Grace Teaches Us To Live Godly Lives In This Present Age (v. 12b).

   a. Self-controlled

   b. Upright

   c. Godly—We *want* to do what He says because we have been persuaded by His loving grace.

   d. Now! In this present age!

5. Grace Causes Us To Persevere (v. 13).

   a. Through the unanswered questions of life (like Job did)

   b. Through the preparation years that lead to the meat of our life's call and work
      - The drudgery
      - The fears of being left behind by everyone else

   c. Through trials, temptations, persecutions

   d. Through the long process that leads to full sanctification

   e. Through the wait for the "blessed hope"—the glorious appearing of Jesus Christ

   f. Through the wait for obtaining the full inheritance of heavenly blessings and promises.

6. Grace's Result (v. 14).

   a. Redemption from wickedness—It doesn't own or control us anymore.

   b. Purified

   c. His very own

   d. Eager to do what is good (the transformation of our will)

      "It is God who is at work in us, both to *will* and to do His good purpose" (Philippians 2:13).

C. How do I Start Living out of Grace?

Your love of God must become true enough that you naturally want to do what it takes.

1. Reckon yourself dead to sin and alive in Jesus (Romans 6:11).

   "I have been crucified with Christ and I no longer live, but Christ lives in me. The life I live in the body, I live by faith in the Son of God, who loved me and gave Himself for me" (Galatians 2:20).

   a. Reckon = to accept as a fact for yourself and in your own experience.

   b. Every time you catch yourself performing for God—trying to earn His favor—you've got to stop what you're doing and kill that manipulative religious spirit in prayer.

   c. Forcefully take the things of the kingdom (Matthew 11:12).

   d. Live in dependence on God.

   "Choosing a life of relationship with God means giving up our independence. It means becoming dependent on someone other than ourselves—Jesus—for the resources of life (e.g., life, wisdom, righteousness, etc.)" —*Grace Works* by Dudley Hall, p. 30

   (1) "The Tree of Life" represents the choice of relationship with God dependent on His wisdom and direction.

   (2) "The Tree of the Knowledge of Good and Evil" represents independence from God, and self-effort for righteousness.

2. Guard the thoughts of your mind (Philippians 4:6-9).

   a. The peace of God, which comes out of a relationship with Him, guards the heart and mind.

   b. Set your mind on the things of God.

   c. Put into practice what you hear from God.

3. Live by faith rather than by feelings.

   "May the eyes of your heart be enlightened" (Ephesians 1:18).

   "Fix your eyes not on what is seen, but on what is unseen" (2 Corinthians 4:18).

   "Fix your thoughts on Jesus" (Hebrews 3:1).

   "Fix your eyes on Jesus, the author and perfecter of our faith" (Hebrews 12:2).

   "Let the Word of Christ dwell in you richly" (Colossians 3:16).

   "It's the *look* that saves, but it's the *gaze* that sanctifies."
   (Anne Ortlund, from *Fix Your Eyes on Jesus*)

   a. Faith in the promise of "No condemnation."

   b. Faith in God's unconditional love, acceptance and forgiveness.

   c. Faith in God's greater power.

4. Meditate on the truth.

   "I have hidden your Word in my heart that I might not sin against You" (Psalm 119:11).

5. Turn to God at the point of temptation and at the point of sin.

6. Worship Him for His love and purity—for those attributes that you need built in you.

7. Ask God to transform your desires and will (2 Corinthians 3:18; Philippians 2:13).

8. Back To Intimacy—to be motivated by His life and His love flowing in and through you…

   a. …where you learn to see the forces of God arrayed on your behalf…

      - …like Elisha asked God to do for his servant when the King of Aram and his army were about to attack them (2 Kings 6). God showed the servant angelic chariots of fire.

   b. …where you receive blessings that can be found in no other way.

Mike Bickle lists seven such blessings in his book, *Passion for Jesus* (pp. 147-156):

"The first step toward experiencing intimacy with Jesus is our decision to pursue Him more than we pursue other good things such as anointing, happiness and success. When you set your heart to seek the Lord, your life will begin to change in many ways. Here are a few:

1. *A Focus on Intimacy Washes Our Spirits.*

    Our spirits will be washed from defilement by the Word of God.

2. *A Focus on Intimacy Protects Our Souls.*

    Our souls will be strengthened against temptation by the breastplate of faith and love affecting our emotions.

3. *A Focus on Intimacy Motivates and Inflames Our Hearts.*

    Our inner man will be motivated and inflamed by a release of divine hunger and zeal as our spirits are exposed to Jesus' flaming heart.

4. *A Focus on Intimacy Satisfies Our Human Spirits.*

5. *A Focus on Intimacy Frees Us From Insecurity and Fear of Man.*

6. *A Focus on Intimacy Heals Inner Wounds of the Heart.*

7. *A Focus on Intimacy Is an Effective Means of Spiritual Warfare.*

"Becoming what you were meant to be is not something you can do on your own! It only happens as we live in relationship with the Father" (The old man must die). —from *Grace Works* by Dudley Hall, p. 29.

Exercises—Grace

1. Ask the Father to reveal to you whether you have been living out of a performance orientation instead of by grace.

2. Ask Him to reveal to you the sins that may underlie this problem—such as pride, independence, the entertaining of a religious spirit, a controlling spirit, envy, covetousness, unbelief, etc.

3. Repent of the sins that He reveals and ask Him to change you from the inside out.

4. Ask the Lord to increase your ability to trust Him.

5. Ask Him to take the load of performance that you have been carrying and to release you into the world of grace.

6. Meditate on the Cross (the death and suffering of Jesus), and ask God to reveal to your heart a deeper level of the reality of His sacrifice and suffering (i.e., His love for you).

7. Establish a regular practice of singing love songs to God—fixing the eyes of your heart upon His glory. During those moments, ask Him to reveal the depths of His love for you in ways that powerfully register in your spirit.

8. Ask the Lord to make your own view of "love" consistent with love's true definition and demonstration.

9. Search the Scriptures, and ask the Lord to show you a list of His promises—those that cannot be seen, but must be believed by faith. Place these verses around the house and other environments so that you can see them and practice believing them. Decide that you are going to believe them no matter what things look like.

10. Establish a practice of taking the time to accept God's forgiveness every time you confess a sin that you have committed. Say it out loud—"Lord, I accept your forgiveness."

11. Ask God to reveal any areas where He has offended your mind so as to reveal a heart of conditional love, and repent of those things.

12. Ask the Lord to reveal areas of your life where you are still in love with the world. Repent of the sin and remove those things from your life.

13. Ask God to give you a deep understanding (one that goes beyond the intellectual level) of how His grace (the unmerited favor of His forgiveness) teaches you to say "No" to ungodliness. Read Dudley Hall's book, *Grace Works*.

14. Ask Him to give you a deep understanding of how His grace teaches you to live a godly life.

The Divine Intent for Sexuality

Mankind (Adam) was created in the likeness and image of God (see Gen. 1:26-28). This likeness and image is reflected in numerous ways: our tripartite nature, our capacity to reflect His glory, our free will, our rule over the earth and our creative capacities. The text further describes "in His own Image" as being "male and female." There is a complementary relationship between the male (masculine) and the female (feminine) that in some glorious way reflects God's image.

The more detailed creation account in Genesis 2:18, 21-24 gives us even more tantalizing clues. Eve was not created from the dust of the ground, as Adam had been. Rather, she was taken from the side of Adam (v. 22). Since God is omniscient—knowing everything, His way of creating Eve is brimming with purpose and design. It is a significant clue as to her role, which as the text tells us is to compliment him by providing companionship and by being a helper to him (see v. 18).

In nature, when you divide something into two parts, there is a natural force within those parts that compels them to reunite. The same can be said of that part of Adam's side that God made into Eve. There is a natural inclination in her to reunite with her original source and become one flesh with him again. And that is what the text tells us. Because Eve was taken out of Adam, *"For this reason,* a man will . . . be united to his wife, and they will become one flesh" (v. 24, emphasis added). We learn from this that God's creative intention is heterosexual monogamy.

Jesus reiterated the importance of this design when speaking to the Pharisees in Matthew 19:4-6:

"Haven't you read ... that at the beginning the Creator "made them male and female," and said, "For this reason a man will leave his father and mother and be united to his wife, and the two will become one flesh?" So they are no longer two, but one. Therefore what God has joined together,
let man not separate."

This picture of faithful, monogamous marriage between a man and a woman is one of the most important in all of God's design in creation. That is why Jesus and the apostle Paul made it very clear that divorce is forbidden except in cases where this heterosexual, "one flesh" bond has been broken through adultery (see Matt. 5:32) or through death (see 1 Cor. 7:8-9, 39-40). Interestingly, in 1 Corinthians 7:15, provision is made for the relationship to be severed at the desertion of a believer by a nonbelieving spouse, leaving one to surmise that even though it is clearly demonstrated by the physical sexual act, this "one flesh" bond is as much a spiritual union as it is a physical one.

Indeed, God's design for human sexuality extends far beyond what is obvious in the physical realm. It is a glorious prefigurement of the ultimate union between Christ, the Bridegroom and His Church, the Bride.

In speaking of how husbands and wives should treat each other, Paul reveals in his letter to the Ephesians one of the great mysteries of the ages—that the covenant bond between a husband and wife has been designed to reveal the selflessly self-giving love that is to be mutually exchanged between Christ and the believer (see Eph. 5:32). In fact the entire purpose of creating us male and female is to point us to that ultimate marriage between God and man.

In Scripture, Christ is referred to as the *second* or *last* Adam (see 1 Cor. 15:45,47). And just as the first Adam's bride came from his side rather than being formed from the dust of the ground, so the second Adam's bride (the Church) came forth from Jesus' side at Calvary (see John 19:34) when His blood was shed for the redemption of all who would believe in Him—the Church. And what God hath joined together, no man will put asunder!

This is why such behaviors as heterosexual promiscuity, adultery, polygamy, homosexuality and gay marriage make no sense. They are a mockery of everything that human sexuality and marriage was meant to declare about the redemption and ultimate destiny of man. They are a gross distortion of the image of God in man. They are lies designed by hell itself to keep people from giving glory to God and from finding intimacy with Him both now and in the age to come. Satan is fighting tooth and nail to destroy human sexuality and marriage. He attempts to pervert our sexual identities and to ruin faithful marriages in order to desecrate the very image of God in mankind and to thwart God's greatest desire, which is to live in a covenant of love with every human being.

You see, God knew at creation that Adam could only freely enter into a covenant of love with someone like himself—someone he could relate to, identify with and know at the deepest, interior levels of knowing. And so, in order to accomplish His desire to live in such a union of love with man, God became a human being—the second Adam (Jesus). Knowing that Christ has lived as one of us, has been tempted and has suffered like us, has been subject to our limitations, we are now able to identify with Him at the deepest, interior levels of knowing, and comfortably choose to live in union with God.

It is clear from Genesis 2:18 and 1 Corinthians 11:9 that God created men and women as compliments and counterparts to each other; that they were created in such a way as to "cleave together" both physically and spiritually, and that they were to live in a lifelong, heterosexual, monogamous relationship. Every perversion of that divine intent (including divorce, adultery, promiscuity, homosexual behavior, prostitution, bestiality, incest, etc.) is thoroughly and repeatedly condemned in both the Old and New Testaments (see 1 Cor. 6:9; Rom. 13:13; 1:24-32; Gal. 5:19-21; Eph. 5:5; 1 Tim. 1:10; Rev. 21:8; 22:15; Lev. 18:22-24; 20:10-21).

A perfectly loving Father does not get pleasure in making arbitrary, pointless rules. There must be something about sexual sin and the break of the monogamous marriage bond that does damage to us, wouldn't you say?

The Damage to Body, Soul and Spirit

Just as God is a unity of three (Father, Son, and Holy Spirit), so are we (body, soul, and spirit). Therefore, anything we do that affects one part (such as the body) also affects the other parts (soul and spirit). Consequently, when we commit sexual sin, which is sin against our own body (see Rom. 8:10; 1 Cor. 6:18), we bring negative consequences upon our soul and spirit as well.

The Bible teaches that sin (of any kind) is a sin against God (see Ps. 51:4). In other words, it is spiritual in nature. Thus, passages such as 1 Corinthians 6:9-10 declare that ongoing, unrepentant sinful lifestyles prevent spiritual union with God and result in eternal separation from Him. Since our spirit is our lifeline to God, this damage is the worst of all.

For a true believer, the Holy Spirit doesn't allow our sin to continue without bringing us to repentance (see 1 John 1:9; 2:3; 3:6, 24). Even though the sin of a believer cannot bring eternal separation from God, (only a permanent and final rejection of Jesus Christ as Savior and Lord can do that), it is certainly one of the ways in which we can grieve (see Eph. 4:30) or quench (see 1 Thess. 5:19) the Spirit.

In addition to body and spirit, sexual sin damages the soul. The apostle Peter made this clear when in 1 Peter 2:11 he stated "sinful desires ... *war against your soul.*" This damage to the soul (the mind, will, and emotions) manifests itself in the memories of sexual sin that plague us from the time of commission to the grave. Further evidence of this damage can be seen in the weakened character and personal will that follow on the heels of sin. And volumes could be written on the emotional damage from sexual sin.

There can be other, often unrecognized, damage to the soul as well. The Bible seems to indicate that when we have sexual relations with someone, we become united with them on more than just the physical level and carry that multi-dimensional bond into all future relationships. Many today refer to the invisible aspect of this union as a "soul tie."

In 1 Corinthians 6:16, Paul points out that since believers are a part of Christ's body, for a Christian to have sexual relations with a prostitute is tantamount to uniting Christ Himself with that prostitute. Since Christ is not physically present in such a case, this hints at a level of union that is more than just physical. Paul also states very clearly in that passage, "he who unites himself with a prostitute is one with her in body." Thus we see that a sinful sex act adversely impacts the entire person—body, soul, and spirit.

Most who have had sexual relations outside of marriage immediately understand the concept of a "soul tie." There is within them a pulling toward those with whom they've had intimate relations in the past. Sometimes it's an emotional pull, a dwelling on their memory, and other times it feels like you just have to see them again. It's as if you still possess a part of them, and they, a part of you. It is an unholy soul tie that must be broken through prayer.

Sexual sin creates a dividing wall between your spirit and God's. God doesn't create the dividing wall. Your sinful behavior and the evil intent behind it does. The relationship with God that you were created to develop as the central purpose for your life is sidetracked. You have set yourself adrift from the One who loves you most, who created you, and who has a plan that He wants to institute in your life.

The good news is that He wants you back. Return to Him now. He will forgive you "seventy times seven times," just as He commanded His disciples to do (see Matt. 18:22). Allow His grace to begin to teach you to say "No" to ungodliness (see Titus 2:11-12) and put yourself into His hands to repair the damage that you've done.

God is trying to protect us from hurting ourselves and blocking our relationship with Him. He is the one who made us. He is the one who knows perfectly how we should operate in the world that He gave us. And rightfully, as Creator, He expects that as moral beings, we should follow Him, rather than any other allurement. We should trust Him rather than our own arrogant presumption of knowing better than He does, so that our lifeline to Him (our spirit) will not be damaged.

You were created to unite with God, to share a communion of spirit with Him, to become like Him in the way that a son becomes like his father. The union of man and wife was intended to be an object lesson—a life picture on the earthly plane of that which should also be occurring on the spiritual plane. That is why all sexual activity that does not conform to this divine intention, even in the marriage bed, by the way (sadism, masochism, sodomy, etc.), is sin that grieves the heart of God.

The spiritual union of Jesus Christ (the Son of God) with His Church (the people who follow Him) is likened in Scripture to the marriage bed (see

Eph. 5:31-32). He wants a virgin (undefiled) bride. When we accept Him as Lord and Savior, He comes in to us and, by the Holy Spirit, plants the seeds of spiritual life within us and we are born again into a pure and virgin state of righteousness. He cloaks us, as it were, with His own righteousness. He becomes our covering—a covering that begins to transform us into His likeness.

When He comes again, as the Bridegroom, for His bride (the Church), He will take us into His marriage chamber to consummate this spiritual marriage. And what God has joined together, no man shall ever put asunder!

The Physical-Spiritual Connection

Human sexuality was created good, holy and pure. It is a sacred aspect of life, no matter how perverted we choose to make it. Sex is just as much a spiritual act as it is a physical and emotional one, and it is only when married couples discover this that their sexual life achieves its intended level. Sexual passion, designed by God to symbolize physically the thoughts, feelings and actions that accompany the spiritual passion He has for His Bride, remains a difficult subject to broach because most of our associations with human sexual behavior are "fallen" ones.

Let's note how some of the aspects of our spiritual marriage with God mirror those found in the physical relationship between husband and wife. Between God and His Bride (believers), there is.....

- a heart of passionate love and desire set on the object of its affections.
- a wooing, a courtship.
- a giving of one's self (body, soul and spirit) into the trust and care of the other.
- an exchange of vows, promises and commitments.
- a personal, interactive relationship.
- intimate moments of deep unity, with an unbridled exchange of love, affection and mutual pleasure.
- the husband becoming one with his wife in the act of planting within her.
- spiritual seeds which bring new spiritual life (e.g., new believers, advancement of the Kingdom, personal spiritual growth, etc.).
- the wife bearing that new life and nurturing it to fullness.
- the image of both husband and wife being passed on to the life that they have created together.

As time progresses in the relationship, a oneness or unity develops where the two become identical in heart and mind.

Thomas F. Jones, Associate Director of "Fresh Start Seminars," has some cogent thoughts on the deeper meanings of our sexuality:

"To define sexuality in mere physical terms misses the most important dimension of human sexuality—the spiritual. Sexuality is not just something that joins our bodies; it also involves the joining of our spirits. . . .

We want spiritual union. We want "belonging." We want to be the object of someone's interest and care. We want reciprocal faithfulness and trust, and we want the assurance and peace that those bring. Any definition of sexuality that excludes those things is inadequate. . . .

Sexuality should be defined, therefore, as the human potential for the complete sharing of our whole selves, both body and spirit, with a person of the other sex. Because our sexuality links the spiritual to the physical, no amount of mere physical activity can create the wholeness for which our hearts long....

The key to success and growth in sexual matters is to set spiritual, rather than physical, goals. Once the passion subsides, physical sexual activity alone will always be a disappointment. Sexual fulfillment does not come from "having sex," but from developing spiritual bondedness.

– from *Discipleship Journal*, Issue 64 July/August 1991 (pp. 35-36). Used with permission. All rights reserved.

Bearing Witness Through Our Sexuality

Our earthly relationships set the pattern and ingrain the behavior for our relationship with God. The fruit of adultery in earthly relationships will bear the fruit of adultery with God in our spiritual relationship. But the faithful and habitual acting out of "one flesh" communion in the marital relationship ingrains in us the pattern that God intends (one of intimate faithfulness with Him), and sets that example for the rest of the world to follow and admire. Having been drawn to the earthly picture of faithful, heterosexual monogamy, people are thereby drawn to the heavenly one: the spiritual union of Christ and the Church. If believers continue to mock God's design for human sexual expression with high rates of promiscuity, marital unfaithfulness and divorce, how will non-Christians ever be drawn to the glory of the heavenly Bridegroom?

In Ephesians 5:24-32, we find God's plan for marriage. We see that God has devised a way to weave the very fabric of His life into the fabric of our being, as golden threads might be woven into a plain fabric. Sexuality, becomes the very picture of the creation and redemption of man, and it demonstrates how we, as created beings, receive into ourselves the very life and image of God, thereby participating in the divine nature of God (see 2 Pet. 1:4), and receiving into ourselves the very life and image of God.

It is an amazing grace to have unveiled the beauty, holiness and meaning behind our human sexuality. It is a precious jewel through which we can bring glory to God. The mind boggles at such a mystery, yet somehow we are emboldened to live holy lives as a result.

As for the person called to remain permanently single, that rare one who is asked to sacrifice the gift of union with a human spouse—God's wisdom unfolds even further. God says:

> *Let not any eunuch complain, "I am only a dry tree." For this is what the Lord says: "To the eunuchs who keep my Sabbaths, who choose what pleases me and hold fast to my covenant—to them I will give within my temple and its walls a memorial and a name better than sons and daughters; I will give them an everlasting name that will not be cut off"* (Isa. 56:3c-5).

For them, some of the deeper levels of that mystical marriage between God and the believer take place even before the marriage supper of the Lamb. He completes them supernaturally in the ways in which a man and woman complete each other in matrimony. They become God's companion and helper at new levels and He takes away their loneliness. In unique ways known only to heavenly beings, His image and glory are displayed in them. It is a holy calling indeed. When grasped as the gift that it is, it becomes the foundation for the bearing of incredible fruit—spiritual progeny for the kingdom of God.

Study Section
The Divine Intent for Sexuality

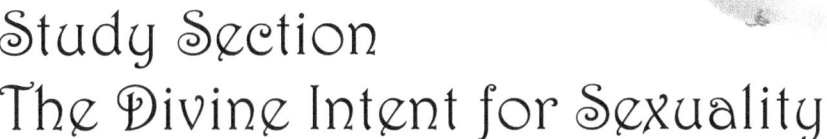

1. GOD'S INTENTION FOR "HETEROSEXUAL MONOGAMY" IN CREATION IS MADE CLEAR IN THE STORY OF ADAM AND EVE (GENESIS 1:26-28 HAS THE GENERAL DESCRIPTION; GENESIS 2:18, 21-24 HAS THE DETAILED ACCOUNT).

    a. Man was made in the image of God (read Genesis 1:26-28).

        (1) "in Our likeness" (v. 26)
            - *Tripartite*
            - *Reflecting the glory of God*
            - *Given a free will*

        (2) "let them rule over…all the earth…and all the creatures" (v. 26, 28)
            - *Rulership*

        (3) "male and female" (v. 27)
            - *Male and Female*—two complimentary parts that when fit together, make "one flesh," with a complementarity between the masculine and feminine (the protecting/initiating/governing and the nurturing/responding/feeling).

            This male/female pairing reflects the Father/Son relationship in the Godhead as well as the lion/lamb characteristics displayed in Jesus.

        (4) "Be fruitful and increase in number" (v. 28)
            - *Creators*—by making children and by the ability to recombine separate things into complex structures of thought and being (e.g., Adam named the creatures in Genesis 2:19).

    b. The separation of "man" into "man and woman" created a complimentary pairing that would have the natural tendency to draw itself back together again into its original state of "one flesh" (see Gen. 2:18, 21-24).

(1) "not good for man to be alone" (v. 18)
- creating a pair that would naturally be drawn into communion

(2) "I will make a helper suitable for him" (v. 18)
- one created to go together with the other as a pair

(3) "God made a woman from the rib He had taken out of the man" (vv. 22-23)
- The woman was actually a part of the man that had been separated out.
- Something taken from something is all the more predisposed to reunite back with its source in order to become complete again.

(4) "For this reason a man will…be united with his wife and they will become one flesh" (v. 24)
- Because they were separated out to form two, they must naturally reunite to reform one again.
- The original unity must be reestablished.
- The complementarity of the two parts must work together to make a whole unit again.

c. When the original image of God is reestablished in the union of one man and one woman, the creative intent of the separation is the result.

(1) creating a baby in sexual intercourse

(2) creating a single-minded team in service of God

(3) creating a force of passionate unity

d. A Summary of the Creation Account Proofs for Heterosexual Monogamy

(1) There was intention and purpose in creating them male and female in order for there to be a mutually supportive, faithfully monogamous relationship that would picture that same intended relationship between man and God, between God and Israel, and between Christ and the Church.

(2) The call to be fruitful and multiply requires heterosexuality.

(3) The command to reunite what God had separated (when He made male and female out of man) is clearly fulfilled in the command to become "one flesh" again.

Jesus said to the Pharisees, "Haven't you read, that at the beginning the Creator made them male and female, and said, 'For this reason a man will leave his father and mother and be united with his wife, and the two will become one flesh?' So they are no longer two, but one. Therefore what God has joined together, let man not separate" (Matthew 19:4-6).

2. PHYSICAL SEXUALITY WAS GOD'S ATTEMPT TO REPLICATE IN THE PHYSICAL THE THOUGHTS, FEELINGS AND ACTIONS THAT ACCOMPANY HIS PASSION IN THE SPIRITUAL REALM.

   a. Between God and His Bride (believers), there is:
      - a heart of passionate love and desire set on the object of its affections
      - a wooing, a courtship
      - a giving of one's self (body, soul and spirit) into the trust and care of the other
      - an exchange of vows, promises and commitments
      - a personal, interactive relationship
      - intimate moments of deep unity, with an unbridled exchange of love, affection, and mutual pleasure
      - the husband becoming one with his wife in the act of

planting within her spiritual seeds that bring new spiritual life (e.g., new believers, advancement of the Kingdom, personal spiritual growth, etc.)
- the wife bearing that new life and nurturing it to fullness
- the image of both husband and wife being passed on to the life that they have created together
- As time progresses in the relationship, a oneness or unity develops where the two become identical in heart and mind.

b. In a lecture given during the April 1991 *IBC* course at the University of the Nations at Makapala, Hawaii, South African Presbyterian minister, Gus Hunter, drew similar parallels between the nature of sexuality in the physical and what it was meant to represent in the spiritual (Used with permission).

"All of our bodily parts are in the image of God. They each represent a function or attribute of God. The method God created for procreation is a part of His image."

"It is out of the interaction between the masculinity and femininity in God that creativity flows." (My note: The sexual act in man is an acting out of this reality—creating a baby). "For this reason, a man will ... be united to his wife ... and become one flesh" (Genesis 2:24). "When the image of God is recreated, creation happens."

"Jesus is both 'Lamb' (femininely submissive to the Father), and 'Lion' (operating with masculine authority over creation), at the same time. He is the Last Adam."

"We then are to be submissive to God and assertively authoritative toward creation." (My note: with what we hear from God. Jesus only did what He heard from the Father. We, too, must return to this original state of yieldedness and trust).

"The masculine (initiative) is born out of the feminine (submissive) not only in nature, but also in the Spirit."

"We, the Bride of Christ, hear from the Lord, nurture it in the womb of our faith, and turn to creation and 'father' the word, working it out with fear and trembling."

"Charles Schultz has put a little bit of every man and woman into the character of Charlie Brown. In a similar way, God has put a picture of Himself (His image) into the unity of the institution of marriage and the marriage act (intercourse)."

"Eve grasped at being the Bridegroom herself (i.e., at being God). Submission was rejected and authority was grasped for her own." (My note: God prophesied this would happen when He said to Eve in Genesis 3:16, "Your desire will be for your husband, and he will rule over you").

3. SPIRITUAL COMMUNION BETWEEN COUPLES AND WITH GOD IS ALSO A PART OF THE DIVINE INTENT IN THE MARITAL RELATIONSHIP AND THE MARRIAGE BED.

   a. The following quotes first appeared in *Discipleship Journal*, Issue 64 July/August 1991—"Singleness" by Thomas F. Jones, Assoc. Dir. of "Fresh Start Seminars" (pp. 35-36). Used with permission. All rights reserved.

   "To define sexuality in mere physical terms misses the most important dimension of human sexuality—the spiritual. Sexuality is not just something that joins our bodies; it also involves the joining of our spirits.

   "(Meeting) our physical needs ... is not all we want. We also want spiritual union. We want 'belonging.' We want to be the object of someone's interest and care. We want reciprocal faithfulness and trust, and we want the assurance and peace that those bring. Any definition of sexuality that excludes those things is inadequate."

   "Sexuality should be defined, therefore, as the human potential for the complete sharing of our whole selves, both body and spirit, with a person of the other sex. Because our sexuality links the spiritual to the physical, no amount of mere physical activity can create the wholeness for which our hearts long."

   "The key to success and growth in sexual matters is to set spiritual, rather than physical, goals. Once the passion subsides, physical sexual activity alone will always be a disappointment. Sexual fulfillment does not come from 'having sex,' but from developing spiritual bondedness."

   "But if sexual intercourse does have a God-given meaning, if it symbolizes the total bondedness and personal commitment of marriage, then it makes perfect sense to remain celibate outside of marriage. Unless two people are prepared for the bond of marriage, it would be a mockery for them to have intercourse since they do not have what intercourse symbolizes."

"Understanding the spiritual nature and potential of our sexuality will set our sights above the merely physical."

4. IN THE FAITHFUL AND HABITUAL ACTING OUT OF "ONE FLESH" COMMUNION IN THE MARITAL RELATIONSHIP, WE ARE INGRAINING THE PATTERN THAT GOD INTENDS FOR MANKIND TO HAVE—ONE OF INTIMATE FAITHFULNESS WITH HIM—INTO OUR SOUL AND SPIRIT, AND SETTING THAT EXAMPLE FOR THE REST OF THE WORLD TO FOLLOW AND ADMIRE.

"If anyone does not love his brother whom he has seen, how can he love God whom he has not seen?" (1 John 4:20-21)

5. OUR ACTIONS TOWARD AND RELATIONSHIPS WITH OUR FELLOW MAN SET THE PATTERN AND INGRAIN THE BEHAVIOR FOR OUR RELATIONSHIP WITH GOD. THE FRUIT OF ADULTERY IN EARTHLY RELATIONSHIPS WILL BEAR THE FRUIT OF ADULTERY WITH GOD IN OUR SPIRITUAL RELATIONSHIP.

6. HAVING BEEN DRAWN TO THE EARTHLY PICTURE OF FAITHFUL, HETEROSEXUAL MONOGAMY, MEN ARE THEREBY DRAWN TO THE HEAVENLY ONE: THE SPIRITUAL UNION OF CHRIST AND THE CHURCH (READ EPHESIANS 5:21-33).

   a. Because the Church submits to Christ, so wives should submit to their husbands (v. 24).

   b. Because Christ loves the Church and gave Himself up for her, so husbands should love their wives through the cleansing power of sacrifice (vv. 25-30).

      (1) "he who loves his wife loves himself" (v. 28) (cf. Genesis 2:23: "bone of my bones and flesh of my flesh"), where Eve was taken out of Adam's body

   c. "We are members of Christ's body" (v. 30), just as Eve was "flesh of Adam's flesh" (Genesis 2:23). And so, "for this reason" (Ephesians 5:31), a man and a woman should unite in sexual union to become one flesh—a profound mystery (v. 32) which pictures the spiritual reality of the reuniting of Christ's members (we, His Church), with the rest of Him.

   d. Therefore, as new creations in Christ, God has devised a way to weave the very fabric of His life into the fabric of our being, as golden threads might be woven into a cotton fabric. Sexuality, therefore, is the very picture of the creation and redemption of man, and how we, as created beings, receive into ourselves the very life and image of God, as we thereby participate in the divine nature of God (2 Peter 1:4).

(1) receiving into ourselves the very life and image of God
- "For the Lord is your Life" (Deuteronomy 30:20)

(2) "that all of them may be one, Father, just as You are in Me and I am in You" (John 17:21)
- If we "become one," instead of uniting with many separate wives (as pictured in the Old Testament polygamous marriages), Jesus unites with one Bride (thus also the transition from polygamy to monogamy from the time of the Patriarchs to the time of Jesus). God's clear intention in calling us to be one pictures His call for us to live in monogamous, covenanted relationships in marriage.

7. THIS IS WHAT WE WERE DESIGNED FOR AND ANY ABROGATION OF THIS INTENT CREATES DAMAGE AND CONFUSION. THERE ARE NATURAL CONSEQUENCES IN SOCIETY AND IN OUR BODIES WHEN WE IGNORE GOD'S DESIGN IN THIS MATTER.

   a. Sinful desires war against your soul.

   "I urge you ... to abstain from sinful desires which war against your soul" (1 Peter 2:11).

   b. He who sins sexually sins against his own body.

   "Flee from sexual immorality. All other sins a man commits are outside the body, but he who sins sexually sins against his own body. Do you not know that your body is a temple of the Holy Spirit, who is in you, whom you have received from God?" (1 Corinthians 6:18-19)

   c. Sexual sin does great damage to your spiritual relationship with God.

   "Do you not know that your bodies are members of Christ Himself? Shall I then take the members of Christ and unite them with a prostitute? Never!" (1 Corinthians 6:15)

   d. When you engage in intimate sexual behavior with someone, you bond with them on a deep emotional, physical and spiritual level and carry that bond into all future relationships.

8. SOME CONCLUDING THOUGHTS—WHICH FIRST APPEARED IN AN ARTICLE IN *DISCIPLESHIP JOURNAL* ISSUE 64 JULY/AUGUST 1991—"BIBLICAL PERSPECTIVE" BY STEPHEN A. HAYNER—PRESIDENT OF INTERVARSITY CHRISTIAN FELLOWSHIP (PP. 24-25). USED WITH PERMISSION. ALL RIGHTS RESERVED.

"Our bodies and our sexuality were God's idea. Somehow we don't hear what God says about sexuality because we don't believe He really approves of it ...'God saw everything that He had made, and indeed, it was very good' (Genesis 1:31) ... God designed our sexual organs and the nerve endings that let us feel pleasure. He even designed our desire to express love physically."

"God wants us to express our sexuality according to His intentions without shame 'The man and his wife were both naked, and they felt no shame'" (Genesis 2:25).

"Sexuality is an integral part of life. The world says, 'You belong to yourself. You can use your body any way you like.' We get confused when we try to reconcile that with God's living in our very personhood ..."

"The biblical view is that we are integrated beings—every part of us is connected to every other part. We are physical, social, emotional, mental, sexual, spiritual beings. What we call 'personhood' is the sum total of all that we are. When our sexuality is isolated and described by merely physical acts, we are depersonalized. Casual sexual activity hurts our ability to be truly intimate, truly loving, and truly human."

"God made sex to be part of a permanent, all-embracing relationship. We can't understand that if we deceive ourselves into isolating sex as a mere biological or genital act. Sexuality was first of all designed to deal with our aloneness."

"The closing verses of Genesis 2 (which are quoted by both Jesus and Paul) offer a picture of the marriage relationship. It is described as 'becoming one flesh.' No human relationship is any closer than this. People must leave their parents and must 'cling' (literally, 'stick together,' 'remain with,' 'be loyally affectionate') to each other in order to experience this. It is a oneness that involves not just the bodies of the man and the woman, but their minds, hearts, and spirits as well."

"Sexuality is about partnership and companionship at the deepest levels. Any understanding of our sexuality that falls outside one of these truths distorts God's plan and ultimately hurts us as persons."

Exercises—Divine Intent

1. Ask the Lord to show you your sexual history, particularly as it relates to the meaning you have put in sexuality and sexual activity.

2. Examine the account of the creation of man and woman, in Genesis chapters 1 and 2. Ask God to give you deeper understanding of His creative intent for sex and ask Him to help you put that deeper meaning into effect in your own sexual life.

3. Ask the Lord to reveal to you the parallels that He intended to draw between the physical sexuality of mankind and certain spiritual realities.

4. Ask God to show you the various things about you as a human being that reflect the image of God and what that means for you.

5. Meditate on Gus Hunter's picture of Jesus as both Lamb and Lion, asking God to show you what that means for your relationships in life.

6. Ask God to uncover areas in your life where you have marred the spiritual meaning that God intended for sex. Repent of those incidents and attitudes. Ask Him to instill deep within your soul an understanding and appreciation of His will in this matter so that you can follow His plan willingly and gladly.

7. Ask God to show you the connectedness between the physical sexual union and the union of Christ with His Church.

8. Meditate on the truth that we are members of Christ's Body (see 1 Corinthians 6:15).

9. Ask the Lord to show you the ways in which you and your spouse (or some couple you know) have become "one flesh" again.

10. Make an irrevocable commitment to the Lord, that with His power, you will honor His design and intention in living in one heterosexual, monogamous relationship, all the days of your life (unless He has given you the calling and gift to remain single, in which case you fulfill this design in marriage to Him).

God, My Father

There is something profoundly simple about the way God works in our lives. Although we in the West try to intellectualize it, God has made His truth plain for all to see and understand. Philip's statement, "Lord, show us the Father and that will be enough for us" (John 14:8), carries a depth of meaning and significance far beyond what we might first imagine. I, for one, had read that statement dozens of times without giving it a thought, until one day, when the Holy Spirit began to show me how foundational this truth is to all of existence.

For us to be healed, it is enough for us to see the Father—to know Him intimately. From that relationship, all of the meaning of life flows. We need to experience the deep, abiding love of God's heart toward us. We need to experience this love—not simply read about it and intellectually agree that it is true. We must pursue God, in worship and prayer—pouring out our love for Him and receiving into ourselves the confidence and assurance of His love for us. Then we truly come alive. "For this is eternal life," Jesus said as He prayed to the Father, "that they may know you, the only true God, and Jesus Christ, whom you have sent" (John 17:3).

A big part of our problem with God as Father is an unhealthy fear of Him based upon our experience with our own father or authority figures, or based on wrong teaching. Sadly, most people who live in bondage to sin don't like God. That is why they will do *anything* to get free except pursue an intimate relationship with Him. They blame Him for the ills of their life. They see Him as a harsh judge with a whip in His hand and a cold, calculating heart. Satan has painted a grotesque picture of God in their minds, depicting Him as an angry God who makes impossible demands and then casts people into hell for failing to keep those demands.

I hated my father for almost 30 years, and so it was unnatural for me to look upon God the Father as a loving being, especially since my dad was a pastor and thus represented the image of God to me even more directly. I cannot remember him ever hugging me, affirming me, telling me he cared for or loved me. But I can remember the day at the age of 10 or 11, while receiving a severe beating from him after trying to run away, that my wounded little spirit couldn't take it any longer, and I declared in my heart that since he hated me, my dad was no longer my father and I was no longer his son. Unfortunately, in doing so I cut myself off from the very earthly being whom God had designed to impart an identity to me. And I went spinning out of control for the next twenty years, clamoring for an identity.

That is how most people feel about God the Father. They think He hates them and so they rebel against Him as a statement of their belief that He is unfair. What a brilliant tapestry of lies Satan has spun. *He has persuaded us to rebel against a God who does not even exist!*

Later, as I began spending regular time with the Lord, worshipping Him, reading His Word, and talking to Him, I began to see the Father for who He really is—an awesome, perfect, unconditionally loving and forgiving Father—one who is perfect in all His ways, flawless in wisdom, one who completes and heals me. This is the true Father in heaven. This is my daddy. If I can trust no one else, I can trust Him completely.

Jesus said, "Anyone who has seen me, has seen the Father" (John 14:9). Do you love Jesus? *Then you know and love the Father as well.* For Jesus is the exact representation of the Father. He is the image of God (see 2 Cor. 4:4c), in whose face we can see the glory of God (see 2 Cor. 4:6c). "In Christ all the fullness of the Deity lives in bodily form" (Col. 2:9).

The Heart of the Father

One night while I was meditating on the biblical accounts of the crucifixion, God revealed a part of His heart to me, and the experience has branded me as His servant forever. Normally, when considering the crucifixion, you contemplate the suffering of Christ. But this night, God the Father was about to show me the crucifixion from *His* perspective.

Without any warning, the heart of the Father swept into my own heart and I could suddenly feel everything that God the Father felt as He watched His Son be crucified. It was a devastating revelation that I was not prepared for. The intensity of emotion was overwhelming. The pain was unbearable.

Imagine if you will, having to watch your son be tortured to death in front of your own eyes. Now imagine that you have all the power in heaven and earth to stop it—but you choose not to. In a sense, you become the executioner. That is what God the Father had to do, and that is the agony that He felt as He watched His Son die.

Mercifully, God only let me feel His suffering for a few seconds, but it was enough. I still commit sins, of course, but they do not come as easily because it is difficult to rebel against a God who suffered so much for me—who loves me with such intensity.

In his book, *Come to Papa,* Gary Wiens writes:

"Because of the joy and pleasure that is found in those kinds of experiences of God's Presence, we find ourselves drawn again and again to the place of seeking to know Him better. . . . [T]he Presence of the Lord is addictive, and we were designed to be captured by this addiction. We were never created to live bored, dissipated lives or to be satisfied with the inferior pleasures of temporary things. We were created to live an exhilarated existence, intoxicated with the beauty and goodness of God. We were meant to be captured by His heart, in love with the One who is madly in love with us" (p. 12).

Toward this end, Paul prayed in Ephesians 1:17-19a:

I keep asking that the God of our Lord Jesus Christ, the glorious Father, may give you the Spirit of wisdom and revelation, so that you may know Him better. I pray also that the eyes of your heart may be enlightened in order that you may know the hope to which He has called you, the riches of His glorious inheritance in the saints, and His incomparably great power for us who believe.

Father Stories

Allow me to share a few more personal stories with you of how God has fathered me since I turned my life over to Him. I want to do this because most of us regard the "pursuit of God" and "the fatherhood of God" as spiritual talk that exists only in the minds of super-spiritual types. We see it as having no practical substance, but that is not true at all. God wants to father us in very real and practical terms as we pursue relationship with Him.

One day I decided to attend a large men's meeting at my church, which was a big stretch for me. I had never felt comfortable in the company of men and would often be overwhelmed with feelings of rejection just being around them—particularly the more macho or athletically-oriented the group. But I knew that God wanted me to have a breakthrough in this area, so I sat there surrounded by 500 men listening to the speaker.

When he finished, we were asked to stand and to give each other a hug, which made me *really* uncomfortable. I didn't like the contrived phoniness of it for one thing. But once everyone is hugging, you've got to go along or else they'll be staring at you wondering, "Why isn't he hugging? What's the matter with him? Let's all lay hands on him and cast that demon out," or whatever.

So I turned around to find somebody to hug and I was met with this Paul Bunyan, lumberjack guy, who nearly crushed me into nonexistence with his arms. Suddenly, however, Paul Bunyan vanished and it was as if God the Father Himself was hugging me. *Astonished* is not even close to the right word. I was *flabbergasted* that God could somehow cause me to know at a deep experiential level that He was hugging me through that man's arms.

I never knew who that guy was and he never knew what God had done through him, but to this day I can vividly remember the healing power that flowed through that hug. In one embrace, God Himself communicated to me the love and the affirmation that I had always longed for from my earthly father.

During my childhood and adolescence, I had grown to hate God the Father. Jesus I had always loved, but the Father I despised. It was a bitter hatred that demonstrated itself in a very rebellious lifestyle. In fact, I deliberately committed certain sins for the express purpose of showing God just how much I hated Him. Years later, after getting saved, that hatred still ran deep in my spirit although it was now covered over with the joy of my salvation. I knew that it had to be lanced, but I was afraid—afraid of what God would do to me if I honestly let out the anger that still brewed in my heart against Him.

One night, however, I decided that if I was to ever go further with the Lord, it had to be laid on the table. So with great trepidation, I let loose the deep pain and emotion, with all the judgments that I had made against the Father, and then waited to be struck dead on the spot. As I braced myself for the heavenly lightning bolt, I was completely taken by surprise when, instead, God hit me with a wave of love. And in the wave, came the message, "You are my son and I love you."

The wave was gentle and yet powerful, and it was liquid love. I became immersed in the exquisite sensation of it. Finally I said, "Father, I just told You how much I hated You and yet You have responded with a wave of love! I don't understand."

He replied, "It's because you have finally been honest with Me. Now I can really help you."

Oh my Lord and my God! What can you say to a God like that? How can you continue to rebel against a Lord as lovely, as sensitive and as understanding as that? You can't! He has captured your heart and you can't continue in willful sin as before. His love cancels the power of sin!

One final story—I was deep in worship during my time with the Lord one night when I suddenly realized that I had begun talking to Him as though I was seven years old. It startled and frightened me, and I remember thinking, "Oh boy, David, you are going off the deep end here. You had better bring yourself back into reality before someone catches you in this condition and sends you away." Just as I said that to myself, the Lord broke in and said, "No, don't stop talking to Me as you have been. I am taking you back to the age when things started going wrong for you so that I can grow you up seamlessly from there. Remain seven for now so that I can heal you." Once again God had astonished me with His unfathomable wisdom. So I locked the door so no one would walk in, and I went back to being seven again with God.

It was amazing what He then began to do. He restarted my emotional growth from the place at which it had shut down as a result of the various traumas of my life. He wasn't interested in patching up a broken vessel. He wanted to recreate a whole vessel like new. And so God the Father began fathering me beginning at the age of seven.

Knowing exactly what the longings of my heart had been back then, He began fulfilling them for me. For example, on one occasion, as I sat in His presence, he caused me to experience myself sitting in his lap while he stroked my hair—something that I had always longed for my father to do.

On another occasion, while in worship, He gave me a vision in which I was playing catch with Him—again, a deep longing in my heart that had never been realized with my earthly father. So He gave me deep interior experiences of those things. And each year, I would grow several more years on the inside, both emotionally and spiritually, so that within just a few years I was relating to God as a teenager and then finally as an adult.

In the healing process, it seems that we must grow through the various stages of maturity—from childhood, to adolescence to adulthood and parenthood. If we missed our childhood with God, we must return to that stage and begin again just as we do when we move through the healing process emotionally (see 1 John 2:12-14).

In Zephaniah 3:17, we read: "(God) will take great delight in you, he will quiet you with his love, he will rejoice over you with singing." Note that the verb in the Hebrew for "take great delight" means to "pick up in the arms and spin around in circles." So what this passage is saying is that God has such delight in you that it is as if He has picked you up in His arms and spun you around in circles. How's that for your self-esteem!

The Father's Discipline

One of the most difficult things about being a dad is learning how to discipline you children in love and without exasperating their spirits (see Col. 3:21). God provides us with the perfect example of just how to do it. He is long-suffering and gracious and has no retributive interest in punishing His children—for several reasons: first, because His Son has already paid the penalty for their sin, and second, because He knows that *it is grace that teaches us to say "No" to ungodliness* (see Titus 2:11-12). And so the discipline of God is rare and carefully measured and has growth in Christlikeness (not retribution) as its goal.

If a believer insists on rebelling at length or if his or her rebellion is leading to a very dangerous place or bringing disgrace upon the name of Christ, then God will send discipline.

The discipline of God, however, is very different than the punishments of the evil one. It is redemptive in nature. The Bible teaches that God simply gives His rebellious children into the hands of the idols that they have chosen (see Ezek. 23:9a,24c), and it is those gods that punish them. Seeing the negative consequences of their ways will then (hopefully) lead them back to God.

Satan comes at us with condemnation, attacking our worth and personhood. God never does that. When God disciplines, the person feels protected, guarded and loved, even while being chastened over his or her behavior.

I'll never forget the first time that God disciplined me. I had just given my life to Christ and had decided that I could still frequent my favorite disco, only I wouldn't bring anyone home for sex. It was typical childish reasoning that did not take into account the many dangers of that environment and the familiar spirits there that knew how to seduce me. Soon after a night spent dancing, I was hitchhiking home and was attacked by the men who picked me up. To this day, I can see the eyes of the man who viciously began to beat me. I could see Satan in his eyes trying to kill me and at the same time I could see God trying to discipline me.

Fortunately, I was able to jump from the car and escape without serious injuries, but as I ran from the scene, I knew that God had just used the evil one to discipline me. In my spirit, I could clearly hear God chastising me for foolishly returning to a club teeming with demonic powers. And so I felt protected, cherished and loved even while I was running for my life.

Read Deuteronomy 8:2-3, 15-17; James 1:2; 1 Peter 1:6-7; Romans 5:3-5; 8:28 to get a scriptural glimpse of how God's fathering requires growth-inducing discipline.

Getting Started in a New, Intimate Relationship with the Father

If the idea of developing an intimate relationship with an invisible God is a bit daunting for you, let me give you a few suggestions to get you started.

 1. Focus primarily on God, His glory, His grace and His power. Sing, worship, pray and read His Word with the goal of knowing God intimately.

 2. Listen for Him to reveal hidden things to you.

 3. Allow Him to relate to you at the age level where your spiritual and emotional growth stopped. Feel free to talk to him like a little child would, if that is where you are in your relationship with Him.

 4. Commit to challenging the old and developing new thought habits.

 5. With the authority Christ has given you, challenge the spir-

itual forces that have participated in the bondage of lying emotions and feelings.

6. Specifically address the tyranny of being controlled by feelings rather than objective truth revealed in Scripture. Practice "truth therapy" in the face of old emotions and beliefs.

7. Identify the major time-stealer in your life and cut it off, using that time to commune with God.

8. Talk to Him at every crossroad, upon making every decision, at the moment of every compulsive or negative thought or feeling. Confess your weakness. Admit your dependence. Ask Him for His power to defeat the enemy.

9. Find a group of devoted, balanced, healthy Christians and join their meetings (home fellowships, men's or women's groups, etc.).

10. Commit yourself to reading every day in the Bible until God speaks to you. Then meditate on that message, asking God to guide and empower the institution of the new truth into your life.

11. Be careful to center your actions in knowing Him, responding in love to Him out of His already demonstrated love for you on the Cross. When you catch yourself going to God with the primary purpose of getting something, then stop, reorient your priorities and approach Him again.

It's amazing what God can do with us once we return to Him with the humbled heart of the prodigal son (see Luke 15:21). After getting saved on a trip to Israel in 1980, I began to seek the Father so that I could learn to love the One I had feared for so many years. Every night, I would kneel at my bed and pour my heart out to Him—telling Him what I was thinking, what I was feeling, what was tempting me, what I didn't understand, asking Him to give me understanding of His Word and His ways, learning to see Him through the exact representation of His Being—Jesus Christ (see Col. 1:15; 2:9). Ever so slowly, I began to love the Father and eventually, even to trust Him. The turnaround came just as the Scripture says it does—God transformed my heart through His grace and love.

There were only two short years between my salvation and my earthly father's passing. In spite of years of virulent hatred toward my father, God was able to heal that relationship as well. When I returned to the States from Israel, I flew to the town where my father lived to tell him what God had done. He was deeply moved, because in the intervening years, God had reached into his heart and brought about significant change as well. There was a gentleness and a tenderness and a grace that hadn't been there before. And in the final two years before his death, my father went from being the man I most hated to the man I most loved.

Study Section—
God, My Father

1. THE HEART OF THE FATHER

    - to love
    - to redeem
    - to forgive
    - to restore
    - to heal
    - to grow
    - to give purpose
    - to guide
    - to protect
    - to provide

    a. Excerpts from *The Father Heart of God*, by Floyd McClung, Jr. Published by Harvest House, Eugene, Or. 1985. Used with permission.

    "Sometimes we want God to perform a miracle and take away all our problems *right now*. Our Father, however, is leading us through a process that is preparing us to reign with Him in heaven. Because He wants to mold and refine us, He allows us to experience temptations which force us to make choices" (p. 75).

    "The struggle is part of the victorious healing process. You are learning invaluable lessons: humility, forgiveness, compassion and endurance" (p. 76).

    "In the process of healing our emotional wounds, God takes the time to build our character, least we remain vulnerable to further hurt" (p. 78).

    "Disappointing circumstances will pass, but one's reaction to them determines a moral and spiritual choice which can influence one's life forever" (p. 84).

    "God allows, even arranges, trying experiences in our lives to expose our character weaknesses and wrong attitudes so that He can deal with them" (p. 85).

b. Scriptural references to the fathering ways of God.

"And you shall remember all the way which the Lord your God has led you in the wilderness these forty years, that He might *humble you, testing you, to know what was in your heart,* whether you would keep His commandments or not. And He humbled you and let you be hungry, and fed you with manna which you did not know, nor did your fathers know, *that He might make you understand that man does not live by bread alone, but man lives by everything that proceeds out of the mouth of the Lord*" (Deuteronomy 8:2-3, NASB).

"He led you through the great and terrible wilderness, {with its} fiery serpents and scorpions and thirsty ground where there was no water; He brought water for you out of the rock of flint. In the wilderness He fed you manna which your fathers did not know, that *He might humble you and that He might test you, to do good for you in the end. Otherwise, you may say in your heart, 'My power and the strength of my hand made me this wealth'*" (Deuteronomy 8:15-17, NASB).

"Consider it all joy, my brethren, when you encounter various trials, knowing that *the testing of your faith produces endurance. And let endurance have {its} perfect result, that you may be perfect and complete, lacking in nothing*" (James 1:2, NASB).

"In this you greatly rejoice, even though now for a little while, if necessary, you have been distressed by various trials, *that the proof of your faith,* {being} more precious than gold which is perishable, even though tested by fire, *may be found to result in praise and glory and honor at the revelation of Jesus Christ*" (1 Peter 1:6-7, NASB).

"And not only this, but we also exult in our tribulations, knowing that *tribulation brings about perseverance; and perseverance, proven character; and proven character, hope;* and hope does not disappoint, because the love of God has been poured out within our hearts through the Holy Spirit who was given to us" (Romans 5:3-5, NASB).

"And we know that *God causes all things to work together for good to those who love God, to those who are called according to His purpose*" (Romans 8:28, NASB).

c. Relating to God's Father Heart

"(God) will *take great delight* in you, He will quiet you with His love, He will rejoice over you with singing" (Zephaniah 3:14-17).

(Note: "take great delight" or "exult" means to "pick up in the arms and spin around in circles").

(In the healing process, we must grow through the various stages of maturity—from childhood, to adolescence to adulthood and parenthood. If we missed our childhood with God, we must return to that stage and begin again just as we do when we move through the healing process emotionally).

e. Getting started in a new, intimate relationship with the Father:

   (1) Focus primarily on God, His glory, His grace, His power. Sing, worship, pray, read His word, with the goal of knowing God intimately.

   (2) Listen for Him to reveal hidden things to you.

   (3) Allow Him to relate to you at the age level where your spiritual and emotional growth stopped. Feel free to talk to him like a little child would, if that is where you are in your relationship with Him.

   (4) Commit to challenging the old and developing new thought habits.

   (5) Challenge the spiritual forces that have participated in the bondage of lying emotions and feelings, with the authority Christ has given you.

   (6) Specifically address the tyranny of being controlled by feelings rather than objective truth revealed in scripture. Practice truth therapy in the face of old emotions and beliefs.

   (7) Identify the major time stealer in your life and cut it off, using that time to commune with God.

   (8) Talk to Him at every crossroad, every decision, every compulsive or negative thought or feeling. Tell Him about it. Confess your weakness. Admit your dependence. Ask Him for His power to defeat the enemy.

(9) Find a group of devoted, balanced, healthy Christians and join their meetings (home fellowships, men's or women's groups, etc.).

(10) Commit yourself to reading every day in the Bible until God speaks to you. Then meditate on that message, asking God to guide and empower the institution of the new truth into your life.

(11) Be careful to center your actions in knowing Him, responding in love to Him out of His already demonstrated love for you on the Cross. When you catch yourself going to God with the primary purpose of getting something, then stop, reorient your priorities and approach Him again.

Exercises—God, My Father

1. Examine the relationship that you have had with your father (or father figure) over the years. Ask God to uncover hidden anger, fear, resentment, judgments, vows, criticisms and other sinful reactions that you have had against him. Then ask the Lord to give you the ability to forgive each one. Make the choice to forgive, independent of your feelings.

2. Ask the Lord to forgive you for the many times when you rebelled against or in other ways failed to honor your father and your mother. Do not allow the sins that your parents committed against you keep you from doing this. It is a command independent of those matters.

3. Write a short paper that answers the question: "When I think of God as my father, I feel…" Discuss your answers with a mature Christian friend or minister who is truly honoring the Lord with their life.

4. Write your heavenly Father a letter, telling Him everything that you have ever thought about Him—good and bad. Describe your feelings, the questions that you have had, the fears and doubts. Ask Him to help you know the truth about Him, deep in your spirit, and to draw you into a deep, intimate relationship with Him.

5. Approach God the Father in prayer as a child, asking Him to reveal Himself as Father to you deep in your spirit. Receive from Him new revelation so that by faith you can receive His love, free from the fears and doubts that have kept you from receiving it fully in the past.

6. Read J.I. Packer's *Knowing God*, A.W. Tozer's *The Pursuit of God* and Floyd McClung's *The Father Heart of God*. Ask God to speak to you and to change you permanently as you read these books.

7. Make a commitment in your heart that from this day forward, no matter what things look like, you are going to assume that God is perfect and good and loving in all His ways. If you are having trouble making this commitment, meditate on the basis for such a com-

mitment—the Cross of Christ-the proof of His love.

8. Ask God the Father to give you His heart for Jesus and His heart for the world. Ask for this regularly.

9. Decide that everything in your life from this point on, will revolve around, and be subject to, a pursuit of intimacy with God the Father.

Root Sources for Improper Sexual Development

Sexual brokenness occurs within the basic developmental processes that shape each and every one of us.

Perhaps the greatest single cause for aberrant development is improper role modeling. We were designed to take on the attributes of those in authority over us. We absorb their values, behaviors and customs—even mannerisms. You've seen pictures of the little boy unconsciously mimicking everything that he sees his father doing. This was built into his very nature. God wants us to take on His values, behaviors and customs as well as those of our own fathers and mothers.

When our earthly role models (primarily father and mother) give us an ungodly example to follow, an aberration of God's intention occurs. This is one of the ways in which the sins of the fathers are visited upon the third and fourth generations that follow them (see Exod. 34:7).

The Influence of Parents

Temperament is a *gift* that, when fitted properly within the fabric of interpersonal relationships, can serve the redemptive purposes of God. Some parents, however, fail to train their children "in the way they should go" (Prov. 22:6) and instead try to change them into their own ideal, thus working against what God has intended. For example, the father who always wanted an athlete for a son may try to change the temperament of his sensitive son through criticism and intimidation, or by forcing him to perform (and fail) in an arena where he has no natural skills or interests. This selfish father is more concerned about how others see him than in the needs and wants of his child. The boy will recognize this and grow to resent it. He will also have problems with developing a healthy sense of self and in accepting who he is. He will more than likely resort to an addictive lifestyle to mask the deep pain of rejection.

Similarly, a father who wanted a son may only affirm his daughter when she acts like the boy he always wanted. Although she will acquiesce to his wishes in order to receive affirmation and attention from him, she will recognize her father's unspoken decree that she is not lovable as she really is and will likely develop a dysfunctional lifestyle in order to cope with the pain.

A father who fails to model masculinity properly, who is cold and distant and who does not bond with his son on an emotional level, can be the primary source for that son's homosexual predilection. A father who molests his daughter can be the source for her homosexual confusion or her promiscuity. A mother who uses her young son to fill the emotional void in her marriage that is not being met by her husband can be the primary cause for that boy's identity or gender confusion.

Children who grow up with dysfunctional parents like these, (or who live in other harmful environments), will eventually grow to resent their lot in life and many of them will blame the God who caused them to be born into such a situation. They will see God as unfair and uncaring. Deep inside, perhaps unknown even to them, they will nurse a deep stronghold of anger at God which they will draw on to justify a sinful lifestyle, and they will be unable to draw close to Him.

If your adopted self-image is negative, God wants to change that error by speaking your true identity into your spirit through His Word, through the words of other believers who He sends to communicate truth to you, and through direct revelation to your soul during times of intimacy with Him.

What then can the healing process be likened to? It's like the guy with a tattoo of a naked lady who comes to the Lord. Since the tattoo cannot be removed, he has clothes tattooed onto the existing picture. The tattoo now depicts a new reality of purity and Godly purpose, but underneath lies a remnant of the old picture that only he knows about. He now must choose to believe in the new reality instead of the old identity. The enemy will try to lie to him and cause him to believe that he is still the man who had the original tattoo put on, but he must choose to believe God instead and accept by faith his new identity in Christ—an identity that reflects objective truth and reality rather than the projections of society or misguided authority figures from his past.

Though the perception of one's identity is initially acquired through life's experiences and the opinions of others, we must eventually choose whose opinion we are going to accept as valid and true—man's or God's. If we accept God's, He will engrave it in our hearts to cover our old perception.

The Bible is very clear in Exodus 20:5, 34:7, Numbers 14:18 and Deuteronomy 5:9 that the sins of the fathers are passed down to (or visited upon) the third and fourth generation of those who hate God. This is a strange concept to grasp at first because it seems to unfairly penalize the children for the sins committed by their parents. But as we look more deeply into the matter, what we observe is a picture of how iniquity works in covenantal situations. We have just seen how it attaches itself to the covenant offspring of a sinner and the ruinous imprint that can be made in his children. Both parents have this influence, but it is particularly true of the sins of the father, since he is the covenant head of the family. The influence of the parents works at three levels: body, soul and spirit.

God has made a way of escape, however, for that child who decides that he or she is no longer going to follow in the sinful ways of his or her parents and who turns to God to be set free. God will break the curse of the fathers from that generation (see Ezekiel 18:14-17). Therefore, as we minister to those with a clear generational line of sins, we must challenge the person to renounce the sin line of their parents, declare that they are no longer going to participate in those works of iniquity, and ask God to break the curse that is over them (and their children) as a result of those generational sins. God will set them free from not only the attraction toward those sins, but also from the physical consequences of such sins that can often be found in diseases such as asthma and arthritis.

The Influence of Teachers

A second major influence for improper identity development in a child is his or her teachers. As young people, we naturally and innocently accept most of what is taught to us. If our teachers fill our minds with lies, then we will believe lies. If they teach us that things taught in the Word of God are wrong, then we will tend to believe them, even against the witness in our own spirits.

When you are told repeatedly by a teacher that you are dumb, bad, a failure, never going to amount to anything, etc., you often unconsciously accept such judgments as accurate observations. Not only is the source of the observation an older and supposedly wiser person, but the judgment is usually proclaimed soundly and loudly into your ear at the very moment when you are behaving in a way that would appear to prove the accusation. In your child's mind, the evidence seals the judgment.

Some teachers create a negative effect by *affirming* the wrong things, such as sexual promiscuity, homosexual tendencies, rebellion against parents or opportunism. The juxtaposition of the lie with benevolence and authority makes the subterfuge all the more insidious.

Then there are the classic scenarios, such as when a teacher seduces and sexually molests a person in his or her class. Teacher sexual abuse is far more common today than it has ever been, especially in high school and college.

The Influence of Friends

A third source of aberrant identity development can be the influence of friends. If our friends exert a godly influence on us, we will tend to conform to their thinking and behavior. Similarly, if they fill our minds with sinful knowledge and entice us with those things that feed our fleshly nature, we will tend to mimic that influence, so as to become identified with them.

It is not unusual, for example, to find that a sexually broken man witnessed at least one incident of exhibitionism by an admired sister, brother, or friend, which then became the catalyst for a life of compulsive masturbation, voyeurism, exhibitionism, or homosexuality.

(I should mention the transfer of demonic spirits that can occur in such a setting. The friend who engages in immoral activity is quite possibly under the influence of a demonic spirit. The one who witnesses their sinful act becomes vulnerable to a transference of that same spirit. Both of them can end up demonized by the same spirit, which is why the witness often ends up in bondage to the same sort of immorality.)

Friends can have significant influence in our lives in more subtle ways as well. Have you ever considered that there might have been unseen factors at work that guided your choice of a "best friend"? Many times we select the person who most accepts us the way we are, or the person who best represents most what we want to be. They remain our "best friend" because of the vital role they play in being a haven of comfort, acceptance and modeling. The more accepting they are of the way we are, or the more they reflect who we want to be, the more power they have over our lives for either good or evil.

Our larger circle of friends can cause us to form negative self-perceptions. They are often highly competitive and wield power through psychological warfare (criticisms, intimidation, comparisons, gossip, etc.). The more we look up to and admire an accuser or a group of accusers, the more influence their words have on us to form a negative self-perception.

The Influence of Heroes

Face it—our early years are spent identifying with and becoming like hero figures. My earliest heroes were Davy Crockett, Swamp Fox and Elfago Bacca—go figure!

Heroes (sports figures, rock stars, TV and movie stars, etc.) have an enormous power in our society because we are a culture of idolaters. If we have already accumulated a negative self-perception from the opinions and treatment of others, and thus are waiting for an excuse to happen, the "fall" of a hero can give us the ammunition that we need to justify our own fall. After all, if one so great as my hero turns to substance abuse or immorality in times of pain or sadness, then who am I to resist those same temptations? In fact, if the one who has embodied everything I have ever dreamed of being finds comfort and justification in sinful behavior, it must be okay.

Hero-worship is a great deception, because eventually, every single one of them will be found out as unworthy of our adulation. God is the only One who can withstand the maturing scrutiny of a man or woman in search of someone to emulate.

The Influence of Outsiders

Many kids have the unfortunate experience of meeting outsiders who negatively influence their growing sense of identity. Some children are sexual molested by strangers. A man who rapes a young boy can be *the* source for the sexual identity confusion or pedophilia that may later develop in that boy. The one who shares pornography with an innocent child can be the source for a host of sexual problems in the life of that child, depending on the kind of pornography and the individual reaction in the soul and spirit of that child.

Others fall prey to forms of opportunistic abuse that may last only seconds—becoming exposed to exhibitionism or other influences that violently jolt them from their world of innocence and thrust them into a fearful world of immoral powers and influences. These kinds of experiences can be deeply traumatizing to children, and even more so to those who are of a more sensitive and innocent nature. And because of the anonymous element, most of these victims are afraid to tell their parents what has happened for fear of not being believed or simply because they have no words with which to describe what has happened. Consequently, they live in a dark and secret world of fear where their sense of well being and moral equilibrium has been harshly compromised—without apparent remedy.

There are millions of people who would, if they had the chance, corrupt and pervert your child's innocence. One recent news program ran a sting where people posed on the Internet as underaged children, and within just a few *hours*, they had *dozens* of child molesters show up at their doors—regular-looking guys who had come thinking that they were about to have sex with a child. It's as if we are once again living in Sodom and Gomorrah.

The greatest negative "outsider" influence in our culture today is, of course, the media, including the Internet. Any five-year-old can now view the most perverted pornography ever imagined by the mind of man on his own computer in his own home (and in many cases, at his local library), and the Supreme Court of the United States has repeatedly struck down laws to stop it. Those images are wreaking horrible destruction in the minds and hearts of our children, day in and day out, in every town and city in the world.

The number one family cable movie network in America (HBO), which can be found in most any hotel room as well as in millions of Christian homes, regularly airs hardcore pornography, and no one blinks an eye.

The largest Internet provider of books in the U.S. (Amazon.com) continues to sell books that encourage and promote pedophilia (child molestation), and yet America yawns as ministries like ours desperately try to get someone to do something to stop them. No one seems to care.

The Influence of the Demonic Realm

Satan and his minions are, of course, sometimes a force for aberrant development. However, their influence is usually derivative—one of encouraging and taking advantage of other more primary influences in order to draw us away from God. Their powers are opportunistic and generated from lies. They use the ground that we (or those who have covenantal influence over us) give them to multiply the damage that flows from our sinful reactions to trial and temptation.

Believers are indwelt or "possessed" by the Holy Spirit and cannot therefore be demon-possessed. However, the word used in the New Testament is "demonized" and refers to a situation where a degree of control or influence has been gained in a person's life by demonic powers, whether believer or unbeliever.

Being demonized is not so much a matter of spatial occupation as it is degree of influence. A demonized person can come to Christ (and receive deliverance), or a person who is already "in Christ" may still need deliverance from one or more unaddressed demonic strongholds, or a believer may have given new ground to the demonic realm through sinful acts and need deliverance for that.

The web of lies that attaches itself to rebellious actions creates a demonic stronghold that we must dislodge with the truth: "The weapons we fight with are not the weapons of the world. On the contrary, they have divine power to demolish strongholds. We demolish *arguments* and every *pretension* that sets itself up against the knowledge of God, and we take captive *every thought* to make it obedient to Christ" (2 Cor. 10:4-5).

It appears that demonizing spirits have an increasing influence over us according to the degree and length of participation in any given sin. This is particularly true of knowing, willful and defiant sin. If I commit a sin out of the uncontrived weakness of an unguarded moment, that is bad enough, but if I repent with genuine contrition, the grace of God is quick to cover my sin. However, if I commit that same sin with full knowledge, in the face of internal pleas from the Holy Spirit to stop (I'm being willful), or out of an angry and deliberate attempt to get back at God for some perceived fault in Him (I'm being defiant), then the chances of a demonic stronghold getting established are far greater. The degree of influence gained by the enemy in that stronghold is greater as well. Should I continue at length in such willful or defiant sin, the likelihood of a demonic outcome increases even more.

One of the odder realities is that some people appear to be demonized by becoming *victims* of sexual abuse. Since demons must earn their ground in a person through their own sin, their ability to demonize a victim may derive from the sinful reactions of that person to the abuse. It is common for a victim of abuse to make bitter judgments and vows, and to pass condemning sentences against God and other people. Although such reactions are understandable, they remain sinful and they allow the demons to gain a degree of influence.

Demons may also gain ground if a child's legal head "uncovers" him or her. If the father or mother is committing sexual abuse, they have not only sinned against their child but they have also rent the spiritual covering, enabling demonic powers to enter in and do even more damage. Believing children still have recourse to God for covering, but they will often will refuse to do so out of anger at Him for having allowed the abuse to happen in the first place.

In addition, we may attract demonic powers by viewing sin, however innocently. Satan doesn't care how innocently you entered his territory. All he cares about is taking advantage of the fact that you are there. Many stories have been told by sex addicts of how their first exposure to pornography was so completely innocent, yet how instantly they became bound to those very images. Many a voyeur will tell similar stories of innocently glancing into a window and seeing someone undressed—and instantly becoming obsessed with viewing others in the same, secretive way. Some would like to attribute this phenomenon completely to brain chemistry, but biblical wisdom suggests that there is more than just chemical imprinting going on.

Finally, we may attract demonic powers by toying with the tools of the demonic realm such as hypnotism, Ouija Boards, Eastern meditation or astrology, however innocently. In any healing/transformation process, there should be an examination of the person's past beliefs and actions to see if any ground has been given to the enemy. Then we should do as the early Christians did—have the person "renounce Satan and all of his works" before entering into prayers of deliverance for them. The process of getting healed from sexual sin and bondage is in a very real sense a matter of uncovering the ground that Satan has gained in a person's life (with God's help) and removing that ground with the tools that God gives them.

Why do some people become demonized while others in the same circumstance are not? Assuming that every variable is the same, it may be as simple as the fact that some demons are better at their job than others—just like people! On one occasion, there may be a more highly skilled demonic power present at a sinful situation than on another occasion. This is pure speculation on my part, however.

Over the years, God has had occasion to correct some of my theology concerning demons. I remember one evening when I was praying against a particular demonic attack, just as I was commanding the demons to leave and to go into the "lake of fire," (referring to Revelation 19:20; 20:10,14-15), the Lord stopped me and said, "You don't have authority to send them into the lake of fire. That will be done by My angels at the appointed time. For you to send them there is to send them nowhere." So that was why such prayers had seemed to have little effect! So I asked the Lord where to send them, and He replied, "Command them to go where Jesus sends them." So I immediately began praying in that manner, and I want to tell you, I don't know where Jesus sends them, but they definitely do not want to go there! When I began praying that way, there was a day-and-night difference in the efficacy of my prayers. The demons are *terrified* of wherever it is that Jesus sends them.

One unexpected bonus to this new revelation was that as I sent the demonic powers to Jesus to send away, I became more aware of my partnership with Him, His presence with me, and His power available on my behalf. My faith for praying spiritual warfare prayers increased dramatically.

On another occasion, I was being assaulted by a barrage of temptations and crying out to the Lord about it. He spoke to me and said, "This is a demonic assault, and you can tell that it is because it hit you out of the blue (with no personal trail of sins or careless choices leading up to it) and carried with it an element of supernatural power." He told me to respond to such a demonic temptation with aggressive spiritual warfare prayer. Then He began to show me how temptations of the heart are different (see Matt. 15:19) because they arise from within me as a result of my own sinful or careless choices. I may have been committing sins, entertaining temptations, being careless in what I have been watching or listening to, or neglecting the spiritual disciplines that protect me from the allure of such things. Temptations of this sort have a more natural feel to them and lack the supernatural element of power. My response should be different as well. Instead of spiritual warfare, my response should be humble repentance from my heart.

Freedom from demonic oppression often comes in multiple stages, especially in the case of those who have suffered serious, multi-tiered, long-term demonization, as I had. In my case, God led me through three major stages over a period of ten years.

When I was saved from a decades-old life of sex, drug, and alcohol addiction, one of the first areas that God addressed with me was demonic strongholds. Within the first week, He directed me to name the demons that were compelling me according to the sin that they were tempting me to commit, and to cast them out in the name of Jesus Christ. So I did, every night, for the next two weeks. At the end of that period, all of the overwhelming compulsions had vanished. I was still left with much brokenness that needed to be healed, and I was still subject to intense temptations from time to time, but the overwhelming power of the demonic that used to rule my life had been broken. I knew my authority in Christ to command them to leave, and they had to obey that authority. I had also been directed specifically by God to cast them out, and so I had received from Him a powerful gift of faith in order to do so. Many who have just come to Christ need other more seasoned believers to pray them through such deliverance, so it is important to listen carefully to the Holy Spirit for exactly what He wants you to do.

Several years later, the Lord took me to another stage of deliverance. He taught me to enter into a *lifestyle* of worship, rather than relegating it to Sunday mornings. He even showed me the kind of songs that He wanted me to sing—love songs, with words that were directed to Him. I began immersing myself in worship, and as I would sing love songs to Him in the evening hours, I could feel an entirely new level of demonic oppression leaving me—a more subtle level of oppression that I had not known was even there until it left. You see, demons cannot stand the worship of God, and if you marinate your environment in such worship, they will leave on their own.

A third stage of deliverance that God took me through began very shortly thereafter, when I started attending conferences where people laid hands on me during ministry times and prayed for whatever the Holy Spirit was telling them to pray for. In those settings, I repeatedly experienced divine appointments, where God sent just the right person to pray for me. The person would have a word of knowledge or wisdom from the Lord that would open up yet one more door on the path to freedom. On many occasions, one or more people would lay hands on me and pray against a still hidden stronghold, or God would show them an empty space in my soul that He wanted to fill, and they would pray for that. I had many revelations from God during those years of deep inner healing prayer while at various conferences, ministry discipleship schools, or in other settings. I have learned an immense amount of wisdom and gained a great deal of freedom through the ministries of people like Leanne Payne, John Wimber, John and Paula Sandford, Francis MacNutt, Peter Horrobin, Doris Wagner, Rebecca Greenwood, and others, and I highly recommend their teaching materials to you.

Having examined the primary *outside* sources of influence, let's now look at some of the many *internal* influences that can also contribute to the development of a bondage to immorality.

The Influence of Self-Judgments

Self-judgments are a natural byproduct of a false self-image that has been branded into us by critical, legalistic authority figures, and they can be a significant catalyst for sinful expression.

If we have been raised under a system of "affirmation by performance," we will probably emerge as our own worst judges upon the inevitable and repeated failures of life. However, somewhere along the line, we will have noticed that if we exhibited the proper self-condemnation upon revealing our sin in front of our legalistic authority figures, they would not exact as heavy an emotional or physical punishment. So we learned to condemn *ourselves* when we failed in order to be emotionally prepared for the impending judgment and condemnation by the authority figures (including imagined condemnation).

Eventually, we reach such an emotionally-damaged stage that we purposely act out our sinful urges as a result of the anger that has grown within us from being so sparsely affirmed and so harshly judged. Essentially, we throw an emotional temper tantrum, rebelling against having been given such an impossible task as to live a perfectly righteous life by our own strength. We rebel in anger over our lot in life, often feeling quite justified in our actions. The self-dialogue usually goes something like this: "If God (or the one who represents God to me here on earth, i.e., father or mother), cares so little for me that He imposes such impossible demands or allows such hurtful things to happen to me, then I am going to do precisely what He does not want me to do!"

Our core sin is often twofold: failing to honor our parents despite their failings (see Deut. 5:16), and refusal to believe in God's goodness. Our decision to doubt God's goodness is a sin of intellectual presumption. We presume that our judgment of the case is more valid than God's (see Job 38:4). We assume therefore, that we are wiser than God (see 1 Cor 1:20), which is pride (see Prov. 16:18).

Our fundamental error is that we are choosing to believe what our *experience appears to show* about God and about our worth and value, rather than what God truly says, thinks, and feels. God can't *make* us believe the truth, so He gives us over to our ignorance so that we will see the true end of it and come back to faith in Him with a new deposit of humility in our heart. He knows that some of us have to prove to ourselves how wrong we are before we will believe how good He is.

The Influence of Childhood Vows

When we are hurt in childhood, we react with simplistic judgments, based on our unrefined and immature sense of justice. We are not able to see grays, only black and white. We are incapable of defining the nuances of a case or reading any of the complexities that may be involved in an event. Neither are we trained in the admonition of the Lord, who says: "Judge not, that ye be not judged" (Matt. 7:1, KJV). We seek justice, but know nothing of grace. And so, we react simply naturally, as fallen creatures. We condemn in our heart, we hold grudges, we pass sentences, we dishonor, and we make vows against those who have caused our pain—vows of rejection, vows of hate, vows that often remain hidden in our subconscious for decades before emerging under the convicting work of the Holy Spirit.

Some of these vows may fuel significant dysfunctions in our life. For example, the young boy who vows in his heart never to love or become like the father whom he has grown to hate, is, in effect, separating himself from the primary means by which God has designed a boy to receive his sense of gender security and identity. This could result in sexual identity confusion (homosexual neurosis) and an unhealthy search for the ideal father figure from which to extract the love and affection that was missing in the father he rejected. That boy may become vulnerable to the deceitfulness of a child molester, who will pretend to offer love and affection in exchange for sexual contact. In many children, the inner anxiety caused by the lack of love and affirmation from a father is so intense that the choice to sacrifice their sexual integrity seems like a small price to pay.

The reality for that boy is that *he is his father*; he is the very DNA of his father and mother, recombined into a unique individual, yet retaining a tendency toward many of the very traits and actions that he most despises in his parents. While a frightening revelation to some at first, this knowledge can become the key in guiding a person in how to pray and how to best order his or her life.

As I have mentioned already, I used to hate my father. One night as I was praying, the Lord pointed out to me that I was composed of the DNA of my father and mother and that, therefore, the hatred that I harbored for my father was the primary source for the self-hatred that I had lived with my entire life. (That self-hatred had been so intense that it had resulted in three suicide attempts). If you hate your father or mother, you are in a very literal and true sense, hating your very self. This is one of the things that makes forgiveness so very vital in the healing process. You cannot proceed to health and maturity without it. We will discuss this further in the chapter on child sexual abuse.

The Influence of the Sinful Heart of Man

It would be a serious mistake to blame our sinful choices solely on the actions of others, our DNA, or whatever else. Jesus told His disciples: "What comes out of a man is what makes him unclean. For from within, out of men's hearts, come evil thoughts, sexual immorality, theft, murder, adultery, greed, malice, deceit, lewdness, envy, slander, arrogance and folly. All these evils come from inside and make a man 'unclean' " (Mark 7:20-23).

A major source of improper sexual development that operates all on its own is the evil heart of man. We are *born* with it, which is why we must be *born again* in order to enter the kingdom of God (see John 3:3ff). Parents, teachers, friends, heroes, and strangers who introduce a world of perversion may be major contributors to our sexual sin problems, but they are building on a foundation that we alone are accountable for—the human heart. Every one of us possesses a heart that is naturally complicit with sin. No process of healing and sanctification would be complete without acknowledging and dealing with that issue.

Our being *born again* by receiving Jesus Christ as Lord and Savior is the start of fixing this problem. He gives us a new heart, the culmination of promises found throughout the Old Testament (see Jer. 31:33b; Ezek. 11:19; 18:31; 36:26-27). When we give our heart and life to Him, a supernatural change takes place within us and we become born again—from above. We receive the promised new heart!

Here's the rub, however. When we receive our new heart, God does not take away our free will. The desires and temptations of the old nature still remain an option for us, and we must make daily choices as to which heart we want to live out of. We can pursue the transformation into the more complete image of God that is offered (see 1 Pet. 2:4-5) or we can return to the ways of the old man (see Rom. 12:2; Eph. 4:23-24; 1 John 2:15). The choice we make will be based on our love for God. The degree of our love for God will be based on how diligently we continue to pursue Him and are thereby exposed to His transforming glory and grace—the "prime directive" (see Heb. 11:6).

In the following chapters, we will discuss some of the more common sexual aberrations, showing how they occur, and what the process of being delivered from them looks like. It is important to remember that I can only describe what sexual brokenness and subsequent sanctification usually look like. The path that any given person must take is tailor-designed by God Himself and will be revealed in the heart of each individual who pursues intimacy with the Father.

Study Section— Root Sources

1. IMPROPER ROLE MODELING, DIS-AFFIRMATION, AND OTHER SKEWED MESSAGES, PARTICULARLY IN ONE'S EARLIEST YEARS (FROM CONCEPTION TO AGE 5) BY:

    a. Parents
        - Temperament is a *gift* that must be fitted properly within the fabric of interpersonal relationships and caused to serve the redemptive purposes of God within that framework. Everyone's natural temperament will serve the purposes of God for their life when guided and utilized in a positive way for God's glory. Parents often fail to work with their child "in the way they should go" (Prov. 22:6), and instead try to change them into their own ideal, thus working against what God has intended. For example, the father who always wanted an athlete for a son and instead gets a sensitive artist will often try to change the personality and temperament of his son through criticism, intimidation, and other forms of psychological torture, or by forcing him to perform (and fail) in an arena where he has no natural skills or interests. This is pure selfishness on the part of that parent. They are more concerned about how others see them than in the needs and wants of their child. The child will recognize this and grow to resent it. That child will also have problems with gaining a healthy sense of self—who they are fundamentally—and their acceptability in being who they really are.
        - Those who created you (your parents), speak into you, by their words and by their treatment of you, who you are. Your self-image is branded into your young soul. This is not a true self-image (i.e., it does not reflect the

reality of what God created you to be). It is a *perceived* self-image. If you have adopted a negative self-image, God changes that error by speaking your true identity into your spirit through His Word, through the words of other believers who He sends to communicate truth to you, and through direct revelation to your soul during times of intimacy with Him.

What then can the healing process be likened to? It's like the guy with a tattoo of a naked lady who comes to the Lord. Since the tattoo cannot be removed, he has clothes tattooed onto the existing picture. The tattoo now depicts a new reality of purity and Godly purpose, but underneath lies a remnant of the old picture that only he knows about. He now must chose to believe in the new reality instead of the old identity. The enemy will try to lie to him and cause him to believe that he is still the man who had the original tattoo put on, but he must chose to believe God instead and accept by faith his new identity in Christ—an identity that reflects objective truth and reality rather than the projections of society or misguided authority figures from his past.

- The perception of one's identity is acquired through the opinions of others and one's experiences. We must chose whose opinion we accept as valid and true, man's or God's. Then God will engrave it in our hearts.

b. Teachers
   - Teachers have a similar formative authority to speak into the life of a young person a perceived identity. When you are told repeatedly that you are dumb, bad, a failure, never going to amount to anything, etc., you often unconsciously accept such judgments as accurate observations. Not only is the source of the observation an older and supposedly wiser person, but the judgment is usually proclaimed soundly and loudly into your ear at the very moment when you are behaving in a way that would appear to prove the accusation.
   - Some teachers create the same effect by affirming the wrong things (e.g., sexual promiscuity, homosexual tendencies, rebellion against parents, opportunism, situational ethics, ontological identity in being an evolved animal, etc.).

c. Friends

- We tend to select our "best friend" according to the person who most accepts us the way we are, or the person who represents the most what we want to be. They remain our "best friend" because of the vital role they play in being a haven of comfort, acceptance and modeling. The more accepting they are of the way we are, the more power they have to impact our lives for the good with their opinions.

- Our larger circle of friends, however, has greater power to cause us to form negative self-perceptions. They are often highly competitive and wield power through psychological warfare (e.g., criticisms, intimidation, comparisons, gossip, etc.). The more we look up to and admire an accuser, the more power their words have on us to form our self-perception.

d. Heroes

- Heroes have an enormous power in our society because we are a culture of idolaters. Particularly when we have already accumulated a negative self-perception from the opinions and treatment of others, the "fall" of a hero can have a great effect in giving us "ammunition" to justify our own fall. After all, if one so great as my hero is weak, then how can I possibly resist the same temptations? In fact, if the one who has embodied everything I have ever dreamed of being finds comfort and justification in sinful behavior, then it must be okay. I am capable of drawing such a foolish conclusion, because as a result of my sin of idolatry, Satan has already blinded my eyes to the truth, and I have lost my ability to judge correctly. My picture of God has already been distorted—otherwise, I would have been a worshiper of Him.

Mike Bickle, in his book, *Passion for Jesus* (pp. 47, 51, 53, 54) puts it this way:

"We individual believers and the church as a whole possess so little of the knowledge of what God is truly like. Our ignorance of His diverse and glorious personality rots our religion. It leads to errors in our doctrines and contributes to the decay of our confidence and passion in worship. Our inadequate ideas about the personhood of God result in failure to develop deep affection for Jesus and to obey Him with fearless abandonment...

...A casual attitude about sin comes from an incomplete understanding of God...

...The whole outlook of mankind might be changed if we could all believe that we dwell under a friendly sky and that the God of heaven, although exalted in power and majesty, is eager to be friends with us...

...The great need of the church is to see, know and discover the indescribable glory of who God is. Seeing the heart, mind and character of God will cure our compromise and instability and motivate us to righteousness and holy passion. Personal, experiential knowledge of the person of Jesus will fuel obedience and zeal. It will put a stop to our restlessness and discontent. A new depth of intimacy with Him will extinguish our boredom and capture our hearts. Just a glimpse of Him."

    e. Outsiders Who Reveal Shocking Worlds or Who Bring Trauma

- People who set out to pervert, corrupt and shock the child by introducing them to adult sexual themes and activities
- People who sexually traumatize the child in one way or another

2. SELF-JUDGMENT

    a. Self-judgments can be a significant catalyst for sinful expression. When we live under a system of "affirmation by performance of the law," upon the inevitable and repeated failures of life, we will emerge as our own worst judges. We will condemn ourselves when we fail in order to be emotionally prepared for and steel ourselves against the expected, painful condemnation and judgment of authority figures. Somewhere along the line, we notice that if we exhibit the proper self-condemnation upon revealing our sin to legalistic authority figures, they do not exact as heavy an emotional or physical punishment.

        (1) Eventually, we will reach such a stage of emotional damage and frustration that we will purposely and passionately act out our sinful urges as a result of the anger that has grown within us over being so sparsely affirmed and given such an impossible task in life as to

live righteously by our own strength.

(2) The fundamental sin here is usually rebellion against parents—failing to honor them and believe in God's goodness despite appearances to the contrary. It is also a sin of intellectual presumption. We presume that our judgments of the case are more valid than God's. We assume therefore, that we are wiser than God. This is pride.

b. Self-judgments are also a natural by-product of a false self-image that has been branded into us by critical, legalistic authority figures.

(1) There is often confusion between "self-identity," "self-esteem" and "self-image."

Pastor Dan Sneed (Conejo Valley Foursquare Church) says that:

Self-identity = who you are in fact
    (2 Corinthians 5:17—Jesus changes our identity)

Self-image = how you see yourself (a mental picture)

Self-esteem = how you feel about yourself

(2) Here too, we eventually rebel in anger over our lot in life—often feeling quite justified in our actions. The self-dialogue usually goes something like: "If God (or the one who represents God to me here on earth—i.e., father or mother), doesn't care enough about me that He allows such things to happen to me, then I am going to do precisely what He doesn't want me to do. I'm going to exact what little love and affection I can out of my miserable lot in life!"

(3) The fundamental sin here is that we are choosing to believe what our *experience appears to show* about God and about our worth and value, rather than what God truly says, thinks, and feels. God gives us over to such ignorant rebellion so that we will see the true end of it and return to faith in Him with a new deposit of humility in our heart. He knows that we have to prove to ourselves how wrong we are before we will believe how good He is.

3. CHILDHOOD VOWS

   a. When we are hurt in childhood, we react with simplistic judgments, based on our undefined and immature sense of justice. We are not able to see grays—only black and white. We are incapable of defining the nuances of a case or in reading any of the complexities that may be involved in the event. Neither are we trained in the admonition of the Lord, who says: "Judge not lest ye be judged." We seek justice, but know nothing of grace. And so, we react simply, and naturally as fallen creatures. We condemn in our heart, we hold grudges, we pass sentences, we dishonor, etc., and we make vows against those who have caused our pain—vows of rejection, vows of hate, vows which often remain hidden in our subconscious for decades before emerging under the convicting work of the Holy Spirit.

   b. Some of these vows may fuel significant dysfunctions in our life. For example, the young boy who vows in his heart never to love or become like the father that he has grown to hate, is in effect, separating himself from his very source of gender security. This could result in sexual identity confusion and a search for the ideal father figure from which to extract the love and affection that was missing in the father he rejected.

4. THE SINFUL HEART OF MAN

   "For from within, out of men's hearts, come evil thoughts, sexual immorality, theft, murder, adultery, greed, malice, deceit, lewdness, envy, slander, arrogance and folly. All these evils come from inside and make a man unclean" (Mark 7:21).

Exercises—Root Sources

1. Ask the Lord to reveal to you the messages that you received from family, friends and other influential people during your childhood that now serve to inhibit your spiritual growth. Ask the Lord to give you power, wisdom and direction as you forgive and otherwise release people from the things they have said and done that have brought you harm.

2. Spend time in communion with the Lord, asking Him to heal the wounds caused by angry lies about your personhood that have been spoken into your mind in the past. Ask Him to reach deep into your very soul and remove the rotted roots of false identity that have been planted there by people influential to you during your childhood and adolescence. Commit yourself to believing the Lord's claim that He has placed infinite value on you by dying for you on the Cross.

3. Ask God to break any generational curses that may have affected you through the sins of your parents or any other curse affecting your sense of value to God that may have come through the words or actions of others. Pray for this "in the name of Jesus," meaning that you have confidence that you are praying the will of God and that by His power and authority conferred on you by Christ Himself when you first believed in Him, you can command such action, and as a result, the curses will be broken.

4. Ask the Lord to speak the truth into your spirit through the Word and through communion with Him. Set out to re-train your thinking about yourself by regularly feeding the truth into your mind and heart. Each time that the lies return, aggressively counter them with the truth that God has given you. Neil Anderson's books, *The Bondage Breaker* and *Victory Over Darkness* will be helpful in doing this exercise.

5. Examine the heroes that you have had in life and those you have today to see if they have modeled and reflected godly values and belief systems. Meditate on the idea of God (Father, Son and Holy Spirit) being your sole hero in life and ask Him to make it so.

6. Ask God to reveal any judgments that you may have held against yourself. Repent of having held them and renounce them, choosing instead to believe that when God says He forgives those who repent, He does indeed forgive.

7. Make a commitment, that by God's power, there will be an end to your habit of judging yourself and others—that forevermore you will let God hold His sole right to be judge.

8. Ask God to fill your heart with His purity and righteousness and to drive out the evil that has resided there. Regularly seek the riches of the kingdom, which are wisdom, purity, love, hope and faith and insist that God impart them to you and express them through you.

Part Two:

Specific Dysfunctions

The Causes of Sexual Identity Confusion: Homosexuality/Bisexuality

In an earlier chapter we examined the divine intent for sexuality—that we were created to be heterosexual and monogamous. As a human being, you were created in the image of God, higher than the animals, on a plane that makes possible an intimate conscious relationship with the One who created you.

We were all created to be heterosexual. Our sexuality in the physical realm is a symbolic foreshadowing of the divine-human relationship that God intends us to have with Him in the spiritual realm. This means that people who find that they are sexually attracted to a member of their own sex suffer from sexual identity confusion ("homosexual neurosis"). Something has occurred in the course of their formative years to damage or veil their naturally created heterosexual design.

Heterosexuality is the natural state of human beings. It comes, however, in time-release form, like a seed in the ground that is designed to lie dormant for a number of years before germinating. Our sexual identity is designed to emerge in concert with the sexual maturation of our physical bodies. During the period of dormancy, however, the seed of heterosexuality, though inactive, needs to be nurtured by a variety of physical, psychological and emotional nutrients in order to germinate at the right time and in a healthy manner. For some, that fragile seed gets damaged through abuse. For others, it suffers from neglect or the absence of necessary formative ingredients, sending such individuals on a search to repair their own internal damage and/or to try to obtain for themselves the missing nutrients. The parts that are missing become magnified by their absence and a frustrated obsession develops over repeated, failed attempts to acquire them through their own efforts. That anxiety becomes eroticized (as anxiety often is) and the missing gender identity becomes the focus of erotic obsession.

Essentially what we are looking at is arrested emotional development caused by trauma or neglect. Should the person suffering from this condition also be exposed to situations or things that produce an early sexual awakening such as sexual abuse or pornography, what is fundamentally an emotional problem can easily be mistaken for a sexual problem.

This is what we are witnessing in our culture today. Emotionally arrested people who have either already experienced puberty or the premature sexualization of their life's experience are mistakenly assuming that the foundation of their unnatural orientation is sexual. As they try to express themselves according to this distortion of reality, they find nothing but frustration when periods of hopeful ecstasy are followed by the inevitable realization that the person of their dreams cannot bring the fulfillment that they are seeking.

The rampant promiscuity in the homosexual community is prima facie evidence of this perpetual cycle of hope and frustration. It's very much like a Hollywood set. Upon first glance, it looks spectacular, like a dream come true, but behind the beautiful facade, there is only emptiness.

Healing for such a person involves (1) an honest determination to face the evidence for what has happened, (2) a decision to renounce patterns of sinful obsession, and (3) a turning to God for His plan to heal the damage and impart the missing pieces. As the person turns to the Father in repentance and reestablishes fellowship with Him, the Father teaches him or her how to starve the false homosexual identity and feed the true heterosexual identity. Over time, the two identities exchange places—the heterosexual identity comes alive and establishes itself as the true and dominant one, and the homosexual identity begins to die, eventually becoming a remnant lie from the past.

Are People Born Gay?

During the past twenty years, there have been numerous attempts by homosexual researchers to prove that homosexual orientation is determined by genes or some other physiological source. *Every single study has failed to do so.* In fact, several studies have actually shown that homosexuality *cannot* be determined by genes.

One study, conducted by Dr. Simon Levay, looked at the hypothalamus glands of cadavers and was reported by the press to have shown that the gland in homosexuals was smaller in size—thus demonstrating a physiological cause for homosexuality. The study had massive flaws, one of which was that some of the cadavers used in the experiment were men who had died of AIDS (a disease that often decimates the brain), making the study of their brains a ludicrous exercise. Nevertheless, the press claimed victory for the gay cause, ignoring the researcher's own clear statements that he had *not* proven anything. Here are his actual words:

> "It's important to stress what I didn't find. I did not prove that homosexuality is genetic, or find a genetic cause for being gay. I didn't show that gay men are born that way, the most common

mistake people make in interpreting my work. Nor did I locate a gay center in the brain."

A second study, by Bailey and Pillard, focused on genetically identical twins. In that study, they hoped to prove a genetic origin for homosexuality by finding genetically identical twins who were both gay. They did find their gay twins, but what was not widely publicized was that they also found numerous "discordant" twins (where one twin was gay and the other was straight). Since the twins were *genetically identical*, then the presence of such discordant twins actually proved that homosexuality could *not* be determined by genes. Most news organizations reported just the opposite.

A third study that tried to prove a genetic cause for homosexual confusion was the 1993 Hamer et al. "Genetic Link" study, which was touted by the press as "proof" that homosexuality is genetically determined but which did not prove any such thing. This was a study of the chromosomes of homosexual brothers in which the researchers found a certain mutation in the DNA. However, what you probably never saw reported was that they also found *heterosexuals* with the same mutation, as well as homosexuals *without* the mutation—thus actually proving that homosexual confusion could *not* be determined by that genetic mutation. When pressed, the gay researchers themselves finally admitted that there must be "non-genetic sources of variation in sexual orientation" as well as "environmental, experiential and cultural factors that influence the development of male sexual orientation."

One other thing that you probably never heard regarding this most famous of the "gay" studies—soon after the study was published, the primary assistant to Dr. Hamer sent him up on charges of fraud before the National Institute of Health for having doctored the data to make it appear to say things it did not say.

Years later, a much larger study was conducted by Rice et al. to determine if Hamer's study had been accurate, and it concluded:

> "It is unclear why our results are so discrepant from Hamer's original study. Because our study was larger than that of Hamer's et al., we certainly had adequate power to detect a genetic effect as large as reported in that study. Nonetheless, our data do not support the presence of a gene of large effect influencing sexual orientation at position XQ 28."

Hamer himself finally admitted:

> "We assumed the environment also played a role in sexual orientation, as it does in most, if not all behaviors. . . . Homosexuality is

not purely genetic . . . environmental factors play a role. There is not a single master gene that makes people gay."

In an article entitled "In Their Own Words: Gay Activists Speak About Science, Morality, Philosophy," published in the *Salt Lake City Tribune* on May 27, 2001, Dr. A. Dean Byrd, (Vice President of the National Association for Research and Therapy of Homosexuality [NARTH]), reported on additional studies that have been conducted on the question of the origins of homosexual confusion:

> "Prominent research teams Byne and Parsons, and also Friedman and Downey, each concluded that there was no evidence to support a biologic theory, but rather that homosexuality could be best explained by an alternative model where "temperamental and personality traits interact with the familial and social milieu as the individual's sexuality emerges."

Are homosexual attractions innate? There is no support in the scientific research for the conclusion that homosexuality is biologically determined.

Regarding the subject of the brain and sexual behavior, Dr. Mark Breedlove (a researcher at the University of California at Berkeley) demonstrated that sexual behavior can actually change brain structure. Referring to his research in the article cited above, Breedlove says:

> "These findings give us proof for what we theoretically know to be the case—that sexual experience can alter the structure of the brain, just as genes can alter it. [I]t is possible that differences in sexual behavior cause (rather than are caused by) differences in the brain."

Every study that has attempted to show a genetic or physiological cause for homosexual confusion has *failed* to do so despite tens of millions of dollars being thrown into the effort. It has been such a massive failure that even some gay activists are beginning to admit it, though mainstream gay organizations and the press continue to write stories that blatantly declare or implicitly assume that proof of a gay gene has been found.

The Lifestyle—Anything *But* Gay

Gay activists are always trying to make it appear as though homosexuality has been proven safe, normal and healthy. They will often point to the fact that the American Psychiatric Association (APA) removed homosexuality from its list of emotional disorders in the 1970s. What they don't tell you is that the decision to do so was made by a small committee led by a homosexual therapist, under threats and intimidation by gay activists who had been storming their meetings and demanding such a change. In other words, the change was not based on any scientific evidence or discovery, but was purely the result of intimidation. Even gay researcher Simon LeVay has admitted that, "Gay activism was clearly the force that propelled the American Psychiatric Association to declassify homosexuality" [as an emotional disorder]. In essence, a political movement has coerced a professional guild into declaring a position on homosexuality that is unproven and untrue.

Let's look closer at just how healthy, happy, and normal homosexuals really are. As one who lived in that lifestyle for over ten years, I can tell you for a fact that there is serious and pervasive emotional brokenness in that population, and an insidious death wish that emanates from profound self-hatred. But we need not rely solely on anecdotal evidence from me or other eyewitnesses who would give similar testimony if the media were to allow it. It turns out that the research statistics speak for themselves.

The truth about freedom and healing may only get a hearing if the truth about the sinful lifestyle is revealed through the statistical evidence. Statistics may be the best way to get through to many in our modern culture who believe they are loving homosexuals by supporting and endorsing their lifestyle. They must see that they are *not loving* homosexuals *but hurting* them by endorsing their destructive lifestyle. To truly love homosexuals involves telling them the truth and showing them the way out that is permanent and eternal—through the forgiveness, healing, and transformation that comes from an obedient and intimate relationship with Jesus Christ.

Statistics Don't Lie

The homosexual lifestyle comes with a high number of unhealthy patterns, including sexual diseases, mental illness, substance abuse, suicide, dysfunctional relationships, domestic violence, pedophilia (adult male attraction for pre-teens) and ephebophilia (adult male attraction for teens).

According to Dr. Jeffrey Satinover, author of *Homosexuality and the Politics of Truth* (Grand Rapids, Mich.: Baker/Hamewith Books, 1996), homosexuals are at high risk for:

- a 25-30 year decrease in life expectancy.
- chronic, potentially fatal, liver disease—infectious hepatitis, which increases the risk of liver cancer.
- fatal immune diseases, including associated cancers.
- frequently fatal rectal cancer.
- multiple bowel and other infectious diseases.
- a much higher than usual incidence of suicide.

A 2001 report by U.C./San Francisco researchers found that HIV infection rates have more than doubled since 1997 (80 percent of these are among homosexual men). HIV infection and AIDS, gonorrhea, and other sexually transmitted diseases continue to be disproportionately represented in the homosexual population.

Another set of statistics concern violence. According to a 1996 study by the National Coalition of Anti-Violence Programs, domestic violence occurs in 25-30 percent of all same-sex relationships—a far higher rate than among heterosexual couples (as cited by Nancy Sutton in "Domestic Violence and Domestic Partners: Two Sides of the Same Coin" and Linda P. Harvey in "Lesbians As Violent Partners," both in *Mission: America*, Fall, 1998). Among gay men, the incidence of domestic violence is nearly double that of the heterosexual population, according to D. Island and P. Letellior in *Men Who Beat Men Who Love Them: Battered Gay Men and Domestic Violence* (1991).

Another problem is substance abuse. One study focused specifically on this issue was published in *Nursing Research*; it reported high levels of alcohol and drug abuse among lesbians.

Gay activists often claim that monogamous gay relationships are commonplace. Statistically, however, monogamous gay relationships do not exist. According to a 2003 study conducted by Dr. Maria Xiridou of the Amsterdam Municipal Health Service and published in the May issue of *AIDS*, homosexual partnerships last, on average, only one-and-a-half years, and men in homosexual relationships have an average of eight partners a year outside their main partnership. Other studies support these results.

The highest increases in suicide, substance abuse, alcoholism, and gay domestic violence are in areas that exhibit the most pro-gay sentiment, such as the Netherlands and San Francisco (Timothy Dailey, *Culture Facts*, Family Research Council, February 11, 2003). In the same study of twins mentioned earlier, published in the *Archives of General Psychiatry*, it was found that active homosexuals are at greater risk for overall mental problems, and are 6.5 times more likely than their twin to have attempted suicide. The suicide rate among gay teens is very high and going higher, not because society disapproves of their behavior, (societal approval of homosexuality has risen dramatically in the past fifty years), but rather because the gay community is telling them that they are born gay and can never change, and the hopelessness of that message is driving them to despair and hopelessness.

According to an article titled "Comparative Data of Childhood and Adolescence Molestation in Heterosexual and Homosexual Persons, by Marie E. Tomeo, et al., published in the *Archives of Sexual Behavior* (vol. 30, p. 539, 2001), 46 percent of homosexual men and 22 percent of homosexual women reported having been molested by a person of the same gender. This contrasts to only 7 percent of heterosexual men and 1 percent of heterosexual women reporting having been molested by a person of the same gender.

The Journal of Sex Research (cited by Lynn Vincent in "Big Problem," *World*, October 26, 2002), found that homosexual pedophiles commit about one-third of the total number of child sex offenses in the United States, even though homosexuals make up no more than 5 percent of the U.S. population. (The actual percentage may be 3 percent, a finding that has been repeated throughout the world by secular research organizations.) In other words, a tiny percentage of the population—homosexual men—commit one third or more of the cases of child sexual molestation. Around 25 to 40 percent of men attracted to children prefer boys, as verified in several studies (Blanchard, et al., 1999; Gebhard et al., 1965; Mohr et al., 1964). Thus, the rate of homosexual attraction is 6 to 20 times higher among pedophiles (cited in "Homosexuality and Child Sexual Abuse," Timothy J. Dailey, Ph.D., *Insight,* June 1, 2002, from Ray Blanchard, et al., "Fraternal Birth Order and Sexual Orientation in Pedophiles," *Archives of Sexual Behavior* 29 (2000): 464.) A significant percentage of books that have appeared on the Gay Men's Press fiction bestseller list contain pedophilia themes (Dailey). It is important to note that over half of all homosexuals are child sexual abuse victims.

Ephebophiles identify emotionally with teenagers of the age they were when they were sexually abused. They are developmentally frozen as a result, lacking a moral compass and quite often, even a conscience. The prevalence of ephebophilia in the gay community lies behind continued attempts by gay organizations to lower the legal age of consent. Additional evidence can be found in the permission given by gay organizations in the past to pedophile groups like NAMBLA (North American Man Boy Love Association) to march in the "Gay Pride" parades throughout the world. Evidence can also be found in abundance at gay clubs and parties, where underage teens are a common fixture and a highly sought-after commodity. The gay community has historically placed a high value on ancient Greek culture, specifically because in that culture teenage boys were commonly used as sexual partners. I would estimate that perhaps 25 percent of the homosexual community struggles with ephebophilia—a much higher incidence than those who struggle with pedophilia.

David Thorstad (a homosexual activist, historian of the gay rights movement and founding member of NAMBLA) writes:

> "Boy-lovers were involved in the gay movement from the beginning, and their presence was tolerated. Gay youth groups encouraged adults to attend their dances ... There was a mood of tolerance, even joy at discovering the myriad of lifestyles within the gay and lesbian subculture" (cited in Dailey, from David Thorstad, "Man/Boy Love and the American Gay Movement," *Journal of*

Homosexuality 20 [1990]: 252.)

In 1985, NAMBLA was admitted as a member in New York's council of Lesbian and Gay Organizations as well as the International Gay Association—now the International Lesbian and Gay Association (ILGA).

The Journal of Homosexuality is the premier "mainstream" English-language publication of the gay movement. One prominent editor is John DeCecco, a psychologist at San Francisco State University who also serves on the editorial board of the Dutch pedophile journal *Paidika*. In 1990 the *Journal of Homosexuality* published a series of essays on pedophilia. None of the essays offered any substantive criticism of pedophilia. Most blatantly promoted man-boy love as the natural right of homosexuals.

Lesbian columnist Paula Martinac has written:

> "[S]ome gay men still maintain that an adult who has same-sex relations with someone under the legal age of consent is on some level doing the kid a favor by helping to bring him or her 'out.' It's not pedophilia, this thinking goes—pedophilia refers only to little kids. Instead, adult-youth sex is viewed as an important aspect of gay culture, with a history dating back to 'Greek love' of ancient times. This romanticized version of adult-youth sexual relations has been a staple of gay literature and has made appearances, too, in gay-themed films." (cited in Dailey, from Paula Martinac, "Mixed Messages on Pedophilia Need to be Clarified, Unified," *Washington Blade,* March 15, 2002).

No matter what statistic you examine, the degree of dysfunctionality within the gay community is off the charts. If the gay community can see that our attempts to rescue them from this deathstyle is grounded in a loving concern not only for their spiritual destiny, but for their physical and emotional welfare here on earth, then we may be able to touch hearts and open ears to the truth.

The Science of Healing

Are there any secular therapists then who have found success in bringing healing to the homosexual? Indeed there are. Psychologist A. Dean Byrd reports:

> "In reviewing the research, Dr. Jeffrey Satinover reported a 52% success rate in the treatment of unwanted homosexual attraction. Masters and Johnson, the famed sex researchers, reported a 65% success rate after a five-year follow-up. Other professionals report success rates ranging from 30% to 70%."

An article in the *Monitor on Psychology* reviewed the research of Dr. Lisa Diamond, a professor at the University of Utah, who concluded "Sexual identity is far from fixed in women who aren't exclusively heterosexual." What is more intriguing is the research of Dr. Robert Spitzer, the prominent psychiatrist and researcher at Columbia University. Dr. Spitzer was the architect of the 1973 decision to remove homosexuality from the diagnostic manual, a gay-affirmative psychiatrist, and a long time supporter of gay rights. His current study focused on whether or not individuals can change. His preliminary conclusions are:

> "I'm convinced from the people I have interviewed, that for many of them, they have made substantial changes toward becoming heterosexual. … I think that's news. … I came to this study skeptical. I now claim that these changes can be sustained."

What was most interesting was Dr. Spitzer's response to a journalist who inquired what he would do if his adolescent son revealed his homosexual attraction. Dr. Spitzer said he hoped that his son would be interested in changing and would get some help. It is interesting to note that the late Dr. Spitzer received considerable "hate mail" and complaints from his colleagues because of his research.

Is homosexuality immutable? Hardly. There is ample evidence that homosexual attraction can be diminished and that changes can be made ("In Their Own Words: Gay Activists Speak About Science, Morality, Philosophy," *Salt Lake City Tribune,* May 27, 2001).

The National Association for Research and Therapy of Homosexuality (now called, The Alliance for Therapeutic Choice and Scientific Integrity) is a professional organization of over a thousand member therapists whose "primary goal is to make effective psychological therapy available to all homosexual men and women who seek change." Their website, (www.therapeuticchoice.com) boldly proclaims:

> "There is no such thing as a 'gay gene,' and there is no evidence to support the idea that homosexuality is genetic or unchangeable…
>
> The right to seek therapy to change one's sexual adaptation should be considered self-evident and inalienable.
>
> We call on our fellow mental-health association to stop falsely claiming to have "scientific knowledge" that settles the issue of homosexuality. Instead, our mental-health associations must leave room for diverse understandings of the family, of core human identity, and the meaning and purpose of human sexuality."

Restored Hope Network, (www.RestoredHopeNetwork.org), is a network of Christian ministries spread throughout the world, many of which are headed by licensed therapists, ordained pastoral counselors and others. Many have reported success rates as high or higher than Masters and Johnson and the other secular therapy groups. All have discovered what the APA's own Dr. Robert Spitzer did—that it *is* possible for a person who is highly motivated to change and to realize a significant degree of transformation in their sexual orientation.

Even lesbian activist Camille Paglia offered the following observations:

> "Homosexuality is not 'normal.' On the contrary it is a challenge to the norm. . . . Nature exists whether academics like it or not. And in nature, procreation is the single relentless rule. That is the norm. Our sexual bodies were designed for reproduction.... No one is born gay. . . . [H]omosexuality is an adaptation, not an inborn trait....
>
> Is the gay identity so fragile that it cannot bear the thought that some people may not wish to be gay? Sexuality is highly fluid, and reversals are theoretically possible. However, habit is refractory, once the sensory pathways have been blazed and deepened by repetition—a phenomenon obvious in the struggle with obesity, smoking, alcoholism or drug addiction (from Byrd)."

The Biblical Witness Concerning Homosexual Behavior

Even if it could be proven that homosexuality had a physiological component, the point would be moot for several reasons:

> 1. *God calls us to live sober lives.* Alcoholism is believed to have a genetic link (although the early studies that supposedly proved that have been overturned), yet God labels drunkenness a sin worthy of eternal damnation (see Gal. 5:19-21). His power is available to us in the areas where we are weak and vulnerable, whether the problem is physiological, emotional or psychological. In relationship with Him, He is able to keep us from falling (see Jude 24) as well as to cleanse us from all unrighteousness (see 1 John 1:9) in times of weakness when we fail to keep the standard of holiness (see 2 Cor. 7:1; Heb. 12:14; 1 Pet. 1:16; 2 Pet. 3:11). The "I can't help it" excuse for continuing in sin cannot be used for sin of any kind.
> 2. *Everyone is born with an inherited propensity to sin.* Yet God expects us to take advantage of His provision to overcome that predilection. This is as true of the homosexual inclination as it is of the basic inclination to sin.
> 3. *God is just.* If genetics or hormones could force a behavior that

God condemns, and if no recourse were made available, God would be unjust for condemning mankind for a behavior that could not be helped. And if God *created* some people to be homosexual, He could not judge their behavior to be sinful, which He clearly does throughout Scripture (see Lev. 18:22; Rom. 1:26-27; 1 Cor. 6:9-11.)

Pro-gay theology is very poor theology that takes advantage of people who do not know any better. It is also unbelievably arrogant, presuming to know better than every Greek and Hebrew scholar, worldwide, throughout all of the history of biblical translation and scholarship. It is eisegesis, not exegesis—reading into the text one's own predetermined theology rather than extracting from the text what is actually being said.

Often, ridiculous "scriptural" claims are made (for example, claims that Jonathan and David or Jesus and John were lovers, that God destroyed Sodom and Gomorrah because they were inhospitable to the angels, that homosexual behavior is only forbidden if the person really isn't homosexual, that the moral laws found in the Old Testament holiness code changed after Christ came). If you ever become trapped in a discussion on one of these rabbit-trails, a quick way to cut through the cloud of dust is to demonstrate that the claims for the text are not found:

- in the texts themselves,
- the context of the passage,
- the context of the early church in which they were written,
- in any extra-biblical writing of that day or centuries hence (except by modern-day gay apologists and others who deny the authority of Scripture)

Pro-gay apologists like to claim that since there is no record of Jesus specifically mentioning homosexual behavior, then it must have been okay with Him. Jesus didn't mention drug abuse or bestiality either. Does that mean they are okay? Can you see the specious reasoning behind such claims?

Additionally, it is important to understand that the New Testament was not intended as a new list of laws, but rather as a way of understanding how the eternal principles that underlie the *unchanging* moral law can be fulfilled through the empowerment that comes in union with the risen Christ. Jesus' teaching assumed a knowledge of existing moral law as God's preexisting standard. After correcting the misunderstandings of the Scribes, Pharisees and Sadducees, Jesus then pointed his listeners to how those principles could only be fulfilled in union with Him. Read Jesus' unequivocal reaffirmation of the Law in Matthew 5:17-20 and Luke 16:16-17, recognizing that the Law to which he referred included the prohibitions against homosexual behavior found in Leviticus 18 and elsewhere.

Another problem with the "Jesus never mentioned it" argument is that it assumes that only the words of Jesus in Scripture are inspired by God. That is not the witness of the Scripture itself nor of Jesus' own testimony of it (See Mark 12:36, 2 Timothy 3:16, 2 Peter 1:21, and 2 Peter 3:16 for proof that other biblical words are equally God-inspired.) It is illegitimate to separate the words of Jesus from those of other biblical writers.

The Bible sees homosexuality as a sinful behavior, not as an identity. It teaches that God has made Himself *clearly* known to men through His creation, yet we have suppressed that truth and refused to thankfully glorify Him as God. As a result, our minds and hearts have become darkened and foolish and we have entered into idolatry of various kinds (see Rom. 1:18ff). One form of that idolatry is the way we look to mortal men rather than to God for our direction, purpose and identity. This is particularly acute in homosexuality, where people begin looking to other human beings for the completion of their identify, rather than to God. It begins with an innocent search for an affirming role model, shifts into envy of those who represent those qualities that seem to be missing, and eventually ends in full-blown idolatry, where various individuals take God's place as the hope for fulfillment.

Romans 1:24-28 tells us that at some point, God gives such an idolater over to their human idols as well as to the depraved and foolish mind that results from such idolatry so that they burn with lust for those who can never satisfy their true needs. It is quite common to hear homosexuals claim that the moment they had their first sexual encounter with a person of the same sex, they knew that they were made to be homosexual. This is the very moment outlined in Romans 1:22,24,28. The certainty that they think they have gained is actually a deception that God has allowed the enemy to bring as a judgment for their idolatry. At the start, I believe that it is a *redemptive judgment,* one designed to bring about their ultimate salvation as they recognize the dead-end path they have taken. However, not all will humble themselves, repent, and turn to the Lord. Those who refuse to forsake their idolatry, according to 1 Corinthians 6:9-10, will not see the kingdom of God.

What Really Causes Homosexual Confusion?

Many who are caught up in the homosexual lifestyle will claim, "I've always felt this way and God wants me to be true to who I am." This argument presupposes the unproven and false claim that God made them homosexual. It also presumes that emotions and feelings reliably and accurately reveal what is true. The fact is, feelings are grossly inaccurate reflectors of reality.

Why do so many homosexuals claim to have always felt that way?

The Causes of Sexual Identity Confusion

Because the primary root cause of most homosexual confusion is a lack of emotional bonding with the parent of the same sex—something that studies have shown needs to occur between the ages of two and five. Since most people cannot remember much of anything before the age of two, this would explain why some homosexually confused people cannot remember feeling any other way. It does not, however, mean that they were born that way.

It is important at this point to make something very clear—the person who experiences homosexual confusion is in most cases morally innocent of wrongdoing at first. Normally, they have had no control over the formation of their condition. At some point, however, they inevitably become co-conspirators in the worsening of their neurosis. How? By committing sins in response to their infirmity, such as entertaining unholy fantasies, acting out sexually, holding on to unforgiveness and making vows against those who may have hurt them, looking to idealized peers to find their identity completion rather than to God or in countless other ways.

Most of the factors that contribute to sexual identity confusion have long been identified—factors that in some way cause the child to develop a deep insecurity, a fear or in some cases a hatred of the opposite sex. Everyone is different, however. We have different personalities and temperaments. A person whose temperament is very sensitive will be affected more profoundly by trauma than will even his own siblings. I've never encountered a homosexually confused person who didn't have a high sensitivity level, even if it was well hidden by a brash exterior.

We also have different sets of peers and some suffer great humiliation because they are artistic, athletically-challenged, too thin, too tall, too short—you name it. We each have a different set of voices speaking into our lives, saying different things at different stages—some affirming and others highly damaging. Such combinations of variables in the human experience create the kinds of insecurities that leave one person ripe for the development of homosexual neurosis and another person unscathed.

Usually, some form of trauma will have been present in the background of the homosexual. For example, over 50 percent of male and up to 85 percent of female homosexuals report being sexually abused as children. Many others report having experienced physical, emotional or verbal abuse.

A male victim of male sexual abuse may question his own sexual orientation, wondering why he was sexually attractive to another male. And if he found pleasure in the act, he may naively conclude that he must be homosexual. Or a young girl who suffers abuse from a male may secretly vow in her heart never to be intimate with a man ever again. A young boy who is molested by his mother may despise her (and the world of women that she represents to him) for betraying her role, or he may grow up fearful that a sexually mature woman may put pressure on him that he cannot handle.

Indeed, the abuse doesn't have to be overt or even sexual to cause such a outcome. It can be far more subtle. In my own family's circle of friends, there was a woman who looked like Marilyn Monroe who would tease me incessantly about girls. As a little boy, that instilled in me a subconscious fear that sexually mature women were potential sources of humiliation and thus should be avoided if possible. Later, when I found myself having to choose between sexual advances from males and females, considering my fears, the males were simply safer and more predictable.

It should be noted that some of the "traumas" in a child's life are more *perceived* than actual. For example, a boy may perceive that his father does not love him and has rejected him when in fact that father may feel great love for his son, but unskilled or afraid to express it. Or, a girl may adopt masculine behaviors because she believes that her parents don't like her because she isn't a boy, when that may not be the case at all. To a child, however, perception is reality and it will be the perception that forms his or her identity.

Real abuse of any kind can create a void within the victim, because the need for healthy affirmation and modeling has not only gone unmet, it has been turned into fear. And if the abuse comes at the hands of a parent, the child loses natural trust and respect for that parent, cutting the emotional cord with the abusive parent, "defensively detaching" from the very person who has been designed by God to impart a secure sense of identity.

Even non-sexual abuse can cause gender-related damage. For example, a boy who witnesses his dad beating up his mom may decide unconsciously to remain identified with her because his dad presents too frightening an image of a male. You see, every infant naturally bonds with his or her mother at birth unless she is a rare exception to the rule and for some reason cannot emotionally bond with her child. As mentioned before, the boy needs to switch his identity to his dad between the ages of two and five. If his dad and all other potential father figures are absent, frightening, abusive, weak or unattractive, that boy may never transfer his identity to the masculine. This is often the cause for effeminacy in a boy. He fears or discounts all that is male and thus holds on to the safe identification that he has had with his mother (the feminine) since birth.

The single most prevalent cause for the development of homosexual confusion in males is the inability to emotionally bond with their father or father figure. As a result, they remain fixed in their infant feminine identification with mom. Their dads never model healthy masculinity to them or affirm them in their emerging manhood. They never show them how to interact with the opposite sex, leaving the boy fearful and uncertain in this area. (There is a much smaller percentage of lesbians who as girls failed to bond with their mother, bringing about similar results.)

These deprivations result in a mental and emotional confusion about where they fit in and how they should act, especially toward the opposite sex. The resulting fear and uncertainty often keeps them from the natural interaction with the opposite sex that could help develop confident interpersonal skills. Their inability to naturally exhibit the proper traits of their own gender often results in ridicule and rejection by their peer group, which results in a further sense of alienation from the idealized state of masculinity or femininity. They feel unacceptable, different and/or cut off from their same-sex peers and they sometimes begin a lifelong, "secret" examination of idealized models of their own gender, looking for that magic key in "successful" peers that will show them what to do to become similarly acceptable.

At about the same time, puberty takes hold, and this examination begins to zero in on the physical evidences of maturation that have begun to display themselves in the school locker room, on TV, or in movies. This is when pornography can be particularly damaging because it depicts in graphic fashion those sexual body parts and behaviors that have come to symbolize the lost sense of sexual identity. In the unconscious search to find points of identity and modeling, they find themselves looking at members of their own gender in the filmed sex scenes or in the locker room, more so than the opposite sex—a behavior that convinces them all the more that they must be homosexual. Even if they succeed in mimicking proper behavior for their gender, they will still know, deep inside, that they are missing something—that they are not fully identified with their peers relative to their behavior toward, and desire for, the opposite sex.

In these ways and others, their basic emotional needs become sexualized, and they naturally begin to confuse the emotional pull that they feel toward members of their own sex with their emerging sexual drive.

With the help of a culture that psychologically steamrolls them into concluding that their need is indeed sexual (and perfectly natural and okay), they will inevitably be persuaded to test it out, to see if they really are a "born homosexual." Once in the arms of another man (or another woman if they are female); receiving the affection from their own sex that their emotional self has been screaming for; attaining intimacy with the object of their obsession; receiving the powerful reinforcing effect of orgasm at the hand of an idealized person--they will quickly conclude that they are indeed sexually destined for this kind of behavior.

The opinion of society plays a significant role in persuading those who might be only slightly inclined or curious about aberrant sexual behavior to pursue it. A culture that sanctions and encourages multiple forms of sexual perversion is a breeding ground for self-induced states of homosexual desire. Any human being, if sufficiently immersed in an environment of insatiable pursuit of fleshly variety and excess, will eventually reach the point of curiosity or sexual need where a homosexual encounter is the inevitable next step. Many heterosexual sex addicts eventually find themselves in this position, to their utter shock and dismay.

Homosexual orientation can also develop in a child who begins masturbation at an early age and who views himself or herself in the mirror while performing the act. The visual picture of his or her own sexual organs becomes progressively identified in their mind as the source of pleasure. This subconscious association becomes reinforced with each successive orgasm.

A child who is exposed to homosexual pornography also becomes a candidate for sexual identity confusion. Pictures of graphic sexual acts instill a fixation in the mind of a young person, particularly if the child has never imagined such things occurring. Even heterosexual pornography can be a contributing factor in the worsening of homosexual confusion. As the young person looks at the pornography, he or she feels more and more inadequate to replicate what is portrayed and is thereby driven deeper into aberrant fears and obsessions.

While some young people have a brief encounter with homosexual play while growing up, the child who repeats the behavior more than a few times is in danger of conditioning him- or herself to respond homosexually. *This is particularly serious if the child is also having sex with older kids or adults.*

Finally, of course, there is the classic scenario of an only son or daughter who is constantly surrounded by very strong or overbearing authority figures of the opposite sex, who encourage and reinforce behaviors in the child that conform to their own gender while regularly ridiculing or making fun of the gender of the child. This is one of the reasons why, in my estimation, gay adoptions are often a form of child abuse.

I could spend the rest of this book spinning scenarios for how certain life experiences conspire with certain personality types to shut down the emotional growth of a child and create homosexual confusion. Suffice it to say that the predominant experiential roots involve some form of abuse (real or perceived) and/or some form of failure to bond emotionally with the same-sex parent or parent figure. Some match of events to personality precipitates homosexuality or bisexuality in an individual.

The variability in each person's temperament and experience means that the outcome is equally variable. In other words, most people who develop homosexual neurosis do so by degree. In fact, from my personal and professional experience, I can safely say that there are a lot more people who have a partial degree of homosexual confusion than those who are exclusively gay—10, 20, 50, 70 and 100 percent, and every percent in between.

For example, among those who are homosexually inclined primarily as a result of child sexual abuse, some were abused much earlier in life than others, so it damaged them to a greater degree. Others were abused repeatedly or for a longer period of time. Some had a safe family to turn to for healing while others had no one to help them deal with the trauma and the self-loathing. Some had more sensitive temperaments than others. Some were desperately needy emotionally, and actually sought out further abuse in exchange for the affirmation and attention that they received from the abuser. Then there are some who, out of sheer perversity, choose to engage in homosexuality from time to time simply out of a desire for variation. These are generally older men or women who have gotten bored or are impotent and in search of something new to kick-start their sex lives. They are often trying to recapture their youth by hiring homosexual prostitutes who physically resemble their image of idealized youth. To their surprise, as they reprogram their sexual responses through this new means of pleasure-seeking, they develop a much deeper degree of homosexual confusion than they may have had before. Such adults incur greater culpability before God for their condition because their decision to enter into perverted sexual behavior was more conscious, willful and deliberate than those who found themselves in their hormonally supercharged youth with a powerful inclination that they did not want. Even so, God's grace extends to them.

Although God only makes heterosexuals, for the reasons cited above and for many more, some people grow up with a sexual identity that has been set askew from its divinely intended mark. Somewhere along the line, their emotional growth stopped and they underwent the sexualization of unmet emotional needs, blocking the healthy emergence of their true heterosexuality.

No "Demon of Homosexuality"

Finally, it is important to understand how the demonic realm contributes to homosexual confusion. While there is no "demon of homosexuality," there are demonic spirits who specialize in homosexual perversion. They begin their work early in the child's life, taking advantage of every opportunity to speak lies into the mind of the child who is being abused, rejected or neglected. Children who are not yet born again are particularly vulnerable to this kind of deception.

Sadly, most children cannot differentiate their own thoughts from demonic ones. When a child sins, the thoughts of condemnation that fill his or her mind are usually demonic in origin, designed to separate them from a loving and forgiving God. The child perceives them as accurate reflections on reality. Soon the child's belief system is grounded in self-hatred, and in my experience this can be found in everyone who suffers from homosexual confusion, as well as all other addictive behaviors.

In counterpart, the demonic realm cultivates an image of God as vengeful, harsh, demanding of perfection and wavering in His love, which makes the child run away from God after sinning, rather than to Him. If a child is abused or rejected, evil spirits are always right there to accuse God of failure to protect or to love.

Obviously, demons can gain influence through sinful behavior, because it affords them further power. Demons can also gain strange ground in us when we sexually unite with a person who has engaged in aberrant behavior. For example, a wife who unknowingly has a bisexual husband may suddenly experience a spirit of perversion working within her that her own personal history cannot account for. What has happened is that the "soul tie" that was made between her husband and his homosexual partner(s) has become linked to her through her sexual relations with her spouse. These ties need to be broken in the power of Jesus' name in prayer and the ground for them (perverted behavior) needs to be eliminated by the guilty party through repentance.

Finally, demons can also obtain ground in a person through the sins of up to four previous generations (see Exod. 20:5; Num. 14:18). This makes a person vulnerable to a particular sin. Such a curse, as we discussed earlier, can be broken by any generation that decides not to walk in that sin (see Exod. 18:14,17-20).

The elements that comprise an individual's homosexual compulsion and confusion are complex, but there is one common feature—a desperate need for love. This need can *never* be met in the gay lifestyle. Many who are in the throes of God's redemptive judgment (see Rom. 1:24) believe that they have found love in their same-sex relationships, but all they have found is romance or a pleasurable experience—feelings that will vanish as quickly as they came.

The Bible defines love as sacrifice and commitment (see 1 John 3:16). It is a selflessly, self-giving lifestyle—something that is light-years away from what people in the gay community experience. They think they have love because they feel romantic or sexually stimulated. Then it goes away, and they move on to someone else—hopelessly trapped in a voracious, promiscuous cycle.

Love is what they are seeking, but it can never be found in sin, because God is holy, and He is love itself (see 1 John 4:16). When the homosexual truly sacrifices and submits his or her passions to God through Christ, then he or she will find true love. In other words, when they forsake that lifestyle for Christ's sake, then they will find true life (see Mark 8:35). If they can see Christ in a believer—if they can experience His sacrificial, unconditional love through one of His sons or daughters—then they will recognize a love that will take them infinitely beyond anything they have ever known or imagined. Then they will pay any price to come home to the Father (see Luke 15:17-21).

Study Section— Sexual Identity Confusion - Causes

A. **FOUNDATIONAL TRUTHS**

1. God Creates You To Be Heterosexual.

   a. The biblical data in the "creation" account reveals three intentions that are clearly built into the very design of human beings:

      (1) There was intention and purpose in creating them male and female because God thinks and acts out of a place of pure wisdom and purpose.

      (2) The call to be fruitful and multiply requires heterosexual monogamy; heterosexual, to make babies; monogamy, to avoid STDs.

      (3) The command to reunite what had been separated—for male and female to "become one flesh" again.

      (4) Scripture condemns every departure from this model, for what it does to society, for what it does to our bodies and for what it does to the image of God in us.

   b. Even if homosexuality was discovered to have a physiological component, the point is moot for several other reasons:

      (1) Even though alcoholism is believed to have a genetic link (although the early studies on that are currently being questioned), God still calls us to live sober lives. He clearly labels drunkenness a sin worthy of eternal damnation (Gal. 5:19-21). His power is available to us in the areas where we fall short, whether the problem is physiological, emotional or psychological and so the, "I couldn't help

it" defense can never be used for sin of any kind.

(2) Everyone is born with an inherited propensity to sin. The formative code of the entire human race has this same inbred mutation. We sin as a natural course of being. Yet God expects us to take advantage of His provision to overcome that predilection so as to live holy lives instead of sinful. This is as true of the homosexual inclination as it is of the basic inclination to sin.

(3) Even if one cannot accept the first two propositions, it could still be properly argued that genetics and hormones could never force (without recourse) a behavior that God condemns man for acting out. If they could, God would be unjust for condemning mankind for a behavior that could not be helped.

c. Scientific studies continue to bear out God's intention that we operate heterosexually.

(1) A number of years ago, *"fetal brain androgen" studies* were said to indicate a physiological component to some sexual identity confusion. However, the studies were few and highly speculative, creating a great deal of unscientific, biased speculation by pro-gay propagandists.

In an article, "Born or Bred?" the February 24, 1992 issue of *Newsweek* magazine reported more recent studies using the size of the hypothalamus gland as "proof" that homosexuals were born that way. Another study of identical twins supposedly "proved" the same thesis according to pro-gay groups. Fortunately, the *Newsweek* article fairly reported the insurmountable evidence against these "political" conclusions. Here are some reasons why:

(2) Regarding *the twin experiment*—"Instead of proving the genetic argument, it only confirms the obvious: that twins are apt to have the same sort of shaping influences. 'In order for such a study to be at all meaningful, you'd have to look at twins raised apart,' says *Anne Fausto Sterling, a developmental biologist at Brown University.* 'It's such badly

interpreted genetics.'"

Newsweek quotes the response of *the dean of American sexologists, John Money (of Johns Hopkins University)* to the "discovery" that there are brain differences involved in sexual orientation as: "Of course it is in the brain. The real question is, when did it get there? Was it prenatal, neonatal, during childhood, puberty?"

"Many scientists (says *Newsweek*) say it's naive to think a single gene could account for so complex a behavior as homosexuality."

(3) Even the man who conducted *the study on the hypothalamus glands of AIDS infected cadavers* admits, "We can't say on the basis of that (the size difference of the gland in some homosexuals) what makes people gay or straight." In fact, *Newsweek* points out, "One of the major criticisms of the study was that AIDS could have affected the brain structure of the homosexual subjects."

Newsweek goes on to say, "The trickier question is whether things might work the other way around: could sexual orientation affect brain structure?" *Kenneth Klivington, an assistant to the president of the Salk Institute,* points to a body of evidence showing that the brain's neural networks reconfigure themselves in response to certain experiences. One fascinating NIH study found that in people reading Braille after becoming blind, the area of the brain controlling the reading finger grew larger. There are also intriguing conundrums in animal brains. In male songbirds, for example, the brain area associated with mating is not only larger than in the female but varies according to the season.

Says Klivington: 'From the study of animals, we know that circulating sex hormones in the mother can have a profound effect on the organization of the brain of the fetus. Once the individual is born, the story gets more complex because of the interplay between the brain and experience. It's a feedback loop: the brain influences behavior, behavior shapes experience, experience effects the organization of the brain, and so forth.'"

Newsweek quotes *the researcher of the hypothalamus study* as admitting he knew "regrettably little" about the sex histories, or the presumed orientation of his subjects. "That's a distinct shortcoming of my study," he said. In the article, he also confesses to going into the experiment with the intention to prove that homosexuality is genetically caused.

Of the study on identical twins, *Newsweek* reports that it had its own "dramatic" shortcomings. Some of the identical twins had one homosexual and one heterosexual. "Many critics have wondered about these discordant twins. How could two individuals with identical genetic traits and upbringing wind up with totally different sexual orientation (if sexual orientation is genetically determined)?" Even the researchers admitted, "There must be something in the environment to yield the discordant twins," reports *Newsweek*.

Newsweek also reveals, "Even within the enlightened ranks of the American Psychoanalytic Association there is still some reluctance to let homosexual analysts practice. As arrested cases themselves, the argument goes, they are ill-equipped to deal with developmental problems. The belief that homosexuality can and should be cured persists in some quarters of the profession."

New York City analyst Charles Socarides says, according to *Newsweek,* that the only biological evidence is "that we're anatomically made to go in male-female pairs." "Some psychiatrists still see the removal of homosexuality from the official list of emotional disorders as a mistake. It was instead innocuously identified as 'sexual orientation disturbance.'"

E.L. Pattullo, former director of Harvard's Center for Behavioral Sciences, recently pointed out in *Commentary* magazine that the scientific evidence *does not* support the claim that sexual orientation is biologically fated and thus entirely impervious to environmental influence." (from Chas Krauthammer commentary in the *Honolulu Advertiser* (April 1993)—columnist for the *New Republic* and *Time*)

(4) *The 1993 Hamer et al. "Genetic Link" study,* touted by the press as "proof" that homosexuality is genetically caused, did not prove any such thing. This was an investigation of 40 pairs of homosexual brothers, whose X chromosomes were studied to see if they shared inherited genetic peculiarities that could be attributed to sexual orientation.

In their research article in the July 16, 1993 issue of *Science* magazine, the researchers admitted that seven of the 40 pairs of homosexual brothers did not co-inherit the variation in the genetic region that supposedly was the locus for the "homosexual gene" found in the other pairs, and that these discordant pairs might be the result of "non-genetic sources of variation in sexual orientation." Neither did they have any control data indicating the presence or absence of the genetic variant in non-homosexual men. At the end of their report, the researchers admitted: "...a single genetic locus does not account for all of the observed variability," and that the sibling pairs that did not fit their conclusions might exist because there could be "environmental, experiential and cultural factors that influence the development of male sexual orientation." Hardly "proof" of a genetic cause for homosexuality.

In an accompanying article in the same issue of *Science,* Robert Pool commented: "The field of behavioral genetics is littered with apparent discoveries that were later called into question or retracted. Over the past few years, several groups of researchers have reported locating genes for various mental illnesses—manic depression, schizophrenia, alcoholism—only to see their evidence evaporate after they assembled more evidence or reanalyzed the original data. 'There's almost no finding that would be convincing by itself in this field,' notes *Elliot Gershon, chief of the clinical neuro-*

genetics branch of the National Institute of Mental Health."

Pool goes on to note: "(Researcher) Hamer warns, however, that this one site cannot explain all male homosexuality."

In a letter to the editor in the September 3, 1993 issue of *Science* magazine, *Evan Balaban of Harvard University and Anne Fausto-Sterling of Brown University* criticize the weaknesses of the Hamer et al. study, noting the lack of an adequate control group and a logical misassumption of the study: "We wish to emphasize that…correlation does not necessarily indicate causation. A gene affecting sexual orientation in some segment of the male population might do so very indirectly. For instance, any gene that might increase the tendency of brothers to psychologically identify with one another might influence their similarity in such matters as sexual orientation and would be picked up in the present study." In other words, the data collected by the study doesn't even begin to prove the hypothesis that it purports to prove.

Finally, the researchers themselves admit, in a letter of response: "We agree that genetic studies can never, in and of themselves, determine the mechanism by which a locus influences a trait." You certainly didn't hear them saying that before being publicly challenged with the erroneous conclusions that had been publicized about the study.

Richard Dawkins, a geneticist at Oxford University says that homosexuality is *not genetic—that genes do not affect behavior.*

d. At the "World Conference of Sexologists" in 1990, *not one sexologist believed that people were born homosexual,* though they acknowledged that certain temperaments leaned toward that.

e. In Feb 1993 the *National Opinion Research Center of the University of Chicago* published a study that showed 2% of men and 1% of women were homosexual. (per D. James Kennedy, 2 1/2% of American men are *former* homosexuals).

f. An NBC Poll on Jan 26, 1993 showed that 58% of Americans were against legalizing gay marriages, although that changed when the Supreme Court decided to legalize it in 2015 (Obergefell v. Hodges).

g. If God created some people to be homosexual, He could not judge their behavior to be sinful, which He clearly does throughout Scripture.

"Do not lie with a man as one lies with a woman; that is detestable" (Lev. 18:22).

"God gave them over to shameful lusts. Even their women exchanged natural relations for unnatural ones. In the same way the men also abandoned natural relations with women and were inflamed with lust for one another. Men committed indecent acts with other men, and received in themselves the due penalty for their perversion" (Rom. 1:26-27).

"Do not be deceived: Neither the sexually immoral nor idolaters nor adulterers nor male prostitutes nor homosexual offenders nor thieves nor the greedy nor drunkards nor slanderers nor swindlers will inherit the kingdom of God. And that is what some of you were. But you were washed, you were sanctified, you were justified in the name of the Lord Jesus Christ and by the Spirit of our God" (1 Cor. 6:9-11).

2. The new, "pro-gay theology" is very poor theology, that takes advantage of people who do not know any better.

a. It presumes to know better than every Greek and Hebrew scholar in the entire world over thousands of years, throughout all of the history of biblical translation and scholarship.

b. It is eisegesis, not exegesis—reading into the text one's own predetermined theology rather than extracting from the text what is actually being said.

c. The "Jesus didn't mention it" argument doesn't hold water either. In Matthew 5:17-20 and Luke 16:16-17 Jesus unequivocally reaffirms the law down to the smallest part of each letter. Also, if all Scripture is

"God-breathed" (2 Tim. 3:16) and has its origin from God, being "carried along by the Holy Spirit" through the agency of men (2 Peter 1:21), it is illegitimate then to try and separate the words of Jesus from those of other biblical writers as though one were inspired and the other not. And finally, Jesus didn't mention child abuse or bestiality either, making the point that it is specious reasoning to cite His silence on the issue of homosexuality as though that pointed to approval. The New Testament was not intended as a new list of laws, but rather as a way of understanding how the eternal principles that underlie moral law can be fulfilled through the empowerment that comes in union with the risen Christ.

d. The "I've always felt this way and God wants me to be true to who I am" argument first of all presupposes the unproven and false claim that there is true intrinsic identity in homosexuality and secondly, presumes that emotions and feelings are accurate arbiters of truth. The fact is, "feelings" are grossly inaccurate reflectors of reality. That many homosexuals will have "always felt that way" is predictable because the homosexual neurosis is often caused by the breakdown in identity bonding, which occurs between the ages of two and five.

3. The recent claim that the early Christian church was pro-homosexual is also bereft of even a shred of truth.

In an article from his June 1994 newsletter titled, "Homo-propaganda: Early Christian Church Blesses Same-Sex Marriages," Mike Gabbard (president of "Stop Promoting Homosexuality, America") quotes a *Hawaii Catholic Herald* story of 6/17/94:

"A new book by former Yale University history chairman John Boswell has added more fuel to the controversy surrounding the legalization of same-sex 'marriages.' Boswell, a homosexual activist, claims in 'Same-Sex Unions in Premodern Europe' that Christian churches dating from the 8th to 17th centuries performed ceremonies that blessed same-sex couple unions.

'The new book raises arguments that certain blessing

ceremonies of the Greek or Byzantine Church called 'adelphopoiesis' (the creation of brothers or the creation of brotherly relations) can be reinterpreted as ecclesiastical blessings of homosexual unions.'

Father Robert Taft, a Jesuit from the Pontifical Oriental Institute in Rome, and expert on Byzantine history and liturgy, disagrees. Taft says Boswell's conclusions are false.

'(Taft) called it ridiculous to claim that the church of Byzantium was blessing homosexual marriages at a time when church laws imposed two to three years' penance for homosexual activity and Byzantine civil law dealt with it as a crime to be punished by 'torture, castration and even execution.'

'Father Taft said the blessing—which makes two people who are not brothers adoptive brothers—reflects the Christian Byzantine cultural context in which close friendship ('philia' in Greek), especially between males, was a 'very high ideal'. The blessing was 'the Byzantine Church's attempt to bring this into the church's liturgical system.'

Taft further stated that considering the blessing as a sexual relationship 'is a very tendentious interpretation…There is nothing in the texts of the rituals themselves that would allow this kind of interpretation.'

Taft is not alone in his conclusions. Father Alkiviadis Calivas, professor of liturgy at Holy Cross Orthodox School of Theology, says '…there is no explicit or implicit thing about marriage connected with the blessing. And as for a homosexual blessing, certainly not. In the early Christian tradition this would be an abomination.'

Paul Meyendorff, a theologian who teaches liturgy at St. Vladimir's Orthodox Theological Seminary in New York, said the 'adelphopoiesis' blessing resembles the type of blessing used in adopting a child, which bonds family members together who aren't biologically related.'"

4. Many factors have been identified as contributing to sexual identity confusion. However, it takes an individual "match" of "events to personality" to actually precipitate active homosexuality or bisexuality in any given individual. The combination of these "events" with "personality" is as different between individuals as are their separate personalities.

5. Although God only makes heterosexuals, some people grow up with a sexual identity that has been set askew from its divinely

intended mark. Somewhere along the line, their emotional growth stopped and they underwent the sexualization of unmet emotional needs, blocking the healthy emergence of their true heterosexuality.

It would be good to visualize the breadth of human sexual identity as a continuum rather than an "either/or" proposition (not to be confused with the "Kinsey Scale"). This continuum is meant to reflect where a person perceives him/her self to be, not what they truly are.

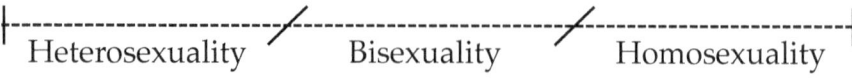

Heterosexuality   Bisexuality   Homosexuality

In order to establish unnatural sexual desire, it takes a perfectly synergized combination of psycho-emotional influences and events, all of which are effected by:
- timing
- number
- family dynamics
- emotional and spiritual health
- event
- severity
- outside influences
- personality
- a state of neediness, dependency or naiveté

"Everything depends on a person's ability to tolerate a given experience."   —Dr. John White (from *Eros Redeemed*)

B. Typical Development of Sexual Identity Confusion

The presence of some of the following situations in a person's life does not mandate their becoming sexually confused. However, in those who are sexually confused, you will find one or more of the causal factors to follow—

1. Confused Sexual Identity Brought on by a Lack of Emotional Bonding With the Same Sex:

    a. In boys, this prevents the change from their initial identification with mother (which naturally occurs in infancy with both boys and girls), to identifying with the father, during the pre-adolescent years.

    b. This prevents the child from identifying itself with it's own sex. It is not uncommon to hear those who have missed out on this bonding say that they never have felt a part of their own gender group (e.g., "one of the guys").

c. Per Sy Rogers (former President of "Exodus International"): their studies have shown that 90% of males and 25-35% of females who have homosexual confusion have had a broken relationship with their same sex parent.

CONTRIBUTING FACTOR # 1

The Peer Factor

In this environment, there is a lack of role-modeling and reassurances of acceptability as a member of one's own gender group, which:

- can result in confusion over how to interact with the opposite sex, creating fear and uncertainty.
- can result in ridicule and rejection from peers.
- can result in a secret examination of idealized members of one's same-sex peer group—searching for identification and "keys" to being acceptable.
- At puberty or at one's sexual awakening, this "emotional" longing becomes confused with the emerging "sexual" drive. The child begins to eroticize the gender he or she has not identified with.
- The reinforcing effects of sexual experiences imprint and reinforce the making of a "sexual" obsession out of this "emotional" problem.
- This can result in the "cannibal compulsion"—a compulsion to take idealized parts or traits of another into oneself (as described by Leanne Payne).
- It can result in "idolatry." God then gives us over to burning with lust with one another, because we have rejected His clear will in order to worship someone else (Rom. 1:25). (Note that Eph. 5:5 equates "idolatry" with "immorality"). Even in the heterosexual world, there are many "idolatrous" relationships, where an insecure but good-looking person feeds from the idolatrous "worship" of a fawning "best friend," who worships the beautiful traits and characteristics of their friend.
- It can result in "symbolic confusion," where unreal, idealized or caricaturized versions of members of both sexes are created in one's imagination, as the tiny child within tries to come to a sense of being—of knowing who and what they are and where they fit in. Then starts the eternal search to avoid or to be like and accepted by, such mythical figures. (Leanne Payne addresses this phenomenon in detail).
- It can result in the "disease of introspection" (another Leanne Payne

term), where the person compulsively uses the conscious mind to ruthlessly examine the unconscious mind and obliterate all self-esteem with impossible standards and accusations. This destroys the intuitive, creative self. Leanne Payne claims that this problem is central to the homosexual neurosis.

- It can result in "same-sex" or "opposite-sex" ambivalence a love/hate/fear relationship with a parent that causes one to desperately want to be near and accepted by that parent, yet afraid of their rejection or ridicule.

Contributing Factor # 2

Societal Pressures

"Love is something more stern and splendid than mere kindness."
—C.S. Lewis

Under the guise of being "non-judgmental" and "open-minded," our culture pressures those entrapped in sexual confusion into pursuing and "accepting" their aberrant sexual feelings.

- This serves to reinforce and "legitimize" the confused feelings.
- Those who suffer from a low-level problem end up strengthening the skewed sexual inclinations that they may sometimes feel through the powerfully reinforcing agent of experience. This horribly victimizes the adolescent who has not yet learned how to spot and avoid psychologically manipulative tactics and who has not yet learned the wisdom of "delayed gratification" and other lessons that only years can teach. Adolescents notoriously fall for adult or peer judgments about their being and personality.

For those who are entrapped in a self-destructive, "on-the-edge" life, societal approval of sexual aberration only serves to encourage them to experiment with what may be fleeting feelings, and thus program their sexual responses improperly.

Contributing Factor # 3

Improper Self-Programming At An Early Age With Pornography And Masturbation

- Early onset masturbation, combined with viewing oneself in a mirror in the process, results in programming one's mind to associate the sight of one's own genitals with sexual pleasure and excitement. These factors are among the highest correlates in studies done on the subject of sexual identity confusion.

- Homosexual pornography, particularly if viewed as a youngster, has a powerful effect in programming sexual orientation. (Even in adulthood, it has the subconscious effect of legitimizing and encouraging skewed inclinations, particularly if coupled with masturbation).
- Even heterosexual pornography can create such feelings of inadequacy (at being able to perform in a similar fashion, in not being as sexually attractive or in not possessing the same physical endowments as those in the pictures), that a person retreats into responding to whoever is drawn to them rather than taking the more arduous path of trying to attract such "unreachable" sexual beings. In the case of young males, there is no shortage of older men who will actively pursue them, who are completely sexually satisfied with watching their victim be sexual without the need for reciprocity and who understand how to take advantage of the insecurities of the young boy by psychologically boosting his sexual ego. These men are often completely sexually satisfied just by being with a young person in a sexual way, whether that person is at all handsome or sexually adept.

Contributing Factor # 4

Homosexual Play

Repeated homosexual play in childhood or adolescence, especially if carried on with older people, has a powerfully imprinting effect on sexual orientation.

Contributing Factor # 5

Dysfunctional Parent

- Sexual identity confusion can result from having an excessively dominating opposite-sex parent, particularly if he or she regularly ridicules your own sex and reinforces your participation in and identification with gender behaviors opposite to your own.
- a father who wanted a son and only affirms and responds to his daughter when she acts like a boy—or vice versa
- a mother who hates men and only affirms her son when he behaves like a little girl
- emotionally distant or hostile parent who did not want a child and never affirms him or her

Contributing Factor # 6

Demonic Influences

- It appears that demonizing spirits have an increasing influence over

us as the degree and length of participation in sexual sin proceeds.
- This is particularly true of "knowing" and "defiant" sin.
- It also appears that we may become demonized (where demonic spirits exert a degree of manipulative control over us) simply by becoming victims of sexual abuse.
- Additionally, we may attract demonic powers by viewing sin, however innocently encountered…
- … or by toying with the tools of the demonic realm (hypnotism, Ouija Boards, eastern meditation, astrology, etc.), however innocently.

2. Sexual Molestation Can Powerfully Effect the Sexual Identification and Orientation of a Person.

   a. It often breeds hatred or distaste for the sex act that was forced upon the victim, and consequently the gender of the perpetrator. This is often the cause behind a female victim's rejection of further sexual intercourse with men—at least on the emotional level.

   b. It may breed obsession with the sex act that was forced upon the victim, resulting either:

      (1) in the repeating of the act later on, in order to recast oneself in the "power" role—this usually being the person who has felt victimized, or

      (2) in repeating the act later on, in order to test if one still retains the power to attract such intense passion toward oneself—this sometimes being the obsession of the one who feels that they were the cause of the molestation.

   c. It sometimes results in a demonic inroad into the life of the abused child.

   d. Per Sy Rogers, among those with homosexual confusion, 40% of males have been molested and 75% of females have been victims of incest during their childhood.

3. Amoral Belief System

   a. Raised in a setting devoid of moral or other Christian input.

   b. Other reasons for someone growing up with deviant behavior having never felt any guilt or shame over it:

- a seared conscience and a selective memory
- a state of denial

C. **HEALING HOMOSEXUAL DESIRES**

1. Confession and Repentance of Sinful Behavior, as Well as Sinful Responses to the People and Events Surrounding the Emergence of One's Sexual Identity.

   "There are two manifestations when Glory comes: for those who are impure, unprepared and uninvited there will be judgment. For those who are welcomed, prepared, anointed, and invited there will be blessing.

   Salvation alone does not give believers the privilege of entering into the Glory of the Lord. If you want an abundant life then live abundantly in the Lord. We need personal repentance. Every day we want to commune in the Glory of the Lord, we need to prepare ourselves with personal repentance unto the Lord."   —Frank Amedia

   Until now, your body (or someone else's) has been your God; your emotions have been your king, and your feelings have been your slave master. Now, you must turn to God for His power to defeat:

   a. Idolatry (Romans 1:18-27)—misplaced love and worship

   b. Rebellion (1 Sam. 15:23)—misplaced homage and obedience

      Agree with God that sexual behavior outside of heterosexual monogamy is wrong. The sexual inclination toward members of one's own sex is not wrong, it is the acting out of those diseased inclinations that is wrong. It is rebellion, which is as the sin of "witchcraft."

   c. Unforgiveness (Mt. 6:14-15)—misplaced position and authority (i.e., making "self" judge).

   d. self-pity—a sin of narcissism that is deadly to honesty

2. Seek God for a Spiritual Healing.

   "We come to know ourselves through moral and spiritual development."   —Leanne Payne

   a. Recognize and acknowledge daily, your absolute need for God's power to heal.

   b. Recognize and acknowledge daily, God's pronounced desire and willingness to forgive and to heal you—

based on the grace won for you by Jesus' work on the Cross.

"God has done everything for you that He requires of you."

"As long as you're letting laws protect you, the Spirit of God can't protect you."

"All His commandments are promises. When He commands you to do something, He's just saying, 'I promise I'm going to do this through you if you trust Me.'"

"Compelled by love, you'll go out in power."

"Obedience is believing."
                    (Dudley Hall—from Grace Works)

c. Take the steps of faith necessary to replace the incorrect associations that you have made between the personality and actions of your earthly father and the character and love of your heavenly Father.

d. Practice the presence of God, throughout each and every day, and receive into your spirit the awareness of the inescapable reality of His unconditional love for you. Always be careful to recognize the immediacy of His forgiveness, at any time, for any reason, for as many times as you sin, no matter what the sin.

"You never want to look at the need before you look at the greatness of God."   —Loren Cunningham

e. Since you must want to change before permanent healing can occur, seek the Lord to increase your will to change. (Leanne Payne teaches that it is the masculine part of us, and of God, that possesses the strength of will).

Aristotle said virtue consists of not merely knowing what is right, but also in having the will to do what is right. He said that the will is trained by practice, by choosing to do right repeatedly until it becomes a habit. In Aristotle's words, "We become just by the practice of just actions." (from a "Focus on the Family" newsletter)

f. Give place for God to work righteous anger in you. Get angry over the destruction Satan has wrought in your life through your sinful behavior! That will serve to keep you from repeating the sins again.

g. Recognize and respond to the *"Mystery of Healing"*—that in intimacy and communion with the Father, we receive into ourselves His will, His purity of thought and desire, the fullness of boundless love, the ability to trust, the wisdom to act rightly and the completion of our personhood—our healing.

This *"mystery of healing"* has everything to do with the intimacy that you develop with the Father, Son and Holy Spirit and the diligence and hunger with which you pursue Him!

h. Receive the power of the Holy Spirit to deliver you (Lk. 11:13). Galatians 5:16 says: "If we walk by the Holy Spirit, we will not carry out the desire of the flesh." God will deliver you from the compulsion to act out your immoral desires, right away. The Holy Spirit is more powerful than all other powers in the universe combined—infinitely more! Temptation may not cease, but the uncontrollable obsession will (1 Cor. 10:13). No other power can force you to do anything anymore unless you give it permission through giving in to your old desires.

i. Recognize the chain of authority in which you are linked and utilize what is now yours through Christ.

(1) All power and authority in heaven and on earth has been given to the One who wants to change you (Mt. 28:18).

(2) His purpose in coming to earth was and is to destroy the work of the enemy (1 John 3:8).

(3) He has given all who follow Him authority to overcome all of the power of the enemy (Luke 10:19, Mt. 10:1).

(4) Those things that seem impossible to you are possible with God (Luke 18:27).

3. Seek God for Mental Healing and He will Lead you Through It. Remember that it is God's power working in and through you (Phil. 2:13), that overcomes the enemy. Learn to turn to Jesus, for His power, and to rely on Him.

a. Reprogram/Renew your mind.

"Be made new in the attitude of your mind" (Eph. 4:23).

"I urge you brothers, in view of God's mercy, to offer

your bodies as living sacrifices, holy and pleasing to God—which is your spiritual worship. Do not conform any longer to the pattern of this world, but be transformed by the renewing of your mind" (Rom. 12:1-2).

"We have the mind of Christ" (1 Cor. 2:16, NASB).

"Whatever is true, noble, right, pure, lovely, admirable, excellent or praiseworthy—think about such things" (Phil 4:8).

"Set your mind on things above, not on earthly things" (Col. 3:2).

"Prepare your mind for action; be self-controlled; set your hope fully on the grace to be given you when Jesus Christ is revealed. Do not conform to the evil desires you had when you lived in ignorance. But just as He who called you is holy, so be holy in all you do" (1 Pet. 1:13-15).

 (1) "Clothe" yourself with Christ through worship and praise. Your attention must be singularly focused on Jesus Christ so that you are in a position to receive the continual impartation of His life.

 "Clothe yourselves with the Lord Jesus Christ, and do not think about how to gratify the desires of the sinful nature" (Rom. 13:14; see also Gal. 3:27) .

 (2) Regularly "feed" on the Word of God (Heb. 5:12-14; Mt. 4:4; Dt. 8:3; Job 23:12; Ps. 119:103; Jer. 15:16).

 (3) Be reinforced in your mind by the exhortations and encouragements that come from fellowshipping with other believers—those who are committed, lovers of God.

 (4) Allow the cleansing effect of "serving" others to renew your mind.

b. Guard your heart and mind.

"The peace of God, which surpasses all comprehension, shall guard your heart and your mind in Christ Jesus" (Phil. 4:7, NASB).

 (1) This happens through intimate, daily communion with God. It changes our perspective.

 "Those who live in accordance with the Spirit, have their minds set on what the Spirit desires"

(Rom. 8:5b).

"Live by the Spirit and you will not gratify the desires of the sinful nature" (Gal. 5:16).

(2) We need to desire it with all of our heart (Jer. 29:13). We often deceive ourselves into thinking that we want something when we don't, but God knows our heart and can reveal to us our self-deceptions.

Consider this exhortation from Thomas F. Jones. First appeared in Discipleship Journal Issue 64 July/August 1991—"Singleness" by Thomas F. Jones (p. 38). Used by permission. All rights reserved:

"While self-control may sometimes be a struggle it is not as difficult as we sometimes think. What it takes is a decision to live in a certain way. Most people who lack sexual self-control have never really made a firm decision to control themselves.

We can never excuse wrong behavior by blaming passion. Imagine yourself in a completely vulnerable situation. You and your lover are totally aflame with desire and on the threshold of intercourse. Nothing can stop you now, right? Then your partner says, 'I'm not sure if I've told you or not, but I have AIDS.' What do you think about control now?

In today's moral climate, many do not fail sexually because they are too weak but because they simply do not see a reason to control themselves...

God's rules (however) point in the direction of maximum spiritual fulfillment, (so) view self-control as a positive affirmation of God-given sexuality."

(3) We need to cooperate with what the Spirit leads us to do. We will repeatedly be faced with a choice between loving Jesus more than we do sin. Our individual decisions will make evident our stance despite our claims and protestations to the contrary.

(4) We need to willingly put on the new self and set our heart against the world.

"Put on the new self, created to be like God in true righteousness and holiness" (Eph. 4:24).

4. Seek God for an Emotional Healing and He will Lead you Through the Process of Being Healed Emotionally.

   a. Replace what you've lost.

      "God shall supply all your needs according to His riches in glory" (Phil. 4:19, NASB).

      (1) God the Father will "bond" with you—sometimes using other people. He will plant certain people in your life who will represent in the flesh, what He is doing in you through the Spirit.

      (2) God will model right behavior for you, through Jesus.

      (3) He will be your perfect Father.

      (4) He will help you replace sinful attitudes with godly ones (e.g., unforgiveness, judgments, vows, etc).

      (5) He will help root out "fear" from your life and replace it with faith.

      "We know and rely on the love God has for us. God is love…There is no fear in love. But perfect love drives out fear" (1 John 4:16-18).

      "God did not give us a spirit of timidity, but a spirit of power, of love and of self-discipline" (2 Timothy 1:7).

      (6) He will teach you how to relinquish control to Him—to trust Him.

      (7) He will heal you on the inside from your emotional traumas, going right to the root cause and healing it at the point of origin.

      (8) He will purify you and return your innocence to you.

"I will sprinkle clean water on you, and you will be clean; I will cleanse you from all your impurities and from all your idols. I will give you a new heart and put a new spirit in you; I will remove from you your heart of stone and give you a heart of flesh. And I will put My Spirit in you and move you to follow My decrees and be careful to keep My laws" (Ezekiel 36:25-27).

    b. God will transfer His wholeness into you. He will not simply patch up the old person—He will make a new creation (1 Peter 2:4-5).

"If anyone is in Christ, he is a new creation; the old has gone, the new has come! All this is from God, who reconciled us to Himself through Christ and gave us the ministry of reconciliation" (2 Cor. 5:17-18).

"As we contemplate the Lord's glory, we are being transformed into His likeness, with ever-increasing glory" (2 Cor. 3:18).

5. Practical Points to Recovery

    a. God's part is to supply the power and the authority—ours is to take up those tools and use them to put to death the old nature. We must "set our heart and mind" against the old sin-bred patterns of thinking, feeling and doing, and toward a love of purity.

"Worship the Lord in the splendor of His holiness" (Ps. 29:2).

In his book, Passion for Jesus, (pp. 138-139), Mike Bickle says:

"When Jesus is revealed, a hunger for purity and righteousness is released...Hunger for purity is one response of a believer who sees the Lord in His glory... The greatest motivation for obedience to the Lord is a growing revelation of who Jesus is—His passions and pleasures and the matchless splendor in His personality."

Purity is more powerful than lust or evil, just as God is more powerful than Satan; infinitely more powerful. The problem is, we don't want purity, or value purity enough to "take it by force" and live in its power—i.e., to live in (abide in) continual communion with God.

"From the days of John the Baptist until now, the Kingdom of Heaven has been forcefully advancing, and forceful men lay hold of it" (Mt. 11:12).

    b. Allow God to identify for you, roots of spiritual, mental and emotional disease. God has the omniscience necessary to identify points of origin for temptation and behavior. If you seek Him for the knowledge, God will methodically but gently expose those things in your life that feed the old skewed orientation, and with your

cooperation, will destroy their power over you.
c. Ask God for the power over these strongholds.
d. Starve the old nature to death! Avoid the people, places and things that God reveals as feeding troughs for your sin nature.

"By the leading of the Spirit, put to death the misdeeds of the body" (Rom. 8:13).

"I have kept my feet from every evil path so that I might obey your Word" (Ps. 119:101).

e. Learn to recognize the schemes of the devil by seeking the Lord to reveal them to you.
   (1) If sexual memories come to you out of the blue (not as a result of an idle mind), but with great power to stimulate, that is a sign that they are borne by demons. Tell them to go where Jesus sends them.
   (2) When all sexual activity outside of the marriage bed has been cast off, the unmarried person may find that the adolescent phenomenon of "wet dreams" returns. This is almost always accompanied by dreams in which immorality takes place. This reveals that there still exists in your mind a "stronghold of sexual immorality" that demons are continuing to stimulate. You must declare your desire to be freed from *all* demonic influence and command that the stronghold be broken in the name of Jesus.

f. Take the kingdom of God by force (Mt. 11:12; Luke 16:16) i.e., wrest your place in the kingdom of God from the illegal attempts of demons to hold onto it, by using your authority to cast them out.

g. Don't rush ahead of what the Lord is doing in some misguided effort to please Him or to "earn your keep."

h. Rejoice in the progress that you make under the Lord's tutelage, but *never* become satisfied to the point that you stop growing in Christ.

i. Frequent men's/women's fellowship groups and home fellowship groups in addition to regular church services so that you can receive the kind of healthy support, modeling and acceptance from your same-sex peer group that has been missing in your life.

j. Find someone with whom you can be accountable—perhaps a discipling relationship within the church.
6. The most important factors for change—all of which increase as you seek greater intimacy and revelation of the Lord are:
   a. The intensity of your desire for change.
   b. The degree of faith with which you hold on to God's promises.
   c. The depth of your love and commitment to Jesus Christ above all others.
   d. The degree of your willingness to be faithful to God's will and direction.
   e. The degree to which you can keep the perspective that it is God's working in you that brings permanent transformation.
   f. The amount of time you spend seeking God in prayer and crying out to Him for help.

   "God rewards those who *diligently* seek Him" (Heb. 11:6).

D. RELATED ISSUES
   1. Loneliness

   Your friends may reject you because you have become alien to them, and a source of guilt.
   a. Don't forsake Christian assembly (Heb. 10:25).
   b. Avoid self-pity. Ruthlessly refuse to let it have any place in you. Combat it with prayer and by serving others.

   Note: There is a grieving over sin and the loss of critical parts of one's childhood that is a necessary part of healing that should not be mistaken for self-pity.

   c. Learn to *practice the presence of God*. He will be your constant companion, so that loneliness will not be a problem.
      • Sit alone in your room (or somewhere where you will not be disturbed) and "wait" on the Lord. Learn to be silent and comfortable with silence. Go there just to be with God—not to get from Him. Go there to find Him, to commune with Him, to discover Him, to be a companion to Him.
      • Don't let the frustration of a busy mind dissuade

you. Learn, by practice, to ignore or put off distracting thoughts. Perhaps keep a pad at your side to write down pressing thoughts that will not go away any other way. At other times, turning to the Bible often helps to drive out a plague of unwanted thoughts.

- As you sit in silence, practice believing by faith that He is with you there. Learn to enjoy the simplicity and beauty of that. Focus on the reality of His presence.

- As you sit there, the Holy Spirit may begin to prompt you to pray about certain things. Do as you feel led. Then return to silence.

- As you sit there, the Holy Spirit may lead you to pick up your Bible (which you should always have at your side in the room) and read. Read until the Spirit begins to speak to you in what you are reading. Stop and pray, or meditate on what He is teaching you.

- As you sit there, sing love songs to Jesus. Talk to Him. Tell Him what you are feeling, what has happened to you that day, etc. If you are troubled about something, tell Him how you feel—what troubles you. Admit your failings, your weaknesses and your faith that He has the answers. Many times you'll find that in the midst of describing your troubles, wisdom to unravel them will come from your own mouth, as God begins to put solutions into your prayers.

- It is important to focus on "worship" and "listening prayer" as the bulk of your activity before the Lord. Enter into petitional prayer preferably as the Holy Spirit leads. However, if there is a pressing issue that seems to prevent all else from taking place, go ahead and pray for that. God knows your heart and will be gracious to respond to that pressing need.

- During your day, stop periodically and acknowledge God's presence. A quick thought of appreciation, praise or request for "help" is very much in order at any time. It is particularly important to stop and turn to the Lord during those moments of the day when you are experiencing a need for His power or wisdom, for example, when you are tempted or facing a dilemma.

- At first you will need to consciously go out of your way to do these things. However, eventually it will become an ingrained habit—one which will bear the fruit of a deep and abiding love and dependence on the one who loves you more than any other.

2. Emotional Dependency

Many people (no matter what their sexual orientation) have a problem with being emotionally dependent on others. Their personality and self-image is so weak or damaged, that they "bend" toward others emotionally in order to absorb a personality or identity, direction in life, or even a sense of justification for their existence. These relationships can be typified by extreme dependence and jealousy and are unhealthy.

Someone who is highly dependent in this way, will seek out someone who possesses the traits they feel they lack, and attempt to create a "best friend" or "lover" relationship. Often, the people they find are those who have an emotional dysfunction of their own—a subconscious need to be idolized. These people may appear to be successful and attractive, but possess deep inner self-doubts. The attention and worship of their dependent friend helps them medicate the pain of their own insecurities.

Sometimes an emotionally dependent person will try to attach themselves to a healthy person, through flattery, gifts, offers of help and prayer, etc. The healthy person naturally responds to these kindnesses with time and attention, but may soon discover that their new friend has emotional needs that they are unable to meet. Due to their inexperience in dealing with emotionally dependent individuals, what starts out as a seeming healthy new friendship often turns into a frightening episode for the healthy party.

Emotional dependency runs rampant in the homosexual community and is almost always an issue that must be dealt with in the healing process. Lori Rentzel has written a brilliant pamphlet on the subject, part of which we'll now examine, as she answers the question: Why are dependencies hard to break? (emphasis added)

"*First*, as painful as dependency is, *it does give us some gratification*. There is emotional security...a sense that we have at least one relationship we can count on and that we belong to someone. Our need for intimacy, warmth and affection might be filled through this relationship. And our egos are boosted when someone admires or is attracted to us. We also enjoy feeling needed. A relationship like this might add excitement and romance when life seems dull otherwise. In fact, the stressful ups and downs of dependencies can become addictive in themselves. Additionally, the focus on maintaining this relationship can provide an escape from confronting personal problems and responsibilities. Finally, many people simply do not know any other way of relating. They are afraid to give up the "known" for the "unknown.

The *second* reason...is that *we can't see them as sinful.* The culture we live in has taken the truth "God is love" and turned it around to mean "Love is god." Romantic or emotional love is viewed as a law unto itself...Viewed in this light, dependent relationships seem beautiful, even noble, especially if there is no overt sexual involvement...Also, we may not be able to see how dependent relationships separate us from God...the euphoric feeling masquerades as closeness to God.

Third, root problems are not dealt with.

Fourth, those who willingly enter dependent relationships become candidates for spiritual deception. When we ignore the Holy Spirit's correction, we make ourselves vulnerable to satanic oppression.

Fifth, we don't want to give up the relationship."

Next, Lori describes several guidelines and suggestions for what the process of healing for emotional dependency might look like:

*"The path out of dependency involves...*turning away from relationships which are based on serving our own needs...and learning new ways of relating as 'new creatures in Christ' (2 Cor. 5:17).

*Begin by making a commitment to honesty...*admitting we are involved in a dependent relationship and acknowledging the sinful aspects of that relationship.

*The next challenge is being honest with another person...*confess to them.

Begin gradually separating yourself from your partner.

*We must also allow God to work...*If we confess to God that we are hopelessly attached to this individual and powerless to do anything about it and invite God to come in and change the situation, the Lord will not overlook our prayers.

Prepare for grief and depression... If we allow ourselves to hurt for a season, our healing will come faster.

Cultivate other friendships.

Discover God's vision for relationships. If we love others as God loves them, we will desire to see them conformed to the image of Christ.

Begin resolving the deeper issues... bring the whole thing before God in prayer...seek out the counsel and prayer of those God has placed in authority over us.

Prepare for the long haul... We need to know ourselves... (and) our adversary...to be willing to believe God loves us, even if we cannot feel His love...to learn God's character through His Word...to stop blaming Him...A close relationship with Jesus Christ is our best safeguard against emotional dependency."

From *Emotional Dependency* by Lori Rentzel. Copyright 1990 by Lori Rentzel. Published by InterVarsity Press, Downers Grove, IL. Used with permission.

3. Celibacy

   The need for affection and loving reassurance is very real, especially in this feeling-oriented world.

   a. People's suspicions of celibates as being abnormal, hurts.

   b. This is where you will learn about the deep waters of self-sacrifice and self-denial that God uses to grow us. We need to mature into forgoing the pleasures of Egypt for a season, for the greater calling and reward that are hidden in the will of God.

   (Note: In the Matson and McWorda study—out of 168 gay couples, not one could maintain monogamy for 5 years).

   c. Keeping an eternal perspective is critical.

   From *Christianity Today*, June 24, 1991, "Death in the Mirror" by Timothy K. Jones (pp. 30-31). Used by permission.

   "Christian faith has always argued that meaning in life will be found *beyond* life. 'In my end is my beginning', the poet T.S. Eliot wrote...In a profound way, where we are headed affects how we travel. And death, for all its mystery and starkness and seeming darkness, leads, for the believer, to something better than life."

d. Our advocate with the Father, Jesus Christ, also led a celibate life.

e. Go to Jesus to receive mercy and grace to help you in your time of need (Heb. 4:15).

f. Let God deal with your newly unmet physical needs. If you really want Him to, He can remove all or part of your sexual cravings until the appropriate time as you head into marriage. He doesn't suppress the drive, He fulfills it in some miraculous way.

Once you have asked God to do this, and He has, if you invite the sexual feelings back into you by giving way to immoral temptation (in unrepentant thought or in actions), it is likely that they will return with an overpowering vengeance. So be careful. Do not request the grace of God lightly or carelessly.

"Those who belong to Christ Jesus have crucified the flesh with its passions and desires" (Gal. 5:24, NASB).

g. It is God who calls us into a "permanent" life of celibacy. Do not presume to take on a calling that is not intended for you. If God has fulfilled your sexual drive miraculously at your request, allow Him to decide if it will be a permanent "gift of singleness" or not. Take things one day at a time.

"Not everyone can accept this word, but only those to whom it has been given. For some are eunuchs because they were born that way; others were made that way by men; and others have renounced marriage because of the kingdom of heaven. The one who can accept this should accept it" (Mt. 19:11, 12).

"Let not any eunuch complain, 'I am only a dry tree.' For this is what the Lord says: 'To the eunuchs who keep My Sabbaths, who choose what pleases Me and hold fast to My covenant—to them I will give within My temple and its walls a memorial and a name better than sons and daughters; I will give them an everlasting name that will not be cut off'" (Is. 56:3-5).

"It is good for a man not to marry. But since there is so much immorality, each man should have his own wife, and each woman her own husband...I say this as a concession, not as a command. I wish that all men were as I am. But each man has his own gift from God; one has this gift, another has that. Now to the unmarried and to the widows I say: It is good for them to stay unmarried, as I am. But if they cannot control themselves, they should marry, for it is better to marry than to burn with passion…Nevertheless, each one should retain the place in life that the Lord assigned to him and to which God has called him…I would like you to be free from concern. An unmarried man is concerned about the Lord's affairs—how he can please the Lord. But a married man is concerned about the affairs of this world—how he can please his wife—and his interests are divided. An unmarried woman or virgin is concerned about the Lord's affairs: Her aim is to be devoted to the Lord in both body and spirit. But a married woman is concerned about the affairs of this world—how she can please her husband. I am saying this for your own good, not to restrict you, but that you may live in a right way in undivided devotion to the Lord" (1 Cor. 7:1-2, 6-9, 17, 32-35).

    h. Sometimes God allows Satan to test us—(see Dt. 8:2; Heb. 12:1-11). The temptation may be the only thing that motivates us to turn our attention and hope toward God. So do not be surprised at lengthy periods of temptation, particularly during periods of spiritual disinterest.

4. Getting Married

    a. There is heavy pressure in churches, among friends, and by one's family to get married. (Don't fall victim to that neo-epicurean group in your church, whose motto is "Eat, drink, and get married!" Many of them go off and become "Moonies," committing mass marriage—a form of mass suicide).

    b. There may be accusing looks from people that will hurt you when you don't meet their timetable or program for courtship and marriage.

    c. Church "Singles" groups often exude an air of desperation.

    d. Don't marry, or even date, to appear straight, or to become straight.

    e. Learn to seek God, to hear Him, and to heed His direction.

    f. Become wed to God first. Then your search for a mate will be properly motivated and balanced.

5. Going Public
   a. You need to find someone with whom you can share your real self. Healing comes in bringing dark areas to the light.

   "Confess your sins to each other and pray for each other so that you may be healed" (James 5:16).

   b. Before saying anything to anyone, it is critical to discern the ability of that person or church to handle the news of your sexual background. Rely on the guidance of the Holy Spirit in these matters.

   c. Only share your background publicly in response to God's clear leading—as an opportunity to glorify Him and to help others.

   d. Always tell a prospective marriage partner. Complete honesty and revelation of who you really are is critical to a healthy marriage. The last thing that you want to see is the look of betrayal on the face of a spouse who has stumbled upon the knowledge of your hidden background.

6. Preventing Sexual Identity Confusion in Your Children
   a. Protect but don't exasperate.
   b. Do sex-identified things with them.
   c. Give nonsexual physical love and affection to them. If you have inner fears of being attracted to them, consult a Christian counselor who has expertise in this field. It is important that you overcome and manage such feelings because your children need that physical touch of affirmation and love without a sexual context.

   "Rules without relationship lead to rebellion."
   —Josh McDowell

   d. Take time daily to interact with them—to reaffirm them in their masculinity or femininity.
   e. Create an atmosphere where your child is free to ask about anything and teach sexual knowledge to them as they express interest and to the depth that they request.
   f. Teach the biblical model and standards for sex.
   g. Teach them the realities of sexual temptation and danger, along with ways to respond to them. Use your

own childhood experiences when appropriate as examples of the consequences of wrong choices and the blessings of godly ones.

h. Carefully check out all children and adults who are given charge over them. Most child sexual abuse is committed by other children under the age of 18.

i. Teach your children that they should not obey authorities who try to engage them in sexual activities, and that they should report those who do, to you, no matter what threats are made against them. Teach them not to tell the perpetrator that they are going to report what he or she has done, in case that may put them in danger, but to tell you anyway as soon as they get the chance.

j. Do not let them go to health spas or to hitchhike.

k. Praise and affirm them.

(From *How To Drug-Proof Your Kids* by Steve Arterburn and Jim Burns, Word Incorporated, Dallas, Tx.)

"All normal human beings respond to praise. In fact, we crave affirmation so much we are likely to do almost anything to receive it. We need to be aware of this with our children. As someone said: 'Whoever gives your kids praise and attention has power over them.'

"If you don't affirm your children, someone else will, and that someone could be a drug dealer *(or child molester—my addition)*. Many people with lifestyles contrary to your own are willing to praise your kids to get what they want from them."

The Healing of Sexual Identity Confusion: Homosexuality/Bisexuality

The two-word answer to the question in the title of this chapter is *spiritual transformation*. And yet, as with any obsessive or addictive behavior, you must want to change before permanent healing can take place. The desire to change will be *imparted* to you as you enter into a continuous, intimate relationship with the loving Father who created you. As you learn from Him, and become intimate with Him, He will supernaturally impart emotional health to you. He will bond with you. He will become the father or the mother you never had. He will deliver you, over time, from the negative mental and emotional consequences of childhood molestation, neglect, or whatever else has been the source of your dysfunctional development.

This is not a quick and easy recipe. It is not a magic pill that you can take for instant healing. It requires the development of a personal relationship with God the Father, made possible through the saving work of His Son, Jesus Christ, who died for you and paid the penalty for the sins of all who would come to Him and receive Him as Lord and Savior.

Like any other relationship, it will take time for you to really get to know and appreciate the Father (who already knows and loves you). As you pursue your relationship with Him, God's Holy Spirit will show you how to let go of your incorrect, negative assumptions about the Father and all the wrong associations that you have made between Him and your earthly father. You will learn how to trust God completely. You will discover how to commune with Him, how to listen to Him and receive His direction for your life. These are all things that will take time—probably years—but every day that you spend in pursuit of Him will be another day of healing. God has *promised* that if you seek Him with all your heart, He will be found by you and will reveal Himself to you (see Jer. 29:13-14).

God will give you the strength you need, when you need it. He will give you *everything* you need, when you need it. But it all revolves around the intimacy that you develop with Him and the diligence and hunger with which you pursue Him.

As you focus on developing that intimacy with Him, God will begin the process of healing those things that caused you to go astray, including your own sinful, self-will. As we learned in chapter three, your will is transformed through direct and repeated experience of God's grace, which writes God's law on your heart, making it your delight and causing you to love Him at deeper and deeper levels.

Even though the full range of healing will be a process, it is possible to be immediately and permanently set free from the ingrained habit of sexually "acting out" with others. It is not uncommon for someone who has been enslaved to homosexuality to be instantly delivered from the *compulsion* to act out their homosexual desires as soon as they trust Jesus as their Lord and Savior and ask God for deliverance with childlike faith.

Once you have received the power of the Holy Spirit—which Jesus will give to anyone who asks (see Luke 11:13), you will then have a force at your disposal that is greater than any power in the universe—indeed, that is far greater than all of the other powers in the universe combined! It is that force—that mighty *river of living water* that surges through the inner being of every believer (see John 4:10,13-14; 7:37-39)—that will deliver you from any power that has compelled you to sin. That is, if you want Him to, He will set you free from those things. Now that you belong to Christ, no other power can force you to do anything, unless you give it ground to do so through disobedience (see John 14:30; 1 John 2:10), a love for sin (see Ps. 52:3; 2 Thess. 2:12; Jas. 4:4; 1 John 2:15), a self-righteous attempt to make yourself holy, or a lack of desire to be free (see Rev. 3:15-16).

Even with the uncontrollable compulsion conquered, you will, however, still retain memories of pleasures past and probably some degree of desire for homosexual relationships. More healing still lies ahead—healing of the brokenness that made you vulnerable to fixing your hope in the creature rather than the Creator (see Rom. 1:25) and that catapulted you into a frenzied search for pleasure to help you escape the painful experiences of your life.

Some temptations give the appearance of being overpowering and unconquerable when they're not. Satan likes to bluff. For example, if sexual memories suddenly assault you with great power, and out of the blue, that is a sign that they are being fed into your mind by demonic powers. In response, you should speak to those powers by telling them to leave you in the name of Jesus Christ, and to go where Jesus sends them. If you know your authority in Christ, believe it, and really want them to leave, they will have to obey.

On the other hand, some temptations will originate from within your own heart (see Mark 7:21-23) as a result of your own careless or rebellious choices. For these, you will be able to see a trail of poor decisions leading up to the temptation. The response to these kinds of temptations should be one of humble repentance.

It is imperative to keep in mind that it is God's power working in and through you that will be the overcoming force in your life (see Phil. 2:13). Therefore, your attention must be primarily focused on Jesus Christ so that you are in a position to receive the continual impartation of His life. It is His life, His righteousness, and His power that you need—not your own efforts at achieving righteousness. Your own self-empowered efforts to become righteous are an abomination to God. They will all be burned up at the judgment seat of Christ, when nothing will survive that He hasn't built into you by His design and with His hand (see 1 Cor. 3:10-15). When you have learned to come before His throne of grace daily to receive His power, direction and healing, marvelous things will begin to happen.

God wants you to be so intimate with Him that you literally take on the mind and the behavior of Christ (see Rom. 13:14; 1 Cor. 2:16; Gal. 3:27.) He promises that if you walk by the Holy Spirit, you will not carry out the desires of your flesh (see Gal. 5:16). It is clear that it is in the shelter of our personal relationship with God that we will see victory over the sins and enticements of our past.

This is what I call the "mystery of holiness," that in intimacy and communion with the Father, we receive into ourselves His will, His purity of thought and desire, the fullness of boundless love, the ability to trust, the wisdom to act rightly, and the completion of our personhood—our healing.

The Sin Aspect

For those of you who have believed that God made you gay, who have identified with that label and justified that lifestyle, it may take a while to come to the place of admitting the length and breadth of your sin guilt. However, it is imperative that sooner or later (the sooner the better), you confess your sins and truly repent of your sinful behavior—at every level. There will be no permanent healing of any kind, including salvation, without genuine repentance. This turning from sin must include not only the overt sinful acts that have been committed over the years, but also the various "sins of response" that you have committed toward the people who were involved in the emergence of your broken sexual identity. God will help you forgive those who have hurt you (see Matt. 6:14-15) and empower you to do so. I will talk about this at length in chapter eight.

Until now, your body (or someone else's) has been your God, your emotions have been your king, and your feelings have been your slave master. Now, they must stand on the unchangeable truth as revealed by God in His Word, even if every feeling, every emotion and every physical evidence appears contrary. In fact, at some point in your life, God will go out of His way to make certain that every feeling, emotion and evidence appears contrary to the truth, so that you learn to trust Him no matter what (see Deut. 8:2-3).

In the healing process, you must learn to turn to God for His power to defeat idolatry (see Rom. 1:18-27) and rebellion (see 1 Sam. 15:23), and agree with God that sexual behavior outside of monogamous, heterosexual marriage is wrong. The sexual inclination toward members of one's own sex is not the sin. It is the embracing and acting out of those diseased inclinations that is wrong.

Self-pity is another obsession common to the homosexual that must be renounced. Self-pity and narcissism are deadly to honesty. Self-pity is the fruit of what Leanne Payne calls the "disease of introspection" whereby an obsession with self causes you to examine your interior thoughts and motivations continually ("Why did I do that?" "Why did I think that?") and crucify yourself with the evidence. This can have the appearance of contrition or repentance, but is in fact an obsession with self and a refusal to accept the power, grace and freedom that God has offered.

You must sit before God and allow Him to bring conviction to the various sins, both hidden and overt, that you have been committing. He will bring them to light, one by one, as you are able to recognize and renounce their evil. He will bring conviction as you read His Word, as you go for prayer at church, home group or conference altar calls, as you listen to sermons or counsel from fellow believers, even as you sing love songs to Him alone. He will do so little by little, so that you do not despair of the enormity of the task (see Exod. 23:29-30; Deut. 7:22-23.)

Some of your sins have been actions and behaviors, others have been wrong beliefs. Some have been mental fantasies, and still others have been interior attitudes, affections and decisions. Some sins have been personal and willful, others have been the outworkings of original sin and inherited family-line curses. All sin has involved a misdirected heart and its fallen loves. It is a complicated matrix that only God can unravel.

As long as we doggedly pursue a love relationship with Him, He will expose the hidden things of darkness and empower new, godly choices. As we gaze upon the glory of the Lord, we will be transformed into His likeness (see 2 Cor. 3:18).

Recognize and acknowledge, *daily,* your absolute need for God's power to transform your heart. Even more, recognize and acknowledge God's pronounced desire and willingness to forgive and to heal you—based on the grace won for you by Jesus' sacrifice on the Cross.

Take the steps of faith necessary to replace the incorrect associations that you have made between the personality and actions of your earthly father and the character and love of your heavenly Father. Toward that end, practice the presence of God the Father throughout each and every day and receive into your spirit the awareness of the inescapable reality of His *unconditional* love for you.

Always be careful to recognize the immediacy of His forgiveness, at any time, for any reason, for as many times as you sin, no matter what the sin.

And since you must *want* to change before permanent healing can occur, ask the Lord to increase your *will* to change.

Give place for God to work righteous anger in you. Get angry over the destruction Satan has wrought in your life through your sinful behavior and those things that continue to tempt you. Satan is trying to kill you and everyone you love. He's trying to destroy the purpose of your life. He's trying to rob you of a deep and intimate relationship with your Creator and the joy and fulfillment of life that that brings. Rehearsing those facts at the point of temptation will help to keep you from repeating those same sins again.

Renewing Your Mind

Your mind is like a computer in many ways. It responds according to the information and emotional patterns that have been programmed into it. For example, if you put a five-year-old in front of a television set and let him watch commercials for ten hours a day, what songs do you think he will be singing, and what items do you think he will want at the store? When Dr. Pavlov rang a bell before feeding his dogs, it didn't take long before the dogs would salivate at the mere sound of the bell—not at the sight of the food.

If you've been feeding your mind with homosexual pornography, using it for masturbation, engaging in homosexual activity, and repeating other behaviors that reinforce a homosexual predilection, how long do you think it will take for your mind and body to stop responding homosexually? All things being equal, it should take about as long as the time you have spent developing and reinforcing the first condition in order to bring you back to ground zero so that you can begin to learn new behavioral responses.

Unfortunately, all things are not equal in this equation. The most significant inequity is that the development and reinforcement of your homosexual behavior probably took place during your formative and young adult years—years that have an inordinately powerful effect on the behavioral course of your entire life.

I do not want to paint a Pollyannish picture of your transformation from homosexual orientation to heterosexual. It will be rough. It will humiliate your spirit. It will humble your soul and deprive your body of things that it craves. At times, it will seem utterly impossible! Indeed, without a full-fledged partnership with Christ, you will be able to do *nothing* that will last (see John 15:5).

You see, up until now, your body has been your god. Your emotions have been your king. Your feelings have been your slave master. And through your sin, Satan has brought his power to bear for your destruction. But now you have one Master. His name is Jesus Christ. And He will have no other gods before Him (see Exod. 20:3)—not Satan, not your mind, not your will, not your emotions, not your feelings and not your programmed behaviors.

So pick up your cross and die to self and Christ will raise you to a life of unimaginable passion and glory. He's offering you beauty for ashes. He's offering you His hand in marriage. And although there will be trials in this life, they cannot compare with the glory that is to be revealed for those who love Him (see Rom. 8:18; 2 Cor. 4:17).

The length of your transformation process generally depends on a number of key factors, any one of which God may give grace to overcome earlier than one would expect in the natural course of things:

- the age at which you began feeding your homosexual inclination,
- how long you've been engaged in homosexual activity,
- the number of issues that have contributed to your homosexual confusion,
- the number of times you have committed homosexual acts,
- how deeply you were involved in it (the variety and depth of activity),
- the intensity of your desire to change,
- the degree of faith with which you hold on to God's promises,
- the depth of your love and commitment to Jesus,
- the degree of your willingness to be faithful to God's will and direction,
- the degree to which you can keep the perspective that it is God working in you to bring permanent transformation,
- the amount of time you spend seeking God in prayer and crying out to Him for help.

You can see from this list how imperative an intimate relationship with God is for anyone who is trying to be healed and to live a righteous life. That's why I earlier referred to it as the "prime directive" of life. God rewards those who diligently seek Him (see Heb. 11:6), and He is capable, despite the many years of homosexual programming that may be behind you, of transforming your affections and reviving your true heterosexual identity.

The good news is that all power and authority in heaven and on earth has been given to the One who wants to change you (see Matt. 28:18); that His purpose in coming to earth was to destroy the work of the enemy (see 1 John 3:8); that He has given *all* who follow Him authority to overcome *all* the power of the enemy (see Luke 10:19); and that even those things that seem impossible to you are possible with God (see Luke 18:27).

Just keep in mind that God is focused on the intention of your heart—how much your desire to pursue holiness is *a response of love* for Him. We tend to look at our progress with performance-oriented, perfectionist eyes, and imagine that God is terribly disappointed when we don't change as quickly as we think we ought. In truth, there are some who will leave the homosexual lifestyle too late in life to realize a significant turnaround in their orientation. The number of their remaining days on this earth is simply not enough to cover all the ground (see Ps. 139:16). However, as they pursue that goal anyway, God is as pleased with them as He is with those who see a complete reversal of orientation. He's not looking for those who achieve perfection. That is impossible. He is looking for those who continuously and genuinely *aim* for perfection (see 2 Cor. 13:11) and press toward the mark of the high calling in Christ Jesus (see Phil. 3:12-14). He's looking for people who will believe that He is able to renew their minds (see Eph. 4:23; Rom. 12:1-2; 13:14; 1 Cor. 2:16; Gal. 3:27; Phil. 4:8; Col. 3:2; 1 Pet. 1:13-15).

As you "clothe" yourself with Christ *by faith,* that is, by being sure of what you hope for and certain of what you do not see (see Heb. 11:1), you will realize more fully that you have been mystically joined to Him as His Bride, the Church, and you will express adoration for your Bridegroom in regular worship. As you worship Jesus Christ in this way, you receive into your mortal body the continual impartation of His life (see 2 Cor. 4:10-11; Col. 3:1-3) and you are transformed into His likeness (see Rom. 8:29; 1 Cor. 15:49; 2 Cor. 3:18). The Lord is our life (see Deut. 30:20).

You will also take on His life by regularly "feeding" on the Word of God (see Heb. 5:12-14; Matt. 4:4; Deut. 8:3; Job 23:12; Ps. 119:103; Jer. 15:16). As you practice the presence of Christ—the Word made flesh (see John 1:1,14) and feed on His living Word, the Scriptures (see Heb. 4:12), you receive your daily portion of his life-giving presence (see John 6:32-35).

You also become more united with Christ by spending time with other believers, finding reinforcement from their ministry, exhortations and encouragements.

Eventually, having "clothed yourself with Christ," you experience the cleansing effect of serving others. There is no better way to forget yourself and to bring down the blessings of God than that.

Guarding Your Heart and Mind

Since it is God's power working in and through you (see Phil. 2:13) that overcomes the enemy, one new habit that you *must* acquire is the habit of turning to Jesus for His power. This goes against the self-sufficient, independent spirit of our culture, and so must be deliberately rehearsed. You must *practice* your weakness (see 2 Cor. 12:9-10; 13:4) in concert with believing in God's power to keep you from falling (see Jude 24; Ps. 37:23), and add to that obedience to whatever the Lord might tell you in the moment of temptation.

One of the promises that God gives believers in the Bible is that "the peace of God, which surpasses all comprehension, will guard your hearts and your minds in Christ Jesus" (Phil. 4:7, NASB). The peace of God that you receive during your times of intimate daily communion with Him provides protection for your heart and mind. Something wonderful occurs in the midst of intimacy with God—a changing of perspective from earthly to heavenly, from temporal to eternal (see Rom. 8:5b). You will begin to see fleshly sin and temptation as the ridiculous fraud that it is. In your wonder and awe at the things that the Father begins to show you in prayer, the stark evil of this world system is unveiled and the strong pull of temptation wanes. God imparts wisdom and perspective, and in the midst of this truth, you are set free from bondage to sinful habits and patterns. You begin to see with the eyes of the heart (see Eph. 1:18-21) and gain new perspective on the matter of self-control.

You will repeatedly be faced with the choice between loving Jesus or some sinful challenger. Your decisions will make evident who or what you love more, despite your claims and protestations to the contrary (see Luke 6:46-49; John 14:15,21,23.) What you should want, of course, is a growing consistency in choosing the Lord and His kingdom.

Time and again, God has shown me areas in my life where I have fooled myself into thinking that I wanted deliverance, when in fact I really didn't want it at all. I had merely been spouting words that I knew God wanted me to say—with no true desire for deliverance. I enjoyed the sin too much. I loved the pleasure and temporary comfort that it brought me. Only when I prayed for God to truly give me the desire to be freed from my love for the sin, did I begin to see deliverance.

It is primarily at the point of "will" and "desire" that God expects you to participate in your healing and deliverance and that is where you face your greatest problem. As a fallen human being, you have neither the will nor the desire to obey God. Neither do you possess the power. The only way to obtain the will, the desire, and the power is by way of the "prime directive," by entering into a close relationship with God. Then you will begin to love what He loves, desire what He desires and will what He wills. In that union, you can also become a conduit of His power over sin (see Jas. 4:7; 1 Pet. 5:9).

Some of you may be saying to yourselves: What if I don't even have the desire or will to enter into this intimate relationship with God? The answer is simple. Simply ask Him to give you that missing will and desire. As long as you are honest with Him, God will always meet you where you are and take you where you need to be. He is a gracious and wonderful Father. So ask and keep asking, for He is rewards those who *earnestly* seek Him (see Heb. 11:6).

One problem that many of us have is that we ask without faith. Our faith is more of a wish, an empty, "I'll believe it when I see it" hope. It is not biblical faith or biblical hope. Let's look at a series of promises from God's

Word to see just what He has promised about answering our prayers. I have italicized the particular conditions found within each promise.

> "But *seek first His kingdom and His righteousness,* and all these things [referring to the basic needs of life] will be given to you as well." (Mt. 6:33)

> *"Ask and it will be given to you. . . .* Everyone who asks receives. . . . How much more will your Father in heaven give *good gifts* to those who ask Him!" (Mt. 7:7a,8a,11c)

> "My God *will supply all your needs* according to His riches in glory in Christ Jesus." (Phil. 4:19, NASB)

> "This is the confidence we have in approaching God: that if we ask anything *according to His will,* He hears us." (1 John 5:14)

> "But when he asks he must *believe and not doubt."* (Jas 1:6a)

> "Whatever you ask for in prayer, *believe that you have received it,* and it will be yours." (Mark 11:24)

> "If you *abide in Me and My words abide in you,* ask whatever you wish, and it will be done for you. *My Father is glorified by this,* that you bear much fruit, and so prove to be My disciples." (John 15:7-8, NASB)

> "You do not have because *you do not ask God.* When you ask, you do not receive, because you *ask with wrong motives."* (Jas. 4:2d-3b)

> "I will do whatever you ask *in My name,* so that the Son may *bring glory to the Father.* You may ask Me for anything in My name, and I will do it." (John 14:13-14)

Since you must embrace the whole counsel of Scripture, and since Scripture interprets itself, you can understand God's promise to answer prayer only in light of the combination of these passages. Seen together, they tell us this: If you are in an abiding (lasting and intimate) relationship with Him and ask in His name (according to His character), in faith, with godly motives, and according to His will, He will supply all of your needs, as well as certain unnamed "good gifts." But you must ask with real faith— a knowing that is so certain that you are already assuming, even as you ask, that your prayer is being answered in the affirmative. That means He has already spoken to you, (either through your intimate communion with Him or through His Word). And finally, the ultimate purpose for answered prayer is to bring glory to the Father. (There goes my Rolls Royce, I suppose!)

These promises can give you a great deal of assurance when you pray for salvation, healing and transformation into His likeness because God has already made it clear that it is His will that you come to Him to be healed and set free from the things of this world and the entanglements of the kingdom of darkness. All you have to do is pay attention to the other conditions (intimacy, faith, God's glory).

You can go higher than your feelings of powerlessness and abandonment and believe God's Word instead by a deliberate act of the will. You can practice believing that God is with you, even when He seems to have abandoned you. Why? Because He promised that He would *never* leave or forsake you (see Heb. 13:5; Matt. 28:20) and because "the angel of the Lord encamps around those who fear him, and he delivers them" (Ps. 34:7).

As you carefully guard your heart and mind by policing what you see, hear and do, God will point out many of the dangers that you may not have recognized (see 2 Cor. 5:17; Eph. 4:24; Col. 3:10; Rev. 2:17).

In his book, *Passion for Jesus,* Mike Bickle explains what keeps us in pursuit of the "good gifts" of the kingdom:

> "When Jesus is revealed, a hunger for purity and righteousness is released. ... Hunger for purity is one response of a believer who sees the Lord in His glory. ... The greatest motivation for obedience to the Lord is a growing revelation of who Jesus is—His passions and pleasures and the matchless splendor in His personality" (pp. 138-39).

Healing Your Emotions

It may seem to you that your life has been a litany of traumas, trials and losses. That's certainly how I felt during the first twenty-nine years of my life. But now that you've decided to forsake the things of this world and follow hard after God, there's hope. As you fully enter into covenant with Him, God wants to heal the damage and replace what you've lost.

If you missed out on bonding with your mom or dad and you are a teenager or older, it is developmentally too late for a human being to do that for you now. However, the One who created everything out of nothing *can* still do that for you! God the Father (who incorporates all the attributes of both mother and father) wants to "bond" with you. He'll do it directly during your moments of communion with Him. Ask Him specifically to do this and pursue Him earnestly. Over a period of months or perhaps years, you will see a miraculous healing in this area.

God will also use other healthy people to invisibly impart this deep bond from His heart to yours. He may do this in the context of men's or woman's groups, or even home fellowship meetings. You will find that in receiving prayers, hugs and affirmations from other believers during such activities, God will bring healing to your soul and your spirit. He will plant key people in your life who will represent in the flesh what He is doing in the Spirit. Recall the story that I related in chapter two about the man God used to hug me and impart the affection of the Father to me.

If you missed having a good father during your childhood, remember that you have an extraordinarily good Father in heaven, who loves you, and who would never do to you what your earthly father did. As we learned in chapter two, God the Father is a *perfect* Father. He is incapable of sin (see Deut. 32:4; Ps. 18:30; Heb. 4:15; 1 Pet. 2:22). He is love itself (see 1 John 4:16). When you read of Jesus, you read also of the Father (see John 10:30; 14:9; Col. 1:15; 2:9; Heb. 1:3). He is the Father that you always wanted.

As you draw closer to the Father, His power will fill you and heal you, and you will become more and more like Him. You will take on His attributes: "God did not give us a spirit of timidity, but a spirit of power, of love and of self-discipline" (see 2 Tim. 1:7).

He will teach you to trust again (see Ps. 32:10), and He will bring you successfully to the ultimate expression of trust—relinquishing the control of your life to Him (see Prov. 29:25 and Isa. 26:3).

He will make up to you for the years that the locusts have eaten (see Joel 2:25) by purifying you (see 1 Cor. 6:11) and returning your innocence to you. He declares:

I will sprinkle clean water on you, and you will be clean; I will cleanse you from all your impurities and from all your idols. I will give you a new heart and put a new spirit in you; I will remove from you your heart of stone and give you a heart of flesh. And I will put My Spirit in you and move you to follow My decrees and be careful to keep My laws.
(Ezek. 36:25-27)

His love will help root out fear from your life and replace it with faith (see 1 John 4:16-18; 2 Tim. 1:7). And if there is anger behind the fear, as there often is, He will bring it to light so that you can repent of it and be set free.

The Lord God, who sees the heart (see 1 Sam. 16:7b; Jer. 17:10; Rom. 8:27) and knows the root cause of your every emotional wound, will heal you precisely at the point of injury. He will not merely patch up old wounds, He will heal them at their point of origin. He will grow you up seamlessly, leaving only a remnant of damage to serve as a reminder of what He rescued you from and as a catalyst for further refining.

If sexual abuse was a source of your homosexual confusion, God will come to you in your times of deep intimacy with Him and heal the effects of those events. God will transfer His wholeness into you. He will not simply patch up the old person—He will make a new creation.

Emotional Dependency

Many people (no matter what their sexual orientation) have a problem with being emotionally dependent on others. Their personality and self-image is so weak or damaged, that they "bend" toward others emotionally in order to absorb a personality or identity, direction in life, or even a sense of justification for their existence. These unhealthy relationships are typified by extreme dependence and jealousy.

A dependent person will seek out someone who possesses the traits they feel they lack, and attempt to create a "best friend" or "lover" relationship. Often, the people they find are those who have an emotional dysfunction of their own, a subconscious need to be idolized. These people may appear to be successful and attractive, but they possess deep inner self-doubts. The attention and worship of their dependent friend helps medicate the pain of their own insecurities.

Sometimes an emotionally dependent person attach to a healthy person through flattery, gifts, offers of help and prayer, etc. The healthy person naturally responds to these kindnesses with time and attention, but may soon discover that this new friend has emotional needs that are too deep to meet. If the healthy party lacks experience in dealing with emotionally dependent individuals, what starts out as a seeming healthy new friendship can turn into a frightening episode.

In the homosexual community, emotional dependency runs rampant; it must almost always be dealt with in the healing process. Let's examine part of Lori Rentzel's brilliant booklet on the subject, as she answers the question: "why are dependencies hard to break?"

> "First, as painful as dependency is, it does give us some gratification. There is emotional security . . . a sense that we have at least one relationship we can count on. . . . We also enjoy feeling needed. A relationship like this might add excitement and romance when life seems dull otherwise. In fact, the stressful ups and downs of dependencies can become addictive in themselves. Additionally, the focus on maintaining this relationship can provide an escape from confronting personal problems and responsibilities. Finally, many people simply do not know any other way of relating. They are afraid to give up the "known" for the 'unknown.'
>
> [Second,] we can't see [dependent relationships] as sinful. The culture we live in has taken the truth 'God is love' and turned it around to mean 'Love is god.' Romantic or emotional love is viewed as a law unto itself . . . [and] dependent relationships seem beautiful, even noble, especially if there is no overt sexual involvement. . . . Also, we may not be able to see how dependent relation-

ships separate us from God . . . the euphoric feeling masquerades as closeness to God.

Third, root problems are not dealt with.

Fourth, those who willingly enter dependent relationships become candidates for spiritual deception. When we ignore the Holy Spirit's correction, we make ourselves vulnerable to satanic oppression.

Fifth, we don't want to give up the relationship."

Lori describes several guidelines and suggestions for what the process of healing for emotional dependency might look like:

"The path out of dependency involves . . . turning away from relationships which are based on serving our own needs . . . and learning new ways of relating as "new creatures in Christ" (2 Cor. 5:17).

Begin by making a commitment to honesty . . . admitting we are involved in a dependent relationship and acknowledging the sinful aspects of that relationship.

The next challenge is being honest with another person . . . confess to them.

Begin gradually separating yourself from your partner.

We must also allow God to work. . . . If we confess to God that we are hopelessly attached to this individual and powerless to do anything about it and invite God to come in and change the situation, the Lord will not overlook our prayers.

Prepare for grief and depression. . . . If we allow ourselves to hurt for a season, our healing will come faster.

Cultivate other friendships. Discover God's vision for relationships. If we love others as God loves them, we will desire to see them conformed to the image of Christ.

Begin resolving the deeper issues . . . bring the whole thing before God in prayer . . . seek out the counsel and prayer of those God has placed in authority over us.

Prepare for the long haul. . . . We need to know ourselves . . . [and] our adversary . . . to be willing to believe God loves us, even if we cannot feel His love . . . to learn God's character through His Word . . . to stop blaming Him. . . . A close relationship with Jesus Christ is our best safeguard against emotional dependency." (from *Emotional Dependency*, © 1990 by Lori Rentzel. Published by InterVarsity Press, Downers Grove, Ill. Used with permission.)

Practical Points on the Road to Recovery

When you have begun to develop an intimate relationship with God, He will begin to speak to you through inner impressions and even sometimes through a still small voice that seems to go directly into your mind and heart without benefit of the ears. He'll cause certain biblical passages to jump to life with direction and purpose for your situation, as if He had written them just for you that day. He'll cause you to hear the same message or point over and over again in a short period of time, or to have several people come up to you and say the same thing about something that has recently been on your heart and in your prayers. You will begin to get the impression that what you are praying for is what God Himself has put into your mind to ask.

In these and many other ways, God will begin to give you direction. Some of that direction will involve steps that He wants you to take in order to compliment the healing that He is bringing about within you.

As He reveals these steps to you, use them to starve the old nature to death! As God shows them to you, avoid the people, places and things that serve as "feeding troughs" for your sin nature. "If by the Spirit you put to death the misdeeds of the body, you will live" (Rom. 8:13).

When you find yourself being sexually tempted, stop and ask God what it was that caused it. Then ask Him how you can avoid it the next time. Then ask Him to give you supernatural power against it, and speak to it as if it were a spirit and bind its power by the blood of Jesus Christ.

If pornography has been part of your problem, God will instruct you to throw all of it in the trash and not buy any more. He will steer you away from certain bookstores with adult sections or even certain aisles of regular bookstores, where the "art books" or the calendars are displayed. He will show you how to guard your heart and mind from the salacious materials found in various apps and on the Internet. He may even tell you to avoid driving down the streets where porn stores or other "triggers" are located—at least until your new man has been made strong enough to resist such enticements. Familiar spirits linger there—demonic powers who know you and how to push your buttons.

God may tell you not to buy certain "socially acceptable" magazines, like *GQ* or *Surfer*, or *Vogue*. He may tell you not to go through certain mail order catalogs any more, knowing that you spend most of your time gazing at the good-looking men or women rather than the clothes. He may tell you not to rent or view certain movies or those with specific ratings, or even watch certain television shows (the ones that feature actors who feed your idolatry).

The Lord will tell you not to drive in the neighborhoods where you used to pick up sexual partners or frequent places where you used to go to stare at the "beautiful people," such as certain beaches or clubs.

He may tell you to forget about the gym or health spa. It does little good to surround yourself with naked men or women when you are trying to receive healing from a sexualized attraction to them. Part of your problem may have been a narcissistic love of your own body, as you observed it reflected in the many mirrored walls of the gym. The last thing you need is to continue staring at yourself like that, or to go where other body-conscious people congregate.

God may tell you to stop picking up hitchhikers. After all, wasn't it just a search for another anonymous sexual encounter that caused you to pick them up in the first place? Oh, I know that you have convinced yourself that you are now only concerned for their safety—so when you pass them by, make sure that you ask God to protect them from harm and to provide them with a safe ride to their destination.

This is a hard one: God may tell you to give up certain friends—people who He knows will only pull you back into bondage or in some way impede your healing. You *must* trust that God knows exactly what He is doing. Take a tip from me: Always do what God asks you to do. He never asks you to do something that isn't for your good.

Surprisingly, He may ask you to stop hugging certain people, until He has built into you the ability to hug in a non-sexual way.

And this is the most difficult one of all: God will eventually point out to you your tendency to stare into the eyes of those who you suspect are sexually ambivalent or gay. You know the look—the one that asks the person if they are vulnerable to being seduced by you—the one that builds your ego by eliciting a blush—the one that used to assure you that you were all right because there were others out there who were looking for identity in the arms of another man (or woman), too.

The list of ways and places that serve to bring subtle and overt temptation is endless. If it's not going into public restrooms, then it's reading the graffiti on the restroom walls. Or maybe it's in watching certain professional sports matches, where you may have developed a habit of feeding on the sight of various athletes. Who knows? God knows. Listen to Him!

When all sexual activity outside of the marriage bed has been cast off, the unmarried man may find that the adolescent phenomenon of "wet dreams" returns. This is almost always accompanied by dreams in which immorality takes place. The presence of the immoral dream indicates that there still exists deep in his heart a "stronghold of sexual immorality" that demons can still access. If this happens to you, declare your desire to be freed from all love of immorality and command that the demonic stronghold be broken in the name of Jesus. Practice hating evil and clinging to what is good (Rom. 12:9).

In a methodical but gentle progression, the Spirit of the Lord will bring all these things and more to light, as He attacks and destroys each stronghold left in you by the enemy. He will do it at the rate you can handle.

The greatest danger you face is your tendency to forge ahead of God to conquer these things by yourself. That is a big mistake, and you will eventually fall flat on your face if you try it. Trust me. Save yourself a lot of time, effort and grief. Wait on the Lord to tell you when and how to deal with the more subtle components of your situation. "Unless the Lord builds the house, they labor in vain who build it" (Ps. 127:1, NASB).

God's part is to bring the revelation and to supply the power and the authority—ours is to take up those tools and use them to put to death the old nature. We must "set our heart and mind" against the old sin-bred patterns of thinking, feeling and doing, and toward a love of purity.

Always keep in mind that purity is more powerful than lust or evil, just as God is infinitely more powerful than Satan. If you have been losing this battle, you can be sure that you have simply not decided that you want or value purity enough to "take it by force" and live in its power. That is the tragedy of so many believers' lives.

Dealing With Loneliness

When you forsake a sinful lifestyle, one of the first things that will happen is that your friends (or former partners in crime) will desert you. They may not do it right away. They may wait politely for a while to see if you are really serious, but the day will come when you will realize that you are no longer included in the inner circle. There may even come a day when your so-called friends will present you with an ultimatum—either return to being like them or get out.

You see, they can no longer feel comfortable around you. An invisible, though quite real, barrier has been erected between you and them—a spiritual one. When you become born again, the Holy Spirit comes to dwell inside of you and you are a new creation (see 2 Cor. 5:17; 1 Cor. 6:9-11; John 14:16-17). You are now born of your Father in heaven (see 1 John 4:4-6), whereas your friends are still sons of their father, the devil (see John 8:42-47). You are no longer of this world (see John 15:19; 17:14,16). Your citizenship and allegiance is now in heaven (see Heb. 12:22-23; Eph. 2:19-22). You have become a stranger to this world, no longer loving the things of the world (see 1 John 2:15-17). This is highly convicting, and therefore uncomfortable, to nonbelievers. It reveals that an unseen spiritual battle is going on between the Spirit in you and the spirits who heavily influence your friends.

Consequently, you will have to deal with loneliness. This is one of the reasons the Bible tells believers not to forsake the assembling of themselves together (see Heb. 10:24), where they can encourage one another. We need to be involved in Christian groups for social reasons as well as for growth and self-protection.

One of the greatest dangers in loneliness is self-pity. One sure solution is prayer, spending time with your Father. Another antidote for self-pity is serving others. In serving, you will find an unending supply of friends and you won't have as much time to think self-pitying thoughts.

As a believer on the road to sexual health, you will have stopped spending your nights in the arms of other people. Your body will still crave the physical affection and sexual release that you used to have. This is where the development of intimacy with God becomes so very important. He can supply all your needs (see Phil. 4:19), even physical ones. It sounds crazy, but it's true!

Ultimately, your loneliness will go away because you will continuously have the sense of His presence. You may be alone, but you will not be lonely. The only exception to this rule is the sense of incompleteness that will linger if you are not yet married and called to be so, as are most people.

Living With Celibacy

I don't want to minimize for a second the very real physical needs of someone suddenly thrust into a life of celibacy, whether temporary or permanent. It can be agonizing at times. For long hours, your body seems to scream for sexual release and physical affection.

Sometimes it's not so much the sexual release as it is the need to be held and stroked and affectionately reassured that you are loved by someone.

We live in a world where the pursuit of feeling and sensation is taught and reinforced every minute of every day—by our friends, our work mates, our radios, our TVs, our books, our movies and the Internet. To live without sex is to be abnormal, or weird. People suspect that you simply must have some secret perversion that you pursue on the sly, and their accusing silence pushes you toward compromise and rebellion against God. So much worldly pressure to satiate the senses makes it extremely difficult to maintain an eternal perspective about pleasure and sensation. We have to choose between the obvious benefits of the pleasures that we can see and those promises of a God we cannot see. We have to believe God, on the evidence of Christ's death on the Cross for us, that He truly does have our highest good in mind in asking us to follow Him, even when He takes us through the deep waters of self-sacrifice and self-denial.

Jesus Christ (who is our advocate before the throne of God) also lived a celibate life. He fully understands the physical needs that we have. Hebrews 2:17-18 tells us that Jesus was made like us in every way so that He could become a merciful high priest for us, and that He suffered when He was tempted and consequently is able to come to the aid of those who are also being tempted. Hebrews 4:15 carries this message, "We do not have a high priest who is unable to sympathize with our weaknesses, but we have one who has been tempted in every way, just as we are—yet without sin. Let us then approach the throne of grace with confidence, so that we may receive mercy and find grace to help us in our time of need."

Jesus referred to men who make themselves eunuchs for the sake of the kingdom of heaven (see Matt. 19:12). By this we see that God can neutralize the sexual needs that you have. Men "make themselves eunuchs" by fervent prayer for God to de-eroticize their body chemistry. They want to remain unmarried without constantly burning with lust, so that they can be servants in the court of the King—preparing the bride (His Church) for the King's pleasure without any thought of pleasure for themselves. God promises a wonderful reward for those who respond to this calling to give themselves fully to His service (see Isa. 56:3-5).

Among the benefits of being single, the apostle Paul said it gave a person more time and more singleness of devotion to the Lord (see 1 Cor. 7:32-35). He encouraged it for those who did not burn with lust as a result (see 1 Cor. 7:1,8-9,27; cf. Rev. 14:4).

The call to permanent celibacy for the purpose of a life of more concentrated devotion to the Lord is a solemn and holy one that should not be taken lightly (see 2 Tim. 1:9). We are all partakers of a heavenly calling (see Heb. 3:1) to live in Christ and to do His will (see Eph. 4:1-6; Phil. 3:14). But there are specific calls to ministry for each individual. So ask Him if He has called you to such a life (see Eph. 1:18). Don't presume upon the Lord's wisdom by taking on a calling that is not intended for you. You will know that He has called you to be a eunuch in His court, at least for a season, when He responds to your repeated prayers to be relieved of your sexual urges.

If God is calling you to permanent celibacy, He will perform a miracle in your body to alleviate the hormonal torment of unrequited sexual desire. He will supernaturally complete you emotionally and spiritually in the way that the unity of a man and a woman in holy matrimony is designed to complete the image of God in the vast majority of people. God will be your spouse. He will cause you to desire, honor and value the call, not out of an unhealed fear of sexual intimacy, but from a place of deep spiritual commitment. He will give you visions or other confirming signs. In various ways, He will make it clear to you, provided you are fervently seeking His will for your life. Those who have an inordinate fear of being called to permanent celibacy are not so called.

For those of you who are single and not called to a life of permanent celibacy, there is good news as well. God can and does release people from overwhelming sexual urges for a limited period of time. There may be a marriage that He has planned for you sometime in the future, and He may, if you ask Him, decrease your sexual urges only for that period of time before the marriage. When the time comes to marry, He will return them to you. That is something worth asking for in this age of perpetual sexual temptation.

You may find that you ask for help in this area and it never seems to come. Beware of the all-too-common trap of praying for deliverance from sexual temptations on the one hand while secretly feeding them on the other. Make sure you ask for sincerity, too, because we are forever asking God for things that, subconsciously, we really don't want.

Be aware also that God may have reasons for temporarily leaving you in a situation where you are being tempted or tested (see Deut. 8:2; Heb. 12:1-11; Rom. 5:1-5; Jas. 1:2-4; 1 Pet. 4:1-2.) Remember that the Holy Spirit *led* Christ into the wilderness so that He would be tempted (see Matt. 4:1). Perhaps that is why Jesus told us to ask the Father not to lead us into temptation (see Matt. 6:13).

It may be that this area of sexual temptation is the only one that so plagues you that you actually turn to God for help. Do you think that the Lord is going to so quickly eliminate the only thing that causes you to come to Him?

God's primary objective is to develop an intimate relationship with you wherein He can impart spiritual life and gifts to you. In order for that to happen, you must regularly seek Him, just like you would any lover. Learn to seek after God regularly and fervently, even when you don't need something from Him. Seek Him just because you love Him and value His companionship. He can answer your prayer about the sexual area, because in providing relief for your need, He won't be cutting off your desire to come to Him.

Masturbation is, of course, a problem with many people who are single, and some who are married. I deal with that subject fully in an upcoming chapter.

Getting Married

Those who come out of a homosexual or bisexual environment usually don't make their background public to the people in the church—and for many very good reasons (see "Going Public" below). Consequently, no one around them really understands the unique struggles that they may be going through pertaining to dating and getting married and they are held to the same expectations as everyone else.

In most churches that means being barraged by well-intentioned couples with requests for relationship status reports. The not-too-subtle will simply keep asking, "So, when are you going to get married?" Others make a point of suggesting likely candidates on a weekly basis. And when you repeatedly ignore or refuse their suggestions, eventually you will see "the look" that accuses, "What's the matter with you?" The final and most humiliating stage is when they start guarding their kids, as if the only possible explanation for your lack of dating must be that you are some kind of closet pervert.

This kind of pressure often causes former homosexuals to begin dating before they are psychologically and emotionally ready. In an effort to avoid being branded a psycho-social misfit, they may try to forge ahead into relationships too soon, before learning the proper social skills or having been healed of an underlying emotional problem.

Many of our churches demonstrate a high degree of prejudice against unmarrieds. Singles are left out of many functions and made to feel like third wheels. This puts a great deal of pressure on everyone, but particularly on those who are secretly dealing with a background of sexual identity confusion. Singles' groups often exude an atmosphere of desperation. Every time you walk into one, you feel as though you are being evaluated and rejected by half of the people in the room. Grim and misleading statistics about the unlikelihood of women in their thirties ever getting married only add fuel to the fire.

Whatever you do, don't allow such pressure to cause you to do something you're not ready to do. To date (and worse, to marry) before you have received proper healing from the Lord can be a disastrous thing to do. Let God tell you when to do it. Getting married will not make you heterosexual. And allaying the church's fears about your background is not a reason to engage in any relationship.

If you are to marry, God has someone for you, and He will bring the two of you together at just the right time. He knows when you are healed and ready to enter a healthy heterosexual relationship. You must learn to trust Him and to hear His voice.

You may find this hard to believe right now, but God can take even the most hardened former homosexual and turn him or her into the most competent and loving spouse and parent that ever lived. After all, He created you! But marry God first, so that you will not go looking to someone else for those things that only God can give.

Going Public

Do you tell your new family of Christian friends about your homosexual past? The answer is both yes and no. Yes, you must tell someone in your spiritual family. Look for someone who is strong in the faith, who can keep a confidence, and who is sensitive to the struggle that former homosexuals face in the transition to heterosexuality. It may take you a long time to find such a person, but keep asking God to provide him or her for you. "Confess your sins to each other and pray for each other so that you may be healed" (Jas. 5:16).

No, you do not necessarily tell everyone. It very much depends on the level of maturity of the people in your particular church. In too many churches, people are afraid of people who have been trapped in sexual sin—particularly homosexuality. If you share your "jaded past" with them, they may respond with fear and suspicion, and you may feel yourself being isolated. The oft-repeated consequence is that the former homosexual leaves the church in bitterness, believing that God has also rejected him or her.

On the other hand, there are many wonderful churches where the congregation understands, for the most part, that they are all sinners redeemed by grace. They believe in the power of God to redeem and restore even the most far-gone sinner to health and wholeness; and they who do not carry around a holier-than-thou arrogance about those who have fallen further than they have. This is the kind of church where the sharing of your past, at the appropriate time, can be a significant aid to your healing.

There is something marvelous that God does when we are open and honest about our shortcomings, when we expose the dark past and present of our lives. In that atmosphere of honesty, the light of truth is able to shine upon those formerly dark and hidden places, and the power of Almighty God can be brought to bear in bringing significant healing in a relatively short period of time.

So, when you emerge from a homosexual or bisexual lifestyle, patiently await the Lord's signal that the time is right to share your past with an individual or with the church. And as with all sharing of testimonies, be careful to share it in such a way that God is glorified—not your colorful past.

If you begin a relationship with someone of the opposite sex that you know has the potential of leading to marriage, it is very important to share your past with that person. This applies no matter what the former sin, because a marriage is supposed to be an intimate and complete knowing of one another—a picture and precursor of Christ's relationship with His Church. In that context, nothing can be hidden.

I'm not suggesting that you share every graphic detail of your past, but that you share the general categories of sin in which you were previously engaged and be willing to answer any more specific questions that your prospective spouse may wish to ask. He or she will let you know when you have shared enough. Indeed, after having witnessed your unsolicited transparency, you may very well be let you off the hook from having to share the complete litany of sins. It is the honesty that your potential partner needs to see, and the willingness to be transparent, not necessarily the greater details of your past.

If you don't share your past with your mate, however, a day will come when someone will, and you will be faced with that awful look of betrayal in the face of the one you love. Trust will fly out the window and there won't be a thing you can do about it.

If you are convinced that you will lose someone if that person finds out about your past, it is far better to lose him or her now than to have your heart ripped apart later, after marriage.

If the one you are interested in cannot accept your past, that's not the right person for you anyway. You need someone who can know you completely and love you anyway. And if you believe that such a person can't exist, go to God in fervent prayer, and He just may surprise you.

In the meantime, there are a number of excellent para-church ministries for Christians who have sexual identity problems. Contact Restored Hope Network (www.RestoredHopeNetwork.org).

Preventing Homosexuality in Your Children

A parent who has had a sexual identity problem faces passing on that problem to his or her children. It happens invisibly and subconsciously, so it takes the illuminating power of God to show you where the danger lies and what to do about it. If you are seriously seeking God's healing and transforming power, you stand a good chance of learning how to properly father or mother your children in the area of sexual identity maturation, just as you do as in other areas.

Many of your actions and reactions, emotions and feelings come automatically from within your subconscious, which has been programmed in childhood and reinforced by subsequent behaviors and events. You don't even realize that you are doing them.

For instance, if you suffer from periodic homosexual feelings, you sometimes will avoid affectionate physical contact with your child for fear of becoming sexually attracted. Admittedly, the thought of responding sexually to your own son or daughter is a frightening one. But you must pursue God's presence and power to overcome this fear, because your children need physical affection and affirmation during their formative years lest they suffer the same lack of healthy same sex-bonding that you did.

Children need their same-sex parents to affirm that they are fully accepted members of their gender group. They need to be complimented and encouraged. Time needs to be spent doing gender-identifying activities. They need to be kissed and hugged, thereby learning how to interact with someone of their own gender in a nonsexual way. If you don't give them these things, someone else will, and it just may be a pedophile.

Take care to protect your children from the pedophiles and ephebophiles that roam every public and private arena where children can be found. This is a delicate tightrope to walk, however, since you don't want to be so overprotective that you provoke your children to seek freedom from you. In addition:

- Learn to pray regularly for God to protect them from things you can't see.
- Know your child's friends, and know their parents.
- Get to know the scoutmasters, coaches, teachers and others who spend time with your child when you are absent. Don't allow your child to "sleep over" with adults that you aren't absolutely certain of, no matter what their office or position. And since most molestations are at the hands of other children or adolescents, be cautious about leaving your child in the care of older

children or teenagers.
- Don't let them go to adult health spas or gyms unattended. These are breeding grounds for pedophiles and ephebophiles.
- Never allow your child to hitchhike. The odds are that they will be picked up by a pedophile or ephebophile almost every time.
- Teach them about sex at the appropriate times and levels. Teach the biblical model and standards for sex and the grand vision for why God made us sexual beings (see the earlier "Divine Intent" chapter). Make certain that you don't spend the whole time lecturing, however. Give your child freedom to express his or her feelings and questions on any topic whatsoever.

One of the biggest mistakes that parents make is to put a veil over certain subjects—to never mention them for fear of stirring an interest in the child or because the parent feels ill-equipped or embarrassed about the subject. If your children go out of the house having been sheltered from a knowledge of the dangers and deceptions that exist out there (even in the smallest of towns), and if they have no idea how to defend themselves, they will be choice prey for all of the perverse influences that await them. They will be like baby chicks in the claws of a chicken hawk. That's why men who prey on children are called "chicken hawks."

One thing is for certain, you can't be everywhere at all times. Even the video arcades are hangouts for pedophiles and ephebophiles these days. So, it is vital that you teach your children the dangers of being approached by strangers and by known adults.

Give them social skills for avoiding potentially dangerous situations. Explain that if someone threatens them or anyone else with violence if they "tell," to come to you as soon as they can and tell anyway, and that you will inform the police about the molester. (Warn them, however, not to tell the molester what you are going to do.)

Teach them never to accept invitations from non-classmates to go to parties, sporting events or anything else until they first check with you. And then make sure you check out the situation carefully.

Teach your children how to escape from threatening situations. Make sure they memorize your home phone number and address and know how to contact the police.

Rather than simply rattling off rule after rule, instill biblical principles and try to elicit from *them* the correct responses to various situations. Teach them how to decide what is right and what is wrong. And don't forget that your life needs to be a model of those biblical principles. They will do what you do, not what you say or read from a book.

Let them know that sex is a healthy, God-given thing when kept to the marriage bed. If you make sex seem dirty, it will only serve to stir up their sin nature. If you make sex seem secretive, you will only increase their desire to uncover it to find out why. Any such "lawmaking" approach will backfire on you—for the law kills, but the Spirit gives life (see 2 Cor. 3:6). Support everything with logical reasons as to why your principles are important to follow. When they ask "why?"—tell them.

At the appropriate times, teach your children about how to respond to sexual temptation and danger. Use your own childhood experiences, when appropriate, as examples of the consequences of wrong choices and the blessings of godly ones.

If you are sharing your homosexual past publicly, then you should share it with your children as early as possible. Talk them through their questions about it and their secret fears that they may "inherit" the problem.

Keep the family computer in the living room, den or kitchen where you can see what they are watching. Put porn-blocking software on your computer and preferably use an Internet company that blocks porn at the server level. If you allow it at all, monitor chat room use very carefully.

Most important of all—cloak your children daily in fervent prayer. For the forces that really want to destroy your children can only be defeated by the power of Almighty God.

Study Section— Sexual Identity Confusion - Healing

A. Healing Homosexual Desires

1. Confession and Repentance of Sinful Behavior, as Well as Sinful Responses to the People and Events Surrounding the Emergence of One's Sexual Identity.

   "There are two manifestations when Glory comes: for those who are impure, unprepared and uninvited, there will be judgment. For those who are welcomed, prepared, anointed, and invited, there will be blessing.

   Salvation alone does not give believers the privilege of entering into the *Glory* of the Lord. If you want an *abundant* life then live abundantly in the Lord. We need personal repentance. Every day we want to commune in the Glory of the Lord, we need to prepare ourselves with personal repentance unto the Lord." —Frank Amedia

   Until now, your body (or someone else's) has been your God; your emotions have been your king, and your feelings have been your slave master. Now, you must turn to God for His power to defeat:

   a. Idolatry (Romans 1:18-27)—misplaced love and worship

   b. Rebellion (1 Sam. 15:23)—misplaced homage and obedience

      Agree with God that sexual behavior outside of heterosexual monogamy is wrong. The sexual inclination toward members of one's own sex is not wrong, it is the acting out of those diseased inclinations that is wrong. It is rebellion, which is as the sin of "witchcraft."

      c. Unforgiveness (Mt. 6:14-15)—misplaced position and authority (i.e., making "self" judge)

      d. Self-pity—a sin of narcissism that is deadly to honesty

2. Seek God for a Spiritual Healing.

 "We come to know ourselves through moral and spiritual development." —Leanne Payne

      a. Recognize and acknowledge *daily,* your absolute need for God's power to heal.

      b. Recognize and acknowledge *daily,* God's pronounced desire and willingness to forgive and to heal you—based on the grace won for you by Jesus' work on the Cross.

 "God has done everything for you that He requires of you."

 "As long as you're letting laws protect you, the Spirit of God can't protect you."

 "All His commandments are promises. When He commands you to do something, He's just saying, 'I promise I'm going to do this through you if you trust Me.'"

 "Compelled by love, you'll go out in power."

 "Obedience is believing."
                       (Dudley Hall—from *Grace Works*)

      c. Take the steps of faith necessary to replace the incorrect associations that you have made between the personality and actions of your earthly father and the character and love of your heavenly Father.

      d. Practice the presence of God, throughout each and every day, and receive into your spirit the awareness of the inescapable reality of His *unconditional* love for you. Always be careful to recognize the immediacy of His forgiveness, at any time, for any reason, for as many times as you sin, no matter what the sin.

 "You never want to look at the need before you look at the greatness of God." —Loren Cunningham

      e. Since you must *want* to change before permanent healing can occur, seek the Lord to increase your *will* to change. (Leanne Payne teaches that it is the masculine part of us, and of God, that possesses the strength of will).

Aristotle said virtue consists of not merely *knowing* what is right, but also in having the will to *do* what is right. He said that the will is trained by practice, by choosing to do right repeatedly until it becomes a habit. In Aristotle's words, "We become just by the practice of just actions." (from a "Focus on the Family" newsletter)

f. Give place for God to work righteous anger in you. Get angry over the destruction Satan has wrought in your life through your sinful behavior! That will serve to keep you from repeating the sins again.

g. Recognize and respond to the *"Mystery of Healing"* — that in intimacy and communion with the Father, we receive into ourselves His will, His purity of thought and desire, the fullness of boundless love, the ability to trust, the wisdom to act rightly and the completion of our personhood—our healing.

This *"mystery of healing"* has everything to do with the intimacy that you develop with the Father, Son, and Holy Spirit and the diligence and hunger with which you pursue Him!

h. Receive the power of the Holy Spirit to deliver you (Lk. 11:13). Galatians 5:16 says: "If we walk by the Holy Spirit, we will not carry out the desire of the flesh." God will deliver you from the *compulsion* to act out your immoral desires, right away. The Holy Spirit is more powerful than all other powers in the universe *combined—infinitely more!* Temptation may not cease, but the uncontrollable obsession will (1 Cor. 10:13). No other power can force you to do anything anymore unless *you* give it permission through giving in to your old desires.

i. *Recognize* the chain of authority in which you are linked and *utilize* what is now yours through Christ.

 (1) All power and authority in heaven and on earth has been given to the One who wants to change you (Mt. 28:18).

 (2) His purpose in coming to earth was and is to

destroy the work of the enemy (1 John 3:8).

(3) He has given all who follow Him authority to overcome all of the power of the enemy (Luke 10:19, Mt. 10:1).

(4) Those things that seem impossible to you are possible with God (Luke 18:27).

3. Seek God for Mental Healing and He will Lead you Through It. Remember that it is God's power working in and through you (Phil. 2:13), that overcomes the enemy. Learn to turn to Jesus, for His power, and to rely on Him.

    a. Reprogram/Renew your mind.

"Be made new in the attitude of your mind" (Eph. 4:23).

"I urge you brothers, in view of God's mercy, to offer your bodies as living sacrifices, holy and pleasing to God—which is your spiritual worship. Do not conform any longer to the pattern of this world, but be transformed by the renewing of your mind" (Rom. 12:1-2).

"We have the mind of Christ" (1 Cor. 2:16, NASB).

"Whatever is true, noble, right, pure, lovely, admirable, excellent or praiseworthy—think about such things" (Phil 4:8).

"Set your mind on things above, not on earthly things" (Col. 3:2).

"Prepare your mind for action; be self-controlled; set your hope fully on the grace to be given you when Jesus Christ is revealed. Do not conform to the evil desires you had when you lived in ignorance. But just as He who called you is holy, so be holy in all you do" (1 Pet. 1:13-15).

(1) "Clothe" yourself with Christ through worship and praise. Your attention must be singularly focused on Jesus Christ so that you are in a position to receive the continual impartation of His life.

"Clothe yourselves with the Lord Jesus Christ, and do not think about how to gratify the desires of the sinful nature" (Rom. 13:14; see also Gal. 3:27).

(2) Regularly "feed" on the Word of God (Heb. 5:12-14; Mt. 4:4; Dt. 8:3; Job 23:12; Ps. 119:103; Jer. 15:16).

(3) Be reinforced in your mind by the exhortations and encouragements that come from fellowshipping with other believers—those who are committed, lovers of God.

(4) Allow the cleansing effect of "serving" others to renew your mind.

b. Guard your heart and mind.

"The peace of God, which surpasses all comprehension, shall guard your heart and your mind in Christ Jesus" (Phil. 4:7, NASB).

(1) This happens through intimate, daily communion with God. It changes our perspective.

"Those who live in accordance with the Spirit, have their minds set on what the Spirit desires" (Rom. 8:5b).

"Live by the Spirit and you will not gratify the desires of the sinful nature" (Gal. 5:16).

(2) We need to desire it with all of our heart (Jer. 29:13). We often deceive ourselves into thinking that we want something when we don't, but God knows our heart and can reveal to us our self-deceptions.

Consider this exhortation from Thomas F. Jones. First appeared in *Discipleship Journal* Issue 64 July/August 1991—"Singleness" by Thomas F. Jones (p. 38). Used by permission. All rights reserved:

"While self-control may sometimes be a struggle it is not as difficult as we sometimes think. What it takes is a decision to live in a certain way. Most people who lack sexual self-control have never really made a firm decision to control themselves.

We can never excuse wrong behavior by blaming passion. Imagine yourself in a completely vulnerable situation. You and your lover are totally aflame with desire and on the threshold of intercourse. Nothing can stop you now, right? Then your partner says, 'I'm not sure if I've told you or not, but I have AIDS.' What do you think about control now?

In today's moral climate, many do not fail sexually because they are too weak but because they simply do not see a reason to control themselves...

God's rules (however) point in the direction of maximum spiritual fulfillment, (so) view self-control as a positive affirmation of God-given sexuality."

- (3) We need to cooperate with what the Spirit leads us to do. We will repeatedly be faced with a choice between loving Jesus more than we do sin. Our individual decisions will make evident our stance despite our claims and protestations to the contrary.
- (4) We need to willingly put on the new self and set our heart against the world.

    "Put on the new self, created to be like God in true righteousness and holiness" (Eph. 4:24).

4. Seek God for an Emotional Healing and He will Lead you Through the Process of Being Healed Emotionally.

    a. Replace what you've lost.

    "God shall supply all your needs according to His riches in glory" (Phil. 4:19, NASB).

    - (1) God the Father will "bond" with you—sometimes using other people. He will plant certain people in your life who will represent in the flesh, what He is doing in you through the Spirit.
    - (2) God will model right behavior for you, through Jesus.
    - (3) He will be your perfect Father.
    - (4) He will help you replace sinful attitudes with godly ones (e.g., unforgiveness, judgments, vows, etc).
    - (5) He will help root out "fear" from your life and replace it with faith.

        "We know and rely on the love God has for us. God is love...There is no fear in love. But perfect love drives out fear" (1 John 4:16-18).

"God did not give us a spirit of timidity, but of power, of love and of self-discipline" (2 Tim. 1:7).

(6) He will teach you how to relinquish control to Him—to trust Him.

(7) He will heal you on the inside from your emotional traumas, going right to the root cause and healing it at the point of origin.

(8) He will purify you and return your innocence to you.

"I will sprinkle clean water on you, and you will be clean; I will cleanse you from all your impurities and from all your idols. I will give you a new heart and put a new spirit in you; I will remove from you your heart of stone and give you a heart of flesh. And I will put My Spirit in you and move you to follow My decrees and be careful to keep My laws" (Ezekiel 36:25-27).

    b.   God will transfer His wholeness into you. He will not simply patch up the old person—He will make a new creation (1 Peter 2:4-5).

"If anyone is in Christ, he is a new creation; the old has gone, the new has come! All this is from God, who reconciled us to Himself through Christ and gave us the ministry of reconciliation" (2 Cor. 5:17-18).

"As we contemplate the Lord's glory, we are being transformed into His likeness, with ever-increasing glory" (2 Cor. 3:18).

5. Practical Points to Recovery

    a.   God's part is to supply the power and the authority—ours is to take up those tools and use them to put to death the old nature. We must "set our heart and mind" against the old sin-bred patterns of thinking, feeling and doing, and toward a *love* of purity.

"Worship the Lord in the splendor of His holiness" (Ps. 29:2).

In his book, *Passion for Jesus,* (pp. 138-139), Mike Bickle says:

"When Jesus is revealed, a hunger for purity and righteousness is released...Hunger for purity is one response of a believer who sees the Lord in His glory... The greatest motivation for obedience to the Lord is a growing revelation of who Jesus is—His passions and pleasures and the matchless splendor in His personality."

Purity is more powerful than lust or evil, just as God is more powerful than Satan; *infinitely* more powerful. The problem is, we don't want purity, or *value* purity enough to "take it by force" and live in its power—i.e., to *live in* (abide in) continual communion with God.

"From the days of John the Baptist until now, the Kingdom of Heaven has been forcefully advancing, and *forceful men lay hold of it*" (Mt. 11:12).

b. Allow God to identify for you, roots of spiritual, mental and emotional disease. God has the omniscience necessary to identify points of origin for temptation and behavior. If you seek Him for the knowledge, God will methodically but gently expose those things in your life that feed the old skewed orientation, and with your cooperation, will destroy their power over you.

c. Ask God for the power over these strongholds.

d. Starve the old nature to death! Avoid the people, places and things that God reveals as feeding troughs for your sin nature.

"By the leading of the Spirit, put to death the misdeeds of the body" (Rom. 8:13).

"I have kept my feet from every evil path so that I might obey your Word" (Ps. 119:101).

e. Learn to recognize the schemes of the devil by seeking the Lord to reveal them to you.

   (1) If sexual memories come to you out of the blue (not as a result of an idle mind), but with great power to stimulate, that is a sign that they are borne by demons. Tell them to go where Jesus sends them.

   (2) When all sexual activity outside of the marriage bed has been cast off, the unmarried person may

find that the adolescent phenomenon of "wet dreams" returns. This is almost always accompanied by dreams in which immorality takes place. This reveals that there still exists in your mind a "stronghold of sexual immorality" that demons are continuing to stimulate. You must declare your desire to be freed from *all* demonic influence and command that the stronghold be broken in the name of Jesus.

    f. Take the kingdom of God by force (Mt. 11:12; Luke 16:16) i.e., wrest your place in the kingdom of God from the illegal attempts of demons to hold onto it, by using your authority to cast them out.

    g. Don't rush ahead of what the Lord is doing in some misguided effort to please Him or to "earn your keep."

    h. Rejoice in the progress that you make under the Lord's tutelage, but *never* become satisfied to the point that you stop growing in Christ.

    I. Frequent men's/women's fellowship groups and home fellowship groups in addition to regular church services so that you can receive the kind of healthy support, modeling and acceptance from your same-sex peer group that has been missing in your life.

    j. Find someone with whom you can be accountable—perhaps a discipling relationship within the church.

6. The most important factors for change—all of which increase as you seek greater intimacy and revelation of the Lord are:

    a. The intensity of your desire for change.

    b. The degree of faith with which you hold on to God's promises.

    c. The depth of your love and commitment to Jesus Christ above all others.

    d. The degree of your willingness to be faithful to God's will and direction.

    e. The degree to which you can keep the perspective that it is God's working in you that brings permanent transformation.

f. The amount of time you spend seeking God in prayer and crying out to Him for help.

   "God rewards those who *diligently* seek Him" (Heb. 11:6).

B. RELATED ISSUES

   1. Loneliness

   Your friends may reject you because you have become alien to them, and a source of guilt.

   a. Don't forsake Christian assembly (Heb. 10:25).

   b. Avoid self-pity. Ruthlessly refuse to let it have any place in you. Combat it with prayer and by serving others.

   Note: There is a grieving over sin and the loss of critical parts of one's childhood that is a necessary part of healing that should not be mistaken for self-pity.

   c. Learn to *practice the presence of God*. He will be your constant companion, so that loneliness will not be a problem.

   - Sit alone in your room (or somewhere where you will not be disturbed) and "wait" on the Lord. Learn to be silent and comfortable with silence. Go there just to be with God—not to get from Him. Go there to find Him, to commune with Him, to discover Him, to be a companion to Him.

   - Don't let the frustration of a busy mind dissuade you. Learn, by practice, to ignore or put off distracting thoughts. Perhaps keep a pad at your side to write down pressing thoughts that will not go away any other way. At other times, turning to the Bible often helps to drive out a plague of unwanted thoughts.

   - As you sit in silence, practice believing by faith that He is with you there. Learn to enjoy the simplicity and beauty of that. Focus on the reality of His presence.

   - As you sit there, the Holy Spirit may begin to prompt you to pray about certain things. Do as you feel led. Then return to silence.

- As you sit there, the Holy Spirit may lead you to pick up your Bible (which you should always have at your side in the room) and read. Read until the Spirit begins to speak to you in what you are reading. Stop and pray, or meditate on what He is teaching you.

- As you sit there, sing love songs to Jesus. Talk to Him. Tell Him what you are feeling, what has happened to you that day, etc. If you are troubled about something, tell Him how you feel—what troubles you. Admit your failings, your weaknesses and your faith that He has the answers. Many times you'll find that in the midst of describing your troubles, wisdom to unravel them will come from your own mouth, as God begins to put solutions into your prayers.

- It is important to focus on "worship" and "listening prayer" as the bulk of your activity before the Lord. Enter into petitional prayer preferably as the Holy Spirit leads. However, if there is a pressing issue that seems to prevent all else from taking place, go ahead and pray for that. God knows your heart and will be gracious to respond to that pressing need.

- During your day, stop periodically and acknowledge God's presence. A quick thought of appreciation, praise or request for "help" is very much in order at any time. It is particularly important to stop and turn to the Lord during those moments of the day when you are experiencing a need for His power or wisdom, for example, when you are tempted or facing a dilemma.

- At first you will need to consciously go out of your way to do these things. However, eventually it will become an ingrained habit—one which will bear the fruit of a deep and abiding love and dependence on the one who loves you more than any other.

2. Emotional Dependency

Many people (no matter what their sexual orientation) have a problem with being emotionally dependent on others. Their personality and self-image is so weak or damaged, that they "bend" toward others emotionally in order to absorb a personality or identity, direction in life, or even a sense of justification for their existence. These relationships can be typified by extreme dependence and jealousy and are unhealthy.

Someone who is highly dependent in this way, will seek out someone who possesses the traits they feel they lack, and attempt to create a "best friend" or "lover" relationship. Often, the people they find are those who have an emotional dysfunction of their own—a subconscious need to be idolized. These people may appear to be successful and attractive, but possess deep inner self-doubts. The attention and worship of their dependent friend helps them medicate the pain of their own insecurities.

Sometimes an emotionally dependent person will try to attach themselves to a healthy person, through flattery, gifts, offers of help and prayer, etc. The healthy person naturally responds to these kindnesses with time and attention, but may soon discover that their new friend has emotional needs that they are unable to meet. Due to their inexperience in dealing with emotionally dependent individuals, what starts out as a seeming healthy new friendship often turns into a frightening episode for the healthy party.

Emotional dependency runs rampant in the homosexual community and is almost always an issue that must be dealt with in the healing process. Lori Rentzel has written a brilliant pamphlet on the subject, part of which we'll now examine, as she answers the question: Why are dependencies hard to break? (emphasis added)

"*First*, as painful as dependency is, *it does give us some gratification*. There is emotional security…a sense that we have at least one relationship we can count on and that we belong to someone. Our need for intimacy, warmth and affection might be filled through this relationship. And our egos are boosted when someone admires or is attracted to us. We also enjoy feeling needed. A relationship like this might add excitement and romance when life seems dull otherwise. In fact, the stressful ups and downs of dependencies can become addictive in themselves. Additionally, the focus on maintaining this relationship can provide an escape from confronting personal problems and responsibilities. Finally, many people simply do not know any other way of relating. They are afraid to give up the "known" for the "unknown.

The *second* reason…is that *we can't see them as sinful*. The culture we live in has taken the truth "God is love" and turned it around to mean "Love is god." Romantic or emotional love is viewed as a law unto itself...Viewed in this light, dependent relationships seem beautiful, even noble, especially if there is no overt sexual involvement...Also, we may not be able to see how dependent relationships separate us from God...the euphoric feeling masquerades as closeness to God.

Third, root problems are not dealt with.

Fourth, those who willingly enter dependent relationships become candidates for spiritual deception. When we ignore the Holy Spirit's correction, we make ourselves vulnerable to satanic oppression.

Fifth, we don't want to give up the relationship."

Next, Lori describes several guidelines and suggestions for what the process of healing for emotional dependency might look like:

*"The path out of dependency involves...*turning away from relationships which are based on serving our own needs...and learning new ways of relating as 'new creatures in Christ' (2 Cor. 5:17).

*Begin by making a commitment to honesty...*admitting we are involved in a dependent relationship and acknowledging the sinful aspects of that relationship.

The next challenge is being honest with another person... confess to them.

Begin gradually separating yourself from your partner.

*We must also allow God to work...*If we confess to God that we are hopelessly attached to this individual and powerless to do anything about it and invite God to come in and change the situation, the Lord will not overlook our prayers.

*Prepare for grief and depression...*If we allow ourselves to hurt for a season, our healing will come faster.

Cultivate other friendships.

Discover God's vision for relationships. If we love others as God loves them, we will desire to see them conformed to the image of Christ.

*Begin resolving the deeper issues...*bring the whole thing before God in prayer...seek out the counsel and prayer of those God has placed in authority over us.

*Prepare for the long haul...*We need to know ourselves...

(and) our adversary...to be willing to believe God loves us, even if we cannot feel His love...to learn God's character through His Word...to stop blaming Him...A close relationship with Jesus Christ is our best safeguard against emotional dependency."

From *Emotional Dependency* by Lori Rentzel. Copyright 1990 by Lori Rentzel. Published by InterVarsity Press, Downers Grove, Il. Used with permission.

3. Celibacy

The need for affection and loving reassurance is very real, especially in this feeling-oriented world.

    a. People's suspicions of celibates as being abnormal, hurts.

    b. This is where you will learn about the deep waters of self-sacrifice and self-denial that God uses to grow us. We need to mature into forgoing the pleasures of Egypt for a season, for the greater calling and reward that are hidden in the will of God.

    (Note: In the Matson and McWorda study—out of 168 gay couples, not one could maintain monogamy for 5 years).

    c. Keeping an eternal perspective is critical.

    From *Christianity Today*, June 24, 1991, "Death in the Mirror" by Timothy K. Jones (pp. 30-31). Used by permission.

    "Christian faith has always argued that meaning in life will be found *beyond* life. 'In my end is my beginning', the poet T.S. Eliot wrote...In a profound way, where we are headed affects how we travel. And death, for all its mystery and starkness and seeming darkness, leads, for the believer, to something better than life."

    d. Our advocate with the Father, Jesus Christ, also led a celibate life.

    e. Go to Jesus to receive mercy and grace to help you in your time of need (Heb. 4:15).

    f. Let God deal with your newly unmet physical needs.

If you really want Him to, He can remove all or part of your sexual cravings until the appropriate time as you head into marriage. He doesn't suppress the drive, He fulfills it in some miraculous way.

Once you have asked God to do this, and He has, if you invite the sexual feelings back into you by giving way to immoral temptation (in unrepentant thought or in actions), it is likely that they will return with an overpowering vengeance. So be careful. Do not request the grace of God lightly or carelessly.

"Those who belong to Christ Jesus have crucified the flesh with its passions and desires" (Gal. 5:24, NASB).

g. It is God who calls us into a "permanent" life of celibacy. Do not presume to take on a calling that is not intended for you. If God has fulfilled your sexual drive miraculously at your request, allow Him to decide if it will be a permanent "gift of singleness" or not. Take things one day at a time.

"Not everyone can accept this word, but only those to whom it has been given. For some are eunuchs because they were born that way; others were made that way by men; and others have renounced marriage because of the kingdom of heaven. The one who can accept this should accept it" (Mt. 19:11, 12).

"Let not any eunuch complain, 'I am only a dry tree.' For this is what the Lord says: 'To the eunuchs who keep My Sabbaths, who choose what pleases Me and hold fast to My covenant—to them I will give within My temple and its walls a memorial and a name better than sons and daughters; I will give them an everlasting name that will not be cut off'" (Is. 56:3-5).

"It is good for a man not to marry. But since there is so much immorality, each man should have his own wife, and each woman her own husband...I say this as a concession, not as a command. I wish that all men were as I am. But each man has his own gift from God; one has this gift, another has that. Now to the unmarried and to the widows I say: It is good for them to stay unmarried, as I am. But if they cannot control themselves, they should marry, for it is better to marry than to burn with passion…Nevertheless, each one should retain the place in life that the Lord assigned to him and to which God has called him…I would like you to be free from concern. An unmarried man is concerned about the Lord's affairs—how he can please the Lord. But a married man is concerned about the affairs of this world—how he can please his wife—and his interests are divided. An unmarried woman or virgin is concerned about the Lord's affairs: Her aim is to be devoted to the Lord in both body and spirit. But a married woman is concerned about the affairs of this world—how she can please her husband. I am saying this for your own good, not to restrict you, but that you may live in a right way in undivided devotion to the Lord" (1 Cor. 7:1-2, 6-9, 17, 32-35).

    h. Sometimes God allows Satan to test us—(see Dt. 8:2; Heb. 12:1-11). The temptation may be the only thing that motivates us to turn our attention and hope toward God. So do not be surprised at lengthy periods of temptation, particularly during periods of spiritual disinterest.

4. Getting Married

    a. There is heavy pressure in churches, among friends, and by one's family to get married. (Don't fall victim to that neo-epicurean group in your church, whose motto is "Eat, drink, and get married!" Many of them go off and become "Moonies," committing mass marriage—a form of mass suicide).

    b. There may be accusing looks from people that will hurt you when you don't meet their timetable or program for courtship and marriage.

    c. Church "Singles" groups often exude an air of desperation.

    d. Don't marry, or even date, to appear straight, or to become straight.

    e. Learn to seek God, to hear Him, and to heed His direction.

    f. Become wed to God first. Then your search for a mate will be properly motivated and balanced.

5. Going Public

   a. You need to find someone with whom you can share your real self. Healing comes in bringing dark areas to the light.

   "Confess your sins to each other and pray for each other so that you may be healed" (James 5:16).

   b. Before saying anything to anyone, it is critical to discern the ability of that person or church to handle the news of your sexual background. Rely on the guidance of the Holy Spirit in these matters.

   c. Only share your background publicly in response to God's clear leading—as an opportunity to glorify Him and to help others.

   d. Always tell a prospective marriage partner. Complete honesty and revelation of who you really are is critical to a healthy marriage. The last thing that you want to see is the look of betrayal on the face of a spouse who has stumbled upon the knowledge of your hidden background.

6. Preventing Sexual Identity Confusion in Your Children

   a. Protect but don't exasperate.

   b. Do sex-identified things with them.

   c. Give nonsexual physical love and affection to them. If you have inner fears of being attracted to them, consult a Christian counselor who has expertise in this field. It is important that you overcome and manage such feelings because your children need that physical touch of affirmation and love without a sexual context.

   "Rules without relationship lead to rebellion."
   —Josh McDowell

   d. Take time daily to interact with them—to reaffirm them in their masculinity or femininity.

   e. Create an atmosphere where your child is free to ask about anything and teach sexual knowledge to them as they express interest and to the depth that they request.

f. Teach the biblical model and standards for sex.

g. Teach them the realities of sexual temptation and danger, along with ways to respond to them. Use your own childhood experiences when appropriate as examples of the consequences of wrong choices and the blessings of godly ones.

h. Carefully check out all children and adults who are given charge over them. Most child sexual abuse is committed by other children under the age of 18.

i. Teach your children that they should not obey authorities who try to engage them in sexual activities, and that they should report those who do, to you, no matter what threats are made against them. Teach them not to tell the perpetrator that they are going to report what he or she has done, in case that may put them in danger, but to tell you anyway as soon as they get the chance.

j. Do not let them go to health spas or to hitchhike.

k. Praise and affirm them.

(From *How To Drug-Proof Your Kids* by Steve Arterburn and Jim Burns, Word Incorporated, Dallas, Tx.)

"All normal human beings respond to praise. In fact, we crave affirmation so much we are likely to do almost anything to receive it. We need to be aware of this with our children. As someone said: 'Whoever gives your kids praise and attention has power over them.'

If you don't affirm your children, someone else will, and that someone could be a drug dealer (or child molester—my addition). Many people with lifestyles contrary to your own are willing to praise your kids to get what they want from them."

Exercises—Sexual Identity

1. Ask the Lord to reveal the root causes of your identity confusion. Then ask Him to show you what to do that will reverse the outcome of those events.

2. Meditate on passages in the Word of God that speak of the evil of homosexuality. Allow that truth to elicit true repentance in your heart. Then ask God to put a love of purity in your heart.

3. Ask the Lord to uncover any fear or hatred of the opposite sex that you may have, buried deep inside. Then ask Him to reverse those fears and beliefs, showing you how to pray and how to think and believe what is true.

4. Ask the Lord to uncover any roots of bitterness, anger, rejection, idolatry and rebellion that may reside deep within your heart. After confession and repentance, ask the Father to show you how to live in the opposite spirit of those things.

5. Seek the Father diligently and faithfully. Ask Him to bond with you and to meet every unmet need from your childhood. Ask Him to fill you with a healthy sense of being the gender that you are. Ask Him to give you a sanctified view of the opposite sex. Ask Him to destroy the work of the enemy in your life and to make you new and pure again from the inside out.

6. Regularly cleanse and renew your mind with the washing of the Word of God. Set your mind and heart on being holy and pure from this day and forevermore. Run to Jesus for the transforming power that will make this dream possible.

7. When you are tempted, commit yourself to immediately turning to God for the power to overcome. Live in weakness and dependence on the God who is all powerful and who is on your side.

8. Remove all factors from your life that feed the old nature. Ask the Holy Spirit to show you what they are. They may include people, places, practices or things.

9. Reconcile with your earthly father and mother, as far as they will allow. If they are deceased, write them a letter of reconciliation.

10. Ask the Lord to reveal any demonic strongholds in your life. Pray against them in the name of Jesus—i.e., with the authority and power that He has bestowed upon you to carry out His will on this earth.

11. Get involved with a men's or women's group in your church. Attend a home fellowship or any other group that allows you to be around a healthy group of affirming Christians. Find someone you can confess your past to and who will keep you accountable.

12. Make an irretrievable commitment that following after homosexual desire will never again be an option in your life.

Child Sex Abuse: The Predator

A growing subculture of sexual abuse victims in the world today may number as high as one-third of the population. And one-third of this group will grow up to sexually abuse other children. This second subculture, one we might call "prey turned predator," is being cultivated through the proliferation of child pornography, by the general devaluing of children in society (as illustrated by abortion and the unimpeded exposure of even young children to pornography through the Internet) and by the failure of the courts to give law enforcement enough freedom to prosecute and treat offenders. Plea-bargaining has destroyed the teeth of our legal system. The common practice of letting parental offenders go scot-free is making elimination and control of the problem a laughable prospect. And the measly attempts that have been made in some jurisdictions to treat offenders are pitiful, even in the estimation of those hired to give the treatment.

Lawyers are being well paid to "defend" a supposed constitutional right to pornography (including child pornography), conveniently forgetting that such a supposed "right" was never upheld during the first two hundred years of our constitutional government. The nation's largest Internet bookseller, (Amazon.com), has sold books by pedophiles, for pedophiles under the excuse of "free speech." Our culture has sunk so deep into denial that on at least one national TV talk show, representatives from NAMBLA, an organization that publicly encourages sex between adults and children, were given license (without any opposing group) to preach their perverse message to the entire country. Many are now pushing for the normalization of pederasty, (aka ephebophilia, the molesting of teenage boys), and even pedophilia. It is a major indictment on the morality of this nation that such organizations are even allowed to exist, much less legitimize themselves on national television.

We like to quote the following Scripture to the child molester, but I suspect it applies just as much to the nation that allows its children to be abused and led into sin. Jesus said: "It would be better for him to be thrown into the sea with a millstone tied around his neck than for him to cause one of these little ones to sin. So watch yourselves" (Luke 17:2-3a).

During my years as a male prostitute, I made a point of picking up kids who were hitchhiking so that I could help them before they were killed or hurt by the kind of men who were picking me up. Probably all of whom were victims of child sexual abuse.

I remember picking up one 14-year-old runaway who could barely walk. He had accepted an offer for a ride in Hollywood and had been gang-raped so brutally that both his legs had been broken. His attackers had also tortured him with cigarettes, leaving scars all over his body. He was lucky to be alive. (Thousands are raped, tortured and murdered every year, and the younger they are, the more they are sought after.)

At a nude beach just north of Los Angeles, I met a group of four guys. They were in their early teens and had run away from Tennessee. My heart broke so that I could barely talk to them because I knew they'd be dead in a few weeks if somebody didn't help them. So, I took them home and let them stay with me. A week or so later, they disappeared.

Many of my closest friends were young hustlers, like I was. To this day, I have not met any finer human beings than some of those young men. They were among the kindest, most vulnerable, compassionate and loving people that I have ever known and I still pray for many of them:

> *Art*—who was picked up and seduced by a man on his way home from school when he was in the seventh grade. I've never met anyone with a sweeter spirit than Art. The last time I saw him, he was in a hospital bed.
> *Curtis*—whose mother was a prostitute and drug dealer. He'd been a male prostitute since the age of twelve in order to bring money into the home. His mother was aware of and supported his profession. I remember telling Curtis one time that I was afraid that if I kept hustling much longer, I would become just like my customers. Curtis told me he'd had that same fear and was going to quit hustling, too.
> *Danny*—whom I picked up near the Los Angeles airport. He was 12 years old and had been hustling for years. His family had kicked him out of the house and his life was a series of one-night stands with whomever would pick him up.
> *Ben*—who had fled his family in British Columbia and at the age of 13 and was the sex slave of a record producer.
> *Ross*—who had come to Hollywood to be a star, only to end up hanging out in health spas in order to get picked up for sex. Though only 17, he had a he-man body and was continually "rented" by men for nude posing sessions and to be sodomized.
> *Brad*—who looked for homosexual relationships ever since catching his bisexual father at home in the arms of a man one day after school. His father had never tried to have sex with him, but the

psychological impact of seeing his dad with another man was so powerful that it drove Brad to mimic that behavior. I met Brad at the home of a child molester who had picked me up. He told me that the man picked him up at school 40 miles away and brought him in to Hollywood for sex every week. He said he hated it when the man sodomized him, but that he was dealing with it as best he could in return for the "love" and companionship that the man gave him.

Jimmy—who lived in a mansion next to Cher and who let men abuse him because his own father was too busy to have anything to do with him. At the age of 15, he would hitchhike around Beverly Hills until someone would have sex with him. He was so sad it broke my heart.

The average child sex abuser will molest 60 young people before he is caught for the first time, and hundreds over the course of his lifetime. (This includes a growing population of female predators.) It should be noted, however, that there *is* a population of pedophiles and pederasts who restrain themselves from molesting anyone, but their numbers are hard to uncover.

Because of the severity of his crime, the pedophile or pederast becomes a master of deception and a specialist in the art of denial and minimization. He concocts intricate rationalizations for the indefensible. Since no one wants to believe that he is doing something wrong, he creates elaborate systems of justification in his mind that are sometimes so ingenious that he fools himself into believing them.

After giving in to behaviors that run contrary to our natural design, it is human nature to try to justify his actions by denying that he has a problem. This only leads to a further acting out of the behavior. Deep inside, he knows that something is terribly wrong, and a profound self-loathing develops from the suppressed guilt. Festering beneath the surface, it creates an inner rage and despair that fuels the pathological behavior even more.

If he has justified his perverted behavior in these or other ways, it is not unlikely that he'll eventually be drawn into acting out variations on that behavior at deeper and deeper levels of perversity and with greater numbers of victims.

The child sex offender truly needs long-term treatment and reconciliation with God. Despite our inclination to send him to jail and throw away the key, we are doing our children a great disservice by not properly treating the sex offender. If we don't help him find healing, the odds are that, because of the out-of-control nature of the condition, he *will* offend again. It takes a gifted and skilled counselor to identify what is going on and properly treat the offender. With man it seems impossible, but with God, all things are possible.

Connections Between Pedophilia, Ephebophilia and Homosexual Confusion

There seems to be a progression of perversity with sexual sin, as with much other sin. For those men whose homosexual confusion resulted from their own childhood sexual abuse, the trail from homosexual neurosis to pedophilia or ephebophilia is sometimes inevitable. This will not be a popular thing to say, but from decades of observation from within the homosexual mind set and its many variant communities, I have noticed one constant: the connection between their homosexual neurosis and a sexual attraction to youths. Although like anything else, this is not true 100 percent of the time, it appears to be true at a much higher rate than found in the heterosexual community. In fact, I would estimate that perhaps between one quarter and one-third of those with homosexual confusion also suffer with one of the even darker disorders of pedophilia or ephebophilia. This inordinately high representation of pedophiles and ephebophiles among homosexuals can be traced to the shared causal factors in all three conditions.

It is a little-known fact that most people with homosexual confusion never act on those feelings. They have a moral structure that prevents them from doing so. The same is true for some of those who struggle with being sexually attracted to children and teenagers. And there are still others who do not act on their feelings because of the legal and social consequences of doing so.

However, I have repeatedly observed in the gay community many who seduce and molest adolescents, and to a lesser extent, children. And I have also observed that those who do so are by and large accepted as a part of this supposedly healthy community. In fact, the sexual use of minors has historically been an accepted part of homosexual life, harking back to the ancient Greeks and their young male sex slaves.

Today, it remains a frequent practice as well as a subject of repartee at gay gatherings. Young teenage (and sometimes preteen) children are a common sight at gay parties. In a large part of the gay underground, there is virtually no social taboo against the blatant display of such desire. This "dirty little secret" in the gay community is behind the endless attempts by gay leaders to lower the age of consent in the legal system; why NAMBLA has in the past been allowed to march in gay pride parades; why the gay press is filled with bestsellers that tell stories about the seduction of underaged kids; why out of the 300,000 kids who are involved in prostitution in America, *one half of them are boys* (serving a gay community that comprises only one to three percent of the total population); and why so many leaders in the gay community are openly avowed pedophiles and ephebophiles—even those who write for their most prestigious journals. (For more on this, read the booklet, *Ephebophilia: The Sin That Dare Not Call Its Name* by David Kyle Foster, available from Mastering Life Ministries at the website:

www.PurePassion.us/shop/store).

Let me emphasize again—this is *routine* in a large segment of gay society—not the exception. However, let me also emphasize that not every homosexual is driven to seduce children or youths. Many are driven to find a father or mother figure instead, and others are driven narcissistically to unite with an image of their idealized self. We need to be careful not to paint them all with the same brush.

My guess is that this search by some gay adults to find fulfillment in the world of youths precipitates from the very cause for their homosexual neurosis. It probably begins like this (I will use masculine pronouns, but the same process can occur in the developing lesbian):

When the emotional growth of the child is interrupted by a lack of bonding with the same-sex parent, the child experiences (or imagines) a separation or rejection by his peers. He no longer is able to grow with his own age group in acting out behaviors appropriate to his gender. He no longer has the internal witness that he belongs or measures up. (Sometimes, he will be able to maintain a surface identity with the group though he has lost it on an inner, emotional level.) Because of this, the child develops an obsession with the age group where he first experienced the rejection, longing for their acceptance.

A different homosexual might develop the same kind of obsession as a result of experiencing some sort of trauma. It may be the trauma of being sexually abused or the trauma of being harshly rejected or humiliated by the opposite sex. The trauma freezes his emotional growth and he remains fixed on rehearsing the trauma again and again as a way of trying to process and overcome it. Though he continues to grow physically, he remains trapped in an obsession fixed on the age at which the trauma first occurred. His later attempts to sexually abuse children of that age are often subconscious attempts to replay his own abuse or attempts to take into himself the lost innocence that his victim possesses.

This helps explain the abnormally high incidence of fixation on youths that so many homosexuals have, who are not only trying to relive their youth, but are still trying to gain acceptance from the age group whose rejection helped bring about their arrested emotional development in the first place. Once they have finally begun committing homosexual acts, however, powerful sexual feelings will tend to mask the true emotional source of their need. Eventually, something inside will tell them that the core need still isn't being met. It is then that they are most likely to begin pursuing younger kids.

Pedophilia/Ephebophilia in General

(For brevity, I will use the term "pedophile" to also represent "ephebophiles/pederasts".)

Someone fearful of rejection and lacking confidence in a given area will often try to compensate by seeking out those who have the least experience in that area. Since pedophiles lack confidence in their sexuality, who better to have sex with than someone who lacks expertise because of inexperience? A child or adolescent knows only what the molester has shown him, which makes the molester the expert and increases his feeling of success.

The perpetrator, feeding from his obsessive need to be accepted by a certain age group, finds the ultimate sign of acceptance in having sex with a young person. He uses money, affection, affirmation, praise and pleasure to accomplish the goal of trying to prove how valuable he can be to youths who he has come to idolize (or hate) because they represent the ones who rejected him.

A pedophile who was seduced or molested by an adult during his own childhood may have entered into a pattern of seductive behavior even while still a child. Now as an adult, he may be subconsciously attempting to recreate those early events in order to "process" them. At the time of his own molestation, his brain had not yet developed enough to process such intense trauma and pain in a healthy way. The person who has been molested or abused as a child is often playing out the memories of that past in his adulthood, only this time from the "power" position—in the role of seducer or abuser.

This is part of the phenomenon whereby personality characteristics and behaviors of trauma-bearing adults become fixed into the psyche of children and are later repeated by them, unconsciously or consciously, sometimes for the rest of their lives.

The ability to seduce children does not depend on good looks but on skillful psychological manipulation. A pedophile receives pleasure just by virtue of the fact that he has the power to cause pain or pleasure in the child. It's as if he is using the child to portray himself in a retelling of his own past (or in a reenactment of a fantasy world of pornography). Thus, he may be abusing the child because he feels as though he himself deserves to be treated that way, and is, in effect, trying to punish himself through the child who now represents his former self. This is why a child molester often cannot recognize the person behind the body that he is abusing. His victim is merely an object and a symbol to him, not a real person. This partitioning of the mind and heart helps him deal with the horror of what he is doing in a way similar to how the Nazis handled their participation in crimes against Jews.

Child molestation can also be a kind of shaking of the fist at God for having allowed the destruction of the pedophile's innocence—an acting out of retribution (by defiling one of God's innocent ones). The cries of pain or pleasure from the child are his cries of pain or pleasure from the past, and reconfirm in his mind the reality of his own abuse or seduction and the presumed rightness of his anger and rebellion against God.

The difference now is that the pedophile is the one with the power to seduce or abuse. He has recast himself in the power role as a way to overcome the feelings of powerlessness that have plagued him as a result of having been abused or seduced in the past. Having been the victim, he must victimize; having been powerless, he must render powerless. It is very much a process of trying to manufacture power in the only situation where the person feels experienced enough to succeed. Oddly enough, the pedophile who operates from this mindset is not primarily concerned with his own orgasm, but with causing one in the child (or with causing pain in the child). His lust is satisfied by causing and witnessing the pain or arousal of the child, because in his mind, he is the child. Inside, he is emotionally frozen at the age at which he was traumatized as a child.

If the child molester was rejected and made fun of in the past and is particularly bitter, his revenge is often exacted by abusing and torturing his victim. Such a perverse mentality lusts after virgin, unconquered innocence, the greatest thrill being to prove to God and all mankind that purity and wholesomeness cannot survive the wiles of his own sensual or coercive power.

I once wrote about my experiences with these kinds of men during my years in Hollywood:

> "I hated them for pretending to love me when they only wanted sex. I hated them because I needed them to temporarily fill a deep psychological void that had developed within me. I hated them because I needed the money. And I hated them because what they were doing to me was driving me to suicide, and they did not care!
>
> When I could see years of hurt and rejection in their eyes, I hated *myself* for caring. At times, some would whimper as they held me, never imagining in their wildest dreams that someone like me would ever be willing to allow them to be sexually intimate with him, yet painfully aware that I was agreeing to it solely for the money.
>
> Child pornographers would regularly pick me up. They would question me to see if I was alone and vulnerable. When I would tell them that I was, they would swoop down on me like hawks and try to get pictures of me. Even though they believed I was 14 years old, they would practically funnel drugs and booze down my throat in order to break down my defenses. They would show me pornography of guys who were the same age as I seemed to be,

and younger, in order to further break down my resistance.

I made an effort to come across as an innocent, straight, all-American boy. As it turned out, it was that very image that intensified their pursuit of me.

Many men at the gym would strike up conversations with me over a period of days or weeks. When they felt that I trusted them, they would invite me to their house "for a beer" or something manly sounding. No sooner would I walk in the door then they would hand me some pornography or offer to show a porno flick. When I would tell them I was straight, many of them even had a ready supply of heterosexual pornography in order to make their seduction as non-threatening as possible.

Nothing is more exciting to a homosexual than scoring a heterosexual. They have all their lines ready, e.g., "No one'll ever know, and you'll get to see what it feels like"; or "Just close your eyes and pretend it's a beautiful girl doing it"; or (if there's a heterosexual porno film playing), "Just look at the film while I do it and pretend that you're with the girl in the movie." Other very effective lines involve building up the boy's male ego by telling him how manly he is or by complimenting him on his body, especially in a gym, where most of the people are heavily narcissistic in the first place.

Most of the child molesters that I met were nice men with great personalities. They were the last sort of people you would ever expect to prey on children—all the way from businessmen and real estate brokers to pool cleaners. Some had a retinue of boys that they saw on a rotating basis. They would try to get us to have sex with each other to reinforce our patterning into homosexual behavior.

In Hollywood, I went to parties that were set up exclusively for the very rich where scores of young boys were brought to be taken home by adults. Some of the biggest movie stars, rock stars, film and television producers and directors and even heads of studios were involved in this horrendous exploitation of children, and still are. One of their great thrills is to parade you around in front of their friends like some trophy. There are even organized groups of them who share boys between themselves like trading cards.

I was dying inside. It was humiliating and demeaning to let these dirty old men touch me, and I didn't know what to do. With every visual and emotional cue I had, I let them know that it was killing me to have them do what they were doing. But they all seemed to feed off of the corruption of innocence in which they were engaged. After all, I was a young preacher's kid!

As soon as they had gotten all they could, however, their attitude changed dramatically. They began to despise me and eventually discard me like so much trash. These proud, successful men resented the fact that they were sexually and emotionally addicted to kids."

That was just one of the gay subcultures that I ran in. There was also the disco crowd, the bar crowd, the art crowd, the rest room crowd, the "personal ad" crowd, and on and on. Because I hated myself so, I sought out people like this in probably over a thousand sexual encounters—people who would treat me shamefully—and I studied them in detail.

There are certain fixations and obsessions that run through the thinking of the average pedophile or ephebophile. Let's examine some of the more common themes:

Power through the corruption of youth. A child molester's obsession with the corruption of the innocent is first of all a desperate attempt to mitigate or assuage his own sense of guilt by confirming in his own mind that these "seemingly" innocent children are not really innocent at all—that everyone is "really" just as corrupt as he is, that the kids' public display of purity and naiveté is simply an act enforced by society and religion. By corrupting this accusatory presence of innocence and wholesomeness, the predator relieves some of his inner pain—much like the obese person who eats another piece of cake to assuage the pain of being fat. He ignores the fact that his painkilling action will only exacerbate his pain in the long run, opting instead for the quick relief of pleasure and self-deception.

Age obsession. The pedophile or ephebophile is usually fixed on a certain age bracket, almost always the age at which he lost peer acceptance as a child. This age group often coincides with the age when he first began to sexualize his unmet emotional need for same-sex bonding, when he first began fantasizing about the peers who had withheld their acceptance. His current activity is an attempt to finally obtain that peer acceptance, preferably from a child or teen who embodies his ultimate childhood desire. If he can cause this child to exhibit the intense pleasure of orgasm—which he causes—then he has gone a long way in convincing himself that he has achieved the long-sought-after acceptance. "After all," he subconsciously reasons, "what can be more proof of acceptance than being allowed to be sexually intimate with someone?" And if he cannot coax pleasure, he will inflict pain.

Unfortunately, obtaining this "acceptance" creates an even stronger desire for more, much like cocaine. That is why there are dozens if not hundreds or even thousands of victims in the life of a pedophile or ephebophile.

Predatory influences. The pedophile or ephebophile has no natural skills to achieve acceptance from youths through normal social means and therefore must coerce or trick them, through drugs, alcohol, money, or the provision of other sexual opportunities—things that the child wants so much that they are willing to suffer the sexual demands of the abuser. The abuser realizes, however, that it was only through coercive means that he obtained sexual favors, which causes the abuser to never really achieve the acceptance that he needs. This may cause him to become bitter and cynical, at which point he begins to hate the very children that he wants to love and emulate. Such a predator often degenerates to a point where he can no longer obtain pleasure without inflicting pain on the child. His perversion becomes a quest to "pay back" (by proxy) those youngsters who rejected him as a kid and who have what he needs but won't give to him naturally.

There are many children who are not forced physically, but rather submit to the pedophile or ephebophile in return for favors or attention. This is the kind of child that the average predator looks for, one who has some desperate physical or emotional need that isn't being met. The child molester can often recognize, just by looking at the child, such a vulnerability. There is a longing, a desperation, a seeking look in the eyes of this kind of child that the pedophile or ephebophile is drawn to, as if, more than spotting someone vulnerable, he has also spotted someone like himself, of the age where his own desperation began, to whom he can, in his own sick fantasy, provide some measure of comfort and assistance. Oddly enough, the relationship may begin as a well-intentioned effort to help the child, but inevitably degenerates into a sexual situation because the pedophile or ephebophile will eventually feel compelled to obtain the fullest and most complete identification with the child.

This is why some men who are drawn to leadership positions over children excel for years as Boy Scout leaders or athletic coaches but eventually become predators. When they meet that one child who looks at them with all of those emotional needs, who tells them with his eyes that he will do anything for them in return for their embrace or affirmation, it's all over. And once that line has been crossed, the pedophile or ephebophile becomes a conscious predator, much like the shark who has tasted the first drop of blood. His hunger actually increases because of the experience of sexual pleasure in the arms of his idol, and because his real need can never be satiated through the means he has chosen. In short order, his discrimination vanishes and he begins trying to orchestrate encounters rather than waiting for the infrequent opportune child.

Sexual inadequacy. Many pedophiles and ephebophiles act out of feelings of sexual inadequacy. Lacking confidence in performing sexually with their own age group, they seek out those who have little or no sexual experience. Someone with no sexual history to draw from for comparison can easily be led to believe that his abuser is a sexual master.

Power—through control. As a result of having had no control during a period in their childhood when they were sexually abused, a pedophile or ephebophile often has an obsessive need to control his life. His attempts to control and dominate children reflect a desperate need to attain, once and for all, the level of control that his abusers exerted over him, and which, at the time, seemed absolute. He feels that achieving this control will give him the subconscious peace he needs never to be hurt again. Sick rationalization can convince him that by taking advantage of a child sexually, he is helping that child learn that he must obtain this control, too.

Power—through shock value. For some pedophiles and ephebophiles, the discovery of orgasm as a child was so amazing and unexpected (and brought on by someone older, whom he admired), that he became obsessed with becoming that older person in other children's lives. His pleasure comes from causing and observing the same wonder and amazement in similarly virgin children. He wants to see the look of shock and fascination on the kid's face, knowing that as the one who introduced this world of pleasure to the kid, he will always hold a permanent place in that child's thinking, just as the adult who introduced him to sex does in his own thinking. This is a position of power and influence, the power to control and permanently affect another person's entire life. They recreate their own childhood molestation, but this time in the power position, subconsciously attempting to overcome the feelings of powerlessness that were formed from their own experience of being molested as a child.

Rationalization. The ability of a pedophile or ephebophile to rationalize away his behavior is incredible. He may convince himself that he is teaching the child valuable lessons in life, in a much kinder way than was taught to him. He may think that he must recreate his sexual abuse to be just as painful as his initiation into adulthood was. He may come to believe that he is providing children with the love and acceptance that they need but aren't getting. He may even convince himself that adult/child sex is healthy, a beneficial way of schooling the child in the ways of sex. The ways of ancient Greece are often cited in such carefully manicured rationalizations.

Pedophiles and ephebophiles are able to lure children because of the dearth of basic parental provision, nurture and guidance in their victims' homes. Ploys include feigned love, concern, acceptance, undivided interest and attention; compliments and affirmations about the child's physical and personal self; places to stay; money; coin and other collections; boats; the use of a car; a job (if the kid wants one); food at the finest restaurants; an endless supply of any drug that the child wants; unlimited alcohol; any kind of sex that the kid has ever fantasized about (including instructions); any kind of pornography that he wants; mansions to live and play in;

swimming pools; endless parties; contact with rich and famous people (connections to make it big); access to private and exclusive clubs; vacations; any kind of recreation that he wants, including movies, games, videos, plays, shows, concerts, amusement parks, horse-riding, sports, etc.

The child predator provides ego satisfaction for the kid who lacks it. In most cases, he literally idolizes children or teenagers as the supreme object of his desire. Therefore, he goes overboard in providing positive affirmation about the child's physical appearance, mental ability, future potential, masculinity, sexual ability, and desirability. He makes the child feel wanted, important, valuable, desirable, attractive, worthwhile, comforted, and provided for. And by bringing the child into his lair filled with other victims, he provides instant popularity with kids of the same age.

Having lost his innocence during childhood, the pedophile, according to Leanne Payne, has a "cannibal compulsion" that causes him to try to ingest this lost innocence back into themselves from the person of their victim.

The Counseling Needs of the Abuser

Author D. Mitchell Whitman says, "Change for the offender involves a complete lifestyle change. He must learn how to cope with feelings, stress, and, in general, life. This means a long process of changing thinking patterns, learning new skills, etc. This probably fulfills a higher purpose than taking away the problem" (see Jas. 1:2-4).

In recommending guidelines for pastoral care of the offender, Whitman goes on to list a number of ideas, from which I have adapted the following highlights. (For the complete list, see pages 133-139 of Whitman's book, *Challenging the Darkness: Child Sexual Abuse and the Church*, published in 1994 by Discovery House Counseling Resources, Bellingham, WA).

1. Hold the offender accountable for his or her behavior.
2. Show grace and mercy in the context of repentance and accountability.
3. Look for repentance as demonstrated by:
   - admission of sin.
   - agreeing to come under the authority of church leadership.
   - willingness to go for a sexual offender evaluation.
   - seeking and receiving treatment from a skilled therapist or sexual offender treatment program.
   - not laying blame on the victim.
   - willingness to sign an "exchange of information" release between the leadership and the authorities.
   - demonstration of financial responsibility toward the victim with regard to medical care and therapy, etc.
   - avoiding all contact with potential victims.

4. Monitor the person's progress during treatment, without condemning or rejecting a repentant offender.
5. Offer spiritual support to the offender through prayer, Bible study, sacraments, counsel, and fellowship with other believers, providing opportunities for confession, prayer, and forgiveness.
6. Offer housing, protection, and other practical support to the offender's spouse and family.
7. Protect the confidentiality of the victim and family.
8. Create a church environment where the offender can experience acceptance and support while working toward healing.
9. At appropriate times, inform the congregation of the problem and the healing and/or disciplinary processes.

The offender may resort to denial and lying, and it may be difficult to determine his or her level of sincerity. When in doubt, err on the side of believing the victim and do not minimize the offense. Never support a "not guilty" plea in court from a person who has committed an offense.

Further advice for how to minister to someone who has sexually abused a child or adolescent can be found in Paula Sandford's book, *Healing Victims of Sexual Abuse,* published by Victory House. Following a scriptural model, she advises ...

- Discovery of the root causes of the problems (see Eph. 5:13; Luke 6:43-45).
- Full confession of the present sin (see Jas. 5:16), which should include asking forgiveness from the victim, the family, and others who have been injured by his or her actions as well as a clear message to the victim that the abuser assumes full responsibility for the molestations.
- Assisting the abuser to choose to forgive all offenses, from childhood on (see Matt. 6:15).
- Helping the abuser repent and ask forgiveness for his/her reaction to those hurts.
- Offering assurances of forgiveness (see 1 John 1:9; John 20:23), praying (aloud, with him/her) for the healing of his/her own wounded spirit (see 2 Cor. 1:1-6).
- Praying (aloud) for the creation of a new and right (mature) spirit within him/her (see Ezek. 36:26; Ps. 51), for the destruction of old habit structures in the "old man" (see Col. 3; Eph. 4:22 ff; Rom. 8:13) and for freedom to receive teaching and nurture.
- Offering disciplines for walking in a new way (see Rom. 6:11-14; 2 Tim. 1:7) and biblical teaching concerning the laws of God, the sanctity of marriage, God's holiness, godly father-

hood, self-sacrifice, the importance of the church body, etc.
- Discerning when the abuser is capable of living a new life which produces the fruit of repentance, season after season.

If all parties persevere with God's help, healing and restoration are achievable. Next, let's examine the needs of the survivor of sexual abuse.

Child Sex Abuse: The Survivor

Survivors do not emerge easily into a place of mental and emotional health. It can take years of therapy, inner healing, and love from skilled Christian counselors, the Church, and their loving heavenly Father. They have lost so much, in such a horrific way, and at such an early age. For starters, their ability to trust has been stripped from them. This is especially true if the perpetrator was a parent or other family member, a trusted authority figure, or family friend. A child being molested by someone like that often concludes to him or herself, "If you can't trust these people, then no one can be trusted."

Survivors of child sexual abuse also have their self-respect torn away. Many of them blame themselves for their own abuse. As children or teenagers, their brains are not yet developed to the point where they can formulate proper intellectual responses or conclusions to such events. As a result, many convince themselves that *they* are to blame. And if they don't draw that conclusion on their own, their perpetrator often plants the suggestion in their minds for them.

Rage, anger, and hatred have been drilled deep into their very souls, robbing them of a healthy sense of well-being. In fact, many survivors report a numbness to their existence, a lack of any sense of being at all, as though they were a nonentity. Their sense of being a whole person has been fractured, blown into scattered pieces. It is only the Lord God Almighty who can heal them and restore to them a joy-filled, complete sense of well-being.

Survivors have had their childhood stolen from them. Instead of innocent thoughts and feelings, they now have dark images and pain-filled sensations. The world is no longer a fun place filled with all kinds of adventures. That's all over. Santa sure does not exist now, and possibly, neither does God.

In his excellent book, *The Wounded Heart,* Dr. Dan Allender speaks of the damage of sexual abuse as involving a profound sense of powerlessness and helplessness that in turn creates doubt, despair, and emotional deadness. Survivors respond their relentlessly painful circumstances by shutting them off through splitting, denial, and memory loss. According to

Allender, this results in the loss of a sense of being intact and alive, a loss of a sense of self. Without the ground of "self," survivors lose the ability to make judgments objectively. Instead, they live out of a profound need for self-protection. Living in a shame-based world of perceived unworthiness often causes them to bring further woe upon themselves through wrong relational choices.

Dr. Allender writes that survivors of abuse suffer a deep sense of betrayal from those who should have been there to protect them as well as from those who abused them. This results in hypervigilance, suspiciousness, distortion, and denial. They lose all hope for real intimacy. They lose hope for justice. And if the very thing that they have despised (the abuse) also brings some degree of pleasure, they enter into a great struggle with ambivalence, feeling two contradictory emotions at the same moment. This creates further confusion, shame, and self-hatred, resulting in chronic patterns of compulsiveness and a fear of pleasure.

"I Want Justice!"

One of the most pressing needs of a survivor of child sexual abuse is for *justice*. Even with a full belief that God will indeed bring justice at Christ's return (see 2 Thess. 1:5-9; Isa. 61:7-8) an abuse survivor needs to deal with the difficult questions of, "Why did God allow it to happen to me?" and "Why didn't He rescue me when I cried out to Him for help?" These questions do not have easy answers. In fact, the complete answers are almost *never* forthcoming, which forces the survivor to come to a place of believing in God's perfect love in the glaring absence of a complete, perfect, and satisfying answer. This is not an easy task when your inner being has been fractured by unspeakable trauma.

Why won't God just answer the question? One night, I was complaining to God about how He allows the innocent to suffer, and He responded, "David, what you are really asking Me is how could I *love you* and allow you to be abused?" Immediately, I recognized the truth. Then He said, "Why don't you stop living out of what you don't know, and start living out of what you do know? You don't know why I allowed you to be hurt so deeply, but you *do* know that I love you. I proved that once and for all on the Cross. When the Cross becomes enough proof for you that I love you, you will find the peace that you have been seeking all these years."

Then it sank in, that in all my griping and complaining about the question of evil, I had been refusing to accept Christ's death on the Cross as the ultimate and final proof of God's love for me and had been demanding further proof instead. What an unmitigated affront to Him! In my insistence that God answer my question, I had been, in essence, placing the idol of western rationalism before Him and demanding that He bow down to it. In my heart, I had been refusing to fully trust Him, fully give myself to Him, fully love Him until He bowed to my intellectual idol. My approach had been actually preventing Him from giving me the answer because He cannot and will never bow to any idol.

So I repented with deep anguish over what I had been doing and declared to the Lord that if He *never* told me why He allows the innocent to suffer, I would accept His demonstrated proof of love on the Cross as all the proof I needed of His love for me and for the entire world, and that I would love Him and serve Him solely on that basis. And I meant it!

This is the life of faith that we are all called to; to see through a glass darkly; to be certain of what we cannot see; to live a life of faith based on what we *do* know of God's infinite love for us, rather than whatever appearances there may be to the contrary.

It should not have surprised me, but after doing that, I was delighted to find that God began to give me some understanding of why evil exists and why He allows the relatively innocent (there are none who are truly innocent—see Rom. 3:10) to suffer. It's not a perfect understanding by any means, but it completely satisfies for me what used to be the most divisive issue between my heart and God's.

Let's first look at the premise of the question: that it is God's responsibility to protect and to maintain justice for everyone. Unfortunately, that premise crashes headlong into a number of problems, not the least of which is God's mercy. You see, He has made a way for us to escape the punishment that we deserve by offering us the atoning sacrifice of His Son on our behalf. Justice is being served, but on the shoulders of His own Son. And so we must first ask ourselves if we are willing to reject that mercy so that justice may be fairly meted out to everyone.

I may object: "But what if my abuser repents and gets forgiven?" I have to be prepared to accept the fact that the people who hurt me may turn to Christ and receive the same pardon for their sins as I have. Although they may still have to live with negative temporal consequences (such as getting arrested and being branded a sex criminal for life), if they accept Jesus Christ as their Lord and Savior, they go free from the eternal punishment that they originally brought upon their heads by abusing me. Is that fair? Only when seen in the light of God's mercy and grace already given to me for the sins that would have sent me to hell.

And so the choice for me is clear. I can live in God's grace and dispense grace to others, or I can live in God's justice and receive justice for my sins. The Bible is very clear that if I am going to receive the pardon from Christ, then I must be willing to pardon those who have hurt me (see Matt. 6:14-15; Mark 11:25; Luke 17:14; Eph. 4:32; Col. 3:13). More about that just ahead.

God also began to give me understanding on other questions about evil. For example:

Why is man's free will so important? In the book of Job (1:9-11; 2:4-5), Satan charged God with coercing or buying Job's faithfulness with blessings—a charge against which God defended Himself by demonstrating that indeed it would have been wrong for Him to have coerced or purchased Job's obedience through too many blessings. Here we see that God has limited Himself in the degree to which He can interfere with the free will of man. God remains sovereign, although self-restrained for a greater good. We see a similar self-limitation by God in the incarnation of Christ (see Phil. 2:5-11), when God temporarily divested Himself of some of His divine prerogatives in order to come as a man and die for the sins of the world.

Since God *is* love, and He is *omnipresent*, the only world that He could have created was one where love could exist. But love, by definition, *requires* a "free will" agent. We must have the freedom to choose evil for our choice to love to carry any moral meaning and thus be genuine.

Besides, we were created in God's image, and part of that image is His free will. That free will in man is what enables us to love and to be filled with God's Spirit.

Why does evil exist? Given the choice to do good or evil, men with a free will continually choose evil (see John 3:19). We (and the fallen heavenly host) are the creators of evil. God is innocent.

If He does not coerce human love and obedience, why does God sometimes interfere in our lives? After all, you hear stories all the time on *The 700 Club* and other talk shows about how God intervened in someone's life to rescue or to bless.

The short answer is this: when God acts in our lives, His action either drives forward His foreordained purposes in the creation and redemption of man, (a right that He has as Creator and Redeemer), or His creatures have invited Him to do so (thus making His interference non-coercive). When we pray, we are inviting God to act. When we obey Him or when we proclaim the gospel, we are releasing Him to act and to bring His promised blessings. For these and many other reasons, God can enter into our lives when we open the door for Him to enter. Our free will remains intact in these instances, because He is coming at our invitation.

Why then didn't He answer my prayers for protection? I prayed many prayers as a kid that were not answered, but I wasn't yet born again when I prayed them. There was as yet no connection between my spirit and God's. I was also leading a very rebellious life.

Even for believers, there are many reasons why God cannot answer our prayers, a prime example being the one I shared above when I was asking God to explain evil while unknowingly preventing Him from giving me the answer. Other variables might include sin, timing, impure motives—the list is endless. This you can know, however—God does not sit in heaven, able to rescue a hurting child, yet callously choosing to let him or her suffer instead. If He does not rescue, it's because for one reason or another He cannot rescue, not because He's not sovereign, but because the circumstances surrounding the situation make it so.

I refer you back to the story that I related in chapter two, when God the Father enabled me to feel the pain in His heart as He watched His pure and perfect Son be tortured on the Cross. There is a perfect example of God, though sovereign, not being able to rescue an innocent because of the unique circumstances surrounding the situation.

If you were traumatized as a child, God was in a similar situation at that time, for one reason or another unable to intervene, yet deeply sharing in your grief and pain. These many years since, He has been longing for you to come to Him so that He can heal the wounds and bring beauty from the ashes. As you seek God for healing, He will carefully lead you by the hand into the frightening world of memory, and part of the pain will be healed as you see Him present and sorrowful over your past experience.

In struggling with these same questions, author, David Seamands writes:

> "This does not mean that all of the harmful things we've been describing were God's intentional will for our lives. God is not the *Author* of all events, but He is the *Master* of all events. This means that nothing has ever happened to you that God cannot and will not use for good if you will surrender it into His hands and allow Him to work.
>
> God does not change the actual, factual nature of the evil which occurs. Humanly speaking, nothing can change this; it is still evil, tragic, senseless, and perhaps unjust and absurd. But God can change the *meaning* of it for your total life. God can weave it into the design and purpose of your life, so that it all lies within the circle of His redeeming and recycling activity" (from *Healing for Damaged Emotions*, Victor Books).

Does Satan have free reign to bring evil into our lives? No. Satan and his demons are restrained from coercing people. Unilaterally, they cannot do anything. They must be released to act. When we choose evil, when we seek after other gods, when we proclaim evil words, when we perform sinful acts, they are released to interfere in our lives.

On rare occasions, demons are released to interfere in man when God is using them to test us. However, God is not of the character to release Satan to test us through *evil* acts such as child abuse. When God releases Satan to test us, it is only when we are ready to pass the test (see 1 Cor. 10:13). Provided we make the righteous choice during those times of testing, we will always grow and be blessed by them.

Why then do the innocent suffer? As I have mentioned, there are no truly innocent. We are all under a curse as a result of our sin and the sins of our forefathers in which we share (see Exod. 20:5; Num. 14:18; Deut. 7:9; Ezek. 18:14-20; Rom. 5:12, 18-19). Also, there is a "corporate" element to good and evil that causes both to spill over into the lives of others. For example, Abraham was told that the world would be blessed through his righteous act (see Gen. 12:3). Jesus seemed to indicate a corporate power in Christian prayer and unity when He said, "Where two or three come together in my name, there am I with them" (see Matt. 18:20). Similarly, the power of evil in the world, though built up through millennia of sinful generations before us, affects our present day lives. Though we may be an innocent victim in any given incident of abuse, we have become a victim, in part because of this corporate spillover effect that pollutes the lives of everyone.

Why do the unrighteous prosper? For the same reason—the corporate nature of good. (They also receive the general blessings of God because for God to provide the blessings of life only to the righteous would in effect be coercive in manipulating men's decision for righteousness).

In summary, evil exists because, given the choice, men chose evil. Men also are culpable in their failure to release God to act through the means given them. These repeated choices for evil empower and authorize a corporate effect of evil into the world that spills over into the lives of the (relatively) innocent.

Survivors Need the Love and Comfort of the Father

Just when they need someone they can absolutely trust, survivors find themselves least likely to trust anyone. They need to gently and carefully be shown the love of the Father for them. They need to experience it for themselves in prayer, in worship, and by the power of the Holy Spirit in counseling. They need to bond with the Father in a healthy way and to develop an intimate relationship with Him.

Many will balk at this suggestion because it was their father who abused them. In such cases, patiently read and pray through the Scriptures that reveal that Jesus is the exact representation of the Father: John 10:30,38; 14:10; 17:11,22 and Hebrews 1:3, which show that the Father is as approachable and loving as Christ Himself.

Survivors who feel threatened by men may find it helpful to discuss the fact that the male pronouns we use for God are meant to reflect His headship and authority, not the nature of His being. Jesus declared: *"God is spirit, and His worshipers must worship in spirit and in truth"* (John 4:24; see also 2 Cor. 3:17).

At first, the use of the word "intimacy" may prove a stumbling block as well, so be conscious of that and help survivors separate their sexual abuse from what is meant by "intimacy with the Father." Chapter four should be very helpful to them in accomplishing this.

Some survivors of sexual abuse believe that they are somehow responsible for their abuse. Perhaps they felt pleasure at some point while being abused or simply stopped resisting the attacks, and have concluded that they are therefore guilty before God. Some may have sought out further abuse because they were so needy for any kind of attention that they were willing to suffer sexual abuse to get it. And for others, their abusers told them they were at fault, "you made me do it," and other variations on that theme. It is crucial that all such thoughts be brought to the surface so that it can then be countered by the truth of what God really thinks. The truth is that they were kids who were coerced, manipulated, and taken advantage of by older kids or adults and are therefore not guilty! They need to hear that from their counselor, but most of all, they need to hear it from God. So it is important to take them into prayer to ask the Holy Spirit to speak the truth to them about what God really thinks.

Survivors Need to Acknowledge "Sins of Response"

Survivors need to recognize and acknowledge the areas in their life where they have sinned against God and others as a result of their abuse and repent of those sins.

You see, when we are harmed by others, we sin in response to those actions. We make vows and judgments and plot revenge in our heart against our abusers, and it seems justifiable to do so. And we would be at least partially justified if we had not accepted the mercy and grace of God for our own sins, which puts us on a different footing with God in these matters. To withhold forgiveness from others now is a sin in and of itself. Committing the sin of unforgiveness gives Satan ground in our life to put and keep us in bondage.

If, as a result of our abuse, we have come to believe that we are "damaged goods" and therefore unlovable, it will be difficult for us to acknowledge personal areas of sin because they seem to us to be proof that we are unlovable. To deflect God's call to repentance in such matters, we will use the horror of our abuse to throw up a smokescreen that will keep everyone focused on our victimhood, rather than on the unlovely sins that we may be harboring.

The church often makes the mistake of demanding prematurely that survivors of sexual abuse must forgive the perpetrators. We know that they must forgive, but we often fail to wait for the leading of the Holy Spirit as to the timing for the forgiveness. This is a critical matter because if you force forgiveness before a person is ready, they will not really be forgiving from their heart. Having forced the words from them, you may have convinced them that they have taken care of the matter and can move on, yet deep inside, they know the forgiveness didn't happen. As a result, they may come to see the whole idea as a ridiculous farce.

I remember a speaking engagement many years ago where I was asked by one of the church deacons to tell a young boy who was kneeling at the altar that he must forgive his molester (who just happened to be in the sanctuary at the time). I looked over at the boy. He was squirming with determination not to do it, as his mother stood behind him with arms folded looking just as determined that he was going to stay there until he did. I walked over and stepped in between the mother and her son and knelt down behind him with my hand on his back. And I began to affirm him—telling him that he was loved by God and that he would grow up undamaged from the abuse, that God was proud of him and was going to do wonderful things in his life. Then I got up and walked away.

You see, that boy first needed to know that someone cared about what had happened to him, God included. He needed to know that it had not been God's will and that God would heal him. Had I forced words of forgiveness on him before he received such assurances, it would only have angered him and caused him to believe that no one understood or cared, God included. So we need to listen to the Holy Spirit for the timing in such things. I am certain that by now that boy has sought God for the ability to forgive his perpetrator and has done so.

There will come a day when God will carefully lead every victim into forgiving those who have sinned against him or her, so that His healing power can root out all the darkness. The forgiveness process can take a great deal of time, but it is crucial to complete healing and restoration.

The power of God is more than sufficient for the task. What you need to remember is to focus on Him, to pursue Him, to simply fix your hope and faith on the Father. He will then guide you into whatever else needs to happen. You will be made whole again, in this lifetime, and your life will be made into a trophy of grace, healing, redemption, and the glory of God.

It is easy to misunderstand what forgiveness means. Let's take a look for a moment at what forgiveness is not:

- Forgiveness is *not* saying that what was done to you was okay.
- Forgiveness is *not* releasing the guilty party from the legal or divine consequences of his or her behavior. Those who have hurt you will still stand before God to answer for what they have done in the body (see 2 Thess. 1:6-10; 2 Cor. 5:10). Your forgiveness does not change that.
- Forgiveness is *not* merely words said to satisfy some legal standard. Forgiveness must flow genuinely from the heart.
- Forgiveness is *not* dependent on the perpetrator's response. It doesn't matter whether the person accepts your forgiveness or

laughs in your face and denies everything. If you have forgiven your abuser from your heart, you have pleased God and obeyed His request in full, and great is your reward in heaven! (see Matt. 5:11-12).
- Forgiveness is not something that you have to achieve on your own.

In my own life, God made it vividly clear to me that my ability to forgive was a gift from His heart to mine. One night I was having the most beautiful time worshipping the Lord, and God said to me, "David, why don't we forgive people tonight?" He began to give me vivid images of various people sinning against me and led me through individual prayers of forgiveness for them. He started with the easy ones and then gradually worked His way up to the two men who I hated more than any on this earth—my father, and a man who had molested someone dear to me. I had hated my father for over twenty-five years, and prior to my salvation, I had planned to murder the other man because I hated him so much.

When God brought these two men to mind, I said, "God, You tricked me! You got me forgiving all these easy ones and now You've tacked these two on the end! You know that I will say the words if You ask me to, but You also know that I won't mean them."

The Lord said, "Look at Me!" I looked up in the Spirit and saw Jesus standing in heaven with His arms outstretched. Moving His right hand a little, He said, "What do I have in my hand?"

I replied, "You have forgiveness in your hand, Lord." (Don't ask me how I knew—I just knew.) Then He said to me, "I can forgive your father. Why don't you take forgiveness from My hand and give it to him."

I remember thinking, "What a concept!" So I reached up in the Spirit and took the forgiveness from Jesus' hand and turned to my father and extended my hand toward him saying, "Father, with the capacity of Jesus to forgive, I forgive you." It was amazing. I could *feel* the forgiveness coursing from Jesus' heart into mine, then down my arm and into my father's heart. He had me do the same thing for the man I had almost murdered. It was finished! It had been such a supernatural empowering that I had no doubt that I had finally forgiven the two men. And sure enough, the acid that used to churn inside at the thought of them ceased, and it has never returned. I had forgiven them by and with the power of God Himself to forgive! So I know with a certainty that no matter how impossible it may seem to you to forgive those who have hurt you, God can and will give you that power if you will seek Him for it.

Now that we've examined what forgiveness *is not*, let's look then at what forgiveness *is:*

- Forgiveness *is* taking yourself out of the judgment seat simply because it belongs to God alone. Imagine yourself arriving at the throne room of God Almighty. What do you think you will do? Do you think you might say, "Hey, what a cool throne!" and run and go sit in it? I don't think so. You will probably hit the floor like a dead man, glorying at the sight of God Himself. So if you are not going to sit on God's throne when you get to heaven, why sit in it now? Get off His throne! It is His seat, and He alone is worthy to sit in it.
- Forgiveness *is* acknowledging that having accepted Christ's forgiveness for yourself, you have no right to withhold forgiveness from others (see Matt. 6:12,14-15).
- Forgiveness *is* an act of God's grace being poured out through your heart.
- Forgiveness *is* a result of being transformed into His image, taking on His mind and heart, clothing yourself with Him.
- Forgiveness *is* actually an opportunity to set yourself free from the bondage created by unforgiveness. It is a removal of a significant part of Satan's ground that has allowed him to re-victimize you so as to emotionally destroy you and your relationship with God.
- Forgiveness *is* an act of the will, not a servant of feelings.

In his book, *Passion for Jesus*, Mike Bickle speaks to the issue of letting go of the hurts of the past as part of the process for healing the inner wounds of the heart. He says:

> "An intimate relationship with Jesus can heal any wound of the human heart.
>
> How are the inner wounds of the heart healed? We have to give everything to God, including our bitterness, self-pity, and desire for revenge. Our grief, anger, shame, and pride—even our hopes, dreams, and ambitions—must be laid on God's altar, along with our personal rights and the desire to run our own lives. Jesus Christ must become the focus of our hearts—not our tragedies, our past, or all that might have been. Only Jesus can transform self-pity into praise or tears into triumph. A focus on intimacy with Jesus heals the inner wounds of the heart."

If you are a survivor of child abuse, you have likely developed a self-protective lifestyle over the years. By seeking comfort and healing from the heart of the Father, you will learn to trust again, slowly but surely. You will begin to see the promise of true intimacy as God intended it to be and gain the courage and freedom to step out once again.

God will free you from your self-exile, simply by loving you and exposing you to what is true, about Him, about yourself, and about what your abuse means. He will begin to reweave your garment of self. It will become redemptive and holy cloth, with His image fixed inside. He will remove despair and give hope, all within the simple, obedient acts of worship, praise, and intimate communion.

As you see God for who He really is, the old images will be replaced with the true. Honesty will be released, and your communion with God will deepen. Shame will die, and hope will be born. The fear of passion will gradually wane as it is driven out by this newborn hope.

Study Section— Child Sex Abuse

Statistics from Dr. Patrick Carnes' PBS television program show—*Contrary To Love*:

Half of all pedophile (adult offenders) were victims of child sexual abuse, usually violently; 99% are passive, lonely males; most child sex abusers are under 18; a common mix for child sexual abuse is, neediness/desire for control/preoccupation with sexual desires/a vulnerable victim. 2.2 million men had *female* abusers. One-third of abused boys become abusers; two-thirds do not!

A. **COMMON THEMES FOR THE ABUSER (FIXATIONS)**

1. Corruption of Youth—assuaging their own guilt by corrupting the accusing presence of innocence.

2. Age Obsession—they desire most, children of the age that rejected them.

3. Predatory Influences—to obtain what they could not get in childhood.

4. Sexual Inadequacy—seeking those with little or no sexual experience makes up for their own sense of inadequacy.

5. Control—seeking to exert the control that they did not have when they were kids (and abused).

6. Shock Value—seeking to recreate their own experience of being sexually abused, from the "power" position, making up for the feelings of powerlessness that were born in their own victimization.

7. Rationalizations—e.g., teaching the child "valuable lessons" on sex, and in a kinder way than they had been shown; that other kids

must experience the pain that they did when they were abused; giving kids the "love" that no one else is giving them; etc.

8. Projection of Themselves Onto Others—the thinking goes, "The kid is really like me and really wants me to do this to him (or her) even if he (or she) pretends otherwise."

B. THE MENTAL AND EMOTIONAL DAMAGE OUT OF WHICH THE ABUSER WORKS

1. During childhood, the pedophile somehow lost his/her innocence. According to Leanne Payne, a "cannibal compulsion" causes them to try to bring this lost innocence back into themselves from the person of their victim. They, in effect, try to ingest or cannibalize that trait or part of their victim that symbolizes this neediness.

2. These kinds of people are riddled with judgments, vows, bitterness, guilt, depression, fatalistic mentality and unforgiveness.

    Lynn Heitritter and Jeannette Vought, in their book, *Helping Victims of Sexual Abuse*, (p. 91), list these psychological traits as common to most types of offenders. (Bethany House Publishers, 1989. Used with permission.)

    a. victims of physical or sexual abuse

    b. low self-esteem and deep feelings of inadequacy

    c. sense of alienation or isolation from others

    d. a feeling of being a helpless victim in an overpowering environment

    e. a need for power and control over others to "prove" self-worth

    f. inability to delay immediate gratification of sexual needs

    g. insensitivity to the needs of others

    h. rigid defense system of denial and rationalization

3. Barriers to treatment success—from, *Helping Victims of Sexual Abuse*, (pp. 106-110)

    a. fear of disclosure

    b. dishonest communication

c. shame

   d. resolving guilt

   e. abandoning power

   f. sexual addiction

C. **THE COUNSELING NEEDS OF THE ABUSER**

   In his book, *Challenging the Darkness: Child Sexual Abuse and The Church*, author D. Mitchell Whitman says:

   "Change for the offender involves a complete lifestyle change. He must learn how to cope with feelings, stress and, in general, life. This means a long process of changing thinking patterns, learning new skills, etc. This probably fulfills a higher purpose than taking away the problem" (cf. James 1:2-4).

   In recommending guidelines for pastoral care of the offender, Whitman goes on to list the following ideas:

   1. Surprise or shock is normal, but avoid absolute disbelief of the allegation.

   2. Hold the offender responsible and accountable for his or her behavior.

   3. Show grace and mercy in the context of repentance and accountability. Repentance is demonstrated by:

      a. admits to their sin

      b. agrees to come under the authority of church leadership

      c. willing to go for a sexual offender evaluation

      d. seeks and receives treatment from a skilled therapist or sexual offender treatment program

      e. declines to lay blame on the victim

      f. willing to sign an "exchange of information" release between the leadership and the authorities

      g. demonstrates financial responsibility toward the victim and family with regard to medical care and therapy, etc.

      h. avoids all contact with potential victims

4. Be prepared for denial, minimization, lies, etc. from the offender.

5. Don't minimize what the offender has done.

6. If in doubt, err on the side of believing the victim.

7. Do not support a "not guilty" plea in court from a person who has clearly committed the offense.

8. Get the offender to sign a "release of information" form so that you can find out from the authorities what they know about the case.

9. See that the offender completes a sexual offender evaluation from a recognized treatment specialist.

10. See that the offender goes through a professional sexual offender treatment program.

11. Monitor their progress during the treatment.

12. Don't condemn or reject the repentant offender.

13. Offer spiritual support to the offender through prayer, Bible study, sacraments, counsel and fellowship with other believers.

14. Provide opportunities for confession, prayer, and the receiving of forgiveness for the repentant offender.

15. Offer housing, protection, and other practical support to the non-offending spouse and family.

16. Protect the rights of confidentiality that the victim and their non-offending family members deserve.

17. Work to create a church environment where the offender can experience acceptance and support as they work toward healing.

18. Inform the congregation of the problem and the healing and/or disciplinary processes at the appropriate times.

—from *Challenging the Darkness: Child Sexual Abuse and the Church*, by D. Mitchell Whitman, (pp. 133-139), Copyright 1994, by Mitchell Whitman, Discovery Counseling Resources, P.O. Box 1456, Bellingham, Wa. 98227. Used with permission.)

Paula Sandford also offers some excellent advice for how to minister and counsel someone who has sexually abused a child or adolescent.

—from, *Healing Victims of Sexual Abuse* by Paula Sandford, (pp. 135-136), Victory House Publishers, Tulsa, Ok. 1988. Used with permission.

1. Discovery of the root causes of his problems (Eph. 5:13; Luke 6:43-45).

2. Full confession of his present sin (James 5:16). This should include asking forgiveness from the victim, the family, and others who have been injured by his actions. It should also include a clear message to the victim that he assumes full responsibility for the molestations. She is not the guilty one.

3. Choosing to forgive those who wounded him from childhood on (Mt. 6:15).

4. Repentance for his reaction to those hurts, asking forgiveness for his responses.

5. Assurances of forgiveness (1 John 1:9; John 20:23).

6. Prayers (aloud, with him) for the healing of his own wounded spirit (2 Cor. 1:1-6).

7. Prayers (aloud) for the creation of a new and right spirit within him (Ezek. 36:26; Ps. 51).

8. Prayers (aloud) for the bringing to death of the habit structures in the "old man" (Col. 3; Eph. 4:22 ff; Rom. 8:13).

9. Disciplines to walk in a new way (Rom. 6:11-14; 2 Tim. 1:7).

10. Teaching concerning the laws of God, the sanctity of marriage, the holiness of God, the functions of a father's love, the blessings of self-sacrifice, the meaning of corporateness, etc.

11. Prayers that the Lord will set him free to receive teaching and nurture, that he may grow up inside to a mature man.

12. Discernment on the part of the counselor to determine when the abuser has come to real repentance and is capable of living a new life which produces the fruit of repentance, season after season.

D. The Healing Path for the Survivor

In his excellent book, *The Wounded Heart*, Dr. Dan Allender comments on this path:

"The answer involves a strategy that seems to intensify the problem: peer deeply into the wounded heart. The first great enemy to lasting change is the propensity to turn our eyes away from the wound and pretend things are fine. The work of restoration cannot begin until a problem is fully faced.

The secular path for change seems to involve some form of self-assertion, setting one's own boundaries and choosing to act on the basis of one's own personal value system. Invariably, the result is a stronger, more self-centered humanist, who lives less for the sake of loving others than for his perceived advantage and benefits.

The deepest damage is never what someone has done to me but what I have done regarding the Creator of the universe. The damage done through abuse is awful and heinous, but minor compared to the dynamics that distort the victim's relationship with God and rob her of the joy of loving and being loved by others.

Denial-based forgiveness—To be told, "The past is the past and we are new creatures in Christ, so don't worry about what you can't change," at first relieves the need to face the unsightly reality of the destructive past. After a time, however, the unclaimed pain of the past presses for resolution, and the only solution is to continue to deny. The result is either a sense of deep personal contempt for one's inability to forgive and forget, or a deepened sense of betrayal toward those who desired to silence the pain of the abuse in a way that feels similar to the perpetrator's desire to mute the victim. Hiding the past always involves denial; denial of the past is always a denial of God. To forget your personal history is tantamount to trying to forget yourself and the journey that God has called you to live.

The best path is through the valley of the shadow of death…The journey involves bringing our wounded heart before God…The path involves the risk of putting into words the condition of our inner being and placing those words before God for His response…The obstacle to life is the conviction that God will damage us and destroy us. The problem is that the path does involve His hurting us, but only in order to heal us…What is the enemy to the healing process? In brief, the answer is shame and contempt. The damage of past abuse sets in motion a complex scheme of self-protective defenses that operate largely outside of our awareness, guiding our interactions with others, determining the spouse we select, the jobs we pursue, the theologies we embrace, and the fabric of our entire lives."

—from *The Wounded Heart: Hope for Adult Victims of Childhood Sexual Abuse.* Copyright 1990 by Dr. Dan B. Allender, NavPress, Colorado Springs, CO. Used with permission.

E. **WHAT THE SURVIVOR HAS LOST**

1. Survivors of abuse lose their ability to trust. If you can't trust these people—usually parents, family members or trusted friends of the family—then who can you trust?

2. They lose their self-respect. Victims usually blame themselves in one way or another.

3. They lose their sense of well-being. Rage, anger and hatred have usually been drilled deep into their very souls.

4. They lose their childhood/their innocence.

Dan Allender speaks to the damage of sexual abuse as involving a profound sense of powerlessness and helplessness which create doubt, despair and emotional deadness. The survivor responds to the relentlessness of their painful circumstances by shutting it off through splitting, denial and loss of memory. This, according to Allender, results in the loss of a sense of being intact and alive—a loss of a sense of self. Without the ground of self, the person loses the ability to objectively make judgments and instead lives out of a profound need for self-protection. They live in a shame-based world of perceived unworthiness that often causes them to bring further woe upon themselves through wrong relational choices.

Dr. Allender writes that a survivor of abuse suffers a deep sense of betrayal from those who should have been there to protect them as well as from those who abused them. This results in hypervigilance, suspiciousness, distortion and denial. They lose all hope for real intimacy. They lose hope for justice. And if the very thing that they have despised (the abuse), also brings some degree of pleasure, they enter into a great struggle with ambivalence—feeling two contradictory emotions at the same moment. This creates further confusion, shame and self-hatred which result in chronic patterns of compulsiveness and a fear of pleasure.

F. **WHAT SURVIVORS NEED**

—From IBC 7/91 lecture at University of the Nations, by Mel Hanna. Used with permission.

The needs of those who have suffered the wounds of injustice are:
- Comfort and understanding
- Forgiveness needs to be released
- Assurance of ultimate justice

> "God's judgment is right…God is just: He will pay back trouble to those who trouble you and give relief to you who are troubled…This will happen when the Lord Jesus is revealed from heaven in blazing fire with His powerful angels. He will punish those who do not know God and do not obey the gospel of our Lord Jesus. They will be punished with everlasting destruction and shut out from the presence of the Lord and from the majesty of His power" (2 Thes. 1:5-10). See also Isaiah 61:7-8.

1. Survivors of abuse need to face the hard questions head-on. If they do not, these questions will forever serve as a hook in their jaw that Satan will use to destroy their fellowship with God.

   Why does evil exist?
   - In the book of Job, Satan charged God with coercing or buying Job's faithfulness through blessings—a charge which God defended Himself against (showing that it indeed would have been wrong for Him to have bought Job's obedience).
   - God is therefore limited in the degree to which He can interfere with the free will of man.
   - He has limited Himself in this way, so that man can truly have a free will. God remains sovereign, even though limited, because His limitation is temporary and self-imposed for a greater good. We see a similar self-limitation by God in the kenosis (incarnation) of Christ (cf. Phil. 2:5-11), where God temporarily divested Himself of some of His godly prerogatives in order to come as a man and die for the sins of the world.
   - Free will in man is necessary in order for man to be able to love. Love requires a free will agent in order

to exist. It cannot be coerced or programmed into a being and still be love. *Man has to be able to chose evil for the choice to love to be meaningful.* It must be this way, because God is love, and it is unthinkable that He would have created a world where love could not exist. Such a world would be a place where He could not exist. That world is called "Hell."

- *Why does evil exist? Because, given the choice to do good or to do evil, men with a free will continually choose evil.*
- God also allows this state of affairs to exist so that He can pour out His love and blessings on those who chose good by submitting their lives to the redemptive Lordship of His Son, Jesus.

If God limits Himself from coercing human love and obedience, how is it that sometimes He does interfere in our lives?

- When God acts in our lives, it is because He has been legitimately released to act. When we pray, we are releasing God to act. When we do good, we are releasing Him to act. When we proclaim the gospel, we are releasing Him to act. He can enter into our lives when we open the door for Him to enter. Our free will remains intact in those instances, because He is coming at our invitation.

Does Satan have free reign to bring evil into our lives?

- No. Satan and his demons are also limited from coercing man. They cannot unilaterally do anything to a man. They also must be released to act. They are released to interfere in our lives when we chose evil—when we seek after other gods, when we proclaim evil words, when we perform sinful acts.
- On rare occasions, demons are released to interfere in man when God is using them to test us. (However, God is not of the character to release Satan to test us through evil acts such as child abuse). Note also that when God releases Satan to test us, it is only when we are ready to pass the test (cf. 1 Cor. 10:13). Provided we make the righteous choice during those times of testing, we will always grow and be blessed by them.

Why do the innocent suffer?

- There are no innocent. We are all under a curse as a result of our sin and the sins of our forefathers, which we share in (cf. Ex. 20:5; Num. 14:18; Dt. 7:9; Ezek. 18:14-20; Rom. 5:12, 18-19).
- There is a "corporate" element to good and evil that causes both to spill over into the lives of others. For example, Abraham was told that the world would be blessed through his righteous act (Gen. 12:3). Jesus seemed to indicate a corporate power in Christian prayer and unity when He said, "Where two or three come together in my name, there am I with them" (Mt. 18:20). Similarly, the power of evil in the world, though built up through millennia of sinful generations before us, affects our present day lives. Though we may be an innocent victim in any given incident of abuse, we have become a victim, in part because of this corporate spill-over effect that pollutes the lives of everyone.
- You might also ask, "Why do the unrighteous prosper?" For the same reason—the corporate nature of good. (They also receive blessing because for God to provide the general blessings of life only to the righteous would in effect be coercive in manipulating men's decision for righteousness).

In summary, evil exists because given the choice, men chose evil. Men also are culpable in their failure to release God to act through the means given them. These repeated choices for evil empower and authorize a corporate effect of evil into the world that spills over into the lives of the (relatively) innocent.

2. Survivors of Abuse Need to Bond With the Father.

   a. They need to learn how to trust the Father, even though He may never show them why they went through what they did.

   Stop living out of what you don't know (e.g., "How could God love me and allow such things to happen," etc.) and instead live out of what you do know (e.g., Jesus' horrible torture and death on the Cross for you) the ultimate proof of His love.

This is the life of faith that we are all called to; to see through a glass darkly; to be certain of what we cannot see; to live a life of faith based on what we do know of God's infinite love for us, rather than whatever appearances there may be to the contrary.

"Stop judging by mere appearances, and make a right judgment" (John 7:24).

"For our light and momentary troubles (cf. vv. 8-9: hard pressed, persecuted, struck down) are achieving for us an eternal glory that far outweighs them all" (2 Cor. 4:17).

—Reprinted from *Healing for Damaged Emotions* by David Seamands, Published by Victor Books, 1981, SP Publications, Inc., Wheaton, Il. 60187. Used with permission. (p. 139):

"This does not mean that all of the harmful things we've been describing were God's intentional will for our lives. God is not the *Author* of all events, but He is the *Master* of all events. This means that nothing has ever happened to you that God cannot and will not use for good if you will surrender it into His hands and allow Him to work.

God does not change the actual, factual nature of the evil which occurs. Humanly speaking, nothing can change this; it is still evil, tragic, senseless, and perhaps unjust and absurd. But God can change the *meaning* of it for your total life. God can weave it into the design and purpose of your life, so that it all lies within the circle of His redeeming and recycling activity.

God is the great Alchemist who, if you will let Him, will turn it all into spiritual gold. He is the Master Weaver who can take every damage, every hurt, every crippling infirmity and weave them all into His design—yes, even though their threads were spun by evil, ignorant, and foolish hands!

When you cooperate with the Holy Spirit in this process of deep prayer and inner healing, then God will not only remake and recondition you, He will not only reweave the design, but will also recycle it into a means of serving others. Then you will be able to look at it and say, 'It is the Lord's doing and marvelous in our eyes.'"

    b. They need to develop intimacy with the Father.

    c. They need to learn how to love God based on His demonstrated love for them on the Cross.

3. Survivors of Abuse Need to Get Rid of Self-Judgments Surrounding the Abuse—to be convinced that they are not the guilty party in the abuse and to forgive themselves. They are *never* the guilty party!

4. They need to see and acknowledge the areas in their life where they have sinned against God and others as a result of their abuse and repent of those sins.

—From *Changing on the Inside,* by John White. Published 1991 by Servant Publications, Box 8617, Ann Arbor, Mi. 48107. Used with permission. (pp. 41,49):

"There are things about ourselves and the people in our lives that we dare not face, because at a deep level we are desperately afraid that reality involves not getting the love we need. Facing our buried negative traits means seeing ourselves as less lovable than we had thought. And that kind of awareness brings fear—fear that no one will love us, that we will be alone and rejected."

Dr. Allender comments on this process:

    "Self-discovery, or owning one's feelings, though necessary and legitimate, often becomes focused on the goal of learning more about oneself in order to require others to take into account one's pain. When self-discovery takes place in a truly biblical way (with the focus on how one can better love others), it annihilates any hope of self-justification and intensifies the need for grace. Biblical self-discovery exposes the abused person's wound and rage, loneliness and self-protective isolation. It doesn't stop at reclaiming repressed feelings, but faces the self-serving comfort found in living with a dead soul. The primary purpose in facing victimization is not simply to know how one feels about it, but to expose more clearly the victim's subtle patterns of seeking life and comfort apart from dependence on God.

    The concept of boundaries is legitimate…(However), the objective must be to bless the other person rather than to make sure we are not abused again. We are to draw a boundary in order to better love the one to whom we are relating. We cannot wholeheartedly give if we live in fear of another."

5. Survivors of Abuse Need to be Shown the Love of the Father for Them.

   In his book, *The Wounded Heart,* Dr. Dan Allender proposes a question that we must ask ourselves before the process of healing can ever really begin:

   "Do I believe that God is a loving Father who is committed to my deepest well-being, that He has the right to use everything that is me for whatever purposes He deems best, and that surrendering my will and my life entirely to Him will bring me the deepest joy and fulfillment I can know this side of heaven?"

   a. that God does not blame them.

   b. that even if there was at times, complicity or pleasure experienced at any point during the abuse, that God forgives it fully and completely.

   c. that Jesus wept over the abuse that they suffered.

   d. that allowing people to sin against God and each other is a necessary part to a world where people are free to love. The meaningful existence of any virtue requires the option to behave in opposition to that virtue. Once we have lived in the midst of every option (both evil and good), and have chosen to live in an atmosphere of perfect love (heaven), then the rightness of God keeping us protected from the influence of evil can be established, and "love" can rightly rule alone and unopposed.

6. They Need to Learn How to Turn to God and Receive His Power to Forgive Those Who Have Hurt Them.

   a. Forgiveness is not:

   (1) saying that what was done was okay.

   (2) releasing the guilty party from the legal or divine consequences of their behavior.

   (3) something that you have to achieve on your own.

   (4) merely words said to satisfy some legal standard.

   (5) dependent on the perpetrator's response.

b. Forgiveness is:
   (1) taking yourself out of the judgment seat simply because it belongs to God alone.
   (2) acknowledging that having accepted Christ's forgiveness for yourself, you have no right to withhold forgiveness from others.
   (3) an act of God's grace being poured out through your heart.
   (4) a result of being transformed into His image, taking on His mind and heart, clothing yourself with Him.
   (5) as much an opportunity to set yourself free as it is an opportunity to set the perpetrator free.
   (6) a removal of a significant part of Satan's ground, that has allowed him to re-victimize you over and over again so as to emotionally destroy you and your relationship with God.
   (7) an act of the will, not a servant of feelings.

   In his book, *Passion for Jesus*, (pp. 152-153), Mike Bickle speaks to the issue of letting go of the hurts of the past as part of the process for healing the inner wounds of the heart. He says:

   "An intimate relationship with Jesus can heal any wound of the human heart.

   How are the inner wounds of the heart healed? We have to give everything to God, including our bitterness, self-pity and desire for revenge. Our grief, anger, shame and pride—even our hopes, dreams and ambitions—must be laid on God's altar, along with our personal rights and the desire to run our own lives. Jesus Christ must become the focus of our hearts—not our tragedies, our past or all that might have been. Only Jesus can transform self-pity into praise or tears into triumph. A focus on intimacy with Jesus heals the inner wounds of the heart."

c. Other tips on forgiving:

   (from *The Trilogy Program newsletter*—Nashville, Tn. Used with permission.)

"(The path to forgiveness depends on) the severity of the hurt incurred, the will to forgive, the presence of a mental disorder, age, moral development, and religiosity. Care must be taken when encouraging forgiveness that the trauma is not minimized or denied. Low feelings of self worth and shame that often follow trauma may be increased by encouraging forgiveness too quickly. Clients should not desire to forgive only out of duty, fear, or a desire to avoid facing the trauma. This could complicate the therapeutic process."

G. A Brief Summary of Dr. Dan Allender's Approach to Healing

Dr. Allender's "biblical route to change" involves:

1. Dying to self through the experience of facing the pain and suffering of the wounds of the abuse. This softens us and causes us to place our trust where it belongs.

2. Biblical expression of honesty as the antidote to the practice of denial. Honesty is "the commitment to see reality as it is, without conscious distortion, minimization or spiritualization." It is a forsaking of the false world that the victim constructed to protect him or her self from the pain of the abuse. It begins with a new commitment to prayer, fasting and reading the Bible and continues with pondering, journal writing and sharing with trusted counselors and friends.

3. Regaining memories of past hurts so they can be dealt with constructively.

4. Biblical expression of repentance, which strips away the self-contempt and hatred of others and replaces it with humility, grief and tenderness. "Repentance is an internal shift in our perceived source of life," from self-protection to trust in God and the "supreme call to love." "(It) involves a refusal to be dead, a refusal to mistrust, and a refusal to despise passion." (Passion is "the deep response of the soul to life: the freedom to rejoice and to weep.")

5. Biblical expression of "bold love," through other-centered loving. Love is "the free gift that voluntarily cancels the debt in order to free the debtor to become what he might be if he experiences the joy of restoration." "Bold love is a commitment to do whatever it

takes (apart from sin) to bring health (salvation) to the abuser." It is "a powerful force and energy to reclaim the potential good in another, even at the risk of great sacrifice and loss." It is a canceling of the quest to seek revenge and a commitment to act in the opposite spirit. "What does it look like to love the average abuser? The answer is simple: set boundaries, deepen relationship where appropriate, grin and bear it, and keep moving toward the qualities of the soul that are not lost in the midst of pain and conflict."

H. **"Becomers" Nine-Step Recovery Program—from *Helping Victims of Sexual Abuse*, (pp. 122-123):**

STEP ONE: I recognize that I am powerless to heal the damaged emotions resulting from my sexual abuse, and I look to God for the power to make me whole.

STEP TWO: I acknowledge that God's plan for my life includes victory over the experience of sexual abuse.

STEP THREE: The person who abused me is responsible for the sexual acts committed against me. I will not accept the guilt and shame resulting from those sexual acts.

STEP FOUR: I am looking to God and His Word to find my identity as a worthwhile and loved human being.

STEP FIVE: I am honestly sharing my feelings with God and with at least one other person to help me identify those areas needing cleansing and healing.

STEP SIX: I am accepting responsibility for my responses to being sexually abused.

STEP SEVEN: I am willing to accept God's help in the decision and the process for forgiving myself and those who have offended me.

STEP EIGHT: I am willing to mature in my relationship with God and others.

STEP NINE: I am willing to be used by God as an instrument of healing and restoration in the lives of others.

I. PREVENTION

1. To Engage a Victim, a molester will:
   - talk to them
   - answer their questions
   - give time to them
   - affirm them
   - give them gifts

2. Joe McCutchen lists four things as having made him vulnerable to being molested:
   - No communication with his parents on the subject of sex, made him think that sex was dirty or embarrassing.
   - The molester was a friend, not an enemy. (85% are relatives or close friends).
   - They usually don't hurt the child.
   - He had been taught an undiscriminating respect for his elders, especially spiritual leaders.

3. Mr. McCutchen lists two things that will help prevent a child from being molested:
   - Open up the lines of communication and give them a healthy view of sex.
   - Teach kids the right to say, "No" over their own bodies—body integrity.

Exercises—Child Sex Abuse

1. If you have ever sexually abused a child or adolescent, ask the Lord to give you a true heart of remorse over your sin—what it has done to the victim and what it has done to your life. Confess, repent and receive forgiveness from the Lord for your sins.

2. Spend quality time in "listening prayer," asking God to reveal the underlying feelings and emotions that have motivated your behavior. Ask Him to guide you into changing the diseased elements of your life. Then respond as the Holy Spirit directs.

3. With God's help, find someone you can confess to and who will keep you accountable. Also seek help from a professional sexual offender treatment program, preferably a Christian one. Contact a local Christian counseling organization for the referral.

4. Read Neil Anderson's *Victory Over the Darkness* and *The Bondage Breaker* and practice believing the things that God says about you. Spend copious hours in worship and praise. It is in those moments where you will be transformed into His image.

5. If you are a survivor of sexual abuse seek help from a competent Christian counselor—one who has expertise and proven success in this area. Begin to face the painful memories of your abuse head-on, asking Jesus to come present in those memories to heal the pain and the hurt.

6. Ask the Lord to show you where you sinned in your responses to the abuse so that you can begin to confess and repent of those things. Willingly forsake any formerly justified "rights" to judge, condemn, blame, run from God, or live inwardly in a self-protective mode that precludes a truly loving and giving, other-centered life.

7. Meditate on the sufferings of Jesus and the Cross and ask the Lord to show you the opportunities that you have to share in them redemptively.

8. Immerse yourself in the truths of Scripture concerning your value to God, your purity in His eyes, the love that He has for you, and other facts that you may have found hard to believe. Make a deliberate choice of your will to believe these truths in spite of those past experiences which have created doubts. Ask the Lord to honor your faith by healing and changing your damaged feelings and emotions.

9. Ask the Lord to give you your childhood as you interact with Him. Feel free to run and play with Him and jump into His loving arms during those intimate moments of worship and prayer.

10. Express forgiveness and mercy toward those who have hurt you in whatever ways are appropriate, as the Holy Spirit leads. If necessary, forgive yourself as well. If this seems impossible, turn to God and ask Him to give you His ability to forgive.

Sexual Addiction

Before delving into this subject, I should make a brief comment about my use of the word "addiction." Unfortunately, the word is used in many clinical settings today to imply a lack of moral culpability for someone's actions. Addictive behavior is seen as the consequence of a "disease" that one suffers from rather than as sin that one must turn from. That is not the sense in which I use the term.

Within Christian counseling circles, there is a more balanced view that recognizes the surface immorality as behavior for which the person is morally culpable, while also noting mechanisms within the mind and body that sometimes mitigate that culpability and need to be brought back into normalcy.

I use the word "addiction" because it *can* be properly harmonized with biblical teaching and because it is a word with instant recognition in our culture. People know what I'm referring to when I say "addiction," and that recognition causes many to listen to what I have to say. The more biblical term, "bondage," is less understood and frightening in its connotations, thus causing many people *not* to listen. If I can get people to listen, I can help them see that there is a God of love who wants to set them free rather than judge them and that if they turn their lives over to Him and cooperate with Him, He will.

I am repeatedly asked to define sexual addiction by those who are unsure whether their interest in sex is healthy or unhealthy, often young men and women who are frightened by the intensity of their sex drive and who are concerned that it might be abnormal. To answer their question, I ask them the same kinds of questions that one would ask about any suspected addiction (drugs, alcohol, gambling, shopping, smoking, overeating, etc.), because all addictions have the same basic foundational causes and patterns of behavior.

Dr. Harry W. Schaumburg is one of my favorite Christian writers and counselors in the field of sex addiction. In his book, *False Intimacy*, he defines it this way:

> "Sexual addiction exists when a person practices sexual activity to the point of negatively affecting his or her ability to deal with other aspects of life, becomes involved in other relationships—

whether real or through fantasy—and becomes dependent on sexual experiences as his or her primary source of fulfillment ... regardless of the consequences to health, family, and/or career."

Dr. Schaumburg identifies the evidences that someone is a probable sex addict as ...

- compelling and consuming behavior
- behavior leading to negative consequences
- out-of-control behavior
- denial of the seriousness of the behavior

He says that sexual addiction is: "an avoidance of the pain often caused by real intimacy. In effect, a sex addict creates a pseudo relationship with something or someone who can be controlled, such as a picture, an actor on the video screen, or a prostitute. ... The primary goal of sexually addictive behavior is to avoid relational pain—essentially, to control life."

Dr. Schaumburg believes that the person who is most likely to develop sexual addiction is one who "feels that life isn't fulfilling, who experiences disappointment in intimacy, who loses hope, and who lacks self-confidence" (all quotes from *False Intimacy* by Dr. Harry W. Schaumburg. Used with permission.)

Fear of intimacy is a key issue with sex addicts. They are deathly afraid of it. They have been deeply hurt by it in the past, and perhaps their family environment modeled an attitude of fear of intimacy or punishment and rejection when intimacy was sought. Let me give you a simple example of how a family environment can create a fear of intimacy in a child. Say you're a seven-year-old boy returning home from school and you burst into the house brimming with excitement over something that you did that day. As you begin to deliver your news to your parents with passion, your dad, rather than listening and sharing in your excitement, mocks you for acting like a girl in getting worked up over nothing, and your mom screams at you for interrupting her day and sends you to your room. Their anger and ridicule caught you at a vulnerable moment. You had opened up your deep heart to them and had gotten slammed for it. As a result, it will be very unlikely that you will risk doing that again. Your parents have just instilled in you a fear of being intimate. If that continues to be the ongoing atmosphere in the home, they will quite possibly (albeit unwittingly) be grooming a budding addict—someone who is afraid of genuine intimacy—and someone who will look for ways to express his need for it where there is no risk of humiliation or rejection.

There is one other piece of fallout from the scenario that I painted above. When that little boy experiences humiliation and rejection at every attempt to share his deep heart, particularly if accompanied by painful verbal or physical abuse, he will begin to develop the belief that he is defective, abnormal, unlovable or just plain bad—the core belief that fuels all addictive behavior.

For the sex addict, intimacy, for one reason or another, is not worth taking any chances for. For them, it is better to pretend than to risk the hurt and rejection of attempting true intimacy. The life of a sex addict is usually saturated with a profound sense of unworthiness, disbelief of the idea of being acceptable to anyone on any deep and meaningful level, and a history of attempted compensation through substitution and fantasy.

The pain of believing that they are unlovable or unredeemable drives many people to engage in compulsive behaviors that provide a strong jolt of pleasure so that, for at least a brief while, they can forget that they feel hopeless, lost, or destined for the trash bin of humanity. But the more they are driven to find stronger jolts of pleasure in even more perverted behaviors, the more convinced they become that they are indeed worthless human beings who God could never love and would never redeem.

So you see, although there are sinful behaviors involved in the life of a sex addict, there is more to the picture than just a simple love of sin and pleasure. In our example of the little boy who grew up to be a sex addict, life's traumas play a part, parental dereliction of duty plays a part, the sinful heart of the boy plays a part, and yes, demons play a part. In fact, the demonic realm was probably at work from start to finish—first bringing in sinful patterns (and possibly spirits) from as many as four prior generations; orchestrating the traumas and rejections of the boy's life; implanting thoughts of self-hatred, fear of intimacy and doubt about God's gracious character; providing the objects or persons who tempted him to commit immoral acts; and finally, hounding the boy with thoughts of self-hatred and condemnation every time he gave in to the sinful pleasures that took away his pain.

In short, sex addicts are often people who have been *slapped silly* by life—on multiple levels and in multiple ways. This does not excuse their sinful behavior, but it helps explain how they ended up in such a trap and what needs to be healed in order for them to get free. According to Dr. Patrick Carnes, (perhaps the country's leading expert on sexual addiction), 97 percent of sex addicts have been emotionally abused and 81 percent have been sexually abused.

A "Sin" That Operates as a "Disease"

Lest we get too preoccupied with the clinical side of the issue and thus distracted from the need for repentance, let's take a closer look at the sin aspect of this condition.

Sexual addiction involves more than just *misguided* subterranean emotional responses, as the addiction-as-disease-only camp would have us believe. While sin is clearly involved on the surface of the matter (namely, sexual immorality), it is involved on a more insidious level as well. Deep in the heart of man lies the real mother lode of evil that fuels and motivates the behavior.

The ironic thing is that the sexual addict uses what God intended as a primary means of intimacy (sexual relations) to achieve just the opposite. This grotesque twisting of what He created is a manifestation of an inner rebellion and anger against God that lingers within the heart of the sex addict. And so, the sex addict will depersonalize the object of their lust and use sex in a *flight* from intimacy rather than as a *means* of intimacy. That is why the sex must be illicit. A great rebellion against God and the created order of things is going on within the psyche of the person.

Of this phenomenon, Dr. Harry Schaumburg writes this (italics mine):

> "Sexual addiction is not a disease over which the sex addict has no control. Sex addicts make significant choices and must be held accountable for those choices. Also, treating sexual addiction as a disease easily leads us to treat the sex addict's behaviors instead of the sin that causes the behaviors.
>
> Only God can help a person overcome sin. Treatment programs can influence a person to stop committing certain sexual acts, but the programs can't address the root cause of those behaviors without bringing the power of Christ to bear on the issues of the heart.
>
> *Sexual addiction primarily stems from the sinfulness of the human heart and a reluctance to be in a passionate, dependent relationship with God.* ... The essence of sin is autonomy from God, a failure to be dependent on Him. Sex addicts' ... refusal to cling to God as the only Person who can fill their deepest longings and ease relational pain did not originate in a shame-based family but in their shameful, deceitful heart. All of us have such a heart ...
>
> When we sin in our hearts toward Him, refusing to be dependent on Him, He gives us over to the control of the sinful things we prefer more than Himself. When God gives us over, He turns us over to the darkness of our hearts, which creates deeper darkness ... *Sexually addictive behaviors are not as dark as the internal commitment to serve self. ... A sex addict truly changes when his or her relationship with God changes."*

And so what we have is a fallen human being who responds to the struggles of life with inner judgments against God, causing a darkened heart with its repeated choices to engage in willful, defiant sin, which invites demonic deception, creating a bondage that then renders the person obsessed and out-of-control. Before it's over, the person is doing things they don't even want to be doing, compelled by the demonic powers that now lead them around by the nose.

We saw this same progression in Chapter Six as we examined how in Romans 1:18-32, the Bible describes those people who decide to worship the creature rather than the Creator and how they are finally given over to their lovers by God Himself. Ezekiel 23 describes this same fate, where God hands people over to their lovers (verses 9, 24c, and 35), and it is those lovers or idols who inflict the deserved punishment (seen also in Ezek. 16:39). God has not permanently forsaken them, but has left them to their own choices, so that they can see the dire consequences of their own decisions and return to Him in repentance.

My life was very much like this. I had what was for me an intensely stressful childhood, for which I blamed God and thereby justified sinful choices. In my anger, I concluded that God either didn't care, or that He didn't exist. If He didn't care, I was determined to make Him sorry for not loving me by sinning mightily against Him. If He didn't exist, I was determined to express my rage over having been told He *did* exist by living a life that trusted no one and by doing whatever it took in terms of pleasure seeking to forget the pain of my existence.

What I ended up doing as I chose to sin repeatedly was to give Satan vast stretches of ground within me to deceive me and to bring me into bondage. Before it was over, I was so out of control that I was willingly walking into situations where I knew my life was at risk, hoping that someone would finally take it for me. I was what the world would call a first class addict, but my "disease" was in truth the aftermath of my own sin.

Yes, my brain chemistry was all messed up, and yes I had suffered much trauma in my life, and yes, I was filled with self-hatred in part because of the actions of others, but I had arrived at the condition that I was in through my own immoral decisions. At every step of the way, I could have humbly turned to God instead for His way of escape. Instead I chose to judge Him and to hate Him and to rebel against Him (even while pretending to love Jesus). I gave Him no choice but to let me suffer the consequences of my own choices, and He allowed Satan to put me in bondage. This is why I say that sexual addiction is a sin that operates as a disease.

Multiple Dynamics at Work

As we've already noted, all sex addicts judge themselves to be incomplete or inadequate. They believe that they are bad people. After committing a sin, rather than thinking, *"I've done a bad thing,"* they will instead say to themselves, *"I am the bad thing."*

In believing this, they put themselves in an impossible position in relation to God the Father. A child naturally turns to look at its father for approval and to see how to act. He *wants* to be like his father. An addict, (with his negative, condemning self-judgments), believes that his heavenly Father hates him, despises him, or at the very least is disappointed in him. He believes that God is angry and is poised in heaven, whip in hand, ready to crack him over the head the next chance He gets! With such a negative image of the Father, a sex addict *doesn't want* to turn to the Father to be shown how to act because he fully expects judgment. Therefore, he never turns to the only person who can help him and who can model for him what it means to be a man (or woman).

The Bible reveals this connection between fear and punishment. Echoing the thought expressed in James 2:13b, "Mercy triumphs over judgment!" 1 John 4:18 tells us, "There is no fear in love. But perfect love drives out fear, *because fear has to do with punishment. The one who fears is not made perfect in love*" (my italics). And so, the one who has a fear of God's punishment is the person who has not yet come to realize that God is love (see 1 John 4:16b) and that since His Son has already paid the penalty for the sins of those who would believe and follow Him, God would rather show mercy than punish the sinner. He does not stand in heaven with a whip. He stands with arms outstretched even to the vilest sinner, saying, "Just come to Me through My Son Jesus Christ, and I will cleanse you and forgive you and put My Spirit within you to move you to follow My laws" (see Ezek. 36:25-27).

Even so, since most sex addicts are so thoroughly convinced that they are unredeemable, some of them will use sex to *confirm their own self-judgments*. Almost as a way of pushing the God who they believe is going to hurt them farther away, they commit even greater and more perverse acts of sexual immorality as a way of proving and confirming their own unworthiness. Their self-talk says, "I am bad, so I will act according to my nature." And so we see that the impulse to form an identity in this world is so great that some people will adopt a highly negative identity rather than living with no identity at all.

Others will use sex to try to *create a sense of worthiness*. The thought of identifying themselves as a bad or worthless human being is so abhorrent that they leap from one sexual conquest to the next, trying to prove to themselves that since so many people want them, they must be worthwhile after all. Their self-talk goes, "I will use sex to prove that I am wanted and worth the attention of others." Unfortunately, the behavior they employ as a cure for their lack of self-worth becomes the very evidence against them that reconfirms their own feelings of failure.

Dr. Schaumburg writes, "Sex addicts need the security of false intimacy, danger, and anonymity that illicit sexual activity provides. They use it to sustain the illusion that they are accepted."

There are other dynamics at work as well. For example, there is always a neurochemical component. Irregular synaptic patterns are often found in the brains of addictive personalities. Imbalances of chemicals like serotonin that provide a sense of well-being also contribute to the impulse to seek out a substance or behavior that will make one feel better. What is not known, however, is whether those conditions precede the initial behavior or the behavior generates the brain irregularities that then precipitate further dysfunctional behavior. As we saw in chapter six, it has been scientifically proven that behavior can directly cause physical changes in brain structures. We also concluded, however, that God has provided a way of escape for any situation, whether it has its genesis in circumstances beyond a person's control (even physical abnormalities) or in willful rebellion.

I have personally experienced how a change in belief system and behavior results in a healing of physical brain irregularities. At the point when I gave my life to Christ, I had been living with deep clinical depression for so long that my history was strewn with suicide attempts and habitual, death-defying, reckless behavior. However, as I began believing the Scriptures rather than my own wisdom and changed my behavior to match the will of God, my lifelong severe depression went away. Whatever irregular synaptic patterns or chemical imbalances that I had simply corrected themselves in response to my change of belief and behavior.

It is critical that we seek God's power and direction for change rather than trying to overcome our bondage on our own. If we are strong-willed enough, we may be able to overcome one behavior or another, but if we don't address what is going on inside that has caused us to seek pleasure in order to mask pain, we will find ourselves trading one addiction for another. Indeed, addictions are interchangeable. Unless the root source has been dealt with, stopping one simply increases another.

As we have previously noted, most addictions have their genesis in early childhood trauma, where self-esteem and self-worth have been significantly compromised. Let's examine at that connection a bit further because it is a key to finding freedom.

Your parents, or significant others, tell you who you are by the way they treat you and the things they say to you during your childhood. Often, a negative self-image is branded into the heart of a young child through verbal, physical, or sexual abuse or neglect. The child literally adopts the opinions of significant others as to who he or she is.

After the child develops a belief about himself or herself (self-image) in response to the "name" they've been given through the opinions and treatment of his or her parents or guardians and the consensus of others (which is reflected in hundreds of interpersonal interactions over the years), the child then behaves according to this belief and thereby seals the judgments of others.

If this "self-image" (belief system) is negative, the child will inevitably develop inner convictions about how unfair it is to have been made that way, or to have been born into a situation that brought so much rejection and pain. They will have feelings of abandonment and of anger over having been given such a lot in life and may form judgments against God, mom and dad, and others who don't seem to be as "defective." The longing to be like someone else often develops into full blown "idolatry" as the person tries to find some sense of completion in being accepted by those who seem to have it all together.

These sins of anger, judgment, criticism, idolatry, covetousness and dishonoring of parents create the ground for demonic strongholds to develop. The naturally inherited autonomy of free will that everyone is given at birth becomes compromised through sins, which empower the manipulation of the enemy. Again, this is the process by which "sin" takes on the characteristics of "disease."

This perception of being inherently bad or defective creates an obsession with self. Sexual addicts are often narcissistic or in some other way hooked into unhealthy, habitual introspection. Their biggest battle is turning from a focus on "self" to a focus on God. This focus on self often breeds an unyielding faith in intellectual understanding as the path out of addiction. Many sex addicts, having blamed God or someone else for their condition, have an unspoken *demand* for intellectual understanding, (as we noted in chapter nine is true of some victims of sexual abuse). They often run from book to book to seminar to seminar, without ever coming to a knowledge of the truth because the truth requires intimacy with the God that they are angry with, and a life of faith through the abandonment of self.

This idolatry of the intellect is primarily a disease found in western culture, about which Malcolm Muggeridge once commented, "We have educated ourselves into imbecility." It is a product of western rationalism, which is the philosophy that emerged from the modernism of the nineteenth century that claimed that man does not need a supernatural revelation from God because he has the capacity to discover truth on his own. In Isaiah 29:14 and 1 Corinthians 1:18-31, God warned us about this form of idolatry, which has as its ultimate end, blind foolishness.

Jesus spoke to this "idolatry of the mind" when He said to the Pharisees of His day: "You diligently study the Scriptures because you think that by them you possess eternal life. These are the Scriptures that testify about me, yet you refuse to come to me to have life" (John 5:39-40).

In addition to suffering from spiritual and intellectual blindness, many sex addicts are addicted to the *thrill* of the out-of-control life that they have been leading. It gives them a "high," and they prefer that high to the humdrum of normal life. They like the thrill of illicit sex. In all honesty, they like it more than they like the Lord.

On still another level, sex addicts are in search of love and acceptance, and like the homosexual, for one reason or another, they have been equating sex with love. To their way of thinking, *false* intimacy is better than *no* intimacy at all; and *pretending* to be loved is better than having to deal with the thought of being consigned to a destiny of *never* being loved.

Can you see what incredible power there is in a lie? It is like the rudder of a ship that controls the entire direction of the vessel.

The sad reality is that sex addicts act the way they do, in large part, because they don't have a clue what love is. And they don't know love because they don't know God. Even though many populate our churches, they have not yet come to know Him, deeply and experientially. The Bible teaches that it is in pursuing that level of *knowing,* (i.e., intimacy), that they will *find everything that they need* to live and to walk in holiness. "His divine power has given us everything we need for life and godliness through our *knowledge* of him who called us by his own glory and goodness" (2 Pet. 1:3, emphasis added).

Sexual addiction involves ritual—in ways not unlike the rituals of a witch doctor, with his ritual beliefs, his dance, his rattle, his chants, his gestures and his potions. For the sex addict, there are certain ritual beliefs that provide the foundation for what they do. There are certain times of the day when they are more likely to "act out." There are certain "triggers" that set them off, such as rejection, stress, criticism or ridicule. There are ritual objects that are used, such as pornography, mirrors, pillows, certain pieces of clothing, etc. There are also certain rooms in the house, places in the city or situations of being alone or on the computer that bring on the compulsion to act out. Their past behavior has actually dug grooves in the brain so that when any of these ritual objects or situations appears, the brain instantly channels the signals toward the familiar responses.

When sex addicts truly repent and begin to develop an intimate relationship with God, the Holy Spirit will begin to identify for them what their ritual places, objects or situations are and help them to establish new channels of belief and behavior in the mind.

Many will engage in obsessive sex to the point of injury (with masturbation, 45 percent of males and 33 percent of females, according to Dr. Patrick Carnes). This happens because sex leaves them feeling empty or bad and they express that frustration in frenzied, self-destructive behavior. The public expression of their sex life is in danger of becoming dangerous and highly secretive. If gone unchecked, their sickness can manifests itself in prostitution, multiple affairs, multiple partners, pornography, compulsive masturbation, exhibitionism, voyeurism, nymphomania, satyriasis, incest, child sexual abuse, homosexuality, bestiality, rape, sadism, masochism, etc. Many sex addicts will eventually involve themselves in several, if not many, of these behaviors in a rapidly escalating descent toward animal regression.

There are inevitably deep waters of *hopelessness* concerning repeated failures to overcome such an addiction. Some develop a toxic, *learned* hopelessness and helplessness. They take everything personally. They see everything as having pervasive power over them. They believe that they are destined to be permanent victims.

Many sex addicts operate out of a "shame-based" emotional framework.

Phrases such as, "I have no right to feel this way" or "I should" or "I ought" dominate such a person's language and often indicate a shame-based personality. These are "people pleasers" who believe they must earn love. When they first encounter unconditional love, they cannot accept it. Gradually, however, with God's help, there comes a dawning of a new self-image, and healing can occur. For healing, four fundamentals are required: (1) healthy relationships in the church where God's love is expressed in response to the revelations of the sex addict's sin, (2) a conscious decision of the sex addict to reform long-held, faulty beliefs about God, others and himself, (3) a willingness in the sex addict to surrender humbly to God, to depend on Him in faith, and (4) the sex addict's willing prayers for God's loving touch.

Healing for the Sex Addict—The Rebuilding of The Spiritual House

As I sought God for deliverance from my own struggle with sexual addiction, one of the most important things that He taught me was to lay the proper foundation—*the Cross*. He literally spoke to me and told me to seek Him for more revelation about what went on at Calvary. He instructed me to go into my room and to meditate on the crucifixion accounts in the four Gospels and to ask Him to deepen my understanding of what had taken place. So for several weeks thereafter, I spent my daily time with the Lord reading the story of Christ's death and resurrection, waiting for God to give me a more profound revelation of Christ's work on the Cross. It was during that time that He gave me the experience that I related in chapter two—of feeling the pain of the Father. But that was not all that He showed me. One evening, He took me to the following Scripture:

The Lord said to Moses, "Make a snake and put it up on a pole; anyone who is bitten can look at it and live." So Moses made a bronze snake and put it up on a pole. Then when anyone was bitten by a snake and looked at the bronze snake, he lived. (Num. 21:8-9)

As I read that Scripture, I saw for the first time how Jesus was prefigured in the Old Testament as the serpent itself, the very epitome of symbolic evil. Jesus became evil itself on the Cross—every hideous and detestable thing ever devised and carried out by man or demon. "God made him who had no sin *to be sin for us"* (2 Cor. 5:21) and "Just as Moses lifted up the snake in the desert, so the Son of Man must be lifted up, that everyone who believes in him may have eternal life (see John 3:14-15).

That is a picture of the continuous provision of grace that God has provided through the death of His Son Jesus. Whenever we have been bitten by the snake (evil, sin) we need only look to Jesus and His sacrifice on the

Cross. He became sin on our behalf—so that we might be healed (the Greek word for "healed" also means "saved"), from the consequences of our deadly sin, and live!

This provision of grace, during this dispensation of grace, gives hope for those who have sinned to the point where they believe they are hopeless, and wrests from Satan one of his most effective tools of bondage—condemnation.

> *This is what the Lord says: "Your wound is incurable, your injury beyond healing . . . But I will restore you to health and heal your wounds," declares the Lord, "because you are called an outcast [one] for whom no one cares."*
> *(Jer. 30:12,17)*

It is critical that you do whatever it takes to intensify your dependence on God. Become intimate with Him through worship, praise, Bible reading, serving others and fellowship at church. Spend a lot of time alone with the Lord, listening to Him, and receiving His health and wholeness into your emotional self. It is your inheritance.

Over a quarter of a century ago, God set me free from 20 years of uncontrollable sexual addiction. If you were to ask me to put in the simplest terms possible what God has done for me in the moments of deep intimacy that I have shared with Him, I would tell you that through direct experience of His person and His kingdom, God has awakened me from the death-sleep of my fantasy world and brought me into the world of reality. He has shown me what He is *really* like; He has shown me what *really* motivated my actions; and He has shown me what the purpose of my life *really* is.

The Bible calls this kind of relationship with God, an abiding relationship. So abide in Him. As you live in an *"abiding"* relationship with God, He will keep you from falling.

Blame, Forgiveness, and Feelings

However, we do not look back into our past in order to fix blame on others, but so as to discover where we have *already fixed* blame, so that those vows and judgments can be repented of and the people forgiven and released. Forgiveness is so very critical to the healing process because:

- when we accepted the forgiveness of God for our sins, we relinquished any rights to hold sins against another (see Matt. 18:23-35);
- because judgment is reserved for God alone and it is a grave sin for us to presume on His office (see Ps. 75:7); and
- because if we do not forgive our fellow man, God will not forgive us (see Matt. 6:14-15).

Develop, *through practice,* new thought patterns and belief systems. Remember how you get to Carnegie Hall? *Practice, practice, practice!* So tear down the strongholds of wrong thinking. Throw down the gauntlet against unhealthy imagining. In essence, you are choosing to live by faith, not by sight.

It is crucial that you grow in your facility to live by faith, rather than by feelings. As I mentioned in chapter 3, this is an epidemic problem in our culture and has been ever since the 1960s when the philosophy of "go with your feelings" became entrenched. It was taught that subjective feelings were the mirrors of truth rather than objective revelation from God's Word. Today our entire culture believes this, so a deliberate choice needs to be made to forsake this tyranny of feelings and to live by every word that comes from the mouth of God instead (see Matt. 4:4).

Ask God to train you in forsaking the "idolatry of feelings" and in making Him the sole God of your idolatry. This is not to suggest that you deny or suppress feelings, but that you learn to discern those feelings that reflect truth from those that reflect fantasy, and respond accordingly.

Your commitment to truth and honesty before God is imperative. Go back and read again the story that I told in chapter 2 about how God responded to my outburst of anger at Him one night with a wave of love, and then told me that He had done so because I had finally come to the place of total honesty with Him—a place where He could finally help me. No matter what it is, tell Him! Completely disclose your innermost thoughts and feelings to Him. Only then can He really help you.

Reread also the story that I told in the chapter called, "Living by Grace," when God told me to stop all lying. As you'll recall, when I obeyed Him, the pressure to return to my sexually addictive behaviors diminished considerably. As it turned out, my openness to lying whenever it seemed convenient had left an open door for Satan to sorely tempt me to dark sins because they were built upon a foundation of lies. Thus, my newfound and more complete commitment to truth dramatically empowered my commitment to sexual purity.

One of Satan's greatest strongholds in people is the view of God that he has helped them to develop. Since the devil is the father of lies (see John 8:44), this view needs serious correcting. So, by an act of the will, you need to choose to believe that God is perfect and loving and flawlessly good, no matter what your thoughts or feelings are to the contrary. He has already proven this on the Cross! Challenge any and all contrary thoughts with your new belief system and with the Word of God, which I called "Truth Therapy" in the "Study Section-Foundations"chapter. Allow the following Scripture to empower your mind with faith: "The weapons we fight with . . . have divine power to demolish strongholds. We demolish arguments and every pretension that sets itself up against the knowledge of God, and we take captive every thought to make it obedient to Christ" (2 Cor. 10:4-5).

Deal with any anger that you may have toward God. Switch from a presumption of guilt to a presumption of innocence when dealing with unanswered questions about why God would or would not do something.

As for other kinds of deception, when thoughts or feelings come that tell you that you've gone too far, or are too bad, or are the exception to God's unconditional love and grace, you must call them "lies" and refuse to entertain them further. You can aggressively respond to such temptations of unbelief with the Word of God and declarative prayer, or sometimes you can put them away simply by ignoring them.

In addition to correcting your view of God, another critical area to address in the healing of sexual bondage is to correct the view that you have of yourself. As one who has thrown him or herself on the mercy of Christ for salvation from your sins and who names Him as your Lord and Savior, you are now a new creation—no longer a bad person, irrespective of your behavior (past, present or future) because you have taken on the merits of Christ and are judged by His merits, not your own. You must decide whether God is lying or telling the truth when He declares these things to those who are in Christ, and choose to act accordingly.

You have a purpose that *will* bring glory to God—a purpose that has not been ruined by your sin, but one which God has the power to resurrect and fulfill through you. It is God's glory to rescue the most depraved of souls and to empower them for holiness and purity as a public statement of His own mercy and might.

Another view that needs to be corrected in the life of most sex addicts is their view of the Christian life. Essentially, their view needs to change from being one of *betterment through legalism* to one of *transformation through grace*. Since the power of God has fulfilled the requirements of the law through the Cross, we are now able to live according to the *spirit* and *principles* that are behind the law rather than the surface *letter*. As we are transformed into His image, we are taking on His mind, His heart and His values. Consequently, our obedience is no longer motivated by the fear of punishment and a focus on the letter, but rather from an understanding of the spirit of the law and an inner delight in keeping it. With our new transformed will, we move in unity with God's very mind and character. In dying to the letter and coming alive to the spirit, we are putting to death that insidious foe called "performance orientation."

As we experience the glorious, unconditional love and mercy of our Father, we begin to *want* to serve Him faithfully. We no longer rebel against the learning of discipline because we have discovered that the God who wants to teach it to us does not operate out of selfishness, manipulation, and control. We've dropped our defensive posture toward Him because we've found out that we do not need to protect ourselves from Him. We have become fully persuaded that His requests of us are always and only for our benefit and the glory of the Son, whom we love. Therefore, we have begun to embrace them enthusiastically and without fear.

One important element in the transformation process is the discovery that we need to have close relationships with other Christians who are strong in the faith—mature believers who will keep us accountable in our walk with the Lord. Old lying thought patterns and belief systems can sneak back up on us in times of discouragement and temptation and a brother nearby who can speak the word of truth into our spirit can be an invaluable resource.

Find a confidant (carefully) with whom you can share your problem and have ongoing prayer and dialogue. Find a Christian support group or ministry with the same focus and avail yourself of its counsel and resources. Read the literature in the field and attend conferences where both teaching and ministry take place. Regularly attend home fellowship, men's or women's fellowship groups, so as to receive the benefit of the life of Christ's body. As the Bible says: "Confess your sins to one another and pray for one another so that you may be healed" (Jas. 5:16b, NASB).

The Christian life is one of *selflessness* rather than selfishness; forsaking the world system and the things that are a part of it; taking up your cross daily; suffering persecution when necessary; a life centered on eternity rather than this finite world; and a life of living with the single-minded goal of bringing glory and honor to the One who died for you, simply because you love Him. Love is what aligns one's mind and heart to the proper "eternal perspective" that brings honor to Jesus Christ. More than anything else, sexual addicts must get their eyes off themselves and onto God. Ask God to train you in moving from a self-focused life into a God-focused life.

Also ask the Lord to reveal any generational or other curses that may have come upon you. If they exist, you must pray that they be broken by the power of the blood of Jesus. Most people are aware that the sins of the fathers are passed down to the children through the third and fourth generation (see Exod. 20:5-6). But what most of us don't know is that this passing down of the sin of one generation to another can be stopped by the free will choice of any generation who chooses to follow the Lord instead. In that generation, God will eliminate the curse (see Ezek. 18:14,17-20). Make such a commitment in prayer together with other mature believers as witnesses and co-warriors in the Spirit.

In a similar vein, get prayer for the "soul ties" that you created with various people through your sexually immoral acts. The idea of a "soul tie" can be found in 1 Corinthians 6:16-17, which contains a direct reference to the "one flesh" union referred to in Genesis 2:24. That unseen "one flesh" connection needs to be severed by a renunciation of the immoral acts that created it and a solemn commitment to discontinue any relationship with those who were involved. If you cannot remember everyone with whom you had immoral sexual relations, pray a general prayer of severance and renunciation for them. In my experience, God will bring to memory those who are particularly important to renounce and will give a general absolution for those long forgotten.

Attention will need to be given to other demonic strongholds as well. I have spoken at length about this in the chapter called "Root Sources," but let me say again: Do not go on a perpetual demon hunt, but do not ignore the subject either. At any point along the way, if you suspect a demonic element behind a problem, ask God to expose that for you so that you can renounce it. If you are a believer, you have the authority to cast demons out in the name of Jesus Christ, but be cautious so that you do not enter into a level of spiritual warfare that you are not yet mature enough to handle. This is where others in the body of Christ can be very helpful.

Keep in mind that demonic strongholds primarily consist of webs of lies. If the lies behind the bondage can be uncovered and renounced, and the sins surrounding them truly repented of, that will break the power of the stronghold. The demon will leave on its own because it no longer has ground to stay. As St. Francis de Sales once said, "All the temptations of Hell do not stain the soul who does not love them."

In my own personal healing process, God led me into a life of nightly worship and praise as an act of spiritual warfare. I so saturated my mind and heart (and the airwaves of my house) with praise and worship, that the demonic powers that still held ground in me left on their own. They couldn't stand the relentless praise of God and took off! (I suspect that another reason for their departure was that as I sang those words of praise, I began to believe them instead of previous lies that I had held to, and that the demonic powers that left had depended on my believing those lies).

Other demonic strongholds in my life did not leave so easily and required spiritual warfare prayers from the body of Christ, with words of wisdom and knowledge exposing the hidden lies that kept them in power. Whatever it takes, and however many times it takes, God will lead you through it all if you remain or abide in an intimate relationship with Him.

As you seek God for deliverance from your bondage to sexual immorality, ask God to reveal the "triggers" that the enemy uses to set off a fall into sin (memories, relationships, criticisms, rejections, failures, loneliness, lies, habits, objects, times, places, etc.), and set your heart and will to do whatever God directs you to do in relation to them. If you can change or eliminate these ritual elements, the power of the addictive cycle can be greatly diminished.

In order for the sex addict to be healed, he or she must discover the source of the pain, with the help of the Holy Spirit, and resolve the issues that surface. In essence, the addict must embrace the pain in order to heal it. The addict has to stop hiding from the things that hurt, and he or she must stop concealing them from those who can help.

The game of pretense has got to end. The sex addict must become vulnerable and tell people that he is hurting. In that regard, it is very important for him to find a situation where he is free to express his hurts and needs without fear of rejection or judgment. That kind of atmosphere is critical to the healing process. Should the addict live in a place where those kinds of people are not to be found, he must all the more intensify his dependence on God and seek His intervention for mental and emotional healing.

Sexual addiction involves relational sins. Much of the process for healing will be the reconciliation and/or resolution of those relationships that have been so debilitating. The sex addict must be prepared to do whatever God directs him to do during worship and prayer or in session with a qualified Christian counselor. That may involve confronting personal impasses or even forgiving others for horrible crimes against childhood innocence.

Healing for the sexual addict also involves a coming to terms with the sinful rebellion that lies deep within and that fuels the sinful behavior. The sex addict is in some way angry with God and has placed unspoken demands on Him for fulfillment, relief, or intellectual satisfaction concerning one or more unanswered questions of life. As a result, he is in a flight from the very intimacy with His Creator that will heal him—a flight that drives him to turn and destroy the image of God in others through depersonalized, idolatrous sex.

As sex addicts deepen their relationship with Jesus Christ, God will show them just how completely they are loved and accepted by Him; how beautiful and perfect they are in His eyes; and how Christ can more fully meet every need that they have.

Study Section— Sexual Addiction

A. What is Sexual Addiction, and How Does it Operate?

1. A Definition:

    In his book, *False Intimacy*, Dr. Harry Schaumburg defines it thusly:

    > "Sexual addiction exists when a person practices sexual activity to the point of negatively affecting his or her ability to deal with other aspects of life, becomes involved in other relationships—whether real or through fantasy—and becomes dependent on sexual experiences as his or her primary source of fulfillment…regardless of the consequences to health, family, and/or career."

    (*False Intimacy* Copyright 1992 by Dr. Harry W. Schaumburg NavPress, Colorado Springs, Co. Used with permission.)

    Dr. Schaumburg describes the evidences of sexual addiction as:
    - Compelling and consuming behavior
    - Behavior leading to negative consequences
    - Out-of-control behavior
    - Denial of the behavior's seriousness

    He says that sexual addiction is: "an avoidance of the pain often caused by real intimacy. In effect, a sex addict creates a pseudo relationship with something or someone who can be controlled, such as a picture, an actor on the video screen, or a prostitute…The primary goal of sexually addictive behavior is to avoid relational pain—essentially, to control life."

    Dr. Schaumburg believes that the person who is most likely to develop sexual addiction is one who "feels that life isn't fulfilling, who experiences disappointment in intimacy, who loses hope, and who lacks self-confidence."

2. Fear of intimacy is a key issue with sexual addicts.

   They are deathly afraid of it. They have been deeply hurt by it in the past, or perhaps their family environment modeled an attitude of fear of intimacy or punishment and rejection if tried. Intimacy, for one reason or another, is a chance not worth taking in their eyes. For them, it is better just to pretend than to risk the hurt and rejection of attempts at true intimacy. In the life of a sex addict, you will probably be able to uncover a life saturated with a profound sense of unworthiness, unbelief at the thought of being acceptable to anyone on any deep and meaningful level, and a history of attempted compensation through substitution and fantasy.

   On a recent talk show, Christian psychologist, Dr. Lynne Logan named six things as barriers to relational intimacy:

   (1) low self-esteem
   (2) unhealed emotional wounds
   (3) fear of love
   (4) fear of abandonment
   (5) unrealistic expectations
   (6) hidden anger

   She went on to list three things that must be developed in a person's life in order for this fear of intimacy to be resolved:

   (1) trust
   (2) commitment
   (3) communication

3. A "Sin" that operates as a "Disease."

   Sexual addiction involves more than just *misguided* subterranean emotional responses, as the "addiction as disease only" camp would have you believe. While sin is clearly involved on the surface of the matter (e.g., sexual immorality), it is involved on a more insidious level as well. Deep in the heart of man lies the real mother lode of evil that fuels and motivates the behavior.

   The ironic thing is that the sexual addict uses what God intended as a primary means of intimacy (sexual relations) to achieve just the opposite. This grotesque twisting of what He created is a manifestation of an inner rebellion and anger against God that lingers within the heart of the sex addict. And so, the sex addict will depersonalize the object of their lust and use sex in a flight from intimacy rather than as a means of intimacy. That is why the sex must be illicit. It is part of a great rebellion against God and the created order of things that is going on within the psyche of the person.

St. Frances de Sales once said, "All the temptations of Hell do not stain the soul who does not love them."

Of this phenomenon, Dr. Harry Schaumburg says:

> "Sexual addiction is not a disease over which the sex addict has no control. Sex addicts make significant choices and must be held accountable for those choices. Also, treating sexual addiction as a disease easily leads us to treat the sex addict's behaviors instead of the sin that causes the behaviors.
>
> Only God can help a person overcome sin. Treatment programs can influence a person to stop committing certain sexual acts, but the programs can't address the root cause of those behaviors without bringing the power of Christ to bear on the issues of the heart.
>
> Sexual addiction primarily stems from the sinfulness of the human heart and a reluctance to be in a passionate, dependent relationship with God.
>
> It is a self-centered energy that demands the right to avoid pain and experience self-fulfillment.
>
> It is a by-product of loneliness, pain, the self-centered demand to be loved and accepted regardless of the consequences, and a loss of a vital relationship with God.
>
> It is a by-product of intense, unmet needs, coupled with the demand for fulfillment and control of relational pain independent of God.
>
> The sex addict wants a quick fix—quick relational relief without the disappointment possible in genuine intimacy.
>
> The essence of sin is autonomy from God, a failure to be dependent on Him. Sex addicts'...refusal to cling to God as the only Person who can fill their deepest longings and ease relational pain did not originate in a

shame-based family but in their shameful, deceitful heart. All of us have such a heart."

Even what Dr. Schaumburg refers to as "fantasy sex" has its roots in sin. He says, "At its core, sexual fantasy is a worship of self, a devotion to the ability of people to fabricate in their minds the solution to what they know is a need and believe they deserve."

The bottom line, is idolatry. Dr. Schaumburg says that "when we sin in our hearts toward Him, refusing to be dependent on Him, He gives us over to the control of the sinful things we prefer more than Himself. When God gives us over, He turns us over to the darkness of our hearts, which creates deeper darkness…Sexually addictive behaviors are not as dark as the internal commitment to serve self. … A sex addict truly changes when his or her relationship with God changes."

4. All sex addicts judge themselves to be incomplete or inadequate.

   a. They believe that they are bad people. Rather than thinking, "I've done a bad thing," they will instead say within themselves, "I am a bad person." This is the primary cause for all addiction.

   A child naturally turns to look at its father for approval and to see how to act. He *wants* to be like his father. An addict (with his negative, condemning self-judgments) doesn't feel deserving to be like anyone else and so has a hard time *wanting* to turn to the Father to be shown how to act.

   b. Some use sex to *confirm* their own self-judgments. Sex is used to either prove or confirm their unworthiness. Their self-talk says, "I am bad, so I will act according to my nature."

   c. Others can use sex to try to *create* a sense of worthiness. This self-talk goes, "I will use sex to prove that I am wanted and worth the attention of others." Unfortunately, the behavior they employ as a cure for their lack of self-worth becomes the very evidence against them that reconfirms their own feelings of failure.

   Dr. Schaumburg says, "Sex addicts need the security of false intimacy, danger, and anonymity that illicit sexual activity provides. They use it to sustain the illusion that they are accepted."

5. There is always a neurochemical component in addiction.

   Irregular synaptic patterns have been found in the brain of addictive personalities. What is unknown is whether the brain irregularity preceded the initial behavior or the behavior created the brain irregularity, which then went on to contribute to further dysfunctional behavior. It has been scientifically proven that behavior can directly effect physical changes in brain structures.

6. Addictions are interchangeable. Stopping one increases another unless the root source has been dealt with.

7. Most addictions have their genesis in early childhood trauma, where self-esteem and self-worth have been significantly compromised. (97% have been emotionally abused; 81% have been sexually abused—per Dr. Patrick Carnes)

   a. Those who created you (parents), or significant others, speak into you who you are by the way they treat you and the things they say to you during your childhood. Often, a negative self-image is branded into the heart of a young child through verbal, physical, or sexual abuse or neglect. The child literally adopts the opinions of significant others as to who he or she is. (This power is biblically illustrated in the Hebrew practice of naming their children according to personality types or prophetic expectations, and the inevitable fulfillment that the prophetic power of the name later had in the life of the child).

b. After the child develops a belief about him or herself (self-image) in response to the name they've been given, the opinions of their parents or guardians, the treatment they've received, and the consensus of those around them (which is reflected in hundreds of interpersonal interactions over the years), the child then behaves according to this belief and thereby seals the judgments of others through reinforcement and the rule of evidence.

c. If this "self-image" (belief system) is negative, the child will inevitably develop inner convictions about how unfair it is that they were made that way, or that they were born into a situation that brought so much rejection and pain into their lives. They will have feelings of abandonment and of anger over having been given such a lot in life and may form judgments against God, their parents, and others who aren't as "defective" as they believe they are. The longing to be like someone else often develops into full blown "idolatry" as the person tries to find some sense of completion in being accepted by those who seem to have it all together. These sins of anger, judgment, criticism, idolatry, covetousness and dishonoring of parents create the ground for demonic strongholds to develop. In essence, the naturally inherited autonomy of free will that everyone is given at birth becomes compromised through sins which empower the enemy to manipulate and influence them.

This is the process by which "sin" takes on the characteristics of "disease."

d. This perception of being inherently bad or defective creates an obsession with self. Sexual addicts are often narcissistic or in some other way hooked into unhealthy, habitual introspection. Their biggest battle is turning from a focus on "self" to a focus on God.

e. This focus on self often breeds an unyielding faith in intellectual understanding as the path out of addiction. Many sex addicts, having blamed God or someone else for their condition, have an unspoken *demand* for intellectual understanding. They often run from book to book to seminar to seminar, without ever coming to a knowledge of the truth because the truth requires an intimacy with the God they are angry with and a life of faith that requires the abandonment of self.

It was Malcolm Muggeridge who said, "We have educated ourselves into imbecility."

And it was Joyce Meyer who said, "When you're trying to figure everything out, you're not trusting God. We spend all our time seeking God for the answers to all our problems when what we should be doing is just seeking God!"

Jesus spoke to this "idolatry of the mind" problem when He said to the Pharisees of His day:

"You diligently study the Scriptures because you think that by them you possess eternal life. These are the Scriptures that testify about Me, yet you refuse to come to Me to have life" (John 5:39-40).

    f. Some sex addicts are addicted to the thrill of the out-of-control life that they have been leading. It provides a "high," and they prefer that high to the boring humdrum of normal life. They like the thrill of illicit sex. They like it more than they like the Lord.

    g. The sex addict is in search of love and acceptance, and they have been equating sex with love.

8. The dynamics of temptation revolve around the person's coping mechanisms for pain and the sins of their childhood that remain unconfessed and therefore unforgiven.

    a. Something they see, hear or feel touches this inner belief system of perceived defectiveness and rejection;

b. that "triggered" belief system triggers an emotional response—a feeling;

c. that feeling triggers an action (usually habitual in nature and mindlessly reflexive because it is responding to a lifetime of inner pain);

d. that action is fueled by inner hurt and anger and is therefore usually rebellious toward the object of its anger—typically, parents or God. The deeper the anger and the more the person blames God or parents (who represent God to them), the more likely that the sin will be darker—such as "immorality" or "violence," as opposed to "overeating," for example.

e. If the reactionary response is one that has become habitual in the life of the person, then it is far more likely that they will go through this temptation cycle without even noticing it.

9. Many engage in obsessive sex to the point of injury. (45% of males; 33% of females, when it comes to masturbation—according to Dr. Patrick Carnes).

    a. Sex leaves them feeling empty or bad.

    b. It becomes a serious problem when it is out-of-control, dangerous, or secretive.

10. There are inevitably deep waters of *hopelessness* concerning repeated failures to overcome addictions.

    Some develop a toxic, *learned* hopelessness and helplessness. They take everything personally. They see everything as having pervasive power over them. They believe that they are destined to be permanent victims.

11. Many sex addicts operate out of a "shame-based" emotional framework.

    Phrases such as, "I have no right to feel this way" or "I should" or "I ought" that dominate a person's language often indicate the presence of a shame-based personality.

    Christian psychologist John Smeltzer, in a lecture given at "Healing '92" conference in Anaheim, Ca., describes the shame-based personality this way:

    They are "people pleasers," who idealize intimacy, relationships and friendships and make them more than they really are. They only know how to have relationships if they can earn those relationships—if they can earn that person's response back. They end up getting "attention" from others in response to their actions, rather than "love." They constantly work for this attention.

    People pleasers please in order to earn people's attention, often becoming loners who try to out perform everyone else in order to prove their worth.

    When people try to genuinely love them, a shame-based person is unable to accept it, believing that they haven't earned it and therefore it is not possible or real. Inside, they are saying to themselves, "If they really knew me, they wouldn't love me," or, "If they do know me and love me anyway, they are making a big mistake."

    John Smeltzer concludes with what he considers to be the way that a shame-based person can be healed. He says that a continual application of God's love is what heals this kind of person. At first, they recoil in disbelief. They experience anguish. (Remember, their identities are immersed in self-loathing and have been for most of their lives). But finally, there comes the dawning of a new image of themselves put there by God through you and by God directly, and healing occurs.

Healing of the shame-based personality takes place in the midst of four fundamental changes:

1. The love of God mediated in relationships in the church and the affection that God's people give in response to the revelations of the sex addict's sin;

2. The person finally becoming persuaded to change their mind about their long held, diseased beliefs about God, others and themselves.

3. The person finally becoming willing to be as a child before God in humble surrender, dependence, faith, and affection.

4. The person's willing prayers for God to touch him or her with His love.

B. Healing for the Sex Addict—The Rebuilding of The Spiritual House

1. Lay the Foundation—The Cross.

   Something that is very helpful is for the client to learn more about the incredible verities behind Jesus' death and sacrifice on the Cross, and to meditate on them until God gives him or her a deeper revelation of Christ's suffering.

   "The Lord said to Moses, 'Make a snake and put it up on a pole; anyone who is bitten can look at it and live.' So Moses made a bronze snake and put it up on a pole. Then when anyone was bitten by a snake and looked at the bronze snake, he lived" (Numbers 21:8-9).

Jesus became "evil" itself on the Cross—every hideous and detestable thing ever devised and carried out by man or demon. That is why Jesus was prefigured in the Old Testament as the serpent itself—the very epitome of symbolic evil—when the Israelites in the wilderness were told to put a serpent on a pole and look to it for healing from their deadly snake bites.

"God made Him who had no sin *to be sin* for us" (2 Cor. 5:21).

"Just as Moses lifted up the snake in the desert, so the Son of Man must be lifted up, that everyone who believes in Him may have eternal life" (John 3:14-15).

"For My Father's will is that everyone who looks to the Son and believes in Him shall have eternal life and I will raise him up at the last day" (John 6:40).

That is a picture of the continuous provision of grace that God has provided through the death of His Son Jesus. Whenever we have been bitten by the snake (i.e., evil, sin) we need only look to Jesus and His sacrifice on the Cross. He became sin on our behalf—so that we might be healed (also "saved" in the Greek) from the consequences of our deadly sin, and live!

This provision of grace, during this dispensation of grace, gives hope for those who have sinned to the point where they believe they are hopeless, and wrest from Satan one of his most effective tools of bondage—condemnation.

"This is what the Lord says: 'Your wound is incurable, your injury beyond healing...But I will restore you to health and heal your wounds,' declares the Lord, 'because you are called an outcast (one) for whom no one cares'" (Jer. 30:12, 17).

In the Cross we see:

- *the evil of sin*, which *causes us to join forces with Him,*

    "Godly sorrow worketh repentance" (2 Cor. 7:10, KJV).

- *the love of God*, which *causes us to love Him,*

    "The love of God is shed abroad in our hearts" (Rom. 5:5, KJV).

- *the power of God*, which *persuades us to cling to Him,*
- *the genius of God*, which *persuades us to surrender our questions to faith in His greater wisdom.*

    "The Cross of Christ means nothing until it takes your breath away." —Harold St. John

2. Intensify your dependence on God—become intimate with Him through worship, praise, Bible reading, serving others and fellowship at church. Spend a lot of time alone with the Lord, listening to Him, and receive His health and wholeness into your emotional self. It is your inheritance.

"Addiction is something you do in the face of pain or emotional injury. When you fail to feed on multiple sources of emotional nourishment, you turn inward to an addictive behavior." (John Smeltzer, "Healing '92", Vineyard, Anaheim, Ca.)

One man, whom God set free from 20 years of uncontrollable sexual addiction, was asked what God had done for him in the moments of deep intimacy that he had shared with the Lord during his healing process. He said that God had brought him out of his world of fantasy and into the world of reality by:

- showing me what He was *really* like,
- showing me what was *really* motivating my actions,
- showing me what the purpose of my life (and life in general) *really* was.

3. Abide in Him. As you live in an "abiding" relationship with God, He will keep you from falling.

   "Abide in Me, and I in you. As the branch cannot bear fruit of itself, unless it abides in the vine, so neither {can} you, unless you abide in Me. I am the vine, you are the branches; he who abides in Me, and I in him, he bears much fruit; for apart from Me you can do nothing. If you abide in Me, and My words abide in you, ask whatever you wish, and it shall be done for you. By this is My Father glorified, that you bear much fruit, and {so} prove to be My disciples. Just as the Father has loved Me, I have also loved you; abide in My love" (John 15:4-5, 7-9, NASB)

   "To those who have been called, who are loved by God the Father and *kept by Jesus Christ...To Him who is able to keep you from falling* and to present you before His glorious presence without fault and with great joy—to the only God our Savior be glory, majesty, power and authority, through Jesus Christ our Lord, before all ages, now and forevermore! Amen" (Jude 1:24).

4. Yield!!! Totally and completely, with full and absolute dependence on the power of God (which is brought forth through intimacy with Him), to overcome your addiction by healing the inner emotional damage that you have suffered throughout your life, and in particular, your childhood.

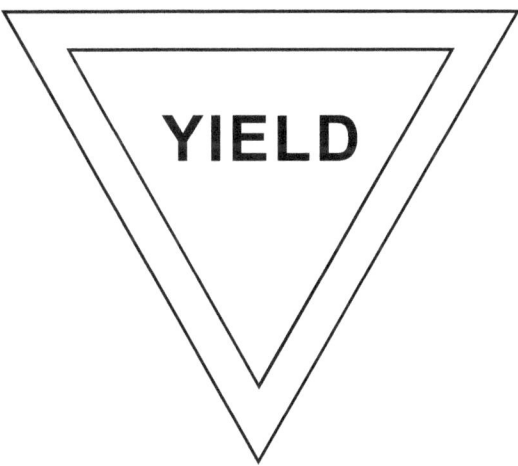

5. Let the Holy Spirit show you the source of your pain, and deal with those issues rather than living in denial (i.e., embrace the pain in order to heal it).

   The traumas and the triumphs of life set the emotional boundaries and belief systems out of which we interpret life. It can be important to re-live the memory of hurtful experiences in order to discover whether or not they precipitated unhealthy or sinful reactions to those who may have hurt us—reactions such as vows, judgments against others, judgments against ourselves, judgments against God, or other permanent negative attitudes or misassumptions.

   ** We do not look back into our past in order to *fix* blame on others, but so as to discover where we have *already* fixed blame, so that those vows and judgments can be repented of and the people forgiven and released.

   Why is forgiveness critical to the healing process?
   - because when we accepted the forgiveness of God for our sins, we relinquished any rights to hold sins against another (Mt. 18:23-35);
   - because judgment is reserved for God alone and it is a grave sin for us to presume on His office (Ps. 75:7);
   - because if we do not forgive our fellow man, God will not forgive us (Mt. 6:14-15).

6. Develop (through practice) new thought patterns and belief systems. Tear down the strongholds of wrong thinking. Throw down the gauntlet against unhealthy thinking. In essence, you are choosing to live by faith, not by sight.

   a. Your growing facility with living by faith, rather than by feelings is crucial.

      "Deception is the most subtle of all satanic strongholds. Have you ever noticed that all people with addictive behavior lie to themselves and others almost continuously?...Lying is an evil defense prompted by the father of lies, Satan (Jn. 8:44) ...Satan's lies are at the heart of addictive behavior. The spiritual side of addictive behavior cannot be overlooked. Faith is the biblical response to the truth, and believing the truth is a choice. When someone says, 'I want to believe God, but I just can't,' he or she is being deceived. Of course you can believe God! Faith is something you *decide to do,* not something you *feel like doing.* Believing the truth doesn't make it true; it's true, so we believe it...Faith doesn't *create* reality; faith *responds to* reality. Your faith is only as great as your knowledge of the object of your faith. If you have little knowledge of God and His Word, you will have little faith."

—From *The Bondage Breaker* by Neil T. Anderson, p. 191. Copyright 1990 by Harvest House Publishers, Eugene, Or. Used by permission.

b. Correcting your view of God

(1) By an act of the will, choose to believe that God is perfect and loving and flawlessly good, no matter what your thoughts or feelings are to the contrary. He has already proven this on the Cross!

(2) Challenge any contrary thoughts with your new belief system and with the Word of God. This is "Truth Therapy" (see "Foundations-Study Section").

"The weapons we fight with...have divine power to demolish strongholds. We demolish arguments and every pretension that sets itself up against the knowledge of God, and we take captive every thought to make it obedient to Christ" (2 Cor. 10:4-5).

(3) Deal with any anger that you may have toward God. Switch from a presumption of guilt, to a presumption of innocence when dealing with unanswered questions about why God would do something or not do something.

(4) When thoughts or feelings come that tell you that you've gone too far, or are too bad, or are the exception to God's unconditional love and grace, you must call them "lies" and refuse to entertain them further. You can aggressively respond to such temptations of unbelief with the Word of God and declarative prayer, or sometimes you can put them away simply by ignoring them.

c. Correcting your view of yourself

   (1) As one who has thrown him or herself on the mercy of Christ for salvation from your sins and who names Him as your Lord and Savior, you are now a new creation; no longer a bad person, irrespective of your behavior (past, present or future) because you have taken on the merits of Christ and are judged by His merits, not your own. You must chose whether God is lying or telling the truth when He declares these things to those who are in Christ, and decide to act accordingly.

   "It is idolatry to believe the people in your past who have told you who you are and how valuable you are when God says different. Some of us have said, in essence, 'I will embrace with my affections what my mind can understand.' Instead, we need to chose to become dependent on God and His Word, not our rational intellect." (John Smeltzer, "Healing '92", Vineyard Anaheim, Ca.)

   (2) As having a purpose that *will* bring glory to God—a purpose that has not been ruined by your sin, but one which God has the power to resurrect and fulfill through you. It is God's glory to rescue the most depraved of souls and to empower them for holiness and purity as a public statement of His own mercy and might.

d. Correcting your view of the Christian life

   (1) Legalism vs. Transformation—the power of God has fulfilled the requirements of the law (in the Cross). We now begin to live according to the *spirit* and *principles* that are *behind* the law because we are being transformed into His image and are taking on His mind, His heart and His values. We stop looking at the *letter* of the law, to obey it, because we increasingly want to keep the *spirit* of the law, as a natural function of our own transformed will. This emanates from a far deeper level of being—one in which we move, from our own center, out of God's very mind and character, having permanently welcomed Him to influence us from within and truly transform us into His image.

   "All who rely on observing the law are under a

curse, for it is written: 'Cursed is everyone who does not continue to do everything written in the Book of the Law'" (Gal. 3:10).

"Through Jesus Christ the law of the Spirit of life set me free from the law of sin and death" (Rom. 8:2).

(2) Allow grace to put to death "performance orientation." (See the chapter on this subject).

(3) The maturity of *seeking to learn* meaningful *structure and discipline* also comes as we experience the glorious unconditional love and mercy of our Father in heaven and begin to *want to* serve Him faithfully and effectively. We no longer rebel against the learning of discipline because through intimacy with the Father, we have discovered that the God who wants to teach it to us does not operate out of the manipulation, control and selfishness that others have. Through personal experience of His love, we are fully persuaded that the teaching in God's school of discipline is always and only for our benefit and the glory of the Son, whom we also love. Therefore, we can embrace it enthusiastically.

(4) The need for relationships with other Christians who are strong in the faith—to keep us accountable in our walk with the Lord—can be very important to someone who is struggling with sexual addiction. The old lying thought patterns and belief systems can sneak back up on us in times of discouragement and temptation. A brother nearby who can speak the word of truth into our spirit during these times can be an invaluable resource.

(5) The Christian life is one of self*less*ness rather than selfishness, forsaking the world system and the things that are a part of it, taking up your cross daily, suffering persecution when necessary; a life centered on eternity rather than this finite world; a life of living with the single-minded goal of bringing glory and honor to the One who died for you, simply because you love Him. Love is what aligns one's mind and heart to the proper "eternal perspective" that brings honor to Jesus Christ. More

than anything else, sexual addicts must get their eyes off of themselves and onto God.

7. Find a confidant (carefully) with whom you can share your problem and have ongoing prayer and dialogue. Find a therapy group or ministry with the same focus and avail yourself of its counsel and resources. Regularly attend home fellowship, men's or women's fellowship groups, so as to receive the benefit of the life of Christ's body.

"Confess your sins to one another and pray so that you may be healed" (James 5:16, NASB).

8. Ask the Lord to reveal any generational or other curses that may have come upon you. If they exist, you must pray that they be broken by the power of the blood of Jesus.

   a. Most people are aware that the sins of the fathers are passed down to the children through the third and fourth generation.

   "I, the Lord your God, am a jealous God, punishing the children for the sin of the fathers to the third and fourth generation of those who hate Me" (Ex. 20:5-6).

   b. What most of us don't know, however, is that this passing down of the sin from one generation to another is conditioned on the free will choice of that subsequent generation to embrace that sin. However, if the next generation chooses instead to follow the Lord, God will eliminate the curse.

   "Suppose this son has a son who sees all the sins his father commits, and though he sees them, he does not do such things...He will not die for his father's sin; he will surely live. But his father will die for his own sin... You ask, 'Why does the son not share the guilt of his father?' Since the son has done what is just and right and has been careful to keep all My decrees, he will surely live. The soul who sins is the one who will die. The son will not share the guilt of the father, nor will the father share the guilt of the son" (Ezek. 18:14, 17-20).

9. End all pretense and hiding. Stop pretending that everything is okay when it isn't. That very lie inhibits the Spirit's work in your

life.

10. Ask God to reveal the "triggers" that the enemy uses to set off a fall into sin (e.g., memories, relationships, criticisms, rejections, failures, loneliness, lies, habits, objects, times, places, etc.), and set your heart and will to do whatever God directs you to do in relation to them.

11. Ask God to train you in moving from a self-focused life into a God-focused life.

   In his book, *False Intimacy*, Dr. Harry Schaumburg addresses this issue of focus:

   > "Self-justification comes easily when we start with our needs and define God as the resource who will meet those needs…It's easy to say that the hope of God improving our lives is what sustains us rather than taking the biblical position that the hope of eternal glory makes our suffering bearable…God's primary purpose is not to offset the pain of living in this sinful world. He doesn't exist simply to solve each and every problem we face in life—or even the ones we perceive will crush us. He calls us to become absorbed in fulfilling His will and purpose, to deny ourselves for the good of others and to His glory. Our joy should be in serving and loving God."

12. Ask God to train you in forsaking the "idolatry of feelings" and in making Him the sole God of your idolatry. This is not to suggest that you deny or suppress feelings, but that you learn to discern those feelings that reflect truth from those that reflect fantasy, and respond accordingly.

13. Ask God to train you in stopping the temptation cycle at its source.

14. The Sexaholics Anonymous model

   Although continually in flux, SA currently teaches that the key to stopping the negative spiritual process that empowers the addict is to recognize and deal with the fundamental "attitude" problem. Underlying the out-of-control behaviors are attitudes and conditions that fuel the addiction machine. They include:

   - resentment
   - rationalizing
   - guilt
   - punishment

- justification
- hostility
- anger
- envy
- rebellion
- rage
- self-obsession (idolatry)
- isolation
- separation
- pride
- blindness
- delusion

SA believes that the solution to sexual addiction lies with:
- fellowship
- stopping the behavior
- starving the lust
- change of attitude in the inner person
- daily surrender as an attitude (humility)
- self-examination (careful to avoid the pride of knowledge)
- face your fears, write them out and burn the list
- taking responsibility to reach out for help
- confession
- having a confidant who helps break the power that fantasy has over you
- forgiving and making amends
- giving up of resentments
- righting wrongs
- turning from self to God
- praying for the objects of your lust (the people)
- letting God into every temptation, emotion, difficulty, success, failure, sadness and joy
- turn from using others to self-denial and giving of self with no thought of return

—From *Sexaholics Anonymous* Copyright 1989 SA Literature, Simi Valley, Ca. Used with permission.

The insights of 12 step groups can be quite helpful, as this list proves and we should avail ourselves of whatever help God leads us to. However, there is a fundamental flaw in 12 step groups that makes them potentially harmful. Not only do they have the potential for teaching and modeling an unhealthy self-focus, but most distressingly, within the group they forbid the public naming of Jesus as the only name under heaven by which we can be saved (and healed). They do teach the need for turning to a god of your own choosing, but in making it right to chose whatever god you want, they model theological relativism and implicitly teach that Jesus Christ is *not* the only way. Jesus said that if we deny Him before men, He will deny us before His Father in heaven.

Look for a second at the potential damage behind this philosophical stance. If I "work the program" and achieve a state of ongoing sobriety without naming Christ, then I become all the more convinced that Jesus is not the only way and that I really don't need Him at all. It would be better if my life fell completely apart so that I might not make that crucial mistake.

(See the chapter on "Miscellaneous Issues" for more discussion on this issue.)

15. The biblical model, as described by Dr. Schaumburg.
    - Face yourself honestly without denial.
    - Recognize your need to change.
    - Face your woundedness.
    - Realize that you can't heal yourself, and turn to God.
    - Trust God to satisfy your needs.
    - Acknowledge your need of repentance.

    "Repentance is not simply a decision or an act of your will to stop addictive behavior. It's not just a new effort you make. Rather, it's an act of God and His grace that occurs as you open yourself to God and the deep work of His Spirit in your heart. Through repentance, you begin to understand that you aren't in control of discovering the source of true fulfillment or protecting yourself from pain. You begin to be disillusioned with the directions you've been heading in. You begin to thirst for real spiritual change."

    - Confess your sins before God.
    - Ask for help, from the Word of God, the Spirit of God, and the people of God.
    - Pursue healthy relationships.
    - Receive a physical examination.
    - Consider joining a self-help group. The advantages

include finding personal support, gaining more information, and having help and encouragement in working through a crisis.
- Change is a lifelong process.

"In this life we must recognize that we will inevitably experience disappointments, pain, and a lack of complete relational satisfaction. When we stop fighting this reality and become willing to accept it, we can be free to move into the world with a real sense of purpose and direction. Like Jesus, we can become committed people who will deny and sacrifice ourselves in order to love others."

Exercises—Sexual Addiction

1. Ask the Holy Spirit to reveal patterns of addictive behavior in your life—things you habitually run to when under stress, pain or defeat.

2. Ask the Lord to work true repentance within you so that you can be truly sorry for having turned to these substitutes instead of to Him to meet your needs. Spend time meditating on the Cross and its meaning for you. Then, confess your sin and receive God's forgiveness.

3. Pray a prayer of dependence, declaring your refusal to strive any more against the bondage and instead committing yourself to a lifestyle of turning to Him to heal and transform you in this area of bondage.

4. Pray a prayer of relinquishment, forsaking the false comforters in your life and embracing the Holy Spirit as your only Comforter in time of need.

5. Ask the Lord to reveal a pattern in your interpersonal relationships of fleeing from intimacy. Confess your fear of intimacy with God and ask Him to break through that fear so that you may develop an intimate relationship with Him. Ask Him to build a stronghold of trust in God in you to replace the one of fear and doubt. Ask and keep asking, relentlessly, until God completes this work in you.

6. Ask the Lord to show you whether or not you have been living out of a shame-based belief system. If you have, ask Him to correct your belief system. Regularly bathe in the Word of God, particularly those passages that speak of God's high value of you. Neil Anderson's, *Breaking Through To Spiritual Maturity* workbook as well as his book, *Victory Over the Darkness* are excellent resources for aiding you in this process.

7. Ask God to identify for you, and then forgive, all those who have sinned against you. God will give you the power to forgive even the most heinous crimes committed against you if you will turn to

Him for that power. This removes a major source of Satan's ground to keep you in bondage.

8. Decide that you are no longer going to live under a "victim" mentality, but that you are going to move out and complete the purposes for which you were born. Take an aggressive stance against the old lies and habit patterns. Counter them with the sword of the Spirit, which is the Word of God. Place scripture phrases around the house or workplace that speak the truth to issues where you have believed lies about God, yourself, others, the purpose of life, etc. Aggressively challenge old thoughts and feelings with these truths and with prayer against them.

9. With God's help, seek out and find a confidante who can speak into your life the truth and who can keep you accountable.

10. Immerse yourself in healthy atmospheres (e.g., church, men's or women's fellowship groups, home fellowship groups, mercy ministries, etc.) things that take you out of focus of yourself and onto serving others.

Pornography

Human beings seem to have a propensity for making images of ourselves and setting them up as idols of marvel and desire. We have certainly spent a lot of time and money on paintings and drawings and sculptures, in photos and film. Oh, we've gotten very good at referring to this worship of the human body euphemistically as "an artistic appreciation of what God has given us," but we are only fooling ourselves.

Paul writes in the book of Romans that because people began serving and worshipping created things rather than the Creator, God gave them over to shameful and unnatural lusts (see Rom. 1:21-27). You can see an almost predictable pattern in the fall of the great civilizations of the world, from an increased worship of the human body to the descent of that society into sexual depravity and disaster.

The modern world is fast approaching the apex of this curve. In our culture today, the human body is indeed the god. We spend billions of dollars making ourselves look beautiful and tan and young and fit. The success of most television, film and advertising campaigns revolve around the sensual depiction of the human body. This obsession has encircled the entire globe. Before we can address the issue of pornography, we must confess our own participation in this evil system of idol worship.

Recognizing the Evil

One of the greatest problems that we have in dealing with pornography is that we do not recognize that it is evil. We minimize, rationalize and deny the evil behind it. And since we refuse to look honestly at the sin, we do not truly repent for what we are doing. We do not repent for being idol worshippers, for grieving the heart of our God.

As parents, we may forbid our children to use pornography, but we do it with a smile and a wink. "After all," we reason, "we did it when we were kids." Some even rationalize it as a means of firming up a heterosexual orientation for their kids and secretly delight in the fact that they respond "normally" to the influence. Is it any wonder that the Attorney General's Commission on Pornography found that teenagers are the number one buyers of both soft and hard-core pornography? (They also found that 85 percent of it is controlled by organized crime.)

What you are paying for when you purchase pornography? Let's not settle for an intellectual, armchair response, but one that stems from my years of experience on the inside, both with the production of and an addiction to pornography. When you put your money down for the purchase of any magazine or video with nudity in it, you are first paying for the exploitation of the actors who were used in the production. The young person who has to take his or her clothes off in order to get a part has already sold some self-respect, and has divided him- or herself from God. You participate in that process by financing that young boy or girl's fall. The Bible says that it would be better for a millstone to be hung around your neck and for you to be thrown into the sea than for you to do that (see Luke 17:1-2).

The kids who are photographed in the nude or in sex acts usually suffer from such low self-esteem that they feel incapable of ever being successful without compromising their values and self-worth. And so they take their clothes off for the director and crew, pasting smiles on their faces and pretending to find the whole thing amusing, while deep down inside, their spirit is being gutted.

Many of these actors have been seduced or coerced or blackmailed into being raped or sodomized or in some other way sexually humiliated by those who control the casting of the production—even so-called "legitimate" productions that you see on TV and at first-run movie theaters. And a great many tens of thousands more, whom you'll never see in pictures, have suffered the same fate at the hands of these kinds of people, only to find that the promises for jobs were lies.

When it comes to explicit pornography, you have an even more hideous reality. In even the most "respected" girlie and boy magazines, there is an incredible amount of sexual abuse and exploitation going on behind the scenes.

In the world of pornography, it is not unusual for young girls and boys to be kidnapped off the streets, force-fed addictive drugs and gang-raped in order to break down their resistance to being used. In some cases, they are brutally treated, tortured and even killed. They are often forced into a life of prostitution. This goes on every day of every week in every major city (and some towns) of this country. And the person who finances it is the person who buys pornography—you and me! Not only do we finance those practices, our porn money is also used for the other activities of organized crime, including murder, rape, prostitution, extortion and who knows what else.

Now let's consider the more subtle damage that pornography does to us. When you have millions of people fixing powerful images in their minds while lusting after airbrushed symbols of perfection, you also have an entire society that is being programmed to view men and women and children as sex objects rather than as human beings. And if we can pretend that they are objects rather than human beings, we can justify to ourselves the fact that we are financing their destruction.

When you add to that equation the fact that most pornography depicts every kind of aberrant sexual activity imaginable, including the violent abuse of women and children, then you have an explosive situation. It is currently blowing up in our faces, with the explosion of incest, sexual child abuse, wife abuse, AIDS and other diseases, and divorce—practices now so common that they barely elicit a yawn anymore. We are reaping what we have sown and have become blinded to our own self-destruction.

I asked the Lord one day why pornography had such power in people's lives. He answered that it was because of the evil that went into its production (this wholesale destruction of people's lives), and because it is pure, unadulterated *idolatry* (practically the "sin of sins" in the Bible). Both factors empower the demonic realm far more than we can imagine and make what appears to be a harmless, impersonal diversion into a very serious matter indeed.

The first part of the remedy for an addiction to pornography is to see it as the evil that it is. There is no single good thing about it. Learn to hate it for what it does to others as well as for what it does to you and your relationship with God.

Recognizing the Grace in Repentance

It is important at this point to make certain that you have a clear understanding of God's grace (carefully read and absorb chapters three and ten), because if you have yet to apprehend God's love and grace in the face of your own evil, it may actually set you back to rehearse the evil that you have been pursuing. As we have noted in chapter ten, most addicts judge themselves to be bad, defective and unlovable. Such lies need to be overturned before you can come to grips with the evil of your actions in a redemptive way. Otherwise, rehearsing the evil only serves to deepen the self-hatred. However, once grace has been understood and embraced, then it is safe to deal with the depravity that you have engaged in.

Coming to grips with your depravity is critical for you to be able to truly repent. As a sex addict, your tendency is to deny or minimize the severity of your actions, which prevents genuine repentance. True "biblical" repentance, is more than being sorry. It involves making a choice of who/what you love more—in this case, pornography or Jesus Christ—idolatry or authentic worship.

Often, we are really only sorry that we got caught and are facing an embarrassing examination by our peers and the difficult road of restoring trust in our primary relationships. Sometimes, we are really only sorry that we are weak, messed up and out of control and we hate being that way. The focus is still on ourselves.

True biblical repentance is something that must be sought and received by the grace of God. By it, you are struck to the core of your being with great sorrow over having hurt and offended a holy, loving God. "Godly sorrow brings repentance that leads to salvation" (2 Cor. 7:10).

In true repentance for involvement with pornography, you cover every base. You confess and renounce your idolatry, admitting to your part (unwittingly or not) in the financing of exploiting others. You *ask for, receive and accept* God's forgiveness. You break the cycle of sin/shame/more sin, by believing God's pledge of forgiveness. The Bible says "If we confess our sins, He is faithful and just and will forgive us our sins and purify us from all unrighteousness" (1 John 1:9). As you believe that Scripture rather than your feelings, you learn to stand cloaked in the righteousness of Christ even when you don't feel as though you are (see Rom. 13:14; Gal. 3:27).

Recognizing the Spiritual Warfare

Another vital element of believing God's Word rather than your own feelings is recognizing that a major portion of the battle takes place in the heavenlies, which is a particularly difficult challenge because you cannot see or feel the spirit realm. However, the Bible is clear that this spiritual warfare occurs, as the following Scriptures demonstrate:

Our struggle is not against flesh and blood, but against the rulers, against the authorities, against the powers of this dark world and against the spiritual forces of evil in the heavenly realms (Eph. 6:12).

Though we live in the world, we do not wage war as the world does. The weapons we fight with are not the weapons of the world. On the contrary, they have divine power to demolish strongholds. We demolish arguments and every pretension that sets itself up against the knowledge of God, and we take captive every thought to make it obedient to Christ (2 Cor. 10:3-5).

Considering the depth of evil found in the pornography industry, it should not be difficult for you to believe that the use of pornography may have been an entryway for a demonic stronghold in your life. Therefore, one of the first things you should do is to ask God to expose any demonic strongholds that may have taken root in you as a result of viewing pornography. Often this occurred during your first exposure to pornography in childhood. A demonically inspired fixation can also result as a consequence of prolonged exposure or from the depth of depravity in the materials that you have seen or used. There may also be a tie between demonic inroads in your life and the acting out of pornographic images in fantasy and masturbation.

Remember, though, that spiritual demonization in a person has to do with degree of influence, not spatial territory. If there is a demonic stronghold, pray against it in the name of Jesus, preferably with other seasoned Christians present and agreeing with you in prayer.

In some cases, the Lord may lead you to renounce and cast off Baal (the god of sexual depravity) in the name of Jesus. The Lord will release His power in you to chase off these demonic forces. You may even physically feel spirits and compulsions lift off you. Or they may leave silently in disgust as you saturate yourself in worship and praise of God.

If you are continually plagued with images of pornography or people that you have lusted over in the past, take those images to the Cross and hand them to Christ. Since it was there that He became sin for us (see 2 Cor. 5:21), He will take them into Himself on that Cross, taking the penalty for those sins upon Himself, and then He will destroy them with His death and His rising. He will break their power for you.

After the power of the Holy Spirit has delivered you from the demonic stronghold, pray for the healing presence and power of God to fill the void left behind. Pray that the diseased perspective will now be replaced with God's health and purity. Pray that the ground in your soul previously held by the enemy will become a permanent habitation for the Holy Spirit.

Recognizing Your Responsibility

It is vital, of course, to get rid of every piece of pornography that you own—not by selling it or giving it away, but by burning and throwing it away. This is a very important step to take, as a practical demonstration to the Lord of your commitment to Him and as a way of eliminating immediate sources of temptation.

Remove yourself also from any place, district or environment where pornography is available. It is also important to extricate yourself from any affiliations or friendships that have contributed to the problem. Put porn-blocking software on the computer or, better yet, acquire an Internet service that blocks it at the server level. Cut up the credit cards that you use to order such materials and services. Change your phone number if you have to. Show the Lord that you are serious, because if you are not serious, then you cannot expect that He will do anything to deliver you. When you become willing to do whatever it takes, then you can expect a great deal of help from the Lord.

When the temptations return, stop and ask yourself: "Who is Lord of my life? Do I love Him more than these things?" After making the decision that you love Jesus the most, turn to Him, away from the sin. You will *always* find His power there for you (see 1 John 2:3,5; Deut. 30:11-20.)

Determine in your heart that, with God's power, you are going to turn away from your sin and follow the Lord in whatever way He instructs you (see John 5:19-20,30). Set your heart against pornography by making an *irrevocable* decision that using it will never again be an option in your life. However, make this commitment with the understanding that it will be God who will actually empower the keeping of the promise. He will do so in honor of your commitment for as long as you want Him to.

That begs the question: How do you sustain your will in wanting God to keep you free from this sin?

    1. By keeping your focus on the beauty and sufficiency of God and the unmatched fulfillment that comes in an intimate relationship with Him. This involves disciplining your life to guard your time and the things you watch and listen to. This often involves consciously changing the things that you set your heart on.

    2. By realizing that since the sin is no longer an option, dwelling on the temptation is little more than torturing yourself over something you will never do.

    3. By remembering the hurt, pain and destruction that sin has brought to your life. Get angry over that! Set your heart and mind against it, for what it does to others (see Luke 17:2), as well as for what it does to you and your relationship with God. "Hate what is evil; cling to what is good" (Rom. 12:9).

    4. By meditating on the Cross of Christ, His suffering and pain for your redemption. There is great hidden power in a heart response of love to Jesus' love poured out in death for us. Read the gospel accounts of His suffering and death and ask God to deepen your understanding, so that you may truly know, deep in your spirit, the incredible nature of what Christ has done for you on the Cross. This revelation alone can change your will permanently into one that is fully persuaded to faithfully follow the Lord all the days of your life.

One very helpful tool that God gave me was to show me the parallels between the enemy that Israel had to face when they entered their Promised Land, and the enemies we must face when entering ours. If you recall the story, God told the Israelites to kill every man, woman and child (and in some cases even the animals) in order to take the Promised Land (see Deut. 7; Josh. 6:21; 8:26; 11:20-22). God told them, "They must be utterly destroyed!" (Deut. 7:2). Seems rather ruthless, don't you think?

There is a message in that for us today. What is our promised land today? Is it not the kingdom of God? And how is the kingdom of God accessed? By faith! Therefore, the battlefield for our promised land today is the mind, and the enemies are all those strongholds of the enemy that reside there. Here's the parallel with the Old Testament battle: we must be just as ruthless in destroying the enemies in our battlefield as the Israelites were commanded to be in their battlefield. If we do not, we will suffer the same fate as they did. The enemies to whom we do not deal a ruthless deathblow will rise up again and lead us back into idolatry.

One of the greatest problems in the Church today is that we are not ruthlessly and violently taking the kingdom of God by force as our Commander in Chief has indicated we should (see Matt. 11:12). In fact, we have little passion at all for holiness. Instead we "supermarket shop" for holiness, saying, "God, make me holy in this area, but leave me alone in this other area."

The kingdom of God is not a supermarket. If you want to be holy, you must want to be made holy across the board. Those who pick and choose where to be made holy and where to remain worldly are not submitted to God. He is not really their Lord at all (see Matt. 7:21; Luke 6:46).

As a way of participating in God's victory over sin in your life according to 2 Corinthians 10:5, ask God (or one of His mightiest angels) to stand at the door of your mind as a bouncer would at the door of a bar. Bouncers are those big guys who demand an ID at the door and if you don't have an ID, you're not getting in. And if you somehow got in without an ID and he finds out, you're going out, and you're going out *now*. God is much more powerful than any bouncer. If a temptation tries to enter the door of your mind and you fervently want God to keep it out, He has the power to make that happen. Indeed, every time you really want God to cast off a temptation, He will—no exceptions! That's how passionate He is to "keep you from falling" (Jude 24).

Aggressively attack every impure thought the minute it approaches your mind. Do not give it time to dwell. The more time it dwells, the more power it gains to remain. We have inherited the kingdom of God by grace, but we take our place in it in this life through aggressive action against the forces of evil, using the weapons, power and direction that God has given us (see Matt. 11:12; Eph. 6:10-18).

If you ask God to cast off a temptation and it remains, that is a sign that you are asking half-heartedly. You are saying the religious words that part of you wants to believe, but another part of your heart still loves and wants the pleasure that the temptation offers. In cases like that, you simply need to stop, confess to the Lord that you still have some love for the temptation, and ask Him to change your heart so that you love Him more than you do the thing that is tempting you. Go deeper into worship and ask Him to transform you into His image as you do so (see 2 Cor. 3:18).

Once you begin to understand how spiritual warfare works and the provision that God has made for your transformation into His likeness, everything changes. In the kingdom of God, which is here now (see Luke 11:20), the Lord turns Satan's schemes upside down and causes them to serve His purpose. In the Kingdom, instead of being a burden that you must carry in your own strength, *temptation becomes an opportunity for righteousness and growth in spiritual maturity.*

Here's one way in which that works. If you are a born-again Christian, Satan cannot tempt you unless God allows him, and God does not allow him to tempt you beyond what you are able to handle (see 1 Cor. 10:13). Since temptation is allowed only at moments when God knows you are able to withstand by His power, it therefore becomes an opportunity for spiritual growth. When you are tempted and turn to God with a full heart, desiring purity and righteousness more than evil and sin, you grow in maturity; more of the divine nature is imparted on your behalf; you are transformed into His likeness in ever-increasing measure. Temptation becomes an opportunity to grow spiritually. In the very areas where you have been chronically tempted, the very areas where you have been the weakest in the past, God uses what Satan means for evil to bring victory. So rejoice with the apostle Paul over your weaknesses, because in concert with God they are turned into strengths (see 2 Cor. 12:9).

You still have a free will, however, and can at any time elect not to resist sin. Additionally, if you decide not to use God's power, and instead try to slug it out on your own, you will eventually fail. And, if you use your free will as a license to sin, you will also fail.

If, however, you turn to God with a heart committed to being made holy every time Satan tempts you, he will eventually realize that by tempting you, he is actually causing you to turn to God, which is the last thing he wants to do. He will then withdraw until a more opportune time when your resolve has weakened or with a new approach and strategy.

Another major area in which you will need God's supernatural assistance is in correcting your mental and emotional response to other people. The old programming from pornographic images and sinful behaviors has to be rectified. Ask God to replace your old view of the sexuality of others with a healthy perspective, to enable you to see them as precious individuals whose bodies deserve to be privately kept for the one they marry, rather than objects of your lust. Remember, to lust after someone is to sin against them. You are reducing them to objects of perverted desire rather than recognizing them as creatures of infinite value and worth.

Reverse misplaced idolatry with regular worship and praise of who God is. Do this with faith and understanding in the power of praise (see 2 Chron. 20:15-17,21-22). As you regularly practice the presence of God in private and corporate praise and worship, ask for and receive into yourself the wholeness and emotional health that God has for you (see Ps. 16:8-11; 2 Cor. 3:18; Gal. 4:19). God will eliminate the neediness or brokenness that fed your obsession with pornography. God meets that need more effectively. It's that simple! There is no other esoteric or hidden key to your healing.

As I have spoken of repeatedly in this book, make it the "prime directive" of your life to enter into relationship with the Father through regular communion with Him so that He can show you the *root* sources of your obsessions and replace that need with Himself (see Ps. 25:14; 32:8; John 6:45). As each one of them is healed, the power of the forces that try to pull you back into sin will slowly wane.

It's really a matter of replacing what the pornography did for you with what God Almighty can do for you. You'll find that it is no contest. What God will fill you with will be beyond what you can possibly imagine or think (see Eph. 3:20). Just give it time, and a great deal of attention.

If you have been the victim of pornographers, you have a much more complex set of issues to deal with, but the process for healing is the same. You will need to forgive those who hurt you. You will also need to learn how to see yourself the way Jesus sees you—with eyes of deep love and forgiveness, as a newborn virgin child.

Know this: God loves you and promises to heal you from your trauma and your sin if you will humbly come to Him and ask for His help, and patiently work with Him as He shows you what to do. He can restore your innocence, because He is a mighty and powerful God. He bought you at the price of the death of His own Son. He sees you clothed in robes of pure white linen, righteous before His eyes because you have clothed yourself with the purity and holiness of Christ. Follow the principles found in this book and in the Scriptures, and find new life in Jesus Christ

Study Section— Pornography

> *We worship the human body, and so
> God has given us over to our lust.*
> (Rom. 1:24-27)

A. SOME THINGS YOU SHOULD KNOW

1. Both the Church and society have become numb to the severity of this problem and the breadth of its influence. *Penthouse* magazine reports that 35% of its readers are born-again Christians—1.67 million of them. The Attorney General's Commission on Pornography reports that teenagers are the number one buyers of both soft and hard core pornography.

2. Pornography is not a victimless crime.

    a. When you buy or use pornography, you are paying for, and thus participating in:
        (1) the exploitation of young people
        (2) the loss of their self-respect and emotional well-being
        (3) the sexual abuse of young people
        (4) the kidnapping, drugging, raping, and forced prostitution of young people
        (5) financing a variety of organized crime activities (Attorney General's Commission on Pornography found that 85% of porn is controlled by organized crime).

    b. Pornography makes sexual objects out of people—to be *used* for your personal sexual gratification.

c. Pornography creates and breeds:
   (1) incest
   (2) child abuse
   (3) spouse abuse
   (4) murder
   (5) AIDS and other venereal diseases
   (6) marital break-up and divorce
d. What gives pornography its power?
   (1) The violence and personal destruction that goes into its creation, empowers demonic forces.
   (2) Pornography is an idol factory.

B. SOME THINGS YOU SHOULD DO

1. See pornography as the evil that it is.
   a. Confess your idolatry.
   b. Renounce your idolatry.
   c. Renounce and cast off Baal (the god of sexual depravity) in the name of Jesus.

2. Admit to your part (unwittingly or not) in the financing of the exploitation of young people.

3. *Ask for, receive, and accept* God's forgiveness. Break the cycle of sin/shame/more sin, by believing God's pledge of forgiveness.

   "If we confess our sins, He is faithful and just and will forgive us our sins and purify us from all unrighteousness" (1 Jn. 1:9).

   Learn to stand in the reality of being cloaked in the righteousness of Christ.

4. Learn and practice true "biblical" repentance, which is more than being sorry. It involves making a choice of who/what you love more—in this case, pornography or Jesus Christ.
   a. Often, we are really only sorry that we got caught and are facing an embarrassing examination by our peers and the difficult road of restoring trust in our primary relationships.

b. Sometimes, we are really only sorry that we are weak, messed up, and out of control, and we hate being that way.

c. True biblical repentance is something that must be sought and received by the grace of God. By it, you are struck to the core of your being with great sorrow over having hurt and offended a holy, loving God.

"Godly sorrow worketh repentance" (2 Cor. 7:10).

d. There also exists a need to enter into what Dr. John White calls "identification-based repentance." This is where you identify yourself with the sins of your nation, your ancestry, or some other group with which you belong or are related—accepting the blame for those sins before God as though you yourself are also to blame.

On page 211 of his book, *Eros Redeemed*, Dr. John White provides the biblical basis for such a concept:

"When identification-based repentance takes place, the grip of ancestral sin is broken, and Christians have authority to declare the chains broken.

"After all, this is precisely what Jesus did in breaking the curse over us. At His baptism, He identified with us in our sin and guilt. (The idea that His baptism was merely 'an example' for us to follow cheapens the magnificence of His action.) What else was He doing when He stood in line? What else, but declare, 'I have come to be one with you in your sin, to share its guilt?' He was to be baptized with a baptism of repentance. What need had He for repentance? ... Jesus had nothing to repent of, nothing to be released from, no chains that needed to be broken. Yet, in order that our chains might be broken, symbolically He repented, identifying with us in our sin, taking our sin on Him as a preparation for becoming our sacrifice. It is that very sacrifice by which He wishes to release us from our habitual sexual sin."

e. When the temptation comes, stop and ask yourself: "Who is Lord of my life? Who do I love more?" After making the decision that it is Jesus who you love more, turn to Him for His power to overcome the temptation and away from the sin, and you will *always* find it there for you.

"And by this we know that we have come to know Him, if we keep His commandments. The one who says, 'I have come to know Him,' and does not keep His commandments, is a liar, and the truth is not in him; but *whoever keeps His word, in him the love of God has truly been Perfected.* By this we know that we are in Him: the one who says he abides in Him ought himself to walk in the same manner as He walked. Beloved, I am not writing a new commandment to you, but an old commandment which you have had from the beginning; the old commandment is the word which you have heard. On the other hand, I am writing a new commandment to you, which is true in Him and in you, because the darkness is passing away, and the true light is already shining" (1 John 2:3-8, NASB).

"For this commandment which I command you today is not too difficult for you, nor is it out of reach. It is not in heaven, that you should say, 'Who will go up to heaven for us to get it for us and make us hear it, that we may observe it?' Nor is it beyond the sea, that you should say, 'Who will cross the sea for us to get it for us and make us hear it, that we may observe it?' But *the word is* very near you, in your mouth and *in your heart, that you may observe it. See, I have set before you today life and prosperity, and death and adversity;* in that I command you today to love the Lord your God, to walk in His ways and to keep His commandments and His statutes and His judgments, that you may live and multiply, and that the Lord your God may bless you in the land where you are entering to possess it. But if your heart turns away and you will not obey, but are drawn away and worship other gods and serve them, I declare to you today that you shall surely perish. You shall not prolong {your} days in the land where you are crossing the Jordan to enter and possess it. I call heaven and earth to witness against you today, that *I have set before you life and death, the blessing and the curse. So choose life in order that you may live, you and your descendants, by loving the Lord your God, by obeying His voice, and by holding fast to Him; for this is your life* and the length of your days, that you may live in the land which the Lord swore to your fathers, to Abraham, Isaac, and Jacob, to give them" (Dt. 30:11-20, NASB).

5. Destroy all such materials that you may have and avoid the places, districts and environments that sell it.

6. Set your heart against pornography by making an *irrevocable* decision that using it will never again be an option in your life.

   This commitment understands that it will be God who will actually empower the keeping of the promise. He will do so in honor of your commitment for as long as you want Him to.

   How do you sustain your will in wanting Him to keep you free from this sin?

   a. by keeping your focus on the beauty and sufficiency of God and the unmatched fulfillment that comes in an intimate relationship with Him. This involves disciplining your life to guard your time and the things you watch and listen to. This often involves consciously changing the things that you set your heart on.

      "The people who know their God *will firmly resist him* (the enemy)" (Dan. 11:32).

   b. by realizing that since the sin is no longer an option, dwelling on the temptation is little more than torturing yourself over something you will never do.

   c. by remembering the hurt, pain and destruction that sin has brought to your life. Get angry over that! Set your heart and mind against it, for what it does to others (Luke 17:2), as well as for what it does to you and your relationship with God.

      "Hate what is evil; cling to what is good" (Rom. 12:9).

   d. by meditating on the Cross of Christ, His suffering and pain, for your redemption. There is great hidden power in a heart response of love to Jesus' love poured out in death for us. Read the gospel accounts of His suffering and death and ask God to deepen your understanding, so that you may truly know, deep in your spirit, the incredible nature of what Christ has done for you on the Cross. This revelation alone can change your will permanently into one that is fully persuaded to faithfully follow the Lord all the days of your life.

7. Recognize the parallels between the enemy that Israel had to face when they entered their promised land, and the enemies we must face when entering ours.

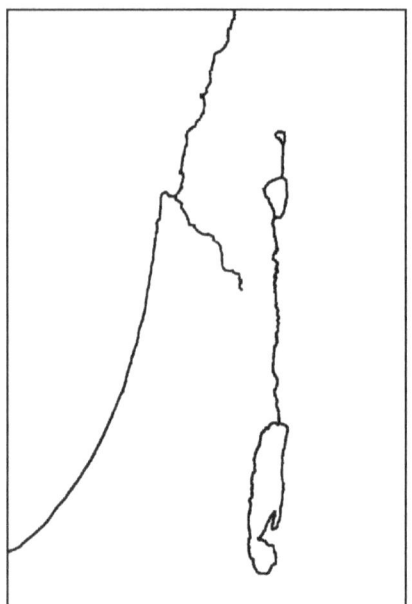

They must be utterly destroyed!

8. Set a guard (bouncer) at the door of your mind.

"{We are} destroying speculations and every lofty thing raised up against the knowledge of God, and {we are} *taking every thought captive to the obedience of Christ*" (2 Cor. 10:5, NASB).

Aggressively attack every impure thought the minute it enters your mind. Do not give it time to dwell. The more time it dwells, the more power it gains to remain. We have inherited the kingdom of God by grace, but we take our place in it in this life through aggressive action against the forces of evil, using the weapons and power that God has given us (Mt. 11:12; Eph. 6:10-18).

9. *See temptation as an opportunity for righteousness* and growth in spiritual maturity.

   a. If you are a born again Christian, Satan cannot tempt

you unless God allows him, and God does not allow him to tempt you beyond what you are able to handle.

"God is faithful; He will not let you be tempted beyond what you can bear. But when you are tempted, He will also provide a way out so that you can stand up under it" (1 Cor. 10:13).

b. Since temptation is allowed only at moments when God knows you are able to withstand by His power, it therefore becomes an opportunity for spiritual growth. When you resist evil with the power of God, you grow in spiritual maturity. God is taking what Satan means for evil and using it for good.

c. You still have a free will, however, and can at any time elect not to resist sin. If you decide not to use God's power, and instead try to slug it out on your own, you will eventually fail.

d. If you use your free will as a license to sin, you will also fail.

e. If, however, you turn to God with a heart committed to being made holy every time Satan tempts you, he will eventually realize that by tempting you, he is actually causing you to turn to God, which is the last thing he wants to do. He will then withdraw until a more opportune time when your resolve has weakened or with a new approach and strategy.

10. Ask God to give you a healthy perspective of the sexuality of others—to enable you to see them as precious individuals whose bodies deserve to be privately kept for the one they marry, rather than objects of your lust.

Remember, to lust after someone is to sin against them. You are reducing them to objects of perverted desire rather than recognizing them as the creatures of infinite value and worth that they are.

"Overcome evil with good" (Rom 12:21, NASB).

11. Reverse misplaced idolatry with regular worship and praise of who God is. Do this with faith and understanding in the power of praise.

"The battle is not yours, but God's. Tomorrow march down against them…You will not have to fight this battle. Take up your positions; stand firm and see the deliverance the Lord will give you…Jehoshaphat appointed men to sing to the Lord and to praise Him for the splendor of His holiness as they went out at the head of the army, saying: 'Give thanks to the Lord, for His loves endures forever.' As they began to sing and praise, the Lord set ambushes against the (enemy) and they were defeated" (2 Chron. 20:15-17, 21-22).

12. As you regularly practice the presence of God in private and corporate praise and worship, ask for and receive into yourself the wholeness and emotional health that God has for you (Ps. 16:8-11).

    "As we behold the glory of the Lord, we are being transformed into His likeness with ever-increasing glory" (2 Cor. 3:18).

    "I am again in the pains of childbirth until Christ is formed in you" (Gal. 4:19).

    God will eliminate the neediness or brokenness that fed your obsession with pornography. God meets that need more effectively. It's that simple! There is no esoteric or hidden key to your healing other than this.

13. Enter into relationship with the Father through regular communion with Him so that He can effectively communicate to you the root sources of your fixation and obsession and so He can replace that need with Himself.

    "The Lord confides in those who fear Him" (Ps. 25:14).

    "I will instruct you and teach you in the way you should go; I will counsel you and watch over you" (Ps. 32:8).

    "It is written in the Prophets: 'They will all be taught by God.' Everyone who listens to the Father and learns from Him comes to Me" (John 6:45).

14. Ask God to expose emotional roots to the problem and heal them.

    Go for the root source—often an incident from childhood, from which your neediness and obsession grew.

15. Regularly seek the Lord in His Word and in fellowship with other believers at church.

    a. In the Old Testament the people of God received daily

manna (bread) from God during their wilderness experience.

b. In the New Testament Jesus has become our manna (bread) from heaven (John 6:25-35). We need to receive Him daily during our wilderness experience of living in this world that is barren of the things of God.

16. Ask God to expose any demonic strongholds that may have taken root in you as a result of viewing pornography.

    Often this occurs during the first incidences of exposure to pornography in childhood. A demonically inspired fixation can also result as a consequence of prolonged exposure or from the depth of depravity existent in the materials that a person has seen or used. There may also be a tie between the acting out of pornographic images in fantasy and masturbation, and demonic inroads in ones life.

17. If there is a demonic stronghold, pray against it in the name of Jesus, preferably with other seasoned Christians present and agreeing with you in prayer.

    "Though we live in the world, we do not wage war as the world does. The weapons we fight with are not the weapons of the world. On the contrary, they have divine power to demolish strongholds. We demolish arguments and every pretension that sets itself up against the knowledge of God, and we take captive every thought to make it obedient to Christ" (2 Cor. 10:3-5).

18. After the power of the Holy Spirit has delivered you from demonic or emotional bondage, pray for the healing presence and power of God to fill the void left behind. Pray that the diseased bent or perspective will now be replaced with God's health and purity. Pray that the ground in your soul previously held by the enemy would become a permanent habitation for the Holy Spirit.

    Remember, spiritual "possession" or habitation in a person has to do with "degree of influence," not "spatial territory."

19. If you have been victimized by pornographers (that includes uncle George or the kid down the street who may have coerced you into posing for pictures), receive from God the ability to forgive those who hurt you.

20. Learn to see yourself as God sees you—a new creation (2 Cor. 5:17), rather than through the picture of the "old man" captured in those pornographic pictures.

C. **STEPS TO FREEDOM FROM PORNOGRAPHY**

(according to Brian Stiller in the video, *The Power To Win*, Windborne Productions, Evangelical Fellowship of Canada. Used with permission).

1. Recognize you have a problem.
2. Confess any hidden sins.
3. Ask forgiveness from God.
4. Be accountable to your spouse.
5. Be accountable to a friend or pastor.
6. Identify places and things that tempt you and avoid them. Plan a daily walk. Put all deception behind you.
7. Face temptation the way Jesus did. Pray and respond with the Word of God.
8. Keep short accounts. Confess each temptation.

D. **STEPS TO FREEDOM FROM PORNOGRAPHY**

(According to Leonard LeSourd, in the article, "Escape the Sexual Trap" in the July/August 1994 issue of *New Man*" magazine. Used with permission).

1. Stop kidding yourself.
2. Make a decision to change.
3. Find a support base for your decision.
4. Cultivate a new lifestyle.
5. Be prepared for the enemy attack.
6. Avoid temptation.
7. Plan each week in advance as completely as possible
8. Reestablish your priorities.
9. Embrace abstinence.

Exercises—Pornography

1. Wait before the Lord, asking Him to reveal deep within your heart the true evil that lies in pornography.

2. Destroy every vestige of pornography that you possess. Eliminate from your environment any other materials that contribute to your lust, even though they may not be pornographic per se (clothing catalogs, etc.).

3. Eliminate everything from your life that contributes to your weakness—e.g., credit cards (if they facilitate the use of pornography); 900 number access on your phone (if dial-a-porn is a weakness); cable TV; video rental cards, etc. Starve the sin. Feed the things that lead to godliness.

4. Ask the Lord to give you a godly, healthy, and pure perspective of other people. Ask Him to change the way you see them into the way He sees them. Ask Him for His eyes and His heart for people.

5. Confess and renounce the god of idolatry that you have been serving. Ask the Lord to expose any demonic elements and renounce them in the name of Jesus.

6. Make a permanent and irrevocable commitment to God that pornography or immorality of any kind will no longer be regarded as an option in your life—without exception. Then ask Him to honor your commitment by empowering it and changing your heart so that you begin to love Him and the things He loves rather than the things of evil.

7. Join the divine army! Decide that you are going to take an aggressive stance against the kingdom of evil and devote the rest of your life to pursuing and operating in the kingdom of God.

8. Practice the mental discipline of immediately ousting any unclean thought that enters your mind by turning to God and calling on His power to drive it out.

9. Ask the Lord to transform your will into His will, so that these exercises are done freely and with great joy.

10. Meditate on the opportunity that temptation offers to choose righteousness and to bring glory to your loving Savior by serving Him in this way. Beat Satan at his own game by turning the tables of temptation right back in his face.

11. Enter into a lifestyle of regular praise and worship—filling your mind with things from above so that the things of the world grow "strangely dim."

12. Share your struggle with another faithful Christian who will listen in confidence and who will pray and exhort you to holiness.

Masturbation

If ever there was a source for secret shame and self-condemnation in this world, masturbation is it. It is the one sexual act that always leaves you feeling alone. And if you were raised under certain religious traditions, it also makes you feel very, very guilty. Why is that? I believe it's something deep inside of us—a witness from God—that something just isn't right. We know that our bodies have been designed for physical union with a person of the opposite sex. It doesn't take a rocket scientist to figure that out. But there's something more. There's the emotional element that goes unfulfilled when you are engaging in sex by yourself. There's a sadness deep within—a feeling of failure—because you are having to resort to this lonely form of self-absorption, when you know that you were created for something much higher and more fulfilling. There's also a subtle, spiritual dissociation going on that you'd like to blame on your guilt-tripping mother, but you suspect has its true source in the heart of God.

The Bible Tells Me So

A search of the Bible finds not even one reference to the practice, though some would have you believe that Onan's act of coitus interruptus was masturbation (see Gen. 38:8-9). Others will point to the seminal emissions referred to in Leviticus 15:16,18,32 and suggest that they refer to masturbation because they made the man unclean. However, the references in verses 16 and 32 (as well as in Leviticus 22:4 and Deuteronomy 23:10) are clearly natural, nocturnal emissions, because no offering needed to be made. Besides, these were rules about ritual and bodily cleanliness, and not necessarily reflections on sinful behavior. For example, the emission referred to in verse 18 is one that occurs during marital intercourse (God-created and blessed) and yet it also makes the couple temporarily unclean by the Old Testament laws.

"But," you ask, "if the Bible doesn't mention masturbation as a sin, can it be so awful?" Whenever the Bible doesn't specifically mention a particular practice, our response should always be to search the Scriptures to find any *correlating principles*. For example, the Bible doesn't forbid smoking marijuana, but the various principles of obeying the law, treating your body as a temple, not getting intoxicated, and not letting anything be master over you, all have a bearing on the question and can therefore lead you to a biblical conclusion that marijuana smoking is sinful.

What then are the correlating principles that provide us with the answer that we are seeking? The first and foremost Scripture is, of course, Matthew 5:28, in which Jesus makes it clear that we are not to lust after someone in our heart. Masturbation almost always involves a stimulating mental picture of someone else. Yet Jesus said that to even look on a woman to lust after her is to have already committed the sin of adultery in one's mind. That is not to say that an erotic thought in and of itself is sin. But once you have welcomed the thought into your mind and have mentally pursued it, it is at that point that you are using another human being to commit sexual sin. That is why all forms of pornography, or any use of the image of another person for lustful purposes is a sin.

In all of our lives there are images of people (from still pictures, movies and from real life) that come to mind to stimulate us to lust. It becomes sin when we give ground to these mental pictures and allow them to linger for our own sexual gratification. The Bible calls this transition point the conception and birth of sin (see Jas. 1:14-16), and it exhorts us to flee from such evil desires (see 2 Tim. 2:22) before they gain ground in our minds and actions.

Satan employs his demons to bring back to our memory past sexual acts and other sex-related things that we have seen, heard or experienced firsthand. Those images feed and perpetuate a bondage to masturbation. Some of the most powerful images that the devil uses are of people from our past or present over whom we've lusted long but with whom we have never had sex. The temptation to fulfill those fantasies, even if only in the mind through masturbation, is enticing. However, depending on who you are lusting over, according to our Lord Jesus Christ, you are committing adultery, fornication, homosexuality, child sex abuse or any other of a host of sins. Such mental assaults must be recognized as the spiritual threats that they are and mercilessly counterattacked by calling on the power and authority of Jesus.

As we saw in the chapter on "The Divine Intent for Sexuality," God's purpose and design in creating us male and female with the capacity to express our love for one another through sexual intercourse is to depict symbolically in the physical realm the unity of human beings with the Creator in the spiritual realm. Sex was designed to be engaged in only within the covenant bond of marriage, where it is to be a selflessly, self-giving prefigurement of the relationship that Christ intends to have with His Bride, the Church. To rightly foreshadow the heavenly fulfillment of our human sexuality is therefore to express it solely between a husband and wife, in love.

Masturbation makes a mockery of this design and purpose. It is a self-centered act born from emotional immaturity and fueled by sinful thoughts and images. It is a behavior that runs counter to God's intent and design for human sexual expression.

The Bible is filled with admonitions not to lust after the sensual things of the world (see Prov. 6:24-25; Rom. 13:13-14; Gal. 5:16-25; Col. 3:5-7; 1 Thess. 4:3-8; Jas. 4:1-4; 1 Pet. 2:11; 1 John 2:15-17). If you discipline yourself to stop the mental pictures in their tracks by calling on the power of Jesus, you will have victory over this plague of memories and images. If you confront the powers each and every time they appear, in Jesus' name, you will be amazed at the power that God has given you over such spirits.

When you first commit to removing them from their place of dominance and control, they will come at you like a plague of locusts, trying to overwhelm you so that you will give up. However, if you are truly turning to God for His power to defeat them, employing by faith your authority in Christ, and if you persevere, once they understand that you mean business, they will withdraw until they can figure out a way to approach you that will catch you off guard. They will save their attacks for times in your life when you have been weakened by one circumstance or another and then try again to regain their position of influence.

One night, I asked God if there were any other Scriptures that had application to this behavior, and to my surprise, He uncovered several more. But first, He simply spoke to me these words: "Do not let anything become master over you." As I rifled through my concordance, I came across the following Scriptures:

> *I will not be mastered by anything (1 Cor. 6:12c, NASB).*
> *A man is a slave to whatever has mastered him (2 Pet. 2:19).*
> *Sin shall not be your master (Rom. 6:14).*

Those who engage in masturbation know very well that it is a behavior that masters them. I've never had a person yet honestly claim to have control over their practice of masturbation. It controls them. It tells them who, when, where, what and how. It seduces them with immoral, erotic images of others—sometimes images so depraved that they can hardly believe their own minds.

Even those Christian leaders who believe it to be generally harmless would agree that there are sinful influences and practices that often complicate the matter and create a practice that can lead to serious bondage and sin.

It is theoretically possible to limit masturbation to infrequent occasions of sexual release, where mental pictures do not inspire or intrude, and where some emotionally dysfunctional incitement does not pertain, but that is not what is going on in 99.9 percent of the cases. In the real world, pure and healthy, mindless masturbation simply doesn't happen. There are too many erotic stimuli in the environment, too many memories of past pleasures, and legions of demons who make certain that our minds are filled with immoral thoughts, particularly when we are engaged in this sort of activity.

There is, therefore, strong biblical evidence that masturbation is a sin. However, those who have fallen into such a bondage are often fleeing from the stress and pain of life and have already developed the foundation of addictive behavior, which is self-hatred and a shame-based way of thinking. For them, a law-based argument from Scripture will probably not be persuasive. They will probably need the same approach that the Lord ultimately took with me during my struggle with this behavior. One night, He simply said to me, "David, I have something better."

The Root Causes for the Bondage

Many professionals would suggest that masturbation is a harmless response to the body's overproduction of sex hormones and that it is an inevitable reaction, particularly in the teen years, to that pressure. Even many respected Christian leaders have taken this position. If, however, you ask a physician if there is any medical or other physiological necessity for masturbation, they will tell you no. There is no physical necessity in the human body to practice masturbation. Whatever a man's body needs to discharge, it does quite naturally with nocturnal emissions. And if we are to say that masturbation is a healthy and godly behavior simply because it brings pleasure, then we have gone entirely outside of the counsel of Scripture.

As with most every other kind of dysfunctional behavior, the roots are to be found in the person's childhood emotional development.

It is well known that masturbation at a very young age can be a sign of emotional disturbance, particularly if it is compulsive. An infant who clutches at his genitals may be suffering from separation anxiety. However, older children (two to eight years old) are more likely reacting to sexual abuse or something else in their environment that is causing deep anxiety. The pleasure of the act is being used as a pain-blocking mechanism, a distraction from whatever is causing distress (rejection, ridicule, failure, stress, abuse, etc).

When tied to such emotional or mental triggers, the chemicals in the brain that are released during self-stimulation quickly become an addictive drug, much like heroin or cocaine. Children like this have trained themselves to respond to stress, pain, and anxiety by turning to a pleasure-inducing solution. As they continue in this pattern, they will fail to develop the emotional skills that are needed to work through the difficulties of life. In other words, they are likely to develop a chronically immature approach to stress-management and problem-solving.

As we noted in the chapter on "The Causes of Homosexuality," early-onset masturbation, combined with viewing oneself in a mirror in the process, results in programming one's mind to associate the sight of one's own genitals with sexual pleasure and excitement. These factors are among the highest correlates in studies of subject of sexual identity confusion.

So, there is no question that children in stressful environments, especially those with sensitive temperaments and no one to help them process their stress in a healthy manner, will adopt immature patterns of coping with that stress that will then persist into their adult years. The earlier this pattern is established, the more "hardwired" or autonomic it will be.

There is also no question that masturbation is one of those coping behaviors that children and adolescents often employ. It's readily available, it's free, and it produces a flood of pleasure-causing chemicals that effectively relieve the immediate sense of anxiety.

This well-known pattern begs another question: How much of a stressful environment is necessary for the pattern to develop? Does it require a hugely stressful environment or can it generate itself from the levels of stress normally present in the lives of most children and adolescents today? I think the answer is obvious. Add to that the wholesale absence in our culture of any moral boundaries on the subject. Add to that the fact that our culture actually encourages and blesses a child's practice of masturbation. Then add to that the fact that most of the parents and authorities in a child's life today model this same immature pattern for problem-solving by regularly turning to stress-relieving behaviors or substances rather than working through life's difficulties in a mature fashion. The kids don't stand a chance. Addictive or "arrested" behavior is pandemic in our culture.

However, this must also be said: if the pattern described above is developing in a child or adolescent, the answer is not to hit the young person over the head with a Bible. The answer is found (with God's help) in uncovering the cause for the anxiety, helping to remove, alleviate and/or work through it in a healthy fashion, and then seeking God together for the renewing, reprogramming and guarding of his or her mind. Children need to be taught the biblical principles for working through problems and for suffering the discomforts of life without resorting to moral compromise.

Additional problems can arise as a person grows older. For example, if someone is deeply shy or inhibited, masturbation can be the vehicle whereby they perpetuate their disposition to remain self-contained and in need of no one. Even for someone with a basic fear of intimacy (such as the sex addict), masturbation can become something that satisfies sexual need enough that a normal, healthy relationship with a member of the opposite sex is never considered. In essence, such people sentence themselves to perpetual loneliness and isolation by privately satiating the only force in their life that might be powerful enough to motivate them to move out of their stunted emotional growth and into the world of interpersonal relationships.

Masturbation is also a "homo" sexual act in that the person is having sex with him/herself. For the person who is already developing homosexual neurosis, it can be a major contributing factor to the further development of that confusion. Even for the heterosexual sex addict, masturbation can significantly contribute to the worsening of that bondage since it is a turning in on one's self—a narcissistic neurosis that feeds introspection and other dysfunctions. This is the very food of both the sex addict and the homosexual.

Helping the Adolescent Through Puberty

What then do we say about masturbation in the adolescent? After all, the sex drive is so very strong during those years. Can't we just give them a break and let them do it?

Is it "giving them a break" to sit idly by while they develop dysfunctional coping mechanisms that may lead to a lifetime of addictive behavior? Is it "giving them a break" to sit idly by while they desecrate the entire function and purpose of their sexuality?

In reality, we're not going to control what they do. They are free moral agents and will do what they want to do. But as adults we are responsible for giving them sound guidance and direction. That is our solemn calling as parents and authority figures. What they do with that is up to them. But to forsake their proper training just because many of them may reject it is a serious dereliction of responsibility on our part, one that we will answer for before God.

In dealing with the child who is going through puberty, we must first acknowledge that there are several factors at work. There is a natural curiosity (especially in boys) to "take apart" and examine new things, a tendency that will continue as they develop new physical sensations and capacities. Coming down hard on an adolescent or child who is engaged in innocent investigation of this sort is precisely the *wrong* thing to do. Remember the biblical principle: imposing "law" in the absence of understanding and a changed heart will only stir up sin and rebellion.

A more effective approach is to do what God did with me—*let them know that there is something better*—a wiser, more fulfilling approach to meeting their newly emerging needs, one that God designed just for them.

Will they listen to you? It depends. You will be far more persuasive in the matter if you have already developed your own intimate relationship with the Lord and have been sharing the joy of it with your child on a regular basis. That witness will stir up in them a love and desire for the Lord Jesus Christ. It will also help if you have been an example to them of the real "weak but strong" Christian that God calls us to be, so that they can learn from your example how to call upon God's power, as well as how to handle failure.

It will be best to have several private discussions with them over a period of several months about the blessing of sex in its proper context and God's provision for helping us to control it. Begin doing this by the age of 10 or 11, or earlier if the school system or their peers have already started to teach about sex. Cast the glorious vision into their hearts that you read about in the chapter called "The Divine Intent for Sexuality."

Early on, develop an open, vulnerable, and honest relationship with your child, so that he or she is free to discuss such issues without difficulty. Tell your child of your own struggles in this area (father to son, mother to daughter) and how God taught you to turn to Him for help when tempted. Talk about the blessings of obedience to God, how His commandments are protective, not restrictive, how they are really promises of what He will accomplish in them by His power if they will honestly and fully pursue Him for the power to do His will.

Finally, let them know that since God made their bodies, He can help them control their bodies. God has the power, if asked, to help quench the fire, or at least to reduce it to a manageable level until the time when they will marry. They may feel reticent about asking God to lighten their sexual desire for fear that He won't bring it back when the time comes for them to marry, but that is a groundless fear.

God expects them to keep their environment as free as possible from stimulants and enticements, but the supernatural miracle of lessening hormonal torment is something God is more than willing to do for the one who truly wants to live a holy life.

Because sexuality is not purely physical but it also has emotional and spiritual dimensions, a young person's intimacy with God can bring about a level of fulfillment that can significantly contribute to success in their battle with natural sexual impulses. The idea that God can meet and fulfill needs expressed sexually will seem weird to them at first, but that weirdness has more to do with our insufficient view of human than with the way things really are.

Additionally, and this is important, when they fail to stay pure in this area, watch that they do not condemn themselves or develop self-hatred or the belief that God is mad at them or doesn't love them anymore. This is one of Satan's most effective traps and can keep a person from even wanting to approach God for help. Remind them that "there is now no condemnation for those who are in Christ Jesus" (Rom. 8:1), and that "If we confess our sins, He is faithful and just and will forgive us our sins and purify us from all unrighteousness" (1 John 1:9).

Masturbation in Marriage

We have already examined numerous biblical texts and discovered that masturbation runs completely opposite to the design and purpose for human sexuality; that it involves a sinful use of the images of others and is tantamount to committing the actual sins of adultery, fornication, homosexuality, child abuse, etc., and that it is a stronghold that masters its participants rather than the other way around. Consequently, masturbation within marriage is equally wrong.

Many would like to use Hebrews 13:4a to excuse whatever activity one chooses within marriage, which in the King James version reads, "Marriage is honorable in all, and the bed undefiled." However, the context of that passage is clearly calling for a pure and holy marriage bed, undefiled specifically by fornication and adultery. It is not giving a blanket license to sexual activities of any kind within marriage. The biblical principles that should be followed for sexual activity within marriage are twofold: (1) Is the behavior consistent with God's design and purpose for human sexuality and marriage? And (2) is the sexual activity mutually desired, causing no harm to either party?

Masturbation transgresses the first condition. A host of other sexual behaviors (for example, anal sex of any kind, sadism, masochism, oral sex to the point of ejaculation, transgender, fetishism, voyeurism, exhibitionism, etc.) transgresses both principles.

What about mutual masturbation in marriage as a way to prevent children? There are far more natural ways to achieve such goals that do not require overturning God's design for human sexual expression. "Natural Family Planning" is the most popular and effective, reportedly more effective than the birth control pill itself (which is often an abortifacient, making it a very serious breech indeed).

Some married couples ask if masturbation is okay while their spouse is out of town, or in the hospital, or is in some other way unavailable. That very question reveals a focus on self-pleasure rather than the biblical call to *give* pleasure to one's spouse and/or to bear the fruit of children. Masturbating to the image of your spouse is not an act of love. Your spouse is not even there. You are having an intimate relationship with a phantom image that you can manipulate at will for your own selfish pleasure. It is a return to using people as sex objects. It is idolatry. If your spouse is unavailable or incapable of having sexual relations for one reason or another, your call becomes the same as that of every single person—to live a chaste and celibate life. Spend that extra time and energy pursuing a deeper level of serving the needs of your divine Spouse. Find your life by giving it away (see Mark 8:35; Phil. 3:8).

I have had many married couples come up to me after conferences, pleading with me to help them. They had expected that when they got married, their prior practice of masturbation would naturally end because they could now have all the sex that they wanted. When the habit did not go away, they were devastated and were left wondering what was wrong with them. No better illustration could I have than this one that masturbation is unnatural and actually battles against the God-ordained path for human sexual expression, as well as marriage itself. It is an expression of emotional immaturity and, in many cases, willful rebellion against God. It does not go away simply because you now have a marriage certificate in your hand. It may disappear for a brief period of time after the marriage, but eventually it will return because it is an ingrained habit formed out of sexual and emotional brokenness and bolstered by sinful beliefs, practices, and concomitant demonic strongholds.

Another shocker happens for many newly married couples when one partner, with a history of masturbation, enters the marriage after having deeply ingrained a mental and physical expectation for orgasm of a certain number of times per week (or day). This sort of patterning does not change the day after the wedding. The new husband or wife will be unlikely to be able to sustain the spouse's frequency expectations. Many wives in such a position are surprised to find themselves feeling glad when their husbands continue to look at pornography and practice masturbation because it takes the pressure off of them to meet such a voracious sexual appetite.

Another problem that masturbation causes once a couple marries is that the husband with a history of practicing it will almost certainly have conditioned his mind and body to come to orgasm more quickly than is desired in sexual intercourse. Until the day of his marriage, there was no one to attend to but himself and therefore no reason to delay orgasm. Little did he realize that he was setting himself up for a problem with premature ejaculation once he got married.

The images of other people used during masturbation become a serious threat to a person's capacity to center on the marriage partner during intercourse. They become a plague that bombards the mind, drawing them away from the intimacy that God intends them to have with the spouse. In many cases, since those images were used repeatedly in the past to bring about guaranteed, intense sexual pleasure, they may actually be *deliberately* called to mind during sex in order to intensify the experience. This is a mockery of what God intended sexual expression to be, as well as being adultery.

Pornography and Masturbation

If pornography is used in masturbation, the problem is severely compounded. There is a chemical imprinting that takes place in the brain when viewing pornography that is significantly strengthened when combined with the pleasure of masturbation.

A second problem is that in the highly controlled environment of pornography and masturbation, your sexual responses are programmed to specific fantasies that usually do not reflect real-life possibilities. This makes it impossible for normal sexual relations with your spouse (or future spouse) to satisfy you. This is one of the main reasons why people become impotent or resort to prostitutes, who will play out the perverted scenarios that their clients have programmed into their minds.

Another problem with combining masturbation and pornography (noted already in the chapter on "Pornography"), is that the individual grows to see people as sex objects rather than as people to love. He or she also idealizes the objects of their lust, which may cause problems later in life when they try to receive the same level of pleasure from a mate who does not match up to those idealized images.

Pornography and masturbation can also serve to fixate the mind in an obsessive search for greater and greater thrills. In a brief span of time, a person's moral defenses may simply collapse, as highly delineated forms of sexual activity that are found in pornography, which are often aberrant or bizarre, are embraced. This can lead to the sexual use of minors, foreign objects and even animals, as well as opening a door to voyeurism and exhibitionism.

As we've already seen, bringing pornography into the picture will significantly increase the chances that a demonic stronghold will develop from the sin of masturbation. It is not for nothing that Scripture warns us: "Be self-controlled and alert. Your enemy the devil prowls around like a roaring lion looking for someone to devour" (1 Pet. 5:8). If the devil is looking for someone to devour, and you are on his turf with your nose buried in a porn magazine, it won't take him long to find out.

In actuality, the reason you have your nose buried in that magazine is because Satan has already been at work in you. His scheme begins long before the big, consequential sin. He works on us for a season in much smaller ways—tilling the ground over a period of time with a flurry of less obvious sins (such as masturbation), so that when the temptation to engage in brazen idolatry comes (such as looking at pornography), you've already weakened yourself with multiple compromises and are vulnerable to a more significant moral collapse.

For those who find it difficult to believe that sexual sin is idolatry, have a look at Ephesians 5:3,5, which reads: "But among you there must not be even a hint of sexual immorality. . . . No immoral, impure or greedy person—*such a man is an idolater*—has any inheritance in the kingdom of Christ and of God" (emphasis added).

If you are an idolater, you draw your life from or putting your hope in someone or something other than God. You are trying to find your completion or fulfillment in the creature rather than the Creator. You are giving of your heart in worship to someone or something other than God and uniting your spirit with that object of worship. The use of pornography is just such a giving of one's spirit to an idol and masturbation is worshipping at the idol of self. Indeed, according to this passage in Ephesians, all sexual immorality is idolatry.

If you find yourself under demonic assault as a result of a life that has been filled with pornography and masturbation, remember my advice in the chapter on the "Healing of Homosexual Confusion": If sexual images sweep over you suddenly and with great power, consider them a demonic attack and speak to the demons, commanding in Jesus' name that they stop and go where Jesus sends them. Then turn to the Lord and ask Him to send them away. Tell Him that you want Him rather than the perverted thoughts of evil.

On the other hand, if the temptation has a more natural feel to it and has a trail of compromises leading up to it, then that is a sin from your own heart. Turn to God in repentance for your sin and for your love of that sin. After all, if your heart didn't love it, it would not tempt you (see Matt. 15:19; Jas. 1:14-15.)

What sort of compromises will you need to repent of? Generally, preceding the point of temptation, there will have been a pattern of carelessness and sin in your use of time, your choice of company, your thought life, or the things you have been watching or reading. There might also be recent turmoil, stress, rejection, anger and hurt, which can breed a spirit of rebellion in the heart against God, who has, in your mind, been unfaithful or unconcerned about you in "allowing" such wearying trials to overtake you.

Let me describe a typical pattern of events that can set someone off into repeating the use of pornography and the practice of masturbation. As I do, remember that people with addictive personalities believe deep inside that they are defective, a condition for which they secretly blame God.

Some *input* (a put-down at work, on a date, by your spouse, etc.), strikes a present, internal *belief* ("I'm unlovable or defective"), creating a *feeling* (despair, anxiety, self-pity, etc.), which elicits a *thought* ("I'm no good and this proves it!").

The pain of being reminded of one's shortcomings triggers a flight into *fantasy*—a flight from intimacy into a safe, make-believe world of acceptance, which gives birth to an *action* (sinful act), which has a *consequence* (arrest, humiliation, self-condemnation)—and that serves as the *input* for a repeat of the cycle.

A core problem is *pride*. It is my pride that reacts in anger and rebellion at being reminded that I am considered to be defective.

Breaking this problem requires a shift in my belief system. That can only come at a transforming level when God Himself speaks the truth into my heart during times of being ministered to by the body of Christ and during times of intimacy with Him.

As you seek God in this matter, ask Him to forgive you and to transform your beliefs and your affections so that they mirror His own. Commit to cleaning up that trail that you know will lead you back into sin if it is not dealt with. Commit to replacing your idols of lust with more and deeper worship of God.

Over a period of time, this "partnership" approach with God has tremendous effects in increasing your faith that God is actually there, powerful, and ready to assist you at any time of need. When He answers your calls of distress, repeatedly and powerfully (which He will do every time you really want Him to), a new joy of gratefulness will grow in your heart for Him.

Let me give you an illustration from my own life about our frightening capacity at self-deception, and consequent habit of asking God for things that we really don't want. When I first got saved and set free from a horrendously out-of-control life that included alcoholism, drug addiction, sex addiction, prostitution, homosexual confusion—all at maximum, death-defying levels—I began a ten-year battle with God over the one lingering issue of masturbation. For the first five years, I convinced myself that it wasn't a sin, but was instead God's provision for single people. I deftly parried all attempts by the Spirit of God to speak to me on the issue simply by ignoring Him and pretending that He wasn't speaking to me. I convinced myself that the convicting thoughts that I had on the matter were the echoing voices of guilt-tripping fundamentalists who, I scornfully decided, were operating out of a fear of sex or a need to control.

During the second five years, however, God finally got through to me that it was indeed a sin and that He had something better. Wanting to please Him, I began asking Him to deliver me from the habit. As the years progressed, I even begged Him to set me free, often with tears streaming down my face. It deeply puzzled me why He had set me free from so many other powerful sins in the past but seemed to be leaving me stranded with this one.

One night as I was engaged in this pleading ritual, the presence of God filled the room and I instantly knew that He had come to set me free. You would have thought that I would have been overjoyed after five years of pleading, but the moment He entered my room, I realized that He had come to set me *free indeed*—which meant that He expected a heart commitment from me that masturbation would never again be considered an option in my life; that it would never again be held out as a "last resort" crutch when life got too stressful or painful. He wasn't demanding perfect performance—only a genuine commitment to it.

When I realized the import of the moment and its ramifications, from within my heart came the words, "Oh, no!" To my surprise, I could sense terror rising up from within me. And for the first time ever, I began to see some of the reasons why I hadn't been set free. Deep inside, I was terrified of living without that crutch, which was by then the only reliable means to instant peace that remained under my control. Additionally, "How could I be a man and be without any expression of my sexuality?" I thought. Here I had weathered the pain of working through the insecurities of my masculinity that had been associated with my homosexual neurosis, and now I was being asked to give up the only natural expression of sexuality left to me as a single person. It was too frightening a prospect. It even made me angry.

I knew then why God had never set me free from masturbation. I had never truly wanted to be free. The behavior was still tied to insecurities that awaited their own full healing. I had only mouthed the religious words that I knew God wanted to hear, like a trained seal. So that night, I turned from God's offer of freedom and returned to the behavior. However, now I knew what the blocking issues were. I knew how to pray more specifically. Most importantly, I knew that I had to pray for God to make me truly willing to be free. And so I did.

Getting Free

Boiled down to its bottom line, *masturbation is both a flight from responsibility and a flight from intimacy.* In broad strokes, that is where we are most likely to discover its root causes, as the Spirit of God leads us through our own personal path to freedom.

Here are a few of the places where God took me in order to reach that very goal. At one point or another, He said the following things to me:

- Ask God for forgiveness for using images and memories of actual people for stimulation. Receive and accept His forgiveness, and sin no more.
- Set your heart against the practice of masturbation. As a permanent and final decision, determine that when the temptation returns, that sin will *never again* be considered an option. That will force you to seek God for the comfort and the satisfaction that you have been achieving through this practice.
- Set your mind on believing that God has something better—that He does indeed have the power and ability to satisfy your physical cravings through supernatural and/or natural means and to bring you to that better place.
- Discipline your mind by calling on the Lord whenever mental images or thoughts come in that are sinful, and obtain the power to overcome the temptation.
- Be ruthless in your pursuit of God's power over this obsession, and rest your faith wholly in God's ability to overcome the problem rather than your own. Be careful to recognize and avoid the traps of self-will and self-effort. These are the breeding grounds for self-righteousness. Remember: "Do not fear, for I am with you; do not be dismayed, for I am your God. I will strengthen you and help you; I will uphold you with my righteous right hand" (Isa. 41:10). "Nothing is impossible with God" (Luke 1:37).

- Never ignore your responsibility to seek God's power and to use it once it has been given.
- Remove every influence that leads you into desiring and repeating the act of masturbation.
- Don't be a slave to your body. Be its master! Being physically stimulated does not mean that you have to obey your body and be drawn into the act.
- Truly desire *permanent transformation!* It will be a long, wearying battle, because Satan will not acquiesce until he knows you mean business. The key to winning the battle therefore, is in coming to the place of love and devotion to the Lord that you fully want Him rather than any other god.
- Take the focus off of yourself and put it on the sufficiency of Christ, through significant time spent in praise and worship of the Lord. Deepen your relationship with the Father through Scripture-reading and prayer as well, and receive His pure and healthy perspective on sex. As you worship God and become more intimate with Him, ask Him to reveal the keys to your deliverance. (A wonderful guidebook in this regard is Hearing God, by Peter Lord.)
- Seek God for a *love* of purity. Be a man or woman after God's own, pure heart. The things that we seek with all our heart are the things that we truly admire.
- Practice "listening prayer." Sit alone and wait on the Lord. Do not bring your own list of requests. Be quiet, and listen for God to bring up what is on His heart to pray about. With honesty, respond to what the Holy Spirit brings up. Tell God what you honestly feel and think about the issue, even if it includes questions about God's participation (or lack of participation), in the matter. You can express your feelings of anger and unbelief toward God. He much prefers honesty to pretense, and He will reward it by showing you the wisdom of His actions (or non-actions), in the matter. Then you can repent of having judged the Lord. You will often find that as you continue to lay out the problem before the Lord (what it is and how it affects you emotionally, intellectually and spiritually), God will bring clarity to the issue from your own mouth. Make the choice to put faith over emotion, and pray with the determination to be obedient to whatever God tells you.
- Ask God to reveal the hidden mysteries behind your particular sexual bondage and to heal you of them (see Dan. 2:27-28,47).
- Ask Him to expose the levels of self-deception that you have lived under that have enabled you to justify continuing to live in sin. He will show you how you have dealt with your guilt by pretending away the offense or by minimizing its gravity and how, after years of this, you fully believe the lies—that you aren't really

sinning, or sinning all that much, or that you want to be free but can't find your way out of the trap you're in.
• Discern and break the "rituals" of addictive behavior. Take note of common settings and change them. Take note of common stress-inducing issues, events and relationships, recognize your sexual responses to these situations, and establish countermeasures in advance, foremost of which should be a determination to turn to the Lord at the first hint of sexualized ritual. Remember that the more you blame God or parents (who represent God), the more likely that your sin will be darker—immorality or violence, as opposed to overeating, for example. Take note of points of inevitability—the moment when you become inexorably drawn into the act. What were you doing at that moment? Look for patterns. Teach yourself to respond in a different manner well ahead of the moment of inevitability. Look for visual points of stimulation such as mirrors, windows, publications, etc., and remove them from your environment as best you can. Set your heart, and *relentlessly* practice, a turning to the Lord for His power to overcome, from the very outset of the ritualization process. Do not base your hopes on these countermeasures alone to solve your problem. Instead, make certain to diligently address the central solution, which is a deep intimacy and fullness with the Father.
• Avoid self-pity and condemnation. These are self-centered exercises in false humility and unbelief. Learn to distinguish them from repentance and sorrow over sin. Believe God's Word when it says there is no condemnation for those who are in Christ Jesus (Rom. 8:1).
• Remember that healing of the problem of masturbation requires: a complete shift in priorities, a sincere desire and determination to be healed, a discovery and healing of the root emotional and sin problems, and a willingness to believe and to act on God's promises.
• Remember that God is always there at any time when you are sexually stimulated—there with the power to quench the fire of the moment.
• If you are physiologically "highly sexed," ask God for His grace to heal that problem and to bring you into physiological normalcy (see Gal. 5:24; Rom. 6:6-7).

If you are already being controlled by the practice of masturbation, there is hope. I know that it seems hopeless, but by Christ's power, you can be delivered from this bondage.

In the chapter on "Foundations for Healing Sexual Brokenness" I told the story of begging God to set me free from my thirty-year bondage to masturbation and then turning Him down when He finally came to do so. He, of course, knew that I would turn down His offer, but graciously bestowed on me that object lesson so that I could see the self-deception that I was under.

Part of the problem was that I was a perfectionist, and didn't want to do anything that I couldn't do perfectly. So I lived under a great deal of self-condemnation regarding this issue. I remember one night, the Lord saying to me, "David, you are much harder on yourself than I ever will be. I've got lots more grace for your failings than you do. Let me set you free through that grace."

Six months after that incident, I was truly ready to be delivered. I had been praying for God to make me willing. I had been working with the Spirit of God on the insecurities that had caused me to be afraid of being free. I had been growing in how to be transformed by His grace (see Titus 2:11-14). And I was finally ready for Him to set me free *indeed*.

One night, while in I was in worship, I asked God to set me free, and His presence entered my room once again, but this time, I said "Yes" to His power to deliver me. The long dark night was over. In the more than twenty-five years since then, even during moments of stress and weakness, there have been very few times when I have resorted to that behavior—which is an absolute miracle! In fact, there have been as many as ten years in between such moments.

And here is the greatest consequence of all: I did not lose my masculinity by giving up the willful habit of masturbation. In fact, since that day of deliverance, though I remain celibate (called to remain single for life, in fact), I have never felt more masculine or complete in my masculinity. I have never felt more sexually fulfilled either. Everything that Satan promised me through that sin has been given me through the *forsaking* of that sin. Hallelujah!

May I remind you again about the "prime directive"—that for any such healing, we must first develop an intimate relationship with God. In that place of intimacy, God reveals to us the hidden mysteries of our bondage and imparts to us power to overcome sin.

If you truly are a seeker of wisdom, then forsake the rationalizations for sin and the pursuit of self-pleasure. Believe that God never takes away without giving back something infinitely more valuable. Once God has delivered you from the "dirty little habit" of masturbation, you will not want to go back. Why? Because after He has delivered you, you will discover that what you had been holding onto was a toxic, filthy rag, and what He has for you in its place, is a glorious robe of righteousness.

Study Section— Masturbation

A. **MASTURBATION IS BOTH A FLIGHT FROM RESPONSIBILITY AND A FLIGHT FROM INTIMACY.**

   1. Biblical Perspective

      a. There is no biblical passage that specifically or directly addresses this behavior.

      b. There are many applicable principles, however.

         (1) Do not lust after someone in your heart (Mt. 5:28).

         (2) Do not commit adultery or fornication (Dt. 5:18).

         (3) Do not covet your neighbor's wife (Dt. 5:21).

         (4) Do not let anything become master over you.

         "I will not be mastered by anything" (1 Cor. 6:12, NASB).

         "A man is a slave to whatever has mastered him" (2 Pet. 2:19).

         "Sin shall not be your master" (Rom. 6:14).

   2. Masturbation and the Adolescent

      a. There is a natural curiosity (especially in boys) to "take apart" and examine new things. Coming down hard on an adolescent or child who is engaged in innocent investigation of this sort is precisely the *wrong* thing to do. Remember the biblical principle, that imposing "law" in the absence of a changed heart and understanding will only stir up sin and rebellion.

      b. A more effective approach is to emphasize that there is *something better*—a wiser, more fulfilling approach to meeting such needs, one that God designed just for man. You will be persuasive in this matter if you:

(1) stir up a love and desire for the Lord Jesus Christ in the child by nurturing your own deep and meaningful relationship with the Lord and sharing the joy of it with your child, and by being an example of the real "weak but strong" Christian that God calls us to be.

(2) have several private discussions over a period of several months, by the age of 10 or 11, about the blessing of sex in its proper context and God's provision for helping us to control it.

(3) develop early on, an open, vulnerable, and honest relationship with your child, so that they are free to discuss such issues without difficulty. Tell them of your own struggles in this area and how God taught you to turn to Him for help when tempted. Talk about the blessings of obedience to God, how His commandments are protective, not restrictive, how they are really promises of what He will accomplish in us by His power if we will honestly and fully pursue Him for the power to do His will.

c. Masturbation that is repeated compulsively in a child or adolescent signals the presence of an emotional disturbance within the child that is causing him or her to turn inward for solace and consolation. The response is not to attack the behavior, but to seek God together for the root problem.

(1) In this context, masturbation is probably serving as a pain-blocking mechanism. The chemicals that are released in the brain upon orgasm are being used as a pain-killing drug, much like any drug addict would do.

(2) The child is programming him or herself to turn to solutions that block problems rather than solve them. This immature life-pattern for problem solving is highly dysfunctional and is the foundation upon which is laid a lifetime of addictive behavior.

(3) Early onset masturbation, combined with viewing oneself in a mirror in the process, results in programming one's mind to associate the sight of one's own genitals with sexual pleasure and

excitement. These factors are among the highest correlates in studies done, on the subject of sexual identity confusion.

3. Masturbation in Marriage

   a. Through the regular practice of masturbation in childhood and adolescence, a "frequency of orgasm" pattern and expectation is established that does not change the day after the wedding.

   b. The masturbation problem may be an emotional problem or purely a sin problem carried over from his or her past. It is important to seek a revelation from the Holy Spirit as to the root cause, as well as the process for healing and deliverance.

   c. The Lord can quench the fire and remove the roots of the problem supernaturally if the person is willing to be delivered.

   d. What about mutual masturbation in marriage as a way to prevent children? If this is truly the only motivation for the act and is carried out by married couples for each other, it would not seem to be a problem. However, I would counsel you to seek God for a peace about issues like this so that your counsel comes from Him, not man.

4. Link to Pornography

   a. Pornography is often used, creating a host of potential problems:

      (1) People come to be seen as sex objects, rather than human beings to whom you center your attention.

      (2) In the highly controlled environment of pornography and masturbation, your sexual responses are programmed to specific fantasies that usually do not reflect real-life possibilities. This makes it impossible for normal sexual relations with your spouse to satisfy you. This is one of the main reasons why some people become impotent or resort to prostitutes, who play out the perverted scenarios that they've programmed their body to respond to through the use of pornography.

(3) Frequent masturbation also serves to program the mind into accepting the highly delineated and limited forms of sexual activity that are found in the pornography—which are often aberrant or bizarre.

5. Other Problems

   a. In the hiddenness of one's secret world of masturbation, a person often begins a search for greater and greater thrills. This can eventually result in the use of children, animals, physical objects, voyeurism and even exhibitionism, as a stimulant, even if only in one's imagination. That then becomes the fodder for actually using such people or things at a future point of weakness or depravity.

   b. Frequent masturbation is often the cause of premature ejaculation later in life, because there is no one there to attend to but one's self and therefore no reason to delay the orgasm.

   c. Masturbation can be the vehicle whereby the inhibited person maintains their propensity to remain self-contained and in need of no one.

   d. Masturbation can become the gateway for a demonic stronghold to develop in your life.

   e. Masturbation is a "homo" sexual act and can be a contributing factor to the development of homosexuality in the person who is already headed in that direction.

   f. Masturbation is a turning in on one's self—a narcissistic neurosis that feeds introspection and other dysfunctional directions.

B. SOME THINGS YOU SHOULD DO

1. "It is God's will that…each of you should learn to control his own body" (1 Thes. 4:3-4).

   a. Set your heart against the practice of masturbation. As a permanent and final decision, determine that this sin will no longer be an option in your life. When the temptation returns, masturbation will *never again* be considered as an option. That will force you to seek God for the comfort and the satisfaction that you have been achieving through this practice.

b. Set your mind on believing that God has something better—that He does indeed have the power and ability to satisfy your physical cravings through supernatural and/or natural means.

c. Discipline your mind by calling on the Lord whenever mental images or thoughts come in that are sinful, and obtain the power to overcome the temptation.

d. Remove every influence that leads you into desiring and repeating the act of masturbation.

e. Being physically stimulated does not mean that you have to obey your body and be drawn into the act. Don't be a slave to your body. Be its master.

"If you do not do what is right, sin is crouching at your door; it desires to have you, but *you must master it*" (Gen. 4:7).

f. If you have been using the images and memories of actual people to stimulate you to masturbate, ask God for forgiveness, receive and accept His forgiveness, and sin no more.

g. You must truly desire *permanent transformation!* It will be a long, wearying battle, because Satan will not acquiesce until he knows you mean business. The key to winning the battle therefore, is in coming to the place of love and devotion to the Lord that you fully want Him rather than any other god.

2. There are two sources for the temptations that lead you into sin:

a. Demonic

"The evening meal was being served, and the devil had already prompted Judas Iscariot, son of Simon, to betray Jesus" (John 13:2).

"Be self-controlled and alert. Your enemy the devil

prowls around like a roaring lion looking for someone to devour" (1 Peter 5:8).

God allows the enemy to tempt us in order to test our hearts, thus giving us an opportunity to pass the test (by choosing God) and thereby grow even stronger in the things of the Spirit.

"You know that the testing of your faith develops perseverance. Perseverance must finish its work so that you may be mature and complete, not lacking anything" (James 1:3-4).

"We are not trying to please men, but God, who tests our hearts" (1 Thes. 2:4).

The process that Satan uses to tempt us begins long before the actual sinful thought. He precedes the sinful thought by tempting us over a period of time to unwittingly till the ground with many, less obvious sins, so that when the sexual thought comes, we are often spiritually weakened and more vulnerable to moral collapse as a result of the flurry of smaller sins.

If sexual images sweep over you suddenly and with great power, consider them a demonic attack and speak to the demons, commanding that they stop and go where Jesus sends them, in Jesus name! Then turn to the Lord and ask Him to send them away—that you want Him rather than the perverted thoughts of evil. Trust that He knows better where to send them than you do.

Over a period of time, this "partnership" approach with God has tremendous effects in increasing your faith that God is actually there, powerful, and ready to assist you at any time of need. When He answers your calls of distress, repeatedly and powerfully (which He will do *every time* you want Him to), a new joy of gratefulness will grow in your heart for Him.

b. Your own heart

"Out of the heart comes evil thoughts, murder, adultery, sexual immorality, theft, false testimony, slander" (Mt. 15:19).

"Each one is tempted when, by his own evil desire, he

is dragged away and enticed. Then, after desire has conceived, it gives birth to sin; and sin, when it is full-grown, gives birth to death" (James 1:14-15).

The source for these temptations can be traced to a pattern of carelessness and sin in your use of time, your choice of company, your thought life, or the things you have been watching or reading preceding the point of temptation. They can also be the result of recent turmoil, stress, rejection, anger and hurt, which sometimes breeds a spirit of rebellion in the heart against God, who has, in your mind, been unfaithful or unconcerned about you in "allowing" such wearying trials to overtake you.

"Despair, is suffering without meaning" (Viktor Frankl).

Despair, is more often (I think), the result of the sins of unbelief—of judging God, and of choosing to assume that He has erred or not kept His promises or fulfilled my expectations.

Some *Input* (a put down at work, on a date, by your spouse, etc.), strikes a present, internal *Belief* ("I'm defective"), creating a *Feeling* (despair, anxiety, self-pity, etc.), which elicits a *Thought* ("I'm no good and this proves it!").

The pain of being reminded of one's shortcomings triggers a flight into *Fantasy* (a safe world of acceptance)—a flight from intimacy, which gives birth to an *Action* (sinful act), which has a *Consequence* (arrest, humiliation, self-condemnation), that serves as the *Input* for a repeat of the cycle.

A core problem is "pride." It is my pride that reacts in anger

and rebellion at being reminded that I am considered to be defective.

3. Be ruthless in your pursuit of God's power over this obsession, and rest your faith wholly in God's ability to overcome the problem rather than your own. Be careful to recognize and avoid the trap of self-will and self-effort. These are the breeding grounds for self-righteousness. Take the focus off of yourself and put it on the sufficiency of Christ, through significant time spent in praise and worship of the Lord (Is. 40:31; Mt. 28:18; Acts 10:38).

   "Do not fear, for I am with you; do not be dismayed, for I am your God. I will strengthen you and help you; I will uphold you with My righteous right hand" (Is. 41:10).

   "Nothing is impossible with God" (Luke 1:37).

4. Never ignore your responsibility to seek God's power and to use it once it has been given.

5. Develop an intimate relationship with the Father through worship, praise, scripture reading and prayer, and receive His pure and healthy perspective on sex.

6. Seek God for a *love* of purity. Be a man or woman after God's own, pure heart.

   "Worship the Lord in the splendor of His holiness" (Ps. 29:2).

   The things that we seek with all our heart are the things that we truly admire.

   "There is no holiness without a Christ-centered, Christ-seeking, Christ-serving, Christ-adoring heart. The plan of salvation requires us to get our hearts into this frame and keep them there" (J.I. Packer, from, *Rediscovering Holiness*).

7. Practice "listening prayer." Sit alone and wait on the Lord. Go there just to be with Him and to listen to what He has to say to you. Do not bring your own list of requests. Be still. Be quiet, and listen for God to bring up from within what is on His heart to pray about.

   Respond to what the Holy Spirit brings up with…

   a. …honesty. Tell God what you honestly feel and think about the issue at hand and the people involved, even if it includes questions about God's participation (or lack of participation), in the matter. You can express the feelings of anger and unbelief that you have harbored toward God. Just try to remain respectful as you do so. He much prefers honesty, than pretending you aren't angry with Him, and will reward it by eventually showing you the wisdom of His actions (or non-actions), in the matter. Remember then to repent of having judged the Lord.

How does God reveal the truth to you? You will often find that as you continue to lay out the problem before the Lord (what it is and how it affects you emotionally, intellectually and spiritually), God will bring clarity to the issue from your own mouth.

b. ... a choice of putting faith over emotion.

c. ... obedient prayer. We learn the mind and will of God through deep communion and fellowship with Him. Then, as we ask according to that revealed will, the result is a dramatically increased rate of answered prayer and a resultant greater love and appreciation of prayer.

8. Ask God to reveal the hidden mysteries behind your particular sexual bondage and to heal you from them.

"No wise man, enchanter, magician or diviner can explain ... the mystery... but *there is a God in heaven who reveals mysteries*" (Dan. 2:27-28).

"Surely your God is the God of gods and the Lord of kings and *a revealer of mysteries*" (Dan. 2:47).

9. Ask the Lord to expose the levels of self-deception that you have lived under that have enabled you to justify continuing to live in sin.

We often deal with sin's guilt by pretending away the offense, or by minimizing its gravity. After years of this, we lose consciousness of such self-deceptions and fully believe the lies— that we aren't really sinning, or sinning all that much, or that we want to be free but can't find our way out of the trap we are in. Consequently, we can arrive at a point where we genuinely believe that we want to be delivered from a sin when, deep inside, we do not. God must peel aside these layers of self-deception.

10. Discern and break the "rituals" of addictive behavior.

    a. Ask God to reveal the ritualistic patterns of cause and effect that underlie your behavior. They exist! Now begin to look for them.

    b. Take note of common settings and change them.

    c. Take note of common stress-inducing issues, events and relationships, recognize your sexual responses to these situations, and establish counter-measures in advance, foremost of which should be a determination to turn to the Lord at the first hint of sexualized ritual.

    d. Take note of points of inevitability—the moment when you become inexorably drawn into the act. What were you doing at that moment? Look for patterns.

    e. Teach yourself to respond in a different manner well ahead of the "moment of inevitability."

    f. Look for visual points of stimulation (e.g., mirrors, windows, publications, etc.), and remove them from your environment.

    g. Set your heart, and *relentlessly* practice, a turning to the Lord for His power to overcome, from the very outset of the ritualization process. Do not base your hopes on these counter-measures alone to solve your problem. Instead, make certain to diligently address the central solution, which is a deep intimacy and fullness with the Father.

11. Avoid self-pity and condemnation. They are self-centered exercises in false humility and unbelief. Learn to distinguish them from repentance and sorrow over sin. Believe God's Word when it says there is no condemnation for those who are in Christ Jesus (Rom. 8:1)!

12. Healing the problem of masturbation requires:
    a. a complete shift in priorities,
    b. a sincere desire and determination to be healed,
    c. a discovery and healing of the root emotional and sin problems, and
    d. a willingness to believe and to act on God's promises.

13. God is always there at any time when you are sexually stimulated

—there with the power to quench the fire of the moment.

14. If you are physiologically "highly sexed," ask God for His grace to heal that problem and to bring you into physiological normalcy (Gal. 5:24; Rom. 6:6-7).

15. The last frontier of sexual temptation is your dream life. Many who achieve sobriety from masturbation, experience a continued demonic assault in their dream life. In males, added despair is created when nocturnal emissions are caused by such dreams.

   a. God wants to be God of all of you—spirit, body, mind, will and emotions, conscious and unconscious. You must not leave this ground of the unconscious mind left open to the enemy. As abstract as it may seem, you must pray that God take the ground of your subconscious mind.

   b. When perverted erotic dreams occur, the response should be confession, repentance, requests for God's power to remove the enemy's foothold in this area, and, if appropriate, spiritual warfare against demonic forces.

      (1) Command, in the name of Jesus, that they leave you completely—mind, soul and spirit, and go where Jesus sends them.
         • The time has not come, nor do you have the authority to send them to the lake of fire or to outermost darkness.
         • Jesus has a very scary place to send them, so let Him participate in this way.
         • This also increases your awareness that Jesus really is right there to participate in and to enforce your prayers.

      (2) Pray also for the Holy Spirit to take possession of that vacated ground.

   c. Why confession and repentance when a perverted dream has occurred? After all, you couldn't help it, right?

      (1) The enemy has no right to manipulate you unless he still has ground in you as a result of unconfessed sin.

(2) The perverted dream is evidence that all the ground in you is not yet fully given over to God. (Remember man's ability to deceive himself?)

(3) It may be a test of your commitment to purity that God is allowing. In either case, the response suggested above is still appropriate.

d. Attack the stronghold immediately. Don't rest for even a moment in the afterglow of your dream. Ruin the pleasure of it so that your mind has nothing to look forward to at the specter of a repeat episode.

Exercises—Masturbation

1. Ask the Lord to show you what He thinks of your practice of masturbation. His response will be less lawgiving than it will be urging you on to something better. (You must have it settled in your mind that habitual masturbation is a sin. Otherwise you will continually compromise your attempts to stop).

2. Repent of your use of pornography, fantasy and lusting after others in your heart during masturbation. Ask God to give you a deep, heartfelt spirit of repentance over these issues and to free you from self-deception. Then, receive His cleansing and forgiveness.

3. Practice the presence of God through listening prayer.

4. Ask the Lord to help you remember how you got started practicing masturbation and what became the main factors behind your continuing. Allow Him to show you the patterns and the underlying forces that have motivated your behavior.

5. Ask God to reveal the objects, times, settings, and other factors and forces behind your ritual behavior with masturbation. Remove or change such influences.

6. Ask the Lord to show you the various ways that masturbation and fantasy have sullied normal sexual relations with your spouse (or sullied your view of sexual relations in general, whether practiced or not).

7. Ask the Lord to show you how masturbation has contributed to a turning in on yourself, whether in narcissism or withdrawal from intimacy with others. If He shows you a history of fear of intimacy, ask Him to begin healing that through intimacy with Him.

8. If normal sexual relations with your spouse does not satisfy you, ask the Lord to begin undoing the programming that you have done to your sexual responses through unreal fantasy. Ask Him to renew your mind from the effects of all the self-pollution that you have done in the past. Begin regularly feeding holy thoughts into your mind, thoughts of purity and goodness, of the beauty and

holiness of sexuality. Ask God to give you a love of purity.

9. Also ask God to deepen your understanding of what sexual intercourse is meant to be in all of its spiritual and physical dimensions. Read the chapter on "The Divine Intent for Sexuality" again and ask God to speak to you through it.

10. Set a guard at the door of your mind to reject the unclean thoughts and fantasies that will return to tempt you. Ask God to set fiery angels of holiness around you to do battle against these demonic temptations when they come. Get aggressive! Look at how masturbation has ruined what is pure and holy in your life and get angry at the evil of this sin!

11. Ask God to expose the many levels of self-deception that you almost certainly have.

12. Yield your heart fully to the Lord and ask Him to change your self-centeredness into other-centeredness.

Voyeurism and Exhibitionism

We have become a society of voyeurs, bred in the incubator of mass communications. From our earliest memories, we are encouraged to watch a variety of films and television programs, many of which depict images of privacy and intimacy that would otherwise remain hidden from view. The nightly news pleads for our attention by bombarding us with one stimulating image after the other, one "up close and personal" item after the other, one scandalous picture story after the other. The Internet, magazines, billboards, even record lyrics constantly fill our minds with formerly forbidden glimpses into other people's most intimate thoughts and actions.

Tabloids dominate newspaper sales. Even television tabloids vie for predominancy, exposing such newsworthy stories as the most recent nude photos of some public figure, or in one case, the sexual acts of exhibitionists in a motel room at the Toronto baseball stadium—through the eye of a telephoto lens no less. I remember when the Toronto story broke, even the local newscasters giggled with glee over the photos and openly wished that they were there. It's normal for modern anchor people to compete for the cleverest joke that will reveal in a "fashionable" sort of way their desire to be "on location" to personally share in the sensual fun.

We've become a culture of voyeurs and exhibitionists. Ask yourself honestly—when you are home alone and something revealing comes on the television screen about someone's sex life, isn't it your natural reaction to freeze, drop everything, and watch? And if you were to come across someone in a sexually revealing situation, and you knew you could not be found out, would you not stay to watch at least some of what you had stumbled upon?

This cultural phenomenon is at least partly the result of our own insecurity. When a society surrounds its people with a constant barrage of images of wealth, success, beauty and fame, it tends to make those watching that much more envious and insecure. We compare ourselves with false media images, and the result is mass insecurity. And so, whenever the opportunity arises to watch successful people engage in activities that we are insecure about, we tend to stop everything to see how they do it, so as to be able to mimic their actions, and to vicariously participate in and share in their professed perfection. And if the perfection of our idols is so far above us as to be clearly unattainable, we gain great satisfaction in viewing images of them in all too human situations.

The problem is that voyeurism and exhibitionism are sin. In the first place, we are not to make idols of anyone or anything. And secondly, we are not to spy on the nakedness of others. When we do such things, our sin hardens us against the Spirit's influence to keep us from sin, and we find ourselves as filthy snowballs rolling down steep hills.

Voyeurism and exhibitionism tend to strike simultaneously in people. The one who likes to look, often becomes one who likes to be looked at in a similarly revealing fashion, particularly if he or she possess the "goods" that will attract others. This is perfectly pictured in the youngster who stumbles upon a couple having sex. Years later, that youngster will also find him or herself with the tendency to engage in sex in places reminiscent of that scene, where he or she might be observed unawares.

After the first exposure to the hidden world of "forbidden nakedness" in childhood or adolescence, the exhibitionistic streak begins manifesting itself on an unconscious level—with unexplained urges to go unclothed or to do sexual things in open places, such as a field or a beach—without really knowing why other than it feels good to do so. Deep down inside lurks the hope that someone will happen upon them and derive the same sensual delight that they had years ago in seeing someone else.

If the exhibitionist is spotted, great stimulation is obtained at the thought of now being the cause of the same excitement in the person now watching. Even the unverified fantasy that someone is watching, out of sight, is sufficient to bring pleasure to the exhibitionist. A powerful fixation and compulsion to publicly repeat the act is nurtured and fed in this way.

The early stages of exhibitionism often mirror early childhood experiences of having seen someone doing something sexual. It becomes a fantasy to repeat that event, this time as the one who provides the setting for pleasuring the voyeur, real or imagined.

In the hidden recesses of the mind, however, it is an oddly narcissistic pleasing of oneself. In their subconscious, they are both the viewer and the performer. While on the surface, they are performing for the person who is watching, in the depths of their mental obsession, they are really performing for the child that they were when they first witnessed such an act. In that way, they become that idealized person of daring and excitement—the potent one whose actions have the power to arouse sexual passion in others.

This early stage of exhibitionism involves the exposing of oneself to those who want to watch. The perversion then makes its full circle—fulfilling the exhibitionist's need to gain a sense of sexual power. After all, they have just made a slave of the one who has watched them—a slave to the exhibitionist's sexual power.

In more serious stages, the exhibitionist will seek to expose him or herself to people who do not want to watch. At this level, the thrill cannot be had without the added dimension of shocking those who will be scared or repulsed. People who reach this level are either those who had a similar experience as children and who are recreating it as adults, or those who are so sexually addicted and self-destructive that they inevitably progress to the most hard-core level of whatever sexual activity in which they find themselves.

These people are acting on two levels simultaneously. At one level, they are begging to be caught and stopped, because they cannot stop themselves. At another, they are so jaded that they believe that everyone secretly wants to see them exposed and only pretend otherwise. In their twisted mind, they are doing a service to those who are too suppressed to ever seek out what they really want, and are "helping" them to discover and express their true desire for unbridled sexual expression.

In some very serious cases, it is an attack against the type of person who repressed them severely during their childhood and who represents the force behind the denial of all sexual expression and reality in their own life. This kind of person will expose him or herself to seemingly the most unlikely of targets, elderly women for example.

And in other cases, as for example when it is directed against children, this level of exhibitionism reflects a serious powerlessness and hopelessness, often born out of having been abused as a child.

For the most part, however, exhibitionism and voyeurism at their tamest levels, have become commonplace and accepted by much of our culture. Nude beaches and health spas are full of them.

I once stayed for the summer in a high-rise building in Chicago that was immediately adjacent to another high-rise along Lake Michigan. Being addicted to these behaviors myself, I carefully studied everyone in the building next door—perhaps 50 or more apartments. Among the majority of healthy, private people was sprinkled a variety of exhibitionists and voyeurs. One man stood watch for hours on end every day with binoculars and telescope, hiding nothing of his desire to see people "perform" for him. Seeing me looking out so often, he eventually began making gestures intended to encourage me to do sexual things—at one point plastering his phone number on his window for me to receive further instructions.

There were also a shocking number of exhibitionists who regularly undressed or performed sexual acts directly in front of their windows for all to see. For the most part, these are insecure people, desperate for attention, who have discovered that there are others who will spend hours waiting to catch the briefest of glimpses of them in a sexually revealing state. These budding exhibitionists put salve on their insecurity by attracting the idolatrous stares of their worshippers. As they perform their ritual acts, one can almost hear their hearts crying out, "Somebody look at me!" "Somebody notice me!" "Somebody consider me important!" "Somebody love me!"

If you are an exhibitionist and/or a voyeur, your healing and deliverance will come tailor-made by the Holy Spirit. The time that you spend developing an intimate relationship with God the Father and His Son Jesus Christ is the necessary foundation for it all. He alone knows the particular circumstances surrounding your compulsions and the steps needed to replace them with healthy desires.

This requires faith, first of all—faith that God really does accept even you, and that He continues to forgive even after you've fallen umpteen times. This faith can be had by meditating on the Crucifixion of Jesus Christ and by contemplating exactly what He did when He hung there for you. You must come to the place of accepting His heartfelt love for you, no matter what your feelings may be saying to the contrary.

You must set your heart against the tyranny of slavery to your feelings and begin to accept what God has promised in Scripture as truth, despite every evidence to the contrary. I am not suggesting that you deny your feelings. Go ahead and let them course through your mind and body and have their little spell. But when that is finished, put your trust in what God has promised and don't allow your feelings to dictate your actions. Feel your feelings, but when it comes time to act, act only according to what God has said. He will never leave or forsake you. And He is faithful and true to forgive every sin that you confess to Him.

There are several dimensions to the healing of sexual sin that always need to be addressed. The first is rebellion. We are a seriously rebellious generation, and your sexual dysfunction is inevitably tied in with a rebellion against the morals and values of your parents and the church. Odds are that you have also rejected and dishonored most, if not all, legitimate authority. Time should be taken to acknowledge the rebellious spirit that lurks deep within you, to confess your partnership with it, to renounce that partnership, and to receive God's forgiveness and power to drive rebellion out of your life.

The second dimension to address in receiving healing for voyeurism and exhibitionism is the emotional. You are undoubtedly on a deeply emotional and psychological search for love and attention. You may not have received the true, unconditional form of these things, which make for a healthy self-acceptance and which fuel the ability to love others in a proper manner. The pain and feeling of abandonment surrounding this void in your life has created a penchant for finding ways to numb the pain—through cheap thrills, drugs, or alcohol. Your feelings of powerlessness, unworthiness and of being out of control anger you and so you strike out against the One (God) who is suppose to love you and provide these things for you by engaging in sinful behaviors. And now, even though you may have reached the point where you want out of this trap, you find that you are addicted and can't get out.

You must believe me when I say, I have been there and have found the way out. It is a lengthy, hard road. And there are very trying times where it seems as if you are regressing rather than progressing, even when you are doing everything right. These are testing points—God's way of pulling us back into the reality of the evil we face and a restored recognition of how utterly dependent we are on His power to bring about the healing. Periodically, however, new levels of freedom do appear, as from nowhere, as your inner man secretly progresses further and further toward mental and emotional health.

As I turned to God daily, worshipping Him in song and prayer, listening for Him, bathing in His presence, feeding on His Word, I was invisibly infused with His healthy emotion and His perfect mind. As I gazed longingly and lovingly upon Him in the Spirit, even when I didn't feel like it, He transferred into me His purity of heart and mind. I began to take on the mind of Christ. I began to know deep within me His undying love and unchangeable commitment to me, and by such recognitions and infusions, I became progressively healed.

He taught me how to turn to Him for power at the point of temptation. He pointed out to me how, at times, I fooled myself into thinking I wanted holiness when I really didn't—mouthing the words that I knew I should say, but not really meaning them. He showed me how to turn to Him for His power instead of trying to tough out righteousness on my own—which it is our nature to do.

He assured me that I needn't ever let shame over failure keep me from turning back to Him—that His forgiveness would always be there. This revelation alone eliminated one of Satan's greatest ploys to keep me from God—that period of time after sinning when I didn't feel worthy or was afraid to turn back to God during which Satan built a barrier that sometimes lasted days, weeks, and even months. Jesus taught me instead that there would never again be any condemnation for me—even while I was sinning—let alone after the sin was finished. He obliterated forever the wall of shame that I had so long hidden behind after falling into sin.

As odd as it may sound, simply the recognition deep within my heart of God's unflinching love and acceptance in the midst of sin, canceled a great area of Satan's rule in my life. It made me love and trust in Jesus so much, that the sins that depended on shame for fuel were left dead in the water. And it helped me to immediately return to Jesus after committing sin. While these may appear to be the ingredients for a license to sin, if the heart is truly set on following Christ and being made pure by Him, then God's grace is actually the "hidden door" to deliverance and healing.

And so, the ingredients for healing are:

1. acceptance of Jesus Christ as Lord and Savior, and of His power to forgive your sins, past, present, and future;

2. setting your heart firmly and without deceit upon receiving God's health and purity into your life;

3. recognition of your absolute and complete dependence on His power and direction in everything;

4. learning how to turn to Him to overcome temptation rather than falling into the trap of self-effort;

5. commitment to spend quality and quantity time with God in order to develop the kind of deep intimacy that it takes to really love Him and receive His nature into your own;

6. doing what He tells you in your prayer and worship time with Him (this may include such things as forgiving others, restoring things, asking forgiveness of others, helping others, ceasing certain activities or associations, etc.);

7. a growing recognition of the schemes of the devil, which will be revealed to you by God during your time of seeking Him and His wisdom;

8. a wholesale shifting from a love of the things of the world and acceptance of its perspective to a love of what God values and esteems, and a taking on of His perspective.

If a serious demonic control has occurred in your life as a result of your behavior or background, God will bring the right people into your life at the right time to handle that. For the most part, however, demonic activity is naturally driven out by your continued and persistent cleaving to the Spirit of God.

Begin by expressing your sincere desire for purity of heart and mind to God, and your willingness to do whatever He shows you to do. At every point of temptation, immediately stop and repeat to God your desire and commitment to be holy. Find a fellow Christian who shares your absolute resolve and commitment to purity, someone you can trust, and share your struggles with him or her. Let them be a physical representative of the Lord for you in this battle. Fill your mind with the things of God. Start living like you really believe that heaven is your home and your dwelling place forever.

God will replace the idolatry of others with worship and praise of Him. He will remove the demonic strongholds that have lived within you, driving them out in the midst of your worship. He will give you an eternal perspective, so that you can see the long term consequences of your behavior. He will give you the ability to see others as beautiful children of God, rather than objects of lust. When the old temptations return, He will be there with great power to send them into utter darkness, the instant you really want Him to. He will even make you want to, by the power His grace has to work within you a desire for His will.

God's stated purpose for us is that we be transformed into the image of His Son. You are a child of God. You are destined for purity and holiness. As a child of God, it is what is now natural to you, and will be for the rest of eternity. Enter in to what God has prepared for you from before the foundation of the earth. It is God's will, and nothing is going to keep God's will from happening—Nothing!

Study Section—
Voyeurism and Exhibitionism

A. SOME THINGS YOU SHOULD KNOW:

1. The media has helped produce a culture of voyeurs. From the advent of motion pictures to the Internet, society has gradually become less and less discriminating about the line between "sinful gazing" and "forbidden," until now we have entire stadium crowds watching people have sex at the ball park (in Toronto) and shown later on the local news with approving comments by the anchor men and women.

   —from *Newsweek* May 13, 1991 regarding Madonna's newest video:

   "When a natural-born exhibitionist exhibits herself, is it the real Madonna you are watching or an artful imitation of reality?...Whether you are wowed by Madonna's honesty or appalled by her shamelessness doesn't really matter: in either event, the movie turns you into a happy voyeur, eagerly awaiting the star's next outrageous move."

2. We vicariously live out our fantasies by watching others do them on film and television, and we think that we're escaping guilt because we are not the ones who are actually committing the acts of immorality.

   —From Billy Graham on radio, who quoted a media source as saying that 27% of every media/entertainment dollar is used to stimulate sexual desire. That runs into the hundreds of billions of dollars.

3. The media has helped create mass insecurity by constantly lifting up idols with which most of us can never compete.

   We unconsciously compare ourselves with the Vogue models

and the studly men in the commercials and films, and form debilitating judgments against ourselves for not matching up.

When I look at you, and compare myself with what I see, I am comparing myself with a higher standard than what really exists, and I am catapulted into either hopelessness or manic striving in order to match up.

From *Free Indeed,* by Tom Marshall, Copyright by 1983 Orama Christian Fellowship Trust, Auckland, New Zealand. Used with permission.

> "We project towards people or situations, not our real self but an 'image' we think will be acceptable, or which, in any case, is expendable, because there is not very much of our real self invested in it. Thus, if it is rejected, we are not too troubled. Other people project similar images towards us, and we in turn behave towards their behavior. None of us ever contacts the real person that lies behind the behavior. Therefore the possibilities for misunderstanding are legion."

4. Voyeurism and exhibitionism often develop together within a person, growing from the same initial cause. As a voyeur, you have experienced the power that the exhibitionist has had over you, and you may want that same power for yourself. The discovery that power and control can be had over others by using one's own body

to offer similar glimpses into the forbidden, is what grows a voyeur into an exhibitionist. This is particularly attractive to one who is desperate for attention, love or affection.

5. These sexual compulsions epitomize narcissistic obsession.

6. A childhood or adolescent experience of seeing someone in a revealing or sexual situation can start the process of obsessing, creating life-long fixations and preoccupations.

7. In the young person who feels sexually suppressed and who possesses a rebellious spirit, this viewing of hidden or forbidden things creates extreme pleasure. This is particularly true if the youngster is from a strict, legalistic family atmosphere or one where "sex" is unmentionable.

8. Pornography is a major stimulus for these obsessions.

9. There are two kinds of exhibitionists:

    a. those who expose themselves to those who have communicated their desire to watch

    b. those who expose themselves to those who do not want to watch
        (1) This is a far more serious level of neurosis.
        (2) These people may be replaying a similar event from their childhood, this time in the "power" or "control" position.
        (3) They may be acting out the next level of dangerous behavior in their fall into serious sexual addiction. Often, at this level, they are subconsciously setting themselves up to be caught, and either punished or helped.
        (4) They may be "paying back" representatives of those who were responsible for their sexual repression and dysfunction (e.g., elderly teachers, grandmothers, etc.).

B. SOME THINGS YOU SHOULD DO:

1. Developing an intimate relationship with the Lord will bring a recognition of God's love and acceptance for you. The absence of

knowing this has been the foundation upon which your sexual obsession has been built.

2. This learning of the absolute faithfulness, love and acceptance that the Lord feels toward you, can be achieved through Bible reading, regular conversations with Him, regular praise and worship of Him, and seeing it demonstrated in the lives of fellow worshipers at church.

3. You need to replace the "shame and self-condemnation" syndrome with the powerfully freeing reality of God's unconditional love and forgiveness. In other words, learn how "grace" works "righteousness."

   "The grace of God…teaches us to say, 'No' to ungodliness and worldly passions,…and to live self-controlled, upright and godly lives in this present age" (Titus 2:11-14).

4. You need to regularly ask for and absorb from Jesus, a sincere desire for purity, and to turn to Jesus for power at the instant of temptation.

5. You must set your heart against slavery to your feelings, learning how to express them without being controlled by them. Feel them, but act only on the truth that God has revealed to you.

6. You must repent of your rebellious past and dishonorment of those who have been put in authority over you, and begin to submit in humility in the way Scripture teaches.

7. You must always remain aware of your complete dependence on God's power in order to overcome sin and to remain pure. This is humility.

8. You must ask God to train you to catch yourself when you are being dishonest about your desire for purity at any given instance. This is necessary even during those times when you sincerely believe that you desire His purity rather than sin.

9. You must always be willing to do what God tells you, or at least, willing to be made willing.

10. You must seek and receive from the Lord, an eternal perspective, His perspective on the things of the world that have attracted you so powerfully in the past.

"We fix our eyes not on what is seen, but on what is unseen. For what is seen is temporary, but what is unseen is eternal" (2 Cor. 4:18).

—From *Christianity Today* June 24, 1991 "Death in the Mirror: Real Meaning in Life is to be Found Beyond Life" by Timothy K. Jones. Used with permission.

> "Christian faith has always argued that *meaning in life will be found beyond life*...Despite the richness of this world, the New Testament reminds us that we are on our way to a reality even clearer and more substantial than we presently experience. 'Here we do not have an enduring city,' the writer to the Hebrews wrote, 'but we are looking for the city to come' (Heb. 13:14). Or, as Paul put it, 'We look not to the things that are seen, but to the things that are unseen' (2 Cor. 4:16,18).
>
> Indeed, *we will never live fully* if we think we can exhaust the meaning of the moment without reference to the longer stretch...*We cannot live rightly until we aim past life. Eternity provides the only goal that makes ultimate sense of each moment.* Awareness of death, and of its opening to a life beyond, has not only framed how I look at life. It has also begun to work a change in how I walk through life. It has, in other words, brought not just new meaning to my moments, but changes to my behavior. As Samuel Johnson reportedly said, 'When a man knows he is going to be hanged in a fortnight, it concentrates his mind wonderfully.' Our awareness of the transitoriness of this life, find, concentrates my priorities, helps me refashion my daily choices.
>
> *To know that life is not a destinationless journey helps me live more completely for a final good, an ultimate end*...To know that 'we have such a hope,' as Paul says, makes us 'very bold' (2 Cor. 3:12). God's gracious assurance and promise of eternal care helps us 'incline to our proper center.' Our daily decisions become oriented around something more profound...*A conviction about what lies beyond is giving me courage to live more fully and more faithfully*...God can take even my frailty and mortality and invest it with eternal significance."

11. You must saturate yourself with the presence of God, through

praise and worship, so that any demonic influence that may have been involved in your problem will have to give up its position in your life and leave.

12. Find a Christian who you can trust to reveal your most secretive sins, so that they may expire in the light of truth, and by the power of combined prayer.

13. Repent of and renounce the sin of envy, and begin seeking God for your contentment.

14. Repent of and renounce the sin of idolatry, and begin looking to God as your sole object of worship.

Exercises—
Voyeurism and Exhibitionism

1. Ask the Lord to help you identify the things in your environment that cultivate the voyeur in you. Eliminate those things from your world as completely as is possible.

2. Ask the Lord to help you identify the people and the media images that are idols for you. Repent of this sin and remove these images from your life as far as is possible.

3. Ask the Lord to help you identify the places and activities where you are drawn into voyeurism or exhibitionism—e.g., the health spa, sporting events, etc. Avoid these places.

4. Ask the Lord to uncover incidents in your past where you were shocked into an obsession with looking at or being looked at in a sexual manner. Repent of your complicity and your love of evil, asking God to reverse the effects of these events. Receive His forgiveness by faith.

5. Ask the Lord to uncover any deep feelings of powerlessness or need to be in control which may have contributed to making you susceptible to these sins. Ask Him to be your source of power and security. Seek Him regularly for this transformation.

6. If the Lord reveals that a legalistic background has contributed to your love of the forbidden, cry out to the Lord and ask Him to train you in living by grace. Ask Him to remove your heart of rebellion and to transform your will by the power of His unconditional love and grace. Read Dudley Hall's book, *Grace Works*.

7. Ask God to give you a vision of the beauty of holiness and the wonder of sexuality as He created it to be.

8. Ask the Lord to enable you to see people as precious children of God, repenting of the sin of having used them as objects of lust.

9. Relentlessly pursue an intimate relationship with God the Father.

Sing love songs to Him. Share your deepest thoughts and feelings with Him. Share the mundane events of your day with Him. Spend the time with Him that you would with anyone you were desiring to marry.

10. By an act of your will, commit to living according to objective truth rather than as a slave to lying thoughts and feelings. This is the beginning of a life of humility.

Transgender Confusion

There is a war of the worlds going on in the shadows of our every day awareness, an unseen battle between the Creator God (YHWH), with His army of heavenly beings, and Satan, with his fallen angels and demonic hosts.

Though already lost, Satan continues to battle in order to enlarge his dark kingdom before its inevitable implosion.

Nowhere is this battle more pronounced today than in the rise of the transgender movement. It is the front lines in Satan's scheme to deface and destroy the image of God that is stamped into our personhood, sexuality, marriages, children, and families.

The problem is that most transgender (TG) people are unaware of the forces that drive them in unhealthy directions.

Forces of Confusion

There exists today a convergence of entities that collude with one another to promote dangerous and damaging lifestyles and identities (such as homosexual and transgendered), as being natural and healthy alternatives to what they dismissively refer to as an antiquated "male-female binary," the idea that there are only two genders.

Entity #1 is a **Wealthy and Powerful LGBT Movement** that for most of its history distanced itself from TG people but who now see it as a cause that can be harnessed to increase their wealth, power, and influence.

Entity #2 is **Wealthy and Powerful Professional Guilds** (such as the American Psychiatric Association and the American Psychological Association), who ceased using science as the foundation for their mental health diagnoses when they began caving to pressure from homosexual activists 45 years ago.

It began in 1973, when gay activists began attacking the meetings of the APA committee that decides what disorders appear in their official *Diagnostic and Statistical Manual of Mental Disorders (DSM)*. The attacks continued until committee members (three of whom were secretly homosexual) relented and removed homosexuality from the list of mental disorders. The decision was not based on any science or new studies. It was based on fear and intimidation.

In a poll several years later (1979), the vast majority of APA members (69%) disagreed with the decision but were ignored. Today, you can lose your license if you disagree with the decision, a threat that forces therapists to keep their mouths shut. When Pure Passion Media attempted to interview therapists for its documentary, *"TranZformed: Finding Peace with Your God-Given Gender,"* only one could be found (the late Dr. Joseph Nicolosi) to go on camera to talk about the dangers of promoting transgenderism.

Entity #3 is **The Media** – Ephesians 2:2 tells us that Satan is the "ruler of the kingdom of the air." Almost all of TV, (including PBS), film and theater, much of radio (including NPR), as well as most newspapers and magazines have thrown themselves wholesale into promoting this great deception, partly because the media is riddled with LGBT people who pull strings from within, but also as a result of the agenda laid out by Marshall Kirk and Hunter Madsen (in their book, *After the Ball*), which was a manifesto for how to manipulate the culture so that it becomes pro-gay and pro-trans. Their scheme has worked so well that any reporter who dares to report on the actual science related to such issues will be vilified and almost certainly fired for daring to be politically incorrect.

Entity #4 is **Public Organizations** like government, education, the AMA, public schools, colleges, and libraries, etc., which have likewise been pressured and deceived into promoting sexually immoral agendas. Today you have gay and trans activists welcomed into *elementary* schools to teach children how to perform the most perverted of sexual acts, how to transition to the opposite sex, and worse. One recent trans activist actually encouraged a group of very young children to become drag queens while he danced around the room in his make-up, wig, and glittery dress.

Entity #5 is **The False Church** – a conglomeration of mainline denominations that have been taken over by nonbelieving liberals and gay/trans activists in order to provide religious cover for the doctrines of demons that they promulgate. Although they do not themselves believe in the authority of Scripture, they invent twisted versions of it in order to sow theological confusion among those who turn to them for divine guidance. As Kirk and Madsen proposed in their gay manifesto: "Use talk to muddy the moral waters ... raise theological objections about conservative interpretations of biblical teachings ... undermine the moral authority of [conservative churches] by portraying them as antiquated backwaters, badly out of step with the times ... set science and public opinion against institutional religion."

But take heed, as the Apostle Paul warned in Acts 20:29-30: "After I leave, savage wolves will come in among you and will not spare the flock. Even from your own number men will arise and distort the truth in order to draw away disciples after them."

Entity #6 is a **Deceived Public** that continues to vote the deceivers into office, whether in government, on school boards, professional associations, or elsewhere. As a result, those parents who have children who present as homosexual or transgender and who naturally turn to the world's experts for guidance are deceived into accepting and encouraging the world's fallen agenda. They want to do the right thing for their child and naively assume that cultural experts know what they are talking about, but it turns into the blind leading the blind.

Pedophilia and pederasty are the next frontier on the activist agenda. Already they have succeeded in having the wording in the APAs DSM changed so that pedophilia is now considered a disorder *only if it causes distress to the perpetrator*.

This same kind of semantic sleight of hand has been used to rename "gender identity disorder" as "gender dysphoria," again playing on the idea that it is disordered only if it causes distress to the transgendered person.

Current American Psychiatric Association Definitions

"Transgender" (TG) is a non-medical, umbrella term describing individuals whose gender identity or expression is at odds with the genetic sex with which they were born, now referred to as "gender dysphoria."

In modern parlance, however, transgendered individuals include transsexuals, transvestites, drag queens, and (incorrectly) intersex individuals.

TG conditions are independent of sexual orientation.

"Transsexual" is a medical term that refers to individuals who have undergone some form of medical or surgical treatment for sex reassignment. But in modern use, the term also includes those who *want* treatment but are unable to get it, for one reason or another.

"Transvestism" or cross-dressing is a term that defines people who derive erotic pleasure from dressing as the opposite sex, but in modern parlance, it includes those who do so whether it causes erotic pleasure or not.

NOT included are those who dress as the opposite sex for political reasons (such as "Joan of Arc") or for reasons related to their job (such as "Queen Hatshepsut" who donned male clothing and a false beard in order to rule Egypt in 1503 B.C.).

"Drag queens" (or kings) are people who dress as the opposite sex for the purpose of entertainment. Some are true transvestites, but others (such as Milton Berle, Jack Lemmon, Tony Curtis, Flip Wilson, Tim Curry and others) have done so simply for laughs.

Some drag queens are driven by a desire to mock the opposite sex by exaggerating their sexuality, but others do it simply for the acceptance that it brings them from a very enthusiastic clientele.

The Problem - Biblically

In the beginning, God made human beings in His image, male and female He created them. He commanded them to multiply through sexual union in a lifelong covenantal relationship with a member of the opposite sex, one that was to prefigure the relationship that Christ would eventually have with His Church (Ephesians 5:22-32).

When they sinned, however, the entire creation fell, all of it, both man and nature. Man's heart was darkened and he began to worship the creature rather than the Creator (Genesis 3; Romans 1:18-32).

Hatred, war, and sexual immorality ensued. The very DNA of man became corrupt. Sickness and disease spread across the earth. Lifespans shortened. Babies died in childbirth, and others were born with defects.

The vast majority of mankind lost all knowledge of the Creator, so they invented mythical gods who reflected their own corruption.

Reports from the Ancient Past

To explain the birth of those born with sexual malformities, mythical gods were invented who shared similar defects. According to Roman historian Plutarch, Cybele was one of the earliest intersex deities, an ancient Phrygian god referred to as "Mother of the Gods" who was worshipped with orgiastic rites in the mountains of Anatolia, and later, Greece and Rome. Depictions of her can be found in artifacts dating back to the earliest civilizations in Mesopotamia, Assyria, and Babylonia.

According to the myth, Cybele was born with both male and female sex organs and characteristics, an hermaphrodite according to Greek mythology.

The Roman poet, Ovid, later wrote that Hermaphroditus (from whom the term is derived), was fashioned by the gods when they merged the son of Aphrodite and Hermes with the water nymph, Salmacis. Ever since, according to myth, hermaphrodites have long been a symbol of androgyny or effeminacy, and have been portrayed in Greco-Roman art as female figures with male genitals.

In the myth, Cybele's beautiful young friend, Attis, castrates himself in order to found a priesthood for her, called the Galli. Various ancient Roman sources refer to the Galli as a middle or third gender.

After Christianity was made the official religion of the Roman Empire in the fourth century A.D., St. Augustine wrote of seeing Galli "parading though the squares and streets of Carthage, with oiled hair and powdered faces, languid limbs and feminine gait."

Jewish rabbinic literature refers to two classes of intersex people.

1. **The Tumtum** are persons whose sex is unknown because their genitalia are hidden. There is a state of doubt about whether they are male or female.
2. **The Androgynos**, on the other hand, are individuals who possess both male and female genitalia and/or characteristics.

These were not to be confused with Eunuchs who were castrated pagan priests or temple prostitutes.

Historically, such intersex individuals have been considered the sex that seems to prevail in their behavior.

"Intersex" Conditions are Not TG Conditions

Today we define "Intersex" persons as those whose sex characteristics, including chromosomes, gonads, sex hormones, or genitals, are abnormal. They constitute between .5 and 1.5% of the population.

The most common intersex condition is Klinefelter's Syndrome, where the sex chromosomes display in variant ways such as XXY, instead of the normal XX or XY. This results in one or more abnormalities during sexual development, such as infertility.

Despite claims by trans-activists to the contrary, most of the ancient references to behaviors that appear to cross normal sexual identity boundaries are for what we now call "intersex" individuals.

Modern TG History in Brief

It was in the early 20th century that a handful of doctors began performing crude sex reassignment surgeries, the most famous of which was on Danish painter, Einar Wegener, who suffered through multiple surgeries in the 1930s in an attempt to become a woman and conceive a child. His story was retold in the 2015 film, *The Danish Girl*, starring Eddie Redmayne. Wegener died as a result of his fifth surgery.

In the 1940s, Dorothy Tipton lived as a male American jazz musician named Billy Tipton. Her own son did not know her secret until she died.

In the 1950s, after his discharge from the Army, George Jorgensen underwent sex reassignment surgery and began calling himself Christine Jorgensen. A now-classic headline declared: *"Ex-GI Becomes Blonde Bombshell."*

In 1965, psychologist John Money persuaded Johns Hopkins Hospital to begin performing sex reassignment surgeries, but after a 1979 study found that those who had such surgeries were not more adjusted to society than their peers, the Psychiatrist-in-Chief at Hopkins Hospital (Dr. Paul McHugh) shut the program down.

Head researcher Jon Meyer declared, "Surgery is not proper treatment for a psychiatric disorder. These patients have severe psychological problems that don't go away following surgery"—a finding reinforced in a major 2011 study out of Sweden.

According to Dr. Paul McHugh:

- Sex change is biologically impossible.
- Transgenderism is a mental disorder that merits treatment.
- People who undergo sex-reassignment surgery do not change from men to women or vice versa. Rather, they become feminized men or masculinized women.
- Transgender feelings do not correspond with physical reality, in a way similar to an anorexic who looks in the mirror and thinks they are "overweight."
- 70%-80% of children who express transgender feelings will, over time, spontaneously lose those feelings.
- "People who promote sexual reassignment surgery are collaborating with and promoting a mental disorder."

Dr. McHugh also admonished those he called "misguided doctors" who administer puberty-delaying hormones to very young children – even though the drugs stunt the children's growth and risk causing sterility. Such actions, says McHugh, come "close to child abuse."

Leaving science aside, the media continues to line its pockets by promoting stories of celebrities who have declared themselves to be transgendered, including:

- Chastity Bono (who now calls herself "Chaz")
- Female model Tracy Beatie (who gained celebrity by giving birth to a child while calling herself "Thomas")
- Olympic athlete Bruce Jenner (who now calls himself "Caitlyn")
- Army soldier Bradley Manning (who now calls himself "Chelsea")

Even the Boy Scouts have yielded to media pressure and have accepted girls into its ranks as well as girls who claim to be boys.

Serious and Significant Problems Among TGs

1. Significantly Higher Risk of Mental Health Problems

2. High HIV, Drug Abuse and Prostitution Rates
   - 28% of male-to-female-TG have HIV
   - 18% of men who have sex with men have HIV
   - Less than 5% of drug users and prostitutes have HIV
   - Less than 3% of female-to-male-TG have HIV
   - Less than 1% of the general population has HIV
   - 30% of TGs abuse drugs and alcohol (vs 9% of general population)
   - One recent study showed that 34% had injected drugs in the past 6 months.
   - A 2011 study showed that 80% of TG in Los Angeles were prostitutes.

3. Surgery Risks and Regrets
   - 25% have bladder and/or stool leakage
   - Infertility
   - Loss of sexual function

4. Significantly Higher Depression Rates, Even After Surgery

5. Twenty Times Higher Suicide Rates, Even After Surgery.

The death rate increases dramatically approximately 10 years after "Sex Reassignment Surgery"—"SRS."

6. Three Times Higher Mortality Rate

7. Three Times Higher Psychiatric Inpatient Care

8. Dangers of Hormone Use
   - Cardiovascular Disease (e.g., Hypertension)
   - Weight Gain
   - Stroke
   - Blood Clots such as Deep-Vein Thrombosis is a side effect of testosterone use.
   - Liver Failure
   - Mood Swings
   - Heart Disease
   - Increased blood sugar (insulin resistance)

9. Higher Lung and Hematological Cancer Mortality Rates

10. Major Problems with False Diagnoses

- From 2009-2014, there had been a 40-50% increase in children wanting to change their gender, but in 2015, that number jumped to a 100% increase (Britain National Health Service)
- 80% of youth with GID eventually accept their true gender.
- The profits are so high and the expertize of "professionals" is so low that people are quickly pushed into SRS with little to no merit for the diagnosis (illustrated by Walter Heyer's testimony in the film *TranZformed*).

An Abrogation of God's Design for Human Sexuality

per Dr. James Anderson of Reformed Theological Seminary:
His entire presentation can be viewed at https://vimeo.com/191056254

A biblical anthropology has to be grounded in the first three chapters of Genesis. It must acknowledge both the order and design of creation, and the disorder and dysfunction introduced by the fall.

Then God said, "Let us make man in our image, after our likeness. And let them have dominion over the fish of the sea and over the birds of the heavens and over the livestock and over all the earth and over every creeping thing that creeps on the earth." So God created man in his own image, in the image of God he created him; male and female he created them. (Gen. 1:26-27) - (Note the basic gender binary.)

And God blessed them. And God said to them, "Be fruitful and multiply and fill the earth and subdue it, and have dominion over the fish of the sea and over the birds of the heavens and over every living thing that moves on the earth." (Gen. 1:28) - (Note the central place that procreation plays in the creation mandate.)

Then the Lord God said, "It is not good that the man should be alone; I will make him a helper fit for him." (Gen. 2:18) - (Note the complementarity between the man and the woman.)

Then the man said, "This at last is bone of my bones and flesh of my flesh; she shall be called Woman, because she was taken out of Man." Therefore a man shall leave his father and his mother and hold fast to his wife, and they shall become one flesh. (Gen. 2:23-24)

The institution of marriage presupposes that basic gender binary.

Genesis 3 records the fall of man. Paul gives us more details in Romans 1, citing the following causes:

- Idolatry
- Darkened hearts
- Sexual confusion

So all of this provides a theological and philosophical context for our response to transgenderism.

[*Author's note*] Deuteronomy 22:5 is the only Scripture that directly impinges on TG disorders:

A woman must not wear men's clothing, nor a man wear women's clothing, for the Lord your God detests anyone who does this.

God's command is grounded in protecting His design for human sexuality, (a principle whose application adjusts as dress norms change in any given culture), as a bulwark against anything that would reveal rebellion against His design or its holy and prophetic meaning.

Dr. Anderson concludes:

> "Gender dysphoria is a genuine condition which is best understood as a psychological disorder or dysfunction (and perhaps also as a deeper spiritual disorder). It doesn't appear to have any simple cause and it isn't something that's chosen.
>
> The different aspects of transgenderism call for different kinds of Christian responses.
>
> We must distinguish a cultural response from a pastoral response. Both are necessary and they are obviously interrelated, but we must not allow one to drive the other.
>
> On the one hand, if we let the culture wars define our pastoral response, then that response will fail to engage with people on a personal level and will lack compassion.
>
> On the other hand, if we let our cultural response be defined by our pastoral experiences, we run the risk of being too passive and accommodating of what is a destructive movement (which will lead to more pastoral problems).
>
> Since the biblical view is that there are only two sexes, male and female, and biological sex is the primary indicator of ontological sex, any treatment for gender dysphoria should proceed on the assumption that a person's biological sex (rather than their gender identity) defines whether they are truly male or female. Consequently, treatments should seek to bring a person's psychology in line with their physiology rather than the reverse.
>
> The sexual revolution and the LGBT movement don't merely invite God's judgment—they are themselves a manifestation of God's judgment (Romans 1:18-32)."

A Way of Transformation for the TG Person

(This assumes you are working with someone who has repented of sin, believed in and surrendered their life to the Lordship of Jesus Christ.)

1. Address any childhood sexual abuse or other trauma that may have confused the child's sense of identity, being and/or sexuality.

2. Correct gender-based misinformation by parents, significant others and/or the culture (as well as any other lies of the enemy that they may have believed). Parents or other family members may have wanted their child to be the opposite sex and either communicated that to him/her outright or more subtly in the ways they gave or withheld affirmation and acceptance when he/she acted like a boy/girl.

- Pray for inner healing for any father-wounds and mother-wounds. Teach them how to be intimate with God the Father as a replacement for a male-hating mother or a female-hating father.
- Deal with any "sins of the father" that may have been passed down (Ex 20:5-6; 34:7; Lev 26:39; Num 14:18; Dt 7:9; Ez 18:14-20) / Generational Curses / Anger at God / Roots of Bitterness and Rejection / Inner Vows / Unforgiveness / Occultic Activity.
- Pray for any peer humiliation that they experienced, (especially related to a rejection of gender), to be reversed by the acceptance of Christ and His Body, the Church.
- Pray to renounce the rejection of their biological sex and/or the self-hatred that it induced.
- Pray with them to accept their biological gender.
- Repent of any use of pornography and masturbation and the core sin behind such behaviors – Idolatry.
- Pray for revelation of and deliverance from any hidden demonic strongholds.
- Pray for any yet undiscovered biological contributors (e.g., hormones, brain chemistry, etc.) to be healed.
- Pray for being washed (Ephesians 5:26; 1 Corinthians 6:11) and having the mind renewed (Romans 12:2) with the Word of God.

3. Overturn any contributing cultural factors

If they grew up lonely and unaffirmed, yet were accepted and celebrated by the trans community (not having understood that their acceptance had more to do with their youth and beauty than anything else), pray that they learn to receive that needed acceptance and affirmation from God instead of man.

Help them to separate themselves from damaging relationships, (friends, music, media, etc.) and to turn their attention to God's Word and serving Him.

Help them find a church, ministry, and other teaching resources that can guide them in the lifelong process of transformation, such as:

Help4Families Ministry
www.help4families.com

Dr. Neil Whitehead's website
http://www.mygenes.co.nz/transsexuality.html
http://www.mygenes.co.nz/transsexual_brain.html

Dr. Robert Gagnon's website
www.robgagnon.net

Thinking Biblically About Transgenderism
http://www.proginosko.com/2016/11/thinking-biblically-about-transgenderism/

www.PurePassion.us

www.TranZformed.org

Transgender by Vaughan Roberts

Transgender Confusion by Denise Shick

Transformation: A Former Transgender Responds to LGBT Issues by Linda Seiler

Exercises— Transgender Confusion

1. Discuss the difference between a transsexual, a transvestite, a drag queen, and an Intersex person.

2. Give examples of transgender people you have met, and describe the impression that they made on you.

3. Ask the Lord to help you identify the sinful reactions that you may have had about them.

4. Pray for the transgender people you have met (or have seen or heard of), especially for the health and mental confusion issues that they live with.

5. Discuss Dr. James Anderson's take on how biblical theology impinges on the transgender lifestyle, its practitioners, and those who promote it.

6. What would you do (as a leader or as a lay person) if an unhealed transgender person began to attend your church?

7. What would you do if they refused to repent or enter into a healing process?

8. If they seem to be genuine in their search for answers, how long would you wait to see indications of healing before asking them to leave?

9. How would you help them find Christ, a renewed mind, healing and/or acceptance by others in the church who are not so welcoming?

10. What would you tell the children in the congregation?

PART THREE:
COMPREHENSIVE HEALING

Why People Remain in Sexual Sin and Bondage

One of the most frustrating times in ministry is when you pour your heart and wisdom into someone, to help them get free from a sin problem, and they fail to change. Such moments drag you through all kinds of thoughts and emotions (e.g., "Have I failed?" "Is what I'm teaching true?" "Is this person an exception?" "Am I being taken for a ride by someone who doesn't really want to be free?") It can really take the wind out of your sails to live with this kind of self-doubt and confusion.

As reluctant as we may be to draw such a conclusion, there may be no other but to recognize that the enemy is using our brother or sister to sap us of the faith and vision that God has for the overall vision and call on our lives. That being the case, it is important to recognize as quickly as possible those cases where people are seeking freedom and transformation without being willing to do what it takes.

I use to be the "Floor Pastor" and trainer for the Los Angeles area counseling center of the "700 Club." One day we discovered that we had a serious problem. Our phone counseling was going on so long with some callers (sometimes an hour or more per call) that the entire CBN telephone ministry was threatened with bankruptcy. The obvious solution was to shorten the phone conversations. But how? Upon seeking the Lord for an answer, He gave me two questions to ask every caller in the early stages of the conversation:

1. "Are you willing to do whatever it takes to get healed, delivered, transformed, etc.?"
2. "What exactly would you like God to do for you right now?"

As we asked these two questions of each caller, the focus of the conversation shifted from the problem to the power, provision and intention of the Lord to bring permanent healing and change. It increased our expectation that God was actually going to give us something concrete to respond to in the midst of our prayer. And sure enough, when we turned to God for answers with this newfound expectant faith, He gave them to us. In fact, it opened a virtual floodgate of words of wisdom and knowledge from the Lord on behalf of the callers.

The phone conversations shortened considerably. What happened was that those who were calling just to talk or get sympathy for their situation but who did not really want to change were suddenly confronted with having to take Spirit-led (and empowered) responsibility for changing things in their lives and many realized that they didn't want to. They were getting too much affirmation and attention by remaining dysfunctional and they weren't about to do anything that would jeopardize that. Within a very short time, such people stopped calling, and our phone time per caller dropped significantly. The ministry was saved and it continues on to this day offering prayer and ministry to those who really need it and who want to change.

How often do you minister with someone who has a sin problem and are unable to do or say anything that will bring permanent change to their life? Let me suggest that what you probably have is a person who either doesn't know what to do to get free, or who is unwilling to do what it takes to get free. Those same two diagnostic questions that the Lord gave me at the "700 Club" may help you to get to the bottom of things with your counselee.

When people are unwilling to do what it takes to get free, they usually don't tell you that. You need to regularly ask God for discernment in this area. Many people who are unwilling to do what it takes, aren't even aware of that fact. They really believe that they are willing and yet are self-deceived.

I regularly find areas in my life where I am fooling myself into believing that I want something when I really don't. For example, I remember begging God in tears for over a decade to free me from a particular habitual sin. Tears, mind you. Begging! One day as I was crying out for deliverance, the power of God fell on me and I knew that the struggle was finally over. God had filled me with a supernatural power that would permanently remove that sin from my life. And yet, as soon as I realized that this meant that I would never again have that sin to turn to, from deep within my heart came the words, "Oh, no!" You see, when I realized that God was playing for keeps, I was finally able to admit to myself that I really didn't believe that I could live without that sin. Deep inside, I was convinced that I had to have that sin as an escape mechanism in my life. And, in fact, I turned away God's delivering power and embraced the sin again. The layers of self-deception in that area had been so carefully constructed that I had for years believed that I wanted freedom from a sin that I still loved and wanted.

The mind and heart of man has an amazing capacity for self-deception, which is why the second diagnostic question that God gave me for the "700 Club" prayer ministry can be so very helpful: "What exactly would you like God to do for you right now?" This question gives both you and the person you are trying to help a tangible way to test their true, inner will. It also enables you to see more clearly when God has answered a prayer, because if you have been specific in your request and the answer comes, then it is all the more obvious that God did it. He then receives the praise, instead of the "spirit of coincidence."

Since that time at CBN, I have done a considerable amount of one-on-one and group counseling through the ministry God has given me to sexually broken people and I have learned that the reasons for people's failure to realize freedom from the sins that beset them are more numerous than those two diagnostic questions can account for. One day I was commiserating over my failure to succeed with a particular counselee and I asked the Lord what the most common reasons were that explained why certain people did not get free. He gave me seven of them.

1. FAILURE TO MAKE AN ACROSS-THE-BOARD COMMITMENT TO HOLINESS.

Many of us want God to free us from one area of sin while we remain unwilling for Him to free us from another. For example, I can spend years crying out to God to deliver me from an addiction to pornography, yet if I am unwilling for Him to deliver me from lying, I have missed the point. Now, God may choose to deliver me from one sin even while I continue in another, but that is His prerogative based on a lot of considerations of which I am totally ignorant. However, if I try to "selectively" live the Christian life, it should not surprise me if He does not respond to such prayers. The Kingdom of God is not a supermarket.

I believe that this is one of the biggest reasons why God does not deliver us from particular sins that are a concern to us. We remain unwilling to cooperate with Him in delivering us from other sins that He has already made known to us. God wants us to commit to holiness across-the-board. As the Holy Spirit brings them to our attention, no area of sin should remain untouched. Walking in the Spirit and in the power of the Kingdom of God requires a full on commitment to holiness. We're not talking about performance here (i.e., sinless perfection), but rather, the intention of the heart and the setting of the heart permanently toward the God of absolute holiness and power.

If we shy away in incredulity at such a prospect, it is because we somehow believe that it has to be our righteous effort that will carry it off, and we know that we are incapable of such a feat. However, the truth was and is and will remain, that God offers to infuse us with His righteous power to "keep us from falling" (Jude 1:24) and to make us "eager to do what is good" (Titus 2:14). We not only have salvation by grace, but sanctification by grace as well. Having already given us everything we need (2 Pet. 1:3), it is God's purpose to empower us to walk holy "in this present age" (Titus 2:12).

Those we counsel as well as the church at large need to make this commitment to walk holy in every area of life. It is our call, our witness and the glory of God to make it so. Though we tend to shy away from committing to something we know we cannot do, once we have made the commitment, we will discover that God is faithful to empower the keeping of it. Our results waver only as our faith and resolve waver. But God remains constant.

2. **FAILURE TO BELIEVE IN AND ACT UPON GOD'S POWER TO DELIVER AND KEEP US.**

Many are ignorant or unbelieving when it comes to the knowledge of God's power, His will and purpose for our lives here on earth, as well as our authority and capability under His guiding and delivering hand. Most need reminding. There are many good books in this area that have been published—most notably Neil Anderson's *The Bondage Breaker* and Tom Marshall's *Free Indeed*. Much of the counseling process for such people is a matter of educating them on who they are in Christ and what God has given them authority to do and be.

This is an area of "faith" that we must pursue and receive revelation on from the Father. In a very real sense, we need to receive for ourselves the "faith of God" (Mark 11:22), which is a gift from God (Eph. 2:8). We need to have God's level of faith. We need to pursue God and wrestle with Him until He blesses us with great faith (Gen. 32:26). Part of this pursuit of faith is accomplished through practicing the presence of God (discussed under reason 5), and part is accomplished through what I call "truth therapy." "Truth therapy" involves regular meditation on the truths of scripture—in this case, those that contradict what we are feeling and experiencing in our battle with sin.

The fact is, our natural thoughts and feelings lie to us constantly. One day I was teaching a seminar, and a woman abruptly stood up and walked out of the room. I was immediately assaulted with thoughts and feelings of failure. I thought to myself: "What did I say to offend her?" "What an insensitive lout I am!" "I've got no business even teaching when I am so obviously deficient in basic interpersonal sensitivity!" On and on my mind went as I began to feel like and believe that I was a first class failure. In just a matter of seconds, right there in the middle of my lecture, I became depressed and defeated. Minutes later, the same lady came back into the room and slipped into her chair. She had been to the bathroom.

When I fail to become planted in the ground of my identity in Christ, His call on my life and His empowerment of that call, I am a sitting duck for the lying thoughts and feelings that periodically invade my soul.

People who fail to embrace the truth of who they are and what they have in Christ are often people who are so enslaved to their feelings that they are incapable of believing anything else. Many are unaware that they can say "No" to feelings and emotions. They think it would be hypocritical or artificial to do so. They are sorely deceived and need to put Christ and His truth on the throne of their lives and learn how to deny and put down the tyranny of the god of emotion. This is not to suggest that they deny their feelings and emotions, but that they discern lying ones, and put them away with the truth that comes from God and His Word.

"Truth therapy" also involves worshipping Christ with our focus on those very attributes of His that we need. Do we need purity of mind, heart and action? Then we need to worship Him for His purity. We need to see Him "through the eyes of our heart" in His holiness. In Ephesians 1:18 Paul prays that, "…the eyes of your heart may be enlightened in order that you may know the hope to which He has called you, the riches of His glorious inheritance in the saints, and His incomparably great power for us who believe." It is through this very enlightenment that we receive the faith to believe and to appropriate the power over sin.

Do we feel powerless against sin? Has the omnipresence of the power of evil in our world tricked us into believing that evil is more powerful than good? If so, we need to repeatedly meditate on and worship the Lord for His power. As we feed these truths into our mind and spirit, they become more real to us. We begin to believe that they are available to us and that they can be built into us by God.

Faith is an indispensable conduit in the flow and outpouring of God's power and kingdom life. Without faith, as the scriptures say, "It is impossible to please God" (Heb. 11:6). We need faith to fully believe in the power of God, in the goodness of God, in His unconditional love for us, in the grace that He extends toward us when we sin, in His concern for us, in the intention of His will to make us holy, in the truth of His Word and in all of the other promises and statements about Him and about life.

3. **FAILURE TO UNDERGO A TRANSFORMATION OF THE WILL THROUGH A BELIEF IN AND EMBRACING OF GOD'S UNCONDITIONAL LOVE.**

Once a person has become fully persuaded of the truth behind God's power and our authority in Him, then freedom from sin becomes a matter of the will. Many people simply are not willing to do what it takes, even with God providing all of the healing and delivering power. They love the sin too much—usually because they don't fully realize, deep within their spirit, that God loves them completely, no matter what they have done, nor how many times, and that He can meet their need better than the sin can.

They need to know that despite continued sin and failure in their life, God's loving arms are still extended out to them with as much love and compassion as if they had been living in perfect victory from day one—as if they had never sinned! They need to truly understand that God's love and acceptance for those who have put their faith in His Son Jesus is not now, nor ever will be, contingent upon their behavior. They must embrace the truth of His unconditional love, for it is from believing in this truth that they are empowered and motivated by love not to sin. Dudley Hall has written an excellent book on this called, *Grace Works*.

This message of the power of grace is most clearly given in Titus 2:12, where the Apostle Paul says, "It is the grace of God…that teaches us to say 'No' to ungodliness and worldly passions, and to live self-controlled, upright and godly lives." How does the grace of God do that?

One day I was busily engaged in a sin (probably for the 10,000th time), and the Holy Spirit spoke to me, saying, "You know, if you will turn to Me right now, I will love you, forgive you and embrace you." I can remember thinking at the time, "That's ridiculous! I'm in the middle of a sin here!" And I ignored the voice of God and continued on. When I had finished my sin, the Holy Spirit again spoke to me and said, "You know, if you will turn to Me right now, I will love you, and forgive you and embrace you." It seemed like such an unreal thing to be hearing, that deep inside I knew it could only be God. I was so intrigued over the possibility that the voice might really be God that I turned to Him in my spirit to see if He would really have me back after I had refused to abort my sin at His first entreaty. When I turned to Him, to my utter surprise and amazement, He swamped me with a wave of love. It was clear to me that my sin was completely irrelevant to Him—that all He really wanted, and all He had ever wanted, was for me to turn to Him and receive His love. It was an awesome moment, as my heart was melted by His unconditional love and grace. I left the room completely changed. He had so taken my heart by His love that I now wanted to do what He wanted me to do. I no longer was suspicious that He was some control freak, out to rob me of my freedom. I was now convinced that He was always and only concerned with one thing—loving me.

God changed my heart, simply by loving me unconditionally. He had broken the power of sin and had transformed my will through grace—taking me from rebellion to submission. I now wanted to do what He wanted. I now fully believed in His loving heart toward me. I was now ready to believe whatever He said and do whatever He suggested. Titus 2:14 had come true in my life in those brief moments as God revealed His unconditional heart of love and grace toward me.

How does the grace of God teach us to say "No" to ungodliness and to live a godly life? By breaking our heart over the relentlessly unconditional love that the Savior holds out to us in spite of our sin. As a result, we fall more and more in love with Him. Our desires change from wanting the impurity of the world to wanting whatever such a wonderful Savior wants. We come to admire Him, to love Him, to believe more deeply in Him, and to desire what He wants. Our hearts are changed from the inside out. Instead of operating out of the willful self-effort of performance, we now operate out of pure heartfelt desire and faith, knowing from the depths of our being that what God wants is without a shred of doubt what we want.

As far as those of us who have been changed in this way are concerned, God is immanently trustworthy and designs His commands around only one principle—what is best for us, His dearly beloved children. Meditating on the proof of His love—His sacrificial, agonizing death on the Cross—is always helpful in coming to believe these things. Satan will try to use the tragedies of life to persuade us differently about God, but meditating on the Cross has greater power to overcome Satan's lies. Jesus' demonstration of love through the Cross is inescapable and incomprehensible except that He did it out of love for mankind.

What we really have been talking about in this third area of counseling for someone in bondage, is how God's unconditional love results in a transformation of the will. As fallen men and women, we too often strive to correct our will through logic and independent self-effort, which eventually fails. God's way is to change our will through the irresistible power of unconditional love. He then will receive the glory for our eventual choice to do His will. "For it is God who is at work in us both to will and to do that which is according to His good purpose" (Phil. 2:13).

When our will has been transformed by the power of almighty God, we find that we have also gained two crucial products of a sanctified will—persistence and obedience. We obey Him because we love Him (John 14:23-24). Our obedience is born out of being fully persuaded by love, not by duty or performance. We are persistent in our pursuit of Him for the same reason—we have been irresistibly drawn by the glory of His love. Without persistence, we cannot get very far in walking with God in holiness (cf. Jer. 29:13; Heb. 11:6), which holiness is a promise from God for this life as well as the next—as it says in Galatians 5:16, "Live by the Spirit, and you will not gratify the desires of the flesh."

4. FAILURE TO SEE HEALING AS A PROCESS WITH A PURPOSE.

Those who come for help are often spiritually naive and think that their sin problem will go away once you've cast out some demon or called to God for that special delivering anointing that will finally rid them of their temptation and sin.

The first counsel that must be given to such believers is that their healing will be a process—a process with a purpose. Even those of us (and I am one of them) who receive an initial, powerful deliverance from the power that certain sins have over us still have a long process of healing to look forward to—a process in which God shows us the root causes of our behavior, the root needs that we are trying to meet, and His more perfect provision to meet those needs. Most of us look at the idea of process with impatience and gloom. We want healing and perfection now! But God is wiser than that. He sees the benefits for us that can only be derived through process. For example, through this process of healing, we develop a relationship of love and dependence on God because we have need to turn to Him often for power over temptation. In the midst of turning to Him often for help, He becomes more real to us. His promises and His presence becomes practical, almost tangible. We get to know Him better. He goes from being one who theoretically loves and empowers us, to one who engages in the deepest fabric of our lives—and that is what life is all about.

Yes, we are to be holy as He is holy—and that is a primary goal and directive. However, the greater goal of knowing Him intimately, is what brings about the goal of holiness. This is clearly stated in 2 Peter 1:3—"His divine power has given us everything we need for life and godliness through our knowledge of Him who called us by His own glory and goodness." And so, it is from our "knowledge" (deep intimate knowing) of Him that everything we need for life and godliness is made manifest.

With the healing of our relationship with God comes the healing of our relationships with others. One flows naturally out of the other, for in our intimate moments with God, He reveals to us the roots of our broken relationships with people and empowers us toward resolution and healing. Bondage is essentially a problem of broken relationships—first with God, and second, with human beings. As these are made healthy, we are made healthy.

Another reason that healing must often be a process is that we are so very ignorant of the complex web of contributing sins that underlie our behavior. We need to learn what these sins are and be persuaded to respond accordingly to what God has shown us. For example, many people who are entrapped in the sin of pornography are unaware that one of the foundational pillars to their surface sin is the very serious crime of "idolatry." If I am unaware that I am engaged in idolatry, then I am not going to confess and repent of that sin, am I? Consequently, no matter how much I plead with God to "deliver" me from the sin of pornography, He cannot, because the deeper sin that fuels the behavior remains.

And so, we see the immense benefit and undeniable necessity behind God's decision to make most of our deliverance from sin a process of revelation, repentance and transformation of the will through coming to know Him as He really is—which brings us to the next reason why some people do not get free from their sin.

5. **FAILURE TO DEVELOP AN INTIMATE RELATIONSHIP WITH GOD THE FATHER.**

Many of us fear intimacy. It's where we got hurt. It's where we got shot down. It's where we are painfully vulnerable.

It amazes me how, when I teach on this topic, people kind of smile patient smiles while they wait for me to go onto something more "practical" for them. For most people, most Christians even, intimacy with the Father is just a romantic notion. They don't see it as a real possibility. Nor do they have any idea how to achieve it or what it will look like when they get it. They're happy to be given "10 Steps to Holiness" that they can perform in the privacy of their own homes, without that messy "I" word. Besides, intimacy means commitment, and loss of independence. Enough said right there!

It's almost as if Satan has put a veil over men's hearts so that they will not do the very thing that will result in their empowerment, freedom and existential fulfillment. At the same time, he's trying to rob God of the thing that God wants most—intimacy with His children.

To answer the question of "What" intimacy is, we need only point to its appearance in certain human relations. It is two hearts becoming one, two minds thinking together in harmony, two bodies moving simultaneously in service to each other. It is the deepest level of knowing, of loving, of feeling—producing the fruit of inner joy and completion.

How do we achieve such a state with the God no one sees? Foundationally, it has to do with our response of love to the sacrifice of Jesus on the Cross and the faith in God that that historic action elicits. This is nurtured through a life-style of worship—something sorely lacking in modern Christian experience. We worship on Sunday, yet if the object of our worship is worthy at all, He is worthy of ongoing, daily worship. And it is in that intimacy of worship that God reveals Himself to us in ways He does not show the common man. It is there that we come to recognize His voice, know His heart, His mind, experience His love, grace and mercy, in the deepest recesses of our hearts. It is there that the "image" is restored—where we receive the transformation of ourselves into the likeness of our Lord—and emerge shining with the glow of His faith, wholeness, holiness, purity and love (2 Cor. 3:18).

Intimacy then is established through a life-style of worship and praise—singing love songs to our Lord and gazing upon His glory in the Spirit—practicing His presence with the same persistence and regularity as we would anything else that is necessary for life. It is also created through knowing Him by scriptural revelation—again, a regular feeding on Him, this time, through His written Word, which He, from time to time, brings alive to our mind and heart. Intimacy is thirdly created through the communion of prayer—simply talking to him—spilling our hearts before Him, and then listening for His response. In these and other ways, intimacy comes when being with Him is a greater priority than doing for Him.

Without a growing relationship of intimacy with God, we cannot receive the revelation, the faith and the security of knowing we are loved that enables and empowers a walk of holiness. Without intimacy, permanent, ongoing holiness is impossible because it is in the womb of intimacy with God where He brings forth the new life of holiness in us.

6. **FAILURE TO HUMBLE OURSELVES IN ABSOLUTE DEPENDENCE ON GOD.**

The sixth reason why someone might remain in habitual sin and bondage is that they may have been living in the pride of self-sufficiency and independence from God, and consequently have not learned yet that they are completely dependent on God's power and wisdom in order to live any kind of meaningful existence. In such a condition, they can neither receive nor use God's power and grace because they are unaware of their need for it. Then there are people who have some idea of their need for God, but haven't understood the full scope of the need yet.

And finally, there are those who theoretically understand their need, but still practice a life of independence from God. To them, humility is a weakness to be avoided and life's problems are challenges that God expects man to deal with on his own.

Man alone, without a continual interaction of dependence on God, is like an infant left out in the middle of a freeway.

Even what wisdom we do have has come to us from God. We're like a word processing program on a computer. We are prestructured to have the capacity to perform certain functions, but without the continual input of an outside force, are virtually useless. Even the pre-structuring comes from that outside force. In like fashion, part of the wisdom that the natural man (who does not know God) seems to have, has been given him by God, and is good and useful (e.g., $E = MC^2$). The rest of it is of his own design and is pure baloney (e.g., Darwinian evolutionary theory). As part of a finite creation, we are completely dependent on God to reveal to us what is true as distinguished from what is a product of our own ignorance. We must continually approach the throne of grace not only for forgiveness, but also for knowledge and wisdom. We are far more dependent in this area than we realize, and don't know anything truly until we have God's assurance that it is true.

The humility of knowing our limitations as well as the depths to which we have fallen as a part of sinful humanity is extremely valuable currency in the Kingdom of God. Take, for example, the teaching in Luke 7:47, when Jesus noted that a person who has been forgiven much will love much and the one who has been forgiven little will love little. If I live in such a state of pride and arrogance that I'm unaware of just how much a sinner I am (the state of the Pharisee), then I am not going to love Jesus very much, if at all. In that frame of mind, I don't believe that there is much to forgive, and so have been forgiven very little. However, the closer I get to Him, the longer I sit at His feet and allow Him to uncover the depths of my sinful heart, the more I am going to grow in the humility of understanding the grace that I stand in, and I will love Him much more.

The same goes for power. Without Jesus, we can do nothing (Jn. 15:5)! We cannot heal ourselves spiritually, mentally or physically. We can do nothing unless God empowers and guides us. That holds true especially in the area of sin. Our first response to temptation must always be a heart of utter dependence turned toward God for power and wisdom. Then and only then can we effectively use the tools that He has given us to overcome the evil one.

7. FAILURE TO LEARN AND PRACTICE SPIRITUAL WARFARE.

That brings us to the seventh area in which we might want to counsel someone who appears hopelessly bound in sin. We need to train them in spiritual warfare—the first six lessons of which we have just discussed. They are an indispensable foundation for victory in spiritual warfare. The weapons of our warfare are mighty to pull down strongholds, but only when employed in the ongoing reality of the first six pillars of incarnational relationship and empowerment.

When we turn to the God with whom we have an ongoing, intimate relationship; our will fully persuaded in wanting what He wants because our hearts have been changed by His loving grace; in great faith because we have practiced His truth and chosen to believe it despite all appearances to the contrary; with a heart filled with the humility of knowing that we are utterly dependent on Him for wisdom and power, as well as life itself; with a heart that is fully turned and committed to holiness in every area of life, then when we go to pick up the weapons of our warfare, we will find that we already have them on. (Referring to truth, righteousness, readiness, faith, salvation, the Word of God—as listed in Eph. 6:14-17). And if we have been wearing our battle dress all along, then we'll have greater facility in using it when it is needed during those inevitable times of trial and temptation.

Spiritual warfare simply involves using the power of God, the wisdom of God, the discernment of God, the peace of God, the faith of God and the love of God to proclaim the will of God at any given moment. It is in the midst of the honor that we have to proclaim the glory of God and His already accomplished victory (see Psalms 149:1, 5), that those things that He already has willed, come to pass. With the prayer and the praise of our heart, released in the full faith and confidence that results from an intimate knowing of Him, the forces of heaven are released to engage and to defeat the enemy.

So, it's easy to see how a process of change and growth is necessary for all of this to come about. And it all starts with step one. My guess is that those who live in the defeat of habitual sin are those who have not yet fully fallen in love with Jesus. They have not yet received the depth of revelation of His love and awesome beauty that transforms the heart and mind. Rather than spending copious hours psychoanalyzing these folks, why not take them afresh to the throne of the Almighty King of Kings—back to the simple, profound truth of His glory and grace. I speak not in theory, but as one who has been healed of numerous severe, lifelong sinful addictions and obsessions. This is the way of God's permanent deliverance and healing. For man, it seems too simple. But once again, God has chosen to make foolish the wisdom of man through the simple truths of His gospel.

In summary then, what are the primary causes for a failure to find deliverance from on-going sin? They are:

1. Failure to make an across-the-board commitment to holiness.

2. Failure to believe in and act upon, God's power to deliver and keep us.

3. Failure to undergo a transformation of the will through faith in God's unconditional love.

4. Failure to see healing as a process with a purpose.

5. Failure to develop an intimate relationship with God the Father.

6. Failure to humble ourselves in absolute dependence on God.

7. Failure to learn and practice spiritual warfare.

Study Section—
Why People Remain in Bondage

1. Failure to make an across-the-board commitment to holiness.

    a. Wanting God to free us from one area of sin while remaining unwilling for Him to free us from another.

    (1) sins God has already spoken to us about.

    (2) sins that are fed by the same underlying fuel (e.g., rebellion), as the one we are seeking freedom from.

    (3) We are attempting to remain the god of our lives, the one who calls the shots.

    Recently I heard a talk show guest give testimony to the condition of his heart before fully giving his life over to Jesus. One of the things that he said was an excellent summary of where many of our hearts are. He said:

    "I didn't mind being religious as long as it didn't cut into my fun."

    b. This has to do with the fundamental intention of our heart to be holy, not the faultless success of that desire.

    c. God will honor our commitment by providing the means to keep it.

    (1) He will "keep us from falling" (Jude 1:24)

    (2) He will "make us eager to do what is good" (Titus 2:14)

    (3) He will give us everything we need (2 Pet. 1:3)

    (4) He empowers us to walk holy "in this present age" (Titus 2:12)

    (5) It is the glory of God to make it so.

2. Failure to believe in and act upon God's power to deliver and to

keep us.

- a. We need to practice the presence of God and make it a permanent habit of daily life.
- b. We need to receive a gift of faith to believe what God says about us and about His power to transform.
- c. We need to persist in seeking this gift.
- d. We need to use the power when He gives it to us.
- e. We need to renew our minds with "Truth Therapy." (see "Foundations" chapter)
- f. We need to discern and reject lying thoughts and feelings.

3. Failure to undergo a transformation of the will through a belief in and embracing of God's unconditional love.

- a. We must ask ourselves: "Am I willing to give up my one good excuse for sin—that I don't believe God is fair, or that He loves or cares for me?"—in order to discover the truth about His love and concern?
- b. We must ask ourselves: "Am I willing to get close enough to God—to enter into intimacy with Him—so that I can experience His love?"
- c. We must ask ourselves: "Am I willing to do whatever it takes to get healed, delivered and transformed?"
    - (1) For example, "Am I willing to give up the sympathy, comfort and attention that being dysfunctional has given me?"
    - (2) Am I willing to give up certain relationships, habits, entertainments, pleasures, etc?
- d. We must formulate specific requests of God.
    - (1) Getting specific tests our true inner will with the reality of what is involved in receiving the requested deliverance or change (e.g., new lifestyle).
    - (2) Specific requests make it all the more evident when God has answered the prayer, and He receives the glory.
- e. Our love of sin must be quenched by the reality of, and

the surpassing greatness of, His love.

    f.   The results of knowing His unconditional love:

        (1) We fall more in love with Him.

        (2) Our desires change into His desires.

        (3) We believe more deeply in Him and trust Him.

        (4) We obey Him because we love Him instead of out of duty or obligation. One "two second" revelation of God's love is worth a lifetime of therapy!

        (5) Like Christ, we persist in the things of God because of a deep knowledge of what has been set before us.

"Jesus…who, for the joy set before Him endured the Cross" (Heb. 12:2).

4. Failure to see holiness as a process—a process with a purpose.

    a.   Forsaking unspoken demands for "instant transformation" that fuel anger and impatience with God.

    b.   If we don't take the time to learn why we did what we did, we are often destined repeat it. For example, one of the sins that underlies the sin of looking at pornography is "idolatry." If I am unaware that I am engaged in idolatry, then I am not going to confess and repent of that sin, am I? Consequently, no matter how much I plead with God to "deliver" me from that sin, He cannot, because the deeper sin that fuels the behavior remains.

    c.   Learning why we sinned a particular sin brings humility.

    d.   Learning why teaches us what needs to take before the Father so that they can be met legitimately.

    e.   The process facilitates a relationship of love and dependence on God because we have need to turn to Him often for power over temptation.

        (1) In the midst of turning to Him often for help, He becomes more real to us.

        (2) His promises and His presence becomes practical, almost tangible.

- (3) We get to know Him better. He goes from being one who theoretically loves and empowers us, to one who engages in the deepest fabric of our lives.
- (4) The greater goal of knowing Him intimately, is what brings about the goal of holiness.

"His divine power has given us everything we need for life and godliness through our knowledge of Him who called us by His own glory and goodness (2 Pet. 1:3).

With the healing of our relationship with God comes the healing of our relationships with others.

5. Failure to develop an intimate relationship with God the Father.
    a. We are afraid of intimacy.
        (1) It's where we have been hurt in the past.
        (2) It's where we are vulnerable and not in control.
        (3) Intimacy is intangible, and therefore not easily pursued.
        (4) We do not know how to achieve intimacy with a spirit.
        (5) Intimacy means commitment and a loss of independence.
    b. We are too intellectual and enamored with the wisdom of men to see the beautiful simplicity of intimacy with the Father as the single cure for all bondage and sin.
    c. It is achieved by relentlessly pursuing God with a heart of humility and a desire to know and to live according to truth.
        (1) meditating on the Cross
        (2) a lifestyle of worship
        (3) a heart set on obedience
        (4) practicing His presence
        (5) regular feeding on the Word of God—the Bible
        (6) regularly communicating with Him in prayer, both in talking and in listening
    d. Intimacy's fruit is abundant.
        (1) God reveals Himself to us.

- (2) We learn His voice.
- (3) We know His heart and mind.
- (4) We experience His love, grace and mercy.
- (5) The "image" of God in us is restored to health—we are transformed into His likeness—and emerge shining with the glow of His faith, wholeness, holiness, purity and love (2 Cor. 3:18).
- (6) We receive the revelation, the faith and the security of knowing we are loved that enables and empowers a walk of holiness.

6. Failure to humble ourselves in absolute dependence on God.

   a. We live in the pride of self-sufficiency and independence from God, habitually unaware of our great need for Him.

   b. Some of us have some idea of our need for God, but haven't understood the full scope of it yet.

   c. Others of us theoretically understand our need, but still practice a life of independence from God because we consider humility a weakness to be avoided and believe that life's problems are challenges that God expects us to deal with on our own.

   d. The truth is that we are completely dependent on God's power and wisdom in order to live any kind of meaningful existence

   e. humility of knowing our limitations as well as the depths to which we have fallen as a part of a sinful humanity is extremely valuable currency in the Kingdom of God.

   f. The closer I get to Him, the longer I sit at His feet and allow Him to uncover the depths or my sinful heart, the more I am going to grow in the humility of understanding the grace that I stand in, and I will love Him much more.

7. Failure to learn and practice spiritual warfare.

   a. The first lesson in spiritual warfare is to put into positive action these seven foundational pillars of a sanctified Christian life.

(1) Make an across-the-board commitment to holiness.

(2) Believe in and act upon the power of God to both deliver and keep you from sin.

(3) Accept as a fact God's unconditional love for you, as proven once and for all at the Cross, and allow it to transform your will into His will.

(4) Believe in the wisdom and love of God in making your healing and transformation a process.

(5) Pursue an intimate relationship with God the Father and receive all of the power, wisdom and purity that you need directly from Him.

(6) Humble yourself in absolute dependence on God.

(7) Practice spiritual warfare against the enemy.

b. In the intimate moments that you share with God, He will reveal spiritual warfare tactics that are tailor-made to your particular weakness and sins. He will reveal their secret strongholds, how to pray against them, and how to keep the ground for Jesus.

c. With these revelations from God, you can pray "in the name of Jesus," under the authority that Christ won for you by His blood and expect to see the demonic powers routed.

d. Spiritual warfare simply involves using the power of God, the wisdom of God, the discernment of God, the peace of God, the faith of God and the love of God to proclaim the will of God at any given moment.

"His divine power has given us everything we need for life and godliness through our knowledge of Him who called us by His own glory and goodness. Through these He has given us His very great and precious promises, so that through them you may participate in the divine nature and escape the corruption in the world caused by evil desires. For this very reason, make every effort to add to your faith goodness; and to goodness, knowledge; and to knowledge, self-control; and to self-control, perseverance; and to perseverance, godliness; and to godliness, brotherly kindness; and to brotherly kindness, love. For if you possess those qualities in increasing measure, they will keep you from being ineffective and unproductive in your knowledge of our Lord Jesus Christ...*For if you do these things, you will never fall,* and you will receive a rich welcome into the eternal kingdom of our Lord and Savior Jesus Christ" (2 Pet. 1:3-8, 10-11).

Exercises—
Why People Remain in Bondage

1. Make an across-the-board commitment to holiness, forsaking all to live for Jesus. Turn your heart toward correction and the humility of unquestioned obedience to God. Allow Him to enter into every area of your life.

2. Allow God to bring the sorrow of true repentance into each area that He targets as sin.

3. When you fail to be sinless in the face of this commitment, refuse to use that as an excuse for returning to habitual sin. Instead, seek and receive God's ever-present grace to forgive and to cleanse from all unrighteousness and return to your commitment.

4. Persistently seek God for the precious gift of faith, so that you may believe in His awesome promises and live the abundant life of power and fruitfulness.

5. Meditate on the Cross and let the power of His grace transform your rebellious heart and will into that given over to the One who loved you unto death.

6. Seek to know Him. Seek intimate revelations of Him. Allow His glory to transform you.

7. Rejoice in Him. Delight in Him. Praise and worship Him. Make knowing Him the greatest pursuit of your life. If you do this, you will not remain in sin.

8. Meditate on the humility of Christ. Read Philippians chapter 2 and ask God to break your pride with His humility.

9. Practice giving up to God what you cannot, nor were meant to, accomplish or control. Cultivate weakness and dependence in the context of an abiding relationship with Almighty God.

10. Read and believe what the Bible says about your authority in Christ against the forces of darkness. Take an aggressive stance against them as the Holy Spirit gives you direction and guidance.

Failure and Self-Condemnation

Throughout this book, I have tried to be candid with you about the complexity, the concentrated effort and the time that will be involved in bringing you to full sexual health. I have been unequivocal about the absolute necessity for Jesus Christ being at the center of the process. And I have tried to be clear about the need for your will to be clear and unwaning in the process.

I would be greatly amiss, however, if I was not candid about the times of failure that you will encounter along the way, and Satan's plan to outflank all of your good intentions with psychological mind games. This is not a "negative confession." It is a reality!

You are, after all, only human. And despite all my warnings to the contrary, you may lapse into old patterns of self-effort and self-striving simply because that is the way you've been doing things your entire life. The pace at which God takes you may become frustratingly slow at times and you may unconsciously launch into attempts to help Him along—to get this thing over with! Particularly in our society, we want what we want when we want it. And if something takes too long, we've always had the luxury of going somewhere else or doing it some other way. Not so with God. His is the perfect way—the way that will bring together every contributing factor into a comprehensive, and therefore complete healing.

God's healing includes the divine-relational, as well as the human-relational aspects. It reaches down into the hidden roots of a need to heal completely, yet waits until the "fullness of time" has been reached before taking action. He will wait until you are ready. He will not force anything on you. He will not act outside of your will.

He will also wait until it is clear in your mind that He alone has brought the healing, so that He does not become an agent of self-righteousness in you. He will bring you to a place of healthy thinking as well as healthy action.

He requires forgiveness and repentance. He requires resolution of will. He requires humility of spirit. He does not put band-aids on problems. But He does perform in you what He requires of you, if you will diligently ask

Him to do so. For you, it is merely a matter of fervently willing Him to do whatever is necessary and then going along with whatever direction He gives you, under the power that He gives you. He does all things perfectly.

So, you can see how the healing might take longer than expected. And you can see how your patience and stamina might be tested—rather, how they will be tested.

When you find yourself falling into sin, or going backwards rather than forwards, as an addictive personality type, you will typically have intense feelings of failure and worthlessness. The dark forces of the spirit world will be only too glad to encourage, even introduce, these thoughts and feelings into your mind. They are thoughts and feelings that you are familiar with—that you've lived with all your life.

There is something about familiarity that makes it a controlling force in us. No matter how negative the thought or feeling, if it is one that we are familiar with, we will be drawn into welcoming it back into our life.

If you have given your life to Christ, you are engaged in a process of shedding all of the familiar, worldly behaviors and belief systems and putting on those that are heavenly. This is very uncomfortable to your natural, fleshly autonomic systems. They have to change, and change is always disruptive and uncomfortable, at least at the unconscious level.

That is why the strength of your relationship with God is so critical. You need His supernatural power to see you through this process, even at its most basic levels.

When you find yourself slipping backwards, it may be because you have allowed the old patterns of thought and behavior to reinvade your world and to gain ground again. At the same time, the demonic realm is, no doubt, plastering your mind with thoughts and feelings of self-condemnation. You feel worthless again. You feel unworthy again. You've probably begun to pass judgments against yourself for turning from what you know God wants, to embrace your old ways.

This is a critical place of spiritual warfare and it is important for you to know what to do when this happens.

If you have been playing games with God and have been using His grace as an excuse for embracing the pleasures of sin, God may allow you to reap the natural consequences of your actions. You may get caught. You may catch AIDS. You may pitch yourself back into a lengthy period of bondage, the second state being much worse than the first (Matthew 12:43-45). God disciplines those He loves (Heb. 12:5-11; Rev. 3:18-19). He will not be fooled or manipulated.

Then there are those who have been raised in a situation where the only attention they ever got at home was when they were disciplined. These folks may purposely sin in an unconscious attempt to attract God's love and attention. For them, being in a state of disciplining is their assurance of being loved. God will probably deal with these people in alternate ways than the norm in order to break them of this perverted pattern of thought and behavior. For He loves them unconditionally and has His eye on them whether they are sinning or not.

As for the thoughts of self-condemnation that accompany our failure, God says that they are lies—that "there is now no condemnation for those who are in Christ Jesus" (Rom. 8:1). We are not accepted by God by our good works either before we are saved, or after. We are accepted by Him because we have accepted His Son as our Lord and Savior. And because of that, God has imputed or reckoned to us the righteousness of Christ (Rom. 4:7-8). To impute something is to count it to someone's record or account. Jesus Christ's record of sinlessness has been counted to us. He purchased the right to do that for us by paying for our sins through His death on the Cross.

And so, when the thought or feeling arises within you—that you are under condemnation for failing to keep God's laws, you can know that that thought or feeling is a lie and has therefore come from the evil one. Reject it! Refuse to give it any place in your life!

Learn to recognize the voice of the enemy that often disguises itself in your mind as your own thoughts. And learn to I recognize the loving, gentle, forgiving and encouraging words that come from God. He has no interest in punishing a repentant heart. He would rather show you how to receive His strength against the enemy the next time the temptation strikes.

God is a good father. Let me illustrate. Say you are a little boy with his dad, trying to ride your bicycle for the first time without training wheels. Since riding on just two wheels is new to you, every once in a while, you wobble and fall. If your dad is an unkind father, he will criticize and humiliate you every time you fall, complaining about how much he paid for the bike and telling you how incompetent and stupid you are. But if your dad is like God the Father, every time you fall, he will run to you, kiss your wounds, tell you it's okay, and encourage you to get back on the bike and try it again. If your dad is like God the Father, his only interest will be in wiping away your tears and showing you how to get back up and do it more successfully the next time. He has no interest whatsoever in punishing or criticizing you, because he loves you, and he knows that you will best learn how to ride the bike if he is supportive and instructive. God's discipline is reserved for defiant, willful, long term rebellion, not for the day to day mistakes that we make as we try to learn how to follow Him. Satan's most effective scheme is in getting us to forget that and to question God's grace.

Your disappointment over having sinned should serve to inspire you to turn back to God, for it is through Him that the power "not to fail" comes. You have that freedom to turn to Him because your sin can never again cause Him to turn away from you. In you, He sees the perfection of His Son. First John 1:9 says, "If we confess our sins, He is faithful and righteous to forgive us our sins and to cleanse us from all unrighteousness" (NASB). Jesus says that "the one who comes to Me I will certainly not cast out" (John 6:37, NASB). The words used in the original language are double negative, meaning, "I will never never cast you out!" No way! By no means! God says elsewhere in the scripture: "I will never leave thee nor forsake thee" (Heb. 13:5, KJV).

If you are allowing self-condemnation to block your growth in Christ, you are showing that you are depending upon yourself to come to Christ, rather than His righteousness. It is indeed humiliating to always be dependent and in need of someone else's work. But that is the kind of spirit that pleases the Lord (Luke 18:9-14; John 15:5; James 4:10; 2 Chron. 16:9).

Briefly then, when you fall into sin, agree with God that your actions are wrong, agree to turn away from the sin, acknowledge that you are helpless to overcome it without the power of God, thank and worship Him for His grace and mercy, and for who He is, and wait upon Him to receive power to resist the temptation.

During these oft-repeated sessions, God will build into you His righteousness and power. As long as you honor and respect God's power within you, it will be with you always. However realize that His strength in you is always subject to your will. If, at any time, you decide that you prefer sin, God will always honor your decision, and allow you thereby to render void His power over sin in you (1 Cor. 10:12). Whatever you do, don't do that! It will be much harder to re-establish what you forsook, the second time around.

The only failure in God's eyes, is the person who refuses to turn to Him for restoration, who thereby is living according to their own standard of righteousness and according to their own judgments (James 4:12). If that is your sin, turn from it now and be restored, for God is gracious to forgive (1 John 1:9).

And always remember, "I have told you these things so that in Me (Jesus), you may have peace. In this world you will have trouble. But take heart! I have overcome the world" (John 16:33)!

Study Section— Failure and Self-Condemnation

> "God loved you without restraint even when sin was rampant within you; how much more will He continue to love you as you seek His grace to be free from iniquity?"
>
> —Francis Frangipane, *The Three Battlegrounds*

A. **SOME THINGS YOU SHOULD KNOW:**

1. Sexual healing is a life-long process, punctuated with significant healings, awakenings and deliverances—all wrought through an increasing dependence on, and devotion to, the Lord.

    "Live by the Spirit, and you will not gratify the desires of the sinful nature" (Gal. 5:16).

2. God's timing is perfect, though it my seem slow.

3. God will not force you or go against your will. He will wait until you are ready and willing to do what He wants you to do.

4. God will wait until you understand that it is *His* power that is working within you.

5. What God requires of you is:

    a. repentance

    b. forgiveness

    c. humility of spirit

    d. resolution of will

    "The proof of desire is in the pursuit." (Rod Parsley, World Harvest Church, Columbus, Oh. TV program 3/92)

6. Understand the tactics of "the evil one":

Remember, Satan is at work in you long before the sexual temptation is ever introduced. He gains power incrementally through "minor" sins, so that he can floor you with things more perverse. His typical treadmill looks something like this:

- Temptation toward self-sanctification and/or self-atonement (i.e., getting you to try to live the Christian life under your own power, or to try to make up for sin by performing good works).
- Temptation toward earning God's love or approval through performance rather than accepting God's grace of unconditional acceptance by faith.
- Temptation through carelessness in guarding your heart and mind in the things you allow into your personal environment.
- Temptation toward rebellion against the constraints of holiness—which blind you to the eternal realities and considerations that have to do with all of God's will.
- Temptation in the "little" things (e.g., anger, gossip, lying, etc.).

After setting us up for a fall through weakening us spiritually in our dealings with unrelated sins, Satan then hits us with the more obvious transgression.

- Sexual temptation
    - Fall
        - Guilt
            - Shame
                - Condemnation
                    - Hopelessness
                        - Temptation
                            - Fall

B. Some Things You Should Do:

1. Repent, forgive, put on humility, set your heart and mind to do the will of Jesus as He reveals it to you and gives you the power to carry it out.

"If My people...will humble themselves...pray...seek My face...turn from their wicked ways, then I will hear...and forgive their sin...and heal" (2 Chron. 7:14).

"My God turns my darkness into light...It is God who arms me with strength and makes my way perfect...He restores my soul" (Ps. 18:28, 32; 23:3).

2. Reject feelings of condemnation and worthlessness as the deceptions of Satan that they are. We're not accepted by God because of our holiness anyway.

"There is now no condemnation for those who are in Christ Jesus, because through Jesus Christ the law of the spirit of life set me free from the law of sin and death" (Rom. 8:1-2).

3. Set your mind and heart to believe the Word of God, despite your own feelings and the appearance of circumstance.

"If we confess our sins, He is faithful to forgive our sins, and cleanse us from all unrighteousness" (1 John 1:9, NASB).

4. Though change is uncomfortable, set your mind and heart to reject those things, beliefs, and patterns of behavior in your life that have been destructive to you, as God reveals them to you in that light.

   a. Note in John 14:30 that Satan had *nothing* in Jesus.
   b. Take captive every thought to make it obedient to Christ (2 Cor. 10:3-5).

5. Strengthen your relationship with the Lord through worship, praise, prayer and the study of His Word.

"I will praise the Lord, who counsels me; even at night my heart instructs me" (Ps. 16:7).

"Call to Me and I will answer you and tell you great and unsearchable things you do not know" (Jer. 33:3).

6. Learn to discern demonic voices, from your own thoughts, and from God's voice.

   a. God's voice is loving, gentle, forgiving, and encouraging.
   b. Satan's voice is condemning, rushed, and often calls into question things that God has already told you.

7. Turn back to God when you fail. He is the only one who can help

you "not to fail" the next time. He has no interest in chastising a repentant heart. He only wants to help you get it right the next time. The only failure in God's eye is the person who refuses to return to Him for restoration after falling.

In his book, *Passion for Jesus,* Mike Bickle comments:

> "When the Lord's presence departs from us in our place of compromise...you and I must arise in obedience and faith and seek Him.
>
> ...He does not condemn us for our immaturity or accuse us of our failures. Instead, He calls things that are not as though they were, because He sees those things in seed form in our hearts (Rom. 4:17).
>
> ...Even when we are weak, even when we fail, the Lord looks at the sincerity and devotion of our hearts and exclaims, 'You are so beautiful to Me!' The knowledge that Jesus continues to enjoy us as we are maturing is a foundational truth that empowers us to mature.
>
> ...Even though your actions sometimes fall short of your intentions, the devout resolution of your heart overwhelms Him with affectionate emotion. He looks at you and yearns over you, longing to draw you into a more intimate relationship with Him.
>
> It is this revelation of Jesus' ravished heart for you that awakens your heart to fervency for Him, igniting your progression in holy passion. And it is His passionate love for you and your response of love and devotion for Him that act as a breastplate of love, guarding your heart with holy affections in times of temptation and in the difficult hours of life (1 Thes. 5:8)."

8. Embrace the humiliation of considering yourself wholly dependent on God. Acknowledge your weakness, His grace, and His power to overcome.

"Jesus said, 'My grace is sufficient for you, for My power is made perfect in weakness.' Therefore, I (Paul) will boast all the more gladly about my weaknesses, so that Christ's power may rest on me...for when I am weak, then I am strong" (2 Cor. 12:9-10).

"To Him who is able to keep you from falling and to present you before His glorious presence without fault and with great joy—to the only God our Savior be glory, majesty, power and authority, through Jesus Christ our Lord, before all ages, now and forevermore, AMEN" (Jude 1:24-25)!

"You are my hiding place; you will protect me from trouble and surround me with songs of deliverance" (Ps. 32:7).

"The Lord is close to the brokenhearted and saves those who are crushed in spirit. A righteous man may have many troubles, but the Lord delivers him from them all" (Ps. 34:18-19).

C. THE DANGERS OF SUCCESS

1. It would be a great danger to your spiritual walk if your success in resisting sin came as a result of self-effort, apart from a dependency on and an appropriation of God's power.

    To believe that you can do it yourself can only result in I becoming self-righteous about your achievements and deluded about the praise-worthiness and the long-term efficacy of your efforts.

2. There can also be hidden danger, even when your success comes as a result of a proper appropriation of God's power and grace.

    After a period of success, there is an ever so subtle temptation to re-take the reigns of your life, and begin living as if you had been the source of the power (i.e., failing to turn to the Lord and rely upon Him each time temptation comes your way). Consider a similar fault in the Israelites of the Old Testament period, found in 1 Chron. 15:13 and Joshua 9:14, where they failed to inquire of the Lord.

Exercises—
Failure and Self-Condemnation

1. Ask God to help you deal with impatience and an inability to trust in His perfect timing for the answer to prayer.

2. Ask God to deal with your unspoken, internal demands and expectations of Him that give you the tendency to automatically blame Him when something doesn't go right.

3. Ask God to help you separate how your parents dealt with you from how God deals with you and to understand the incredible nature of the fatherhood of God.

4. Ask God to expose Satan's tactics against you in bringing discouragement, condemnation, fear and doubt, and a pull toward the self-centered, fleshly nature. Then ask God to show you what to do in the face of those tactics.

5. Ask God how to recognize and eliminate those minor infractions in life that mount up and weaken you (set you up) for a fall in the larger areas of sin. Ask Him to give you the depth of love and commitment to Him that will enable you to target these more minor areas of sin as well as the larger ones.

6. Set your heart and mind to believe the Word of God at all times and in every circumstance in spite of any seeming evidence to the contrary.

7. Spend copious hours in worship and praise, in prayer and Scripture reading.

8. Read Peter Lord's book, *Hearing God,* or Leanne Payne's book, *Listening Prayer,* and practice listening for the voice of the Lord.

A Comprehensive Game Plan for Sexual Healing

Become Born Again

The first step on the path to sexual healing is to accept Jesus Christ as your Lord and Savior. He is the One who created you. He is the One who paid for your sins by allowing Himself to be crucified on a cross. By the wounds that He suffered, all who come to Him can be healed both spiritually (1 Pet. 2:21-24) and physically (Mt. 8:16-17), in fulfillment of the Isaiah 53:4-5 prophecy concerning Him. Jesus is the only One who can bring complete healing into your life.

He said that unless a man is born again, or born "from above" (referring to a spiritual birth through Him), he cannot enter the kingdom of God (John 3:3). When Adam and Eve sinned, they died spiritually (Gen. 2:16-17; 3:2-3). When you were born, you were born spiritually dead, separated from God, because you are a descendant of Adam and have inherited his fallen nature (1 Cor. 15:22). God is the only One who can rectify all that and He has chosen to do so through the offices of His one and only Son, Jesus. That is why there is no other way to be saved (Acts 4:12).

Recognize the Adversary

It is important to understand and believe that there is a devil in the invisible spiritual realm who walks about the earth like a roaring lion seeking whom he may devour (1 Pet. 5:8). The Bible refers to him as Abaddon or Apollyon, which means "destruction" (Rev. 9:11); the accuser of believers (Rev. 12:10); the adversary or enemy (1 Pet 5:8); the angel of the abyss (Rev. 9:11); Belial (2 Cor. 6:15); Beelzebub, or "Lord of the Flies," used by the Jews as an epithet for Satan (Mt. 12:24); the devil (Mt. 4:1); the god of this age (2 Cor. 4:4); a murderer (John 8:44); a liar and the father of lies (John 8:44); the prince of demons (Mt. 12:24); the ruler of the kingdom of the air (Eph. 2:2); the prince of this world (John 14:30); the ruler of this world (John 12:31); the ruler of darkness (Eph. 6:12); a serpent (Gen. 3:4); the dragon (Rev. 20:2); the tempter (Mt. 4:3); the evil one (Mt. 13:19); the king of Tyre and formerly, the anointed cherub that covers (Ez. 28:12, 14); the king of Babylon, star of the morning and son of the dawn (Is. 14:4, 12).

Before the creation of the universe, Satan (then Lucifer) was created, along with all of the other angels (cf. Job 38:4, 7). He was indeed the most beautiful of angels before sin was found in him and he fell, taking a third of the angels with him in his rebellion (Ez. 28:19; Is. 14:4, 11-19). In the garden of Eden, he recruited man into his rebellion (Gen. 3). In these last days, he comes as an angel of light (2 Cor. 11:14) to further deceive. And in the end, he will be thrown into the lake of fire to suffer forever and ever (Rev. 20:2-3, 10).

Satan holds the power of death over unbelievers (Heb. 2:14, 15), and wields a certain measure of authority over this world (Luke 4:6). But his work can be destroyed by the power of Jesus (1 John 3:8), given to His followers (Luke 10:18-19). The devil inflicts disease (Job 2:7), accuses the redeemed (Zech. 3:1), steals spiritual truth from our minds (Mt. 13:19), sows counterfeits in the church (Mt. 13:38-39), performs false miracles (2 Thes. 2:9), has dominion over (Acts 26:18) and blinds the minds of unbelievers (2 Cor. 4:4).

As Christians, we are exhorted to not give Satan a foothold in our lives (Eph. 4:27). We're to put on the armor of God in order to stand against the devil (Eph. 6:11). We're to resist the devil (James 4:7; 1 Pet. 5:9), but always by the power of God that is available to us when we seek it.

Demons (Eph. 6:12) are those angelic beings that followed Satan in his rebellion and who now serve him against God and all humanity. They do whatever they are told, including possession and control (Mt. 8:28-32); the inflicting of disease (Mark 9:17); and deceiving people, through their minds (1 Tim. 4:1) and through miracles (Rev. 16:13-14). But realize that Jesus Christ came to destroy all the power of the enemy (1 John 3:8). In Jesus, you can have the victory over Satan and his demons (Luke 10:19).

Develop a Mature Perspective on Life

There are a number of components to the "eternal perspective" that we must be diligent to keep.

We must always remember that we have been born into a battle—the battle of evil against good (Satan against God), and that as members of Christ's body, the Church, we will suffer wounds from, the battle. Jesus was very clear on that point. He said that we will have tribulation in this world (Jn. 16:33), but that we share the ultimate victory with Him (1 Cor. 15:57). In the meantime, we will share in His sufferings (Rom. 8:17; Phil 3:10; 1 Pet. 4:13), because as Jesus said, "No servant is greater than his Master. If they persecuted Me, they will persecute you also" (Jn. 15:20). "I send you out as sheep in the midst of wolves . . . and you will be hated by all on account of My name" (Mt. 10:16, 22, NASB). "If you should suffer for the sake of righteousness, you are blessed" (1 Pet. 3:14, NASB, see also 1 Pet. 4:14; Mt. 5:10; James 5:10-11). "For if we endure, we shall also reign with Him" (2 Tim. 2:12, NASB). "Knowing that the testing of your faith produces endurance. And let endurance have its perfect result, that you may be perfect and complete, lacking in nothing" (James 1:3-4, NASB). "By your endurance you will gain your lives" (Luke 21:19, NASB). "(Be) imitators of those who through faith and patience inherit the promises" (Heb. 6:12, NASB).

These promises primarily relate to the testing and persecution that you will suffer because of your faith in Jesus and the righteousness that He calls you to. That righteousness is an affront to this world because Satan is its ruler, and those who do not belong to Christ are unwitting soldiers in his army. They are; repelled by the things of God by virtue of their position in that army and the spirit of sin that controls them. The battle is not against the people, however, it is against the spirit that manipulates and controls them. You will do well to retain this perspective.

A second component to the "eternal perspective" is who we are in relation to God—that we are created beings who are incapable of doing anything truly and perfectly good without the redemption, the restoration, the equipping, and the work of God in and through us to accomplish it. *He is the One who both wills and does in us and through us what we can never do on our own.* So, our place is as servants of the One who redeemed us—to do as He directs with the power and abilities that He gives—to always remember that we have nothing that wasn't given to us by Him, and that without Him we can do nothing. Therein lies true humility, which is simply a heartfelt acceptance and incorporation of this truth into our daily lives.

A third component of an "eternal perspective" is a constant awareness of the power, presence and purity of the One we serve—a healthy "fear" or reverence for Almighty God. This fear will both give you the will to resist temptation, as well as the courage to resist anything that the evil one brings against you.

A fourth component is a "time" perspective. Psalm 90:12 says, "Teach us to number our days, that we may present to Thee a heart of wisdom" (NASB). We need to constantly remind ourselves that our time on this earth is short (James 4:14), and extremely valuable—that what we do here in this brief span of some 40-80 years will bring fruit that will last forever and ever. The spiritual maturity and good deeds done by the direction of the Holy Spirit will in some way determine an eternal course for us in heaven.

We need to daily consider that our years here on earth, though crucial to our eternal state, are but a speck in the vast expanse of a timeless future, and that whatever hardships or persecutions fall to us in God's incredible plan are but fodder for endless joys to come.

A fifth component is a "place" perspective. It is vitally important to our spiritual growth and service to Christ that we always reckon ourselves as strangers on this planet—that we have a home made in heaven (Lev. 25:23;

1 Chron. 29:14-15; Ps. 119:19). In speaking of men of great faith, the Apostle Paul said, "(They) confessed that they were strangers and exiles on the earth. Those who say such things make it clear that they are seeking a country of their own. And indeed if they had been thinking of that country from which they went out, they would have had opportunity to return. But as it is, they desire a better country, that is a heavenly one. Therefore God is not ashamed to be called their God; for He has prepared a city for them" (Heb. 11:13-16, NASB).

The Apostle Peter refers to Christians as "aliens and strangers in the world" (1 Pet. 2:11). The Apostle Paul said that we are "fellow citizens with God's people and members of God's household" (Eph. 2:19), and that "our citizenship is in heaven" (Phil. 3:20).

Lastly, an eternal perspective can be formed in us only as we reckon ourselves dead to this world and the things of the world that would entice us to do otherwise. The Apostle John exhorted us: "Do not love the world, nor the things in the world. If anyone loves the world, the love of the Father is not in him. For all that is in the world, the lust of the flesh and the lust of the eyes and the boastful pride of life, is not from the Father, but is from the world. And the world is passing away, and also its lusts; but the one who does the will of God abides forever" (1 John 2:15-17, NASB).

We need to ask God for eyes to see how Satan is using the world and our five senses to blind us to eternal realities—how what we watch, what we eat, what we say, what we think upon, what we feed into our minds and bodies affects our intimacy and walk with Him. These things are often the last to go, for we have become lovers of things rather than lovers of God, and Satan is going to employ the ruse of our "freedom" and the tyranny of "time" to lure us back into the ways of this world.

Seek God fervently for His perspective on everything you do and say, and respond ruthlessly to those things that He cautions you about. And be honest with yourself! Stop this game of pretending to ask God for His opinion without the full longing for it in your heart.

Renounce Known Sin and Seek God's Power Over It

We have to decide once and for all to renounce all sin—that it will no longer be master over us (Rom. 6:14)—that Christ will be our *only* Master (Mt. 6:24). Too often, we parcel out to God little pockets of sin, one by one, as we weary of them or as we come to the place of having satisfied the lion's share of our desire for them. We abuse the grace of God under the guise of weakness or "being only human." And what we don't realize is that not only are we adding to Christ's sufferings by this, we are also adding to our own, by thwarting God's plan for us and crippling our own spirit.

"The grace of God has appeared, bringing salvation to all men, instructing us to deny ungodliness and worldly desires and to live sensibly, righteously and godly in the present age, looking for the blessed hope and the appearing of the glory of our great God and Savior, Christ Jesus" (Titus 2:13, NASB).

God will not be mocked. We will reap what we sow! As believers, we may have escaped eternal damnation, but we have not escaped all judgment from God. We will indeed be judged on that last day when the deeds of the righteous and the unrighteous will be made known, and many believers *will* suffer loss, though not their salvation (1 Cor. 3:15). "For we must all appear before the judgment seat of Christ, that each one may receive what is due him for the things done while in the body, whether good or bad" (2 Cor. 5:10). "Watch yourselves, that you might not lose what you have accomplished, but that you may receive a full reward" (2 John 8, NASB).

God created each of us for a purpose. He said, "I know the plans I have for you; plans to prosper you and not to harm you, plans to give you a hope and a future" (Jer. 29:11; cf. Prov. 16:19) You have been called to salvation "according to His purpose" (Rom. 8:28). "For we are His workmanship, created in Christ Jesus for good works, which God prepared beforehand, that we should walk in them" (Eph. 2:10, NASB).

Throughout scripture, Jesus exhorts us over and over again to be ready for His appearing (Mt. 24:42-25:46), at which time He will say to some, "Well done thou good and faithful servant" (Mt. 25:21, KJV). The crown of righteousness awaits those who *love* His appearing (2 Tim. 4:8). Your faith will be tested by fire and will hopefully be found to result in praise, glory and honor at the appearing of Jesus Christ (1 Pet. 1:7; 1 Cor. 4:5). Only those deeds which have been wrought in God will survive the test (John 3:21). So live so as to have confidence in the day of judgment (1 John 4:17), and so you will not shrink away from Him in shame at His coming (1 John 2:28).

So, it is imperative that we seek for God's plan and for His enablement to carry the plan through, always remembering that it is God who works in us "to will and to act" according to His good purpose (Phil. 2:13).

Jesus is the true vine. Just as a branch cannot bear fruit by itself, unless it abides in the vine, neither can we, unless we abide in Him. If we abide in Him, as He does in us, then we can bear much fruit. But apart from Him, we can do nothing (John 15:15).

Learn to Worship and Praise the Lord

Many people are put off by the constant reminders in scripture to praise God and to give Him all the glory. On the surface, it sounds too much like some cosmic egomaniac desperately trying to bolster his low self-esteem.

The problem, however, lies with our fallen perspective. We're forever trying to measure God according to our own impure experience and have a certain amount of difficulty imagining a Being who is perfect, flawless and incapable of error—indeed, incapable of needing our praise and worship at all.

If God is indefectible, and the source of everything that is good, then He rightly deserves all of the glory. God is also a God of absolute truth. And so, His insistence on receiving all praise and worship is, in effect, an insistence on living according to the truth. Our seeking after and ascribing to Him all the glory is, in reality, a seeking after and embracing of truth, and is therefore necessary. It is also a needed reminder for us, that we do *not* deserve glory, as we so often presume after doing something good. In that sense, it is a good humility builder.

Since truth is an integral part of God's nature, a benefit of declaring the truth of His glory through praise is that we are uniting ourselves to Him, cleaving to Him, having His nature imparted to us as we praise Him. And so the scriptures declare that God "inhabits" the praises of His people (Ps. 22:3, KJV). The Hebrew word used means "to dwell," "to inhabit," or "to be enthroned upon."

There is no one single part of the Christian life that is more important than spending copious hours praising and worshipping God, for it is in that time of truth and intimacy that He imparts His life and character to us, and we are made to be like Him. The Apostle Paul referred to this process as Christ being "formed in us" (Gal. 4:19). At the end of our time here on earth, what God wants to see more than anything else, is how much of Himself has been formed in us. Isn't that just like a father's wish for his son?

Another benefit of praise and worship is that it scatters and defeats the enemy. Evil Spirits cannot stand to hear the praises of God's people and will often flee at the sound. It is a key weapon of our warfare in the spiritual realm.

Divine power is imparted during praise (2 Chron. 20:22). We receive assurance of peace, inner healing, power to defeat the enemy and a host of like benefits as we ascribe glory to God, to whom belongs all glory and dominion (1 Pet. 4:11). It is a sacrifice of thanksgiving to the One who saved us (Jer. 17:26; Heb. 13:15). It is something that the whole earth is engaged in (Hab. 3:3), even infants and nursing babes (Mt. 21:16). It is something innate in nature itself (Luke 19:37-40). Even the heavens declare God's glory (Ps. 19:1). It is what we are to set our mind upon (Phil. 4:8), for it is what is continually taking place in heaven (Rev. 4:8-11), which is our home.

Learning the Power of Prayer

Most of us suffer from a lack of desire for prayer born out of a lack of results from prayer. After all, if we actually saw immediate results from prayer—miraculous, powerful results, we'd, be highly motivated to pray would we not? We're used to getting what we want quickly—practically anything we want, whereas in prayer, God seems either unconcerned or uninterested. It's not easy talking to a blank wall, as if there were an invisible Spirit there, when we can't see an immediate response.

We make our first mistake when we interpret a lack of quick results as a sign of God's disinterest or as a sign of our unworthiness to be heard. First of all, God's movements and actions are always perfect, which means that they are also perfectly, timed. In that sense, He is prevented by His own perfection from answering prayers in the way we prescribe. That often means delayed results. If we give up too early, we often lose what God intends for us.

He also must consider the request itself. If it is not according to His will, He cannot do it, because He is perfect and can only do things perfectly. Only those things which are perfect can ever be according to His will. That is why we are told in scripture that we must pray according to His will (1 John 5:14). As we grow in intimacy with Him, and become more and more like Him, we begin thinking like Him and our requests adhere more often to His will. That is why we receive whatever we ask if we abide in Him and His words abide in us (John 15:7). A similar concept is found in the exhortation to ask "in His name" in order to receive what we ask for (John 14:13-14).

While in the process of "putting on the mind of Christ" so that we ask the things He is able to grant, we can still ask Him for wisdom about what to ask for (James 1:5-8). He is certainly willing and capable of revealing that information.

A good place to start is to pray back to God the prayers that are already found in scripture. How easy could it be to find the will of God than that? From the Psalms, we learn one of the most important prayers: "Help me O God!" (Ps. 12:1; 79:9; 109:26-27). In Mark 9:24, the prayer is: "Help me overcome my unbelief!"

Other important things to pray for are: faith that does not fail; the will to follow Jesus; the power to be obedient to His holy calling; the unleashing of the Holy Spirit in the world; for the Lord to raise up and send out workers for the harvest of souls to come; for His unblemished love; for a hunger and diligence to seek Him and His will; for the gifts of the Spirit, in order to more effectively minister to others; to know His will; for the healing of your damaged body or emotions; for humility; for compassion for others; for wisdom; for discernment; etc. And don't give up, even when you see these things beginning to be formed in you!

Faith is a critical component to answered prayer. Mark 11:22-26 teaches us that if we have the "faith of God" we will believe that we have received the requests we make, and they shall be ours. Having the faith of God is another major byproduct of a life of intimacy with Him.

Our hearts are deceitfully wicked (Mt. 15:19). We too often ask God for things out of impure motives (James 4:3). We're sometimes so blinded by our adultery with the things of the world that we aren't even aware of improper motives. That is when we need to pray with King David: "Search me, O God, and know my heart; test me and know my anxious thoughts. See if there is any offensive way in me, and lead me in the way everlasting" (Ps. 139:23-24).

And, of course, if we have unconfessed, unrepented sin in our lives (including such things as unforgiveness, anger, bitterness, etc.) God may not answer our prayer.

The Bible even says that sometimes we don't have, simply because we don't ask (James 4:2). We give up too easily. We allow Satan to convince us that we are unworthy to ask anything of God, despite the clear biblical teaching to the contrary (Rom. 8:1; Eph. 3:12; Heb. 4:16; 10:19, 35).

Perseverance and passion are also vital components to prayer. We are to ask and keep asking (Mt. 7:7). We are to wrestle with God, as it were, for the things we passionately seek (Gen. 32:24-30). In the process, we learn for ourselves what is really important to us. And it is those things that the Father delights in giving us.

Jesus taught that the kingdom of God (the rule and reign of God on earth) is advancing forcefully and forceful men lay hold of it (Mt. 11:7-12). We must begin to take seriously our call in this world—a call to arms as soldiers in the war against all that is evil. And if we truly want to be healed; if we really want to be made pure in word, thought and deed; if we seriously want to serve the living God; then we must set our hearts to do whatever it takes. We must deal ruthlessly with the sources of sin in our lives. We must relentlessly pursue God—with all our heart, with diligence and perseverance. And we must do it with a humility of spirit that recognizes Him as the source for the tools of success in this war—a humility that willingly and honestly gives Him all the glory.

If we can come to that point of commitment, nothing will be impossible, and our prayers will light up the heavens. What does it take to come to that point? All it takes is for us to really want it and to seek God relentlessly for it. He *will* respond! Should you find yourself without this desire, ask God for it until He gives it to you. He *will* give it to you if you persevere in prayer for it. And in the throes of giving yourself wholly to the Lord, you *will* be healed from the psychological and emotional damage that caused your sexual problem.

Learning to Trust and Use the Word of God

The person on the street will tell you that the Bible is an unreliable document because it is a collection of flawed memories of human beings that has been rewritten so many times as to have lost any semblance of accuracy.

The Bible has many charges to bring against the man on the street, which makes him want to draw such conclusions. And since he has never seriously investigated the overwhelming evidence against his assertions, his conclusions are quite understandable. The odds are that he is genuinely ignorant of the indisputable evidence that the Bible is the actual Word of God, containing no errors whatsoever in its original writing and only a handful of negligible mistakes in transcription.

Today's Bible is, in fact, the most accurate we've ever had simply due to the thousands of archeological discoveries that have been made in this century. For example, there are over 5,000 whole or partial manuscripts of New Testament books that have been unearthed over the years. This massive source for cross-referencing brings to naught any argument for an inaccurate Bible. We have partial manuscripts of the Gospel of John that date back to the early second century, putting it in the same generation as the original author. This kind of documentation is unparalleled in all of antiquity.

The discovery of the Dead Sea scrolls has effectively put to rest any doubt as to the accuracy of our modern versions of the Old Testament. However, the best place to start with determining the veracity of the Bible is to examine the thousands of prophecies that have been written there. When you match the historical progression of prophecy and fulfillment, and then try to figure the odds of so many thousands of prophecies coming true exactly as predicted (prophecies such as the prediction of the precise name of a king (Cyrus, King of Persia) two hundred years into the future—see Is. 44:21-28; 45:1, 5; Jer. 25:12 and Ezra 1:1), you will see that the Scripture had to have been breathed from the very mouth of God. As it claims—"All Scripture is God-breathed" (2 Tim. 3:16). Researchers in this area have determined that the odds against the prophecies being as numerous and as accurate as they are, are so astronomical as to indisputably support the Bible's own claim to divine authorship.

The second indisputable evidence for the veracity and authority of Scripture is the fact that when you respond to its claims and promises for your life according to the conditions it requires, it proves itself true in you own personal experience.

God will back up His Word. When He promises something in Scripture, and lays out the conditions for the promise, *anyone* who takes Him up on it will see the promised results. For example, in Jeremiah 29:13, God promises, "You will seek Me and find Me when you seek Me with all your heart."

So, call Him on it! What have you got to lose? Seek Him *with all your heart*, and He *will* reveal Himself to you.

There are many such promises in Scripture, but when you use them, always note the conditions to the promise. Also be careful to consider each scripture of like kind when determining the conditions that apply. This is where a facility with the scriptures, established through regular Bible reading, is important. For example, there are a number of scriptures where God promises to give us whatever we ask for in prayer, but each has a condition attached to it:

God's Promise	The Condition
Whatever I ask for, I will receive	if I keep His commandments and do the things that are pleasing in His sight (1 John 3:22)
I will get what I ask God for	if I pray according to God's will (1 John 5:14-15) (cf. Col. 1:9)
God will do what I ask	if I ask in Jesus' name (John 14:13)
The Father will give me whatever I ask in Jesus' name	if I go and bear fruit that will last (John 15:16)
Ask whatever you wish and it shall be done for you	if you abide in Me, and My words abide in you (John 15:7) (cf. 1 John 3:24)
God will give me the desires of my heart	if I delight myself in Him (Psalm 37:4)
All my basic needs will be met	if I seek first the kingdom of God and His righteousness (Matthew 6:33)

So, in preparing to ask for the promise of "getting whatever you ask for in prayer," take the time to deal with the applicable conditions to your life and relationship with God. As you might expect, such a grand promise as the one in our example requires a significant interactive relationship with God. However, not all of God's promises are so far-reaching, so neither are their conditions. But when you pray according to what the scripture says, you will see the promised results—a phenomena that clearly vindicates the divine authorship of the Bible.

The Apostle Peter says: "Above all, you must understand that no prophecy of Scripture came about by the prophet's own interpretation. For prophecy never had its origin in the will of man, but men spoke from God as they were carried along by the Holy Spirit" (2 Pet. 1:20-21).

Peter goes so far as to specifically refer to the writings of Paul as Scripture (2 Pet. 3:15-16). And Paul clearly states: "We thank God continually because, when you received the Word of God, which you heard from us, you accepted it not as the word of men, but as it actually is, the Word of God, which is at work in you who believe" (1 Thes. 2:13).

Jesus Himself referred to the writings of David as having been spoken by the Holy Spirit (Mark 12:36), and the Apostle Paul refers to the writings of Jeremiah as coming from the Holy Spirit

Jesus also claimed that not the smallest part of a letter of any of the words of Scripture would pass away until all of it had been fulfilled (Mt. 5:18) (i.e., that every letter and every word of Scripture was critically important to God precisely as it has been written down). In John 10:35, Jesus said that Scripture cannot be broken. In Mt. 22:41-46, He based His claim to deity on a single word from the Old Testament. This kind of argumentation demands a belief in an error-free, God-breathed Scripture. Paul does the same thing in Gal. 3:16, basing his whole argument on the very specific "plural" use of a word in Scripture.

After satisfying yourself as to the critical place of Scripture in your life, the next step is to ingest it into your system on a regular basis. It is your spiritual food, as necessary for your spiritual health as food is for your physical health. Through it, the Holy Spirit will speak to you, by enlightening certain passages and making them appropriate to your personal situation. In a very real sense, it is made a "living word" to your soul by this supernatural action of the Holy Spirit. By it, God will teach, guide, comfort, correct and train you in righteousness

Learning to Forgive

If you are sexually dysfunctional or are addicted to any kind of behavior or substance, the odds are extremely good that deep inside, you are angry. You may have been unfairly abused or shortchanged in life in some way. You may have many good excuses for having done the things that you have done, but you've since discovered that the way you've been dealing with the pain and anger of your problems has actually been making things worse, not better. Now you're faced with the question of how to get healed and on the right track.

It's important to see that the anger, bitterness, resentment or unforgiveness that you've nourished over the years as a result of your pain has actually made things worse. It has created an emotional block that secretly opposes all attempts at healing and reconciliation. It is harming *you* rather than the person against whom you hold it.

Consequently, the first thing you must do is to believe and trust God when He assures you that He will judge all men (Acts 17:31; Ps. 62:12; Jer. 17:10; Mt. 16:27; Rev. 20:12; Ecc. 3:17). Jude 15 assures us that God will "judge all the ungodly of all the ungodly acts they have done!"

But also remember that it is God alone who has the right to judge (Ps. 75:7). James 4:12 tells us: "There is only one Lawgiver and Judge, the one who is able to save and destroy." It is God alone who can see into the heart of man and accurately judge his actions. It is God alone who is pure and undefiled and capable of judging with complete impartiality. For you or I to usurp this prerogative of God's, is a grave offense. To set ourselves up as judges in the face of God's declaration that: "Vengeance and retribution is Mine" (Dt. 32:35; Heb. 10:30) is to judge God's law (James 4:11).

Secondly, when Jesus Christ forgave you of every offense that you have ever, or ever will, commit, you absolutely lost the right to hold anything against anyone, ever again. Jesus' parable about the unmerciful servant makes this point very clear (Mt. 18:21-35).

With the understanding that the forgiveness that you accepted from Christ wasn't deserved, forgive everyone who has ever done you wrong. This is imperative. I didn't say it was easy, but it is imperative (Mt. 6:12-15). Particularly for those of you who have been brutally treated, this may be one of the most difficult things you will ever have to do. But it must be done, and God will give you the ability to do it if you will come to Him with sincerity in your heart and ask Him to enable you.

You will know that you have forgiven someone "from your heart" when the thought of them no longer causes a caustic reaction inside. For some of you, this is something only God Himself can accomplish, so turn to Him now and begin to receive His power to forgive in the intimacy of praise and worship.

Thirdly, believe in and receive by faith God's promise to forgive you (Acts 10:43; 13:38; 26:18; Eph 1:7; Col 1:13-14; 1 Jn 1:9). Those who have victimized you over the years, including Satan, may have done an excellent job at making you think that you are the guilty party, or an evil person. If you are the victim of child sex abuse or involuntary homosexual inclinations, I hope by now you understand that you are not judged for those unfortunate situations.

Even if you are guilty of sin, as we all are, God has declared that anyone who comes to Him in repentance will be forgiven. For you to refuse to forgive yourself after God has declared you forgiven is tantamount to claiming that you have a higher standard than God, or that you know better than God. No one knows better than God! No one has a higher standard than God! And He says that you are forgiven. So do not doubt, but believe Him!

Lastly, ask the Lord to search your heart to see if you are harboring unconscious judgments against Him. Out of the pain of your past, you may very well have developed a subconscious anger and bitterness toward God for allowing the trauma to occur. It is out of such evidence as Christ's death on the Cross for you that you will be able to release God from those hidden judgments. So, in response to Christ's demonstration of love for you on the Cross, release God from all judgments and conditions for your love.

Make the Learning of Humility a Priority in Your Life

Too often we do not give pride the serious attention it deserves. Read just a few examples of what God thinks:

"May the Lord cut off all flattering lips and every boastful tongue" (Ps. 12:3).

"The Lord pays back the proud in full" (Ps. 31:23).

"Blessed is the man…who does not look to the proud" (Ps. 40:4).

"Whoever has haughty eyes and a proud heart, I will not endure" (Ps. 101:5).

"You rebuke the arrogant who are cursed" (Ps. 119:21).

"The Lord hates…haughty eyes" (Prov. 6:16-17).

"I hate pride and arrogance" (Prov. 8:13).

"The Lord tears down the proud man's house" (Prov. 15:25).

"The Lord detests all the proud of heart. Be sure of this: they will not go unpunished…Pride goes before destruction, a haughty spirit before a fall" (Prov. 16:5, 18).

"The Lord Almighty has a day in store for all the proud and lofty, for all that is exalted. They will be humbled" (Isaiah 2:12).

"I will put an end to the arrogance of the proud" (Isaiah 13:11, NASB).

"Do not be arrogant, for the Lord has spoken Give glory to the Lord your God before He brings the darkness" (Jer. 13:15, 16).

"I am against you, O arrogant one…(You) will stumble and fall and no one will help you up" (Jer. 50:31, 32).

"The pride of your heart has deceived you…who say to yourself, 'Who can bring me down to the ground?…I will bring you down,' declares the Lord" (Obad. 1:3).

"The soul (of the proud one) is not right within him" (Hab. 2:4, NASB).

> "Behold, the day is coming, burning like a furnace, when all the arrogant and every evildoer will be stubble; and the day that is coming will set them ablaze, say the Lord Almighty. Not a root or a branch will be left to them" (Mal. 4:1, NASB).
>
> "There will be terrible times in the last days. People will be lovers of themselves…boastful, proud" (2 Tim. 3:1, 2).
>
> "The boastful pride of life is not from the Father, but is from the world" (1 John 2:16, NASB).

Now let's look at what God says about humility:

> "When he humbled himself, the anger of the Lord turned away from him" (2 Chron. 12:12, NASB).
>
> "Though the Lord is exalted, yet He regards the lowly; but the proud He knows from afar" (Ps. 138:6, NASB).
>
> "When pride comes, then comes dishonor, but with humility comes wisdom" (Prov. 11:2, NASB).
>
> "Before honor, comes humility" (Prov. 15:33, NASB).
>
> "The reward of humility and the fear of the Lord are riches, honor and life" (Prov. 22:4, NASB).
>
> "A man's pride will bring him low, but a humble spirit will obtain honor" (Prov. 29:23, NASB).
>
> "I will dwell…with the contrite and lowly of spirit in order to revive the spirit of the lowly and to revive the heart of the contrite" (Isaiah 57:15, NASB).
>
> "To this one I will look, to him who is humble and contrite of spirit, and who trembles at My word" (Is. 66:2, NASB).
>
> "He has showed you, O man, what is good. And what does the Lord require of you? To act justly and to love mercy and to walk humbly with your God" (Mic. 6:8).
>
> "Whoever humbles himself as (a) child, he is the greatest in the kingdom of heaven" (Mt. 18:4, NASB).
>
> "Whoever exalts himself shall be humbled; and whoever humbles himself shall be exalted" (Mt. 23:12, NASB).
>
> "(Christ) humbled Himself by becoming obedient to the point of death…Therefore also God highly exalted Him" (Phil. 2:8-9, NASB).
>
> "God opposes the proud but gives grace to the humble" (Jas 4:6).

"Humble yourselves in the presence of the Lord, and He will exalt you" (James 4:10, NASB).

"Clothe yourselves with humility toward one another...Humble yourselves under the mighty hand of God, that He may exalt you at the proper time" (1 Pet. 5:5-6, NASB)

Do you get the feeling that God hates pride and loves humility? Humility, remember, is not a pious look or a string of self-deprecating pronouncements. Those are born out of either a self-righteously proud spirit or an unhealthy search for acceptance.

True humility comes from deep within the spirit and displays itself as an honest reckoning of others as more important than oneself. The Bible tells us to: "Do nothing out of selfish ambition or vain conceit, but in humility consider others better than yourselves...Look not only to your own interests, but also to the interests of others" (Phil. 2:3-4).

A natural by-product of humility is servanthood. When Jesus washed His disciple's feet (John 13:1-17), He was displaying the natural working of His humble spirit, a humility that gave its most amazing demonstration on the Cross (Phil. 2:8).

Humility is not easily gotten, particularly in our culture where it is viewed as an absurd weakness. It can be gotten, however, in one of two ways.

If you are proud, God may choose to humble you before the judgment, like right now. When the Israelites left Egypt, they were humbled by God leading them forty years in the wilderness. He said in Dt. 8:2-18:

> "You shall remember all the way which the Lord your God has led you in the wilderness these forty years, that He might humble you, testing you to know what was in your heart, whether you would keep His commandments or not. And He humbled you and let you be hungry, and fed you with manna which you did not know, nor did your fathers know, that He might make you understand that man does not live by bread alone, but by everything that proceeds out of the mouth of the Lord...
>
> "Beware lest ... when your silver and gold and all that you have multiplies, your heart does not become proud, and you forget the Lord your God...who led you through the great and terrible wilderness...that He might humble you and that He might test you, to do good for you in the end. Otherwise, you may say in your heart, 'My power and the strength of my hand made me this wealth.' But you shall remember the Lord your God, for it is He who is giving you power to make wealth" (NASB).

From this passage we learn that it is God who enables us to do all that we do, and therefore to Him that we should turn in thanksgiving and obedience; that our very existence is inextricably tied into a relationship with Him. We must understand, and live as if, He were the source of everything we need and the power behind everything that we accomplish. In that frame of mind, there is no place for exalting oneself.

The passage also teaches us that God will put us through various trials in this life, in order to instill these truths into our hearts. He wants to bless us and do good for us, but cannot as long as we are proud of heart.

The second way to get humility is through an intimate relationship with God. As you come to know Him more and more, humility will grow naturally within you as a consequence of the awe and inspiration you receive from the things He shows you. I am not talking about becoming an expert in the knowledge of God, but a relational knowing—one that is born at first from scripture, but more critically from personal interaction with Him in prayer and worship.

Discerning the Voice of God

We sometimes get the impression from scripture that God only speaks to men and women of biblical stature and importance to the kingdom of God. However, nothing could be further from the truth. God wants to have as intimate and communicative a relationship with you and me as He did with Billy Graham or the Apostles.

How then can we tell when God is trying to communicate to us? It is primarily through the nature and content of the message that is being sent. For example, when God wants to speak to us, He often orchestrates events and input around us in such a way as to repeatedly drive home an idea to us. It's almost like the waves of the seashore relentlessly lapping or pounding at the door of your mind. The repetitive and unusually coincidental nature of this process will be accompanied with the thought, "God may be trying to tell me something."

God will use people, media, the Bible—virtually any source of information to tailor this repeated coincidence of ideas. Over time, you will begin to recognize more quickly when this is happening.

God speaks audibly to a few people on rare occasions, but more often uses a "still small voice" in your inner man. It's not a voice that you hear with your ears, but one that seems to emanate from the very center of your spirit and that speaks directly to your heart or to your brain.

As your devotion and intimacy with God deepens, this form of communication will likely increase. It is important therefore, to be able to discern God's voice from your own thoughts, and from demonic communication. This is where the content and nature of the voice becomes very important.

The demonic world is always communicating thoughts to your mind.

Many of the temptations you face in your thought life are directly generated and empowered by these forces. For the most part, these kinds of messages are obvious by virtue of the content that they carry (e.g., unbiblical, immoral, etc.). Sometimes however, demons will try to impersonate the voice of God in order to divert you from what God wants you to do to a course that seems right on the surface. It can even be a morally neutral or godly sounding message but is opposed to what God wants you to do.

You need discernment in these instances. Whereas God's voice will be positive, affirming, encouraging and unrushed, Satan's voice will be negative, condemning, discouraging or may call for impulsive or hurried behavior. It may call for a giving up of something God has promised or a turning from a direction God has given. It often puts in doubt or in some way denies things God has said in His Word.

Demonic communication often uses guilt to attack your self-image, rather than to call you to repentance and a return to God in a way that leaves your self-image in tact. There is an important but subtle difference between these two uses of guilt. God will point out that you did something that was wrong. Satan, on the other hand, will say that YOU are what is wrong—that you are a bad person. And in God's eyes, nothing could be further from the truth.

The result of demonic communication is a distancing from God rather than a drawing close to Him. It will encourage rash, hurried, impulsive behavior. It contains a reactionary, rebellious response to matters rather than a faith-affirming reliance on God.

In case of doubt, there are several things to do. First, the Bible instructs us to "test the spirits to see whether they are from God" (1 John 4:1). Biblical tests of spirits include asking them if they confess that Jesus Christ came in the flesh (1 John 4:2; 2 John 7); if they confess that Jesus is the Son of God (1 John 4:15); if they believe that Jesus is the Messiah (5:1); if they love the Father (5:1); and the most effective one, asking them to say, "Jesus is Lord" (1 Cor. 12:3). Any spirit would have to pass each of these tests if they were of God.

If you are uncertain whether God is saying something to you or it's your own thought, it is always appropriate to ask the Lord for confirmation. He knows exactly what to do that will satisfy your mind that He is indeed speaking to you. It will be different with each person. However, if you are using a plea for confirmation merely to delay or defy God's request, then do not expect that He will give you any such confirmation.

This matter of discerning the voice of God is a very important one, not only for receiving insights into the course your healing should take, but also for fulfilling the purpose for which you were created—those good works that God prepared beforehand that you should carry out in this life (Eph. 2:10).

Make the Pursuit of God the Obsession of Your Life

Many of you have been taught to live rigidly balanced, circumspect lives—that a passionate pursuit of something is always bad or crazy. This is particularly true in dysfunctional families, where the immediate family members of the problem person inevitably establish a strong system of control in the family in order to hide the problem from the rest of the world. Great pains are taken to create a very controlled environment, so that the family is not unduly embarrassed by the behavior of the problem- member.

As a result, when you finally broke free from this stifling environment and rebelled against whatever you rebelled against, you probably became obsessive in one or more areas. What you hadn't realized was that you and your family had been living obsessive lives all along—obsessively bent on maintaining and controlling proper social appearances. It will be natural for you to react obsessively to things, because you have never learned how to live a balanced life. Your model has been one where obsession was used destructively—to deceive the outside world and thereby perpetuate the family problem.

It may surprise you to learn that it's not wrong to passionately pursue something in life, as long as it is the right thing, and as long as it's done honestly. God says that it is our predetermined destiny to become conformed to the image of Jesus Christ (Rom. 8:29). That is why you are on this earth. That is why you were born. Why not, then, channel your predilection for obsession into a whole-hearted pursuit of God? What Satan means for evil, God can use for good (Gen. 50:20). You will have no greater satisfaction out of the traumas of your life than to turn them over to God by pursuing Him with all your heart. If you do this, you will see Him turn the bad into good, by wresting from Satan every ounce of victory that he had in your life and by making up to you the years that were ruined by the evil one (Joel 2:25).

The Bible exhorts us to make the most of our time, to not be foolish but to understand what the will of the Lord is (Eph. 5:16-17). And insofar as you have time beyond the responsibility of job and family, spend yourself pursuing God—I don't mean knowledge about God, but God Himself! Make Him the obsession of your life. You will never regret it, and through it all, you will be healed.

Living by Faith, Not Feeling

In this rationalistic, scientific culture of ours, faith has been relegated to the feeble and ignorant. Ours is a society that believes only what it sees, touches, tastes, smells or calculates from known, quantifiable evidence. To believe in a God who is invisible is acceptable only in a theoretical sense, but to live one's life according to that "hope" is considered absurd!

In recent decades, however, a slight shift has taken place. The demonic realm has begun to show its hand through increased supernatural phenomena, and we have accommodated this new information by extending our self-obsession to include a worship of ourselves as God!

Because society was already convinced of how wonderful man was, it had already exalted experience as a legitimate determinant of reality. So, when spirits began telling us that we were God, it was not too difficult a shift to make in our thinking.

In essence, we are a culture who now worships itself as God, not only in mind and body, but also in destiny and purpose. We sanction this "religion" through feeling and experience, explaining away anomalies by pronouncing all truth to be relative. How convenient!

We are a people driven and controlled by our feelings. We establish truth according to our experience. We've been blinded by our self-obsession into adopting the foundational offense of Satan's kingdom—rebellion against the rule of God.

We must come out from among these rebellious people (2 Cor. 6:17-18). We must utterly reject this cultural blasphemy and separate ourselves philosophically from those who would lure us back into it. Believe it or not, we do not have to respond to every feeling or emotion that comes along. God gave us a mind and the inner witness of the Holy Spirit to guide us into all truth (John 16:13). Feeling and experience must not rule over us. They are not infallible guarantors of truth. Neither should they be our standard. The Bible alone holds that place in our lives. Experience must always be subservient to the principles outlined in God's Word.

Faith always has an object. That object for us is God. And so our faith must be in response to what He tells us. When we stand in faith, it must be for something He has revealed to us—a promise, a hope, a direction. We have faith because of the infallibility of the One who speaks to us. We have faith because He enables us.

Faith is faith because its object is unseen—a promise from God that is not yet manifest, yet hoped for (Heb. 11:1). Without faith, it is impossible to please God (Heb. 11:6). We must believe not only that God exists, but that He rewards those who diligently seek Him (Heb. 11:6).

Faith is a gift from God (Eph. 2:8). It is not something we can work up by our own strength. It comes by hearing ("understanding" is implied) the Word of Christ (Rom. 10:17). It is to believe what God says despite all evidence to the contrary. It is foolishness to men. In fact, it is designed to make foolish the wisdom of man (1 Cor. 1:18-31) so that no one can boast before God.

You must decide whether you are going to remain a slave to your lusts and feelings (Titus 3:3) or whether you are going to make your body the slave of faith in God's principles (1 Cor. 9:27). The Bible says that you are no longer to be a slave to sin (Rom. 6:6). You are to no longer allow it to reign in your body (Rom. 6:12). "Sin shall not be master over you" (Rom. 6:14, NASB). "Do you not know that when you present yourselves to someone as slaves for obedience, you are slaves of the one whom you obey, either of sin resulting in death, or of obedience resulting in righteousness?" (Rom. 6:16, NASB). "Just as you presented your members as slaves to impurity...so now present your members as slaves to righteousness" (Rom. 6:19, NASB).

Set your heart this day, not to serve your feelings, but to live by faith in God according to His perfect Word.

Love as a Commitment

One other casualty of our society's enslavement to "feeling and experience" is a profoundly deficient understanding of "love." We grow up believing that love is a feeling that comes and goes—that it exists by the whim of our emotions. When the client tells the marriage counselor, "I'm no longer in love with my spouse," it usually means, "The feeling of affection and attraction has died."

Love is not a feeling. It is not an emotion. Feelings and emotions are a part of the full-rounded experience of love, but they are not love, nor are they accurate barometers of the presence of love. They are more reliably indicators of an emotional call to action.

Love is a commitment. Jesus made this point over and over again. He said, "If you love Me, you will obey what I command...Whoever has My commands and obeys them, he is the one who loves Me...If anyone loves Me, he will obey My teaching...He who does not love Me will not obey My teaching" (John 14:15, 21, 23, 24).

Love for God has its natural outworking in obedience. 1 John 5:3 says, "This is love for God: to obey His commands" (see also 2 John 6).

Love demonstrates itself in practical, committed action, not feeling or emotion! Jesus went on to further make this point by saying, "Love each other as I have loved you. Greater love has no one than this, that one lay down his life for his friends" (John 15:12-13). When Jesus was with Peter after His resurrection, He drove home the point that if Peter truly loved him, he would feed His lambs and take care of His sheep (John 21:15-17).

Christ's love for us was demonstrated in the hard things of life. His love drove Him to the Cross (Rom. 5:8). After urging us to use the gifts of the Holy Spirit for "service" to one another, the Apostle Paul declared that "love must be sincere" (Rom. 12:6-9) and that brotherly love is the equivalent of devotion to one another (Rom. 12:9-10). Both Jesus and Paul equated the doing of the Ten Commandments to loving God and your neighbor (Mt. 22:36-40; Rom. 13:8-10). And the thirteenth chapter of First Corinthians is the supreme document establishing love as a commitment, an action—not a feeling.

Before you do anything else, stop and ask the Lord to put *real* love into you—love for both God and your fellow man. For it is God who pours out His love into our hearts by the Holy Spirit (Rom. 5:5). Ask the Father to place in you the same love that He has for His Son. You will notice a difference. You will begin to desire to help others, and yes, you will "feel" a compassion and empathy you never dreamed possible. But even when that feeling seems to have vanished, you will still be loved by God, and you should still retain the commitment to serve your brother from the heart. That is love.

Now that you have understood what love really is, determine in your heart this very minute to stop all of your attempts to earn God's love and approval. It cannot be earned. It is freely given. It is unconditional. You didn't earn it in the first place, nor is there anything you can do to keep it. It is yours forever.

Unfortunately, this world portions out a false love, based on performance. You're used to having to earn it. If you get good grades, you get love. If you are good in bed, you get love. If you behave, you are assured that you are loved. There are always strings attached.

Some of you have only received false love. No one has ever told you that you were valuable to them, and if they did it was only to exploit you. You've been put down and told you are of no value, useless and without purpose in this world. People have been telling you that, not because it is true, but because by putting you down, they make themselves look better in their own eyes. They have a very low self-image and have been using you as a doormat to step on while trying to exact some sense of self-worth for themselves.

Chose this day, who you are going to believe—God or the people who build their own egos by destroying yours. You may not feel loved by God or anyone, but remember that love is not to be gauged by feelings.

God has already demonstrated His love for you, practically, on the Cross. Even though He knew that you would sin against Him, He died for you anyway (Rom. 5:8). And He says that He will, under no circumstances, cast anyone away who comes to Him (Heb. 13:5; John 6:35-37; 11:25-26).

Now that you have learned to accept God's love without trying to earn it, give it away to others by forgiving and serving them. As you do, you will not only be healed, but God will fill you to overflowing with His infinite supply of love.

Your Call to Ministry

One of the greatest impetuses for my healing was the realization that God wanted to use me to help others in the same condition that I had been in. It was the Apostle Paul who wrote:

"Blessed be the God and Father of our Lord Jesus Christ, the

Father of mercies and God of all comfort; who comforts us in all our affliction so that we may be able to comfort those who are in any affliction with the comfort with which we ourselves are comforted by God" (2 Cor. 1:3-4, NASB).

It gives a real boost to your self-worth to realize that the Lord wants to use you to help others. If you are done with pretense, if you are in love with Jesus, if you have set your heart toward living under His power and direction, if you are sold out to the kingdom of God and the purposes of God in this world, you are ready to be used by Him to help others.

There is a purpose to your suffering after all. There is a redemptive plan of God that goes far beyond anything you could ask or think (Eph. 3:20). God has a destiny for you and no matter how far down you've gotten or how old you are, He is able to rescue a lion's share of that plan.

You were born for a purpose (Jer. 29:11). Once you have given your life to Jesus Christ, you have crossed over to the winning side. He has a position and a plan for you to fulfill. You are a saint, by declaration of God the Father, and have a destiny carved in stone—to serve in the kingdom of God.

In God's eyes, you are a person of infinite worth and value. That is why He died for you. And with God's power and your cooperation, your life can really mean something—I don't care who you are or what you've done. God's glory is made all the more evident by using the weak things of the world to conquer the strong (1 Cor. 1:27).

Your past is just that. Now you must seek the Lord and receive His calling for you. Don't make the mistake of trying to create your own calling. The Bible says:

> "Trust in the Lord with all your heart, and lean not on your own understanding. In all your ways acknowledge Him, and He will make your paths straight. Do not be wise in your own eyes; fear the Lord and turn away from evil. It will be healing to your body, and refreshment to your bones" (Prov. 3:5-8).

Your calling could be anything from helping widows and orphans to a ministry of praying for people, but everyone has a ministry and no ministry is unimportant (1 Cor. 12).

Pursue the Lord in worship and prayer, and follow His direction. Seek Him with an open mind and a heart filled with devotion. Tell Him that you will go wherever He wants you to go and do whatever He wants you to do, and marvel at what God can do!

Study Section— Comprehensive Game Plan for Sexual Healing

A. BECOME BORN AGAIN. (JN. 3:5-8)

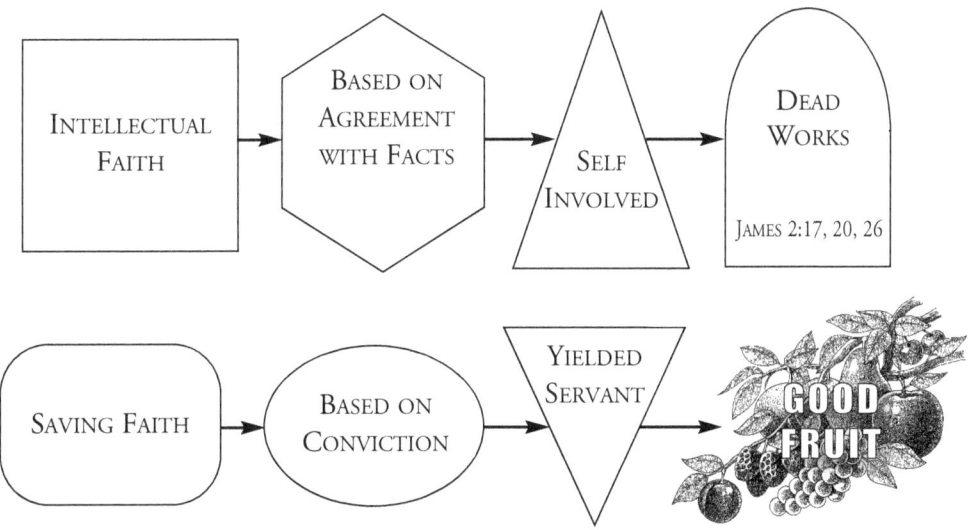

The late Dr. D. James Kennedy's *Evangelism Explosion* gave us two good questions to ask a person, that help determine if they are saved or not.

If you were to die tonight, are you sure that you would go to heaven?

> An uncertain answer reveals the issue of insecurity— often due to a sinful life.

If you went to heaven and Jesus asked you why He should let you in, what would you say?

An answer other than, "Because I accepted Jesus Christ as my Lord and Savior and am counting on His death on the Cross as payment for my sins" (or similar words), reveals an understanding of salvation that is insufficient. The person may be counting on their good works or an unreal definition of "God's goodness" to save them.

B. KEEP BEING FILLED WITH THE SPIRIT. (EPH. 5:18; ACTS 4:31; 13:52)

Although there is some disagreement on this issue among believers, most understand that the Bible commands that we "keep being filled with the Holy Spirit" in order to live the Christian life—that there is an ongoing need to cleave to God and to receive His life and godliness through the power and activity of the Holy Spirit.

C. RECOGNIZE YOUR ADVERSARY.

"When we come against the power of the devil, it must be from a heart in submission to Jesus."

—from, *The Three Battlegrounds,* by Francis Frangipane. Used with permission.

"As you begin to appropriate, not just the name of Jesus, but His nature as well, the adversary will withdraw. Satan will not continue to assault you if the circumstances he designed to destroy you are now working to perfect you."

D. DEVELOP A MATURE PERSPECTIVE ON LIFE—AN ETERNAL PERSPECTIVE.

1. Life is a battle with purpose.

"We know that suffering produces perseverance; perseverance, character; and character, hope" (Rom. 5:3-4).

"The testing of your faith develops perseverance. Perseverance must finish its work so that you may be mature and complete, not lacking anything" (James 1:3-4).

"These are the nations the Lord left to test all those Israelites who had not experienced any of the wars in Canaan (He did this only to teach warfare to the descendants of the Israelites who had not had previous battle experience)...They were left to test the Israelites to see whether they would obey the Lord's commands, which He had given their forefathers through

Moses" (Judges 3:1-2, 4).

2. You will suffer in order to bear the fruit of spiritual growth. Your healing is a "process" for growing you up into Christlikeness.

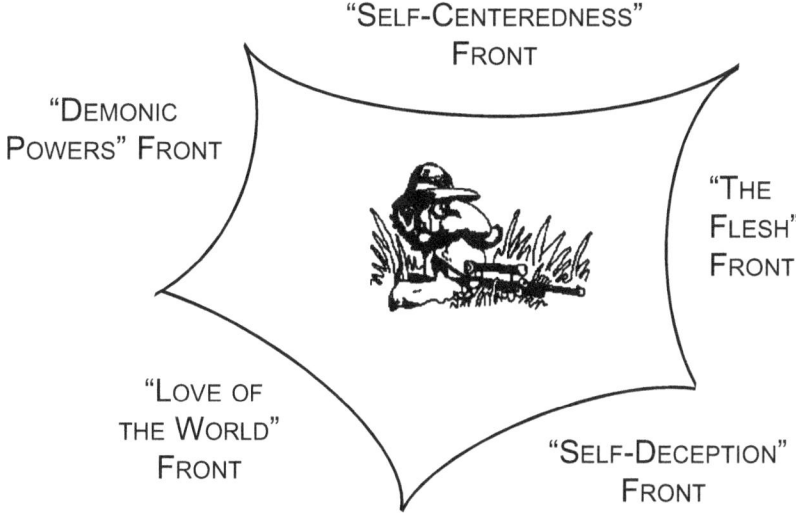

"Little by little, I will drive them out before you until you have increased enough to take possession of the land" (Ex. 23:30; see also Dt. 7:22-23).

"(Jesus) learned obedience from what He suffered" (Heb. 5:8).

3. You need God.

    God led you forty years, to test and humble you, to show you that *it is He who gives You the ability to overcome* and to be healthy (cf. Dt. 8:1).

    "It is God who arms me with strength and makes my way perfect" (Ps. 18:32).

4. The fear of God is the beginning of wisdom (Ps. 111:10).

    The Hebrew word for "fear" = a reverential awe and respect, tinged with actual fear of His power and might.

"The greatest defense you can have against the devil is to maintain an honest heart before God" (*Frangipane*).

5. You were created for a purpose (Jer. 29:11).

6. You have a limited ("numbered") time on this earth in which to carry out your purpose.

    "From one man He made every nation of men, that they should inhabit the whole earth; and *He determined the times set for them and the exact places where they should live*. God did this so that men would seek Him and perhaps reach out for Him and find Him, though He is not far from each one of us" (Acts 17:26-27).

7. You are a stranger on this earth (Ps. 119:19; John 15:19; 1 Pet. 2:11; Heb. 11:13; 13:14)

8. You are to reckon yourself dead to the things of this world (Rom. 6:9-14; 1 John 2:15; Col. 2:15; Gal. 5:24-25; 6:14)

9. The Kingdom of God is at hand!

    "You go and *proclaim the Kingdom of God*" (Luke 9:60).

    "Heal the sick and tell them, 'The Kingdom of God is near you'" (Luke 10:9).

    "Yet be sure of this, *the Kingdom of God is near*" (Luke 10:11).

    "If I drive out demons by the power of God, then *the Kingdom of God has come to you*" (Luke 11:20).

    "Do not be afraid, little flock, for *your Father has been pleased to give you the Kingdom*" (Luke 12:32).

    "*The Kingdom of God does not come visibly*...for *the Kingdom of God is within you (lit. 'in your midst')*" (Luke 17:20-21).

    "*The Kingdom of God is not a matter of talk, but of power*" (1 Cor. 4:20).

    "*I confer on you a Kingdom*, just as My Father conferred one on Me" (Luke 22:29).

    "*Unless a man is born again* (from above), he cannot see the Kingdom of God...*he cannot enter the Kingdom of God*" (John 3:3, 5).

"My Kingdom is not of this world...it is from another place" (John 18:36).

E. **RENOUNCE KNOWN SIN AND SEEK GOD'S POWER OVER IT.**

"Often the battles we face will not cease until we discover and repent for the darkness that is within us. If we will be effective in spiritual warfare, we must be discerning of our own hearts; we must walk humbly with our God" (*Frangipane*).

1. Be honest with God.

"You have set our iniquities before you, our secret sins in the light of your presence" (Ps. 90:8; see also Ps. 44:21 and Rom. 2:16).

"He who conceals his sins does not prosper, but whoever confesses and renounces them finds mercy" (Prov. 28:13).

2. Learn how "grace" works. Sexually bound people are notorious for having a "legalistic" faith system.

3. "Sin *will not* be master over you" (Rom. 6:6-7, 14; Gal. 5:24).

At first glance, there seems to be a paradox here. The Bible clearly indicates that we can do *nothing* without the help of God (Jn. 15:5)—that "the battle belongs to the Lord" (1 Sam. 17:47). "The Lord will fight for you; you need only to be still" (Ex. 14:14; see also 2 Chron. 20:15-17; 32:8).

However, the Bible is also clear that we bear responsibility for acting against the forces of evil in our lives. For example:

"If you do what is right, will you not be accepted? But if you do not do what is right, *sin* is crouching at your door; it desires to have you, but *you must master it*" (Gen. 4:7).

The only conclusion then is that out of a realization of complete dependence on God, we are to turn to Him for power and authority (something that comes as a byproduct of relationship with Him), and then turn to resist the enemy with God's sword (power) in our hands (like David did with Goliath) (James 4:7; 1 Pet. 5:9).

—From *Changing on the Inside* by John White. Published by Servant Publications. Used with permission.

"God will have it no other way. Passivity will get us nowhere.

He calls us to dynamic interaction, to plunge into the waves He sends to us—with our own arms and legs, day by day, moment by moment. We are not to sit passively on an island whose waves lift and carry us. We are called to will to participate in what is willed...

Now, some people might say, 'I think I understand. This would involve exercising my will to put into practice everything that is found in the Bible. But that's exactly where my problem lies. I've tried it and I can't.'

That is not at all what I mean. True, we should put every good thing we know into practice. How different things would be if we did! But I agree: we are unable to do so. We are not the masters of our fate, the captains of our souls. We are swimmers meeting the waves that come to us.

More accurately, in repentance we are children plunging for the first time into the waves. If we are to succeed at swimming, we need more than the will to swim. What we need is a teacher, preferably a dad who can support us and instruct us while we learn to kick.

Repentance involves learning. I need to interpret the movement of the water and how it relates to my strokes and my own buoyancy. As I learn to move through the water and to react appropriately to the movement of the waves, I begin to ride atop them with less effort.

So it is with repentance and the lifestyle changes that follow. I need to sense the forces that I encounter, the good and the evil which impinges on my spirit. I need to know how to interpret what is happening to me and to sense and collaborate with the power of God. I need to ski with my senses tuned to snow and changing slope, to sail with every nerve attuned to the changing wind. For this is what is going on when we live in the middle voice."

F. **WORSHIP AND PRAISE THE LORD.**

Dr. John Woodbridge, in his book, *More Than Conquerors*, quotes A.W. Tozer's definition of "worship" as:

"To feel in your heart and express in some appropriate manner a humble but delightful sense of admiring awe and astonished wonder and overpowering love."

1. Take the focus off of your problem and put it on the Lord.

"Look to the Lord and His strength; seek His face always. Remember the wonders He has done, His miracles" (Ps. 105:4-5).

2. Worship fulfills the demands of truth.

3. God imparts Himself as we embrace the truth of His glory (Ps. 22:3).

4. Christ is then formed in us (Gal. 4:19).

"Victory begins with the name of Jesus on your lips; but it will not be consummated until the nature of Jesus is in your heart" (*Frangipane*).

5. Praise defeats and scatters the enemy.

The "Displacement Theory" of Francis Frangipane is that demons or strongholds are displaced by the growing presence of the Lord within us or in any given society.

6. Divine power is imparted during praise (2 Chron. 20:22).

G. LEARN THE POWER OF PRAYER—OF LISTENING AND TALKING TO GOD.

1. Lack of desire often comes from lack of results.

2. Incorrect expectations are another cause.

3. Prayer releases God to act.

Let me repeat some of the points that I made in an earlier chapter. Note the charge against God that Satan made in Job 1:6-12 and 2:1-7. He charged God with undue interference and influence in having allegedly coerced Job's faithfulness through material blessings. Since God responded by proving the charge untrue (by allowing Satan to take away all of Job's blessings and to afflict him), it must have been a chargeable offense, if true. Otherwise, God would not have bothered to defend Himself or Job. The alleged offense must have been something that God was not allowed to do.

What possible restraint could God be under that He cannot do what He wants to do whenever He wants? The answer: God is under the restraints imposed by the world He chose to make. He chose to make a world where men have a free will to chose good or evil. If men are to have a truly free will, then God's perfect justice demands that they not be unduly coerced in making their moral choices.

Neither Satan nor God are allowed to unilaterally interfere in someone's life, unless the individual person (as a free will agent), somehow invites or releases them to interfere.

How is God or Satan released into a place of influence in our lives? God is probably released through righteous acts, acts of faith, good deeds, worship and praise, the proclamation of God's Word, and through prayer.

This helps us to understand why God asks us to pray, when He already knows what we want. In some way, prayer releases Him to act. When we invite God to enter into our lives, His interference changes from what otherwise would be coercion, to legitimately requested aid.

What about instances when God seems to interfere in someone's life who does not ask for help? That is where an accumulation of righteous acts comes in; that is where a life focused and centered on God comes in; that is where the prayers of others on our behalf comes in; and that is where the "corporate" nature of good comes in.

How is Satan released to interfere in our lives? He is probably released through sinful acts, through lies and slander spoken from our mouths, through the summoning of his powers in occultic activity. When we lie, for example, we give evil spirits a little more power and influence or "rights" to participate in our lives. When we believe lying thoughts or emotions instead of the truth revealed through God's Word, we empower an increase in satanic delusion and influence in our lives.

4. Practice "listening prayer."

    Take the time to enter into communion with Him, to hear His voice, to feel His heartbeat, to discover what His will is at that point, before verbalizing anything.

5. Pray the prayers of Scripture, which already reflect His will.

6. As you become like Him, your requests will begin to match what He wills.

    "If we ask anything according to His will, He hears us…and we know that we have what we asked of Him" (1 Jn. 5:14-15).

7. Repent.

—From *Changing on the Inside* by John White

"Each one of us is different and repentance comes to us in different ways. One reason change may be slow in coming, however, is that at some level we are not yet ready for it or are even resisting it. Remember, repentance is in essence a decision—a response to the work of the Holy Spirit. It is a decision we can make unconsciously, but it is a decision nevertheless. Until we are ready to respond to the Spirit's prompting, therefore, deep change will not happen in our lives." (See White's "12 Steps"—modified as a way to prepare ourselves to respond to God.)

8. Forgive.

9. Have the faith of God (Mark 11:22-24).

10. Ask from pure motives.

"The Lord searches every heart and understands every motive behind the thoughts" (1 Chron. 28:9b).

Motivation check:

- Are you seeking and feigning love for God because of what you can get from Him?
- Are you obeying God's law in order to become acceptable or righteous in His eyes?
- Do you serve others for the praise that you will receive?
- Do you do what you do in order to find or create an identity, rather than out of the identity that God has already given you?

("God's Grace" - Lecture by Lee Bennett—University of the Nations, Makapala):

PRACTICE > ROLE > PROVISION > IDENTITY = RELIGION

IDENTITY > PROVISION > ROLE > PRACTICE = GRACE

IDENTITY = "sonship" as a gift from the Father—a place of abiding and rest.

PROVISION = our inheritance as children of the Father—everything that we need to live, including the Holy Spirit.

ROLE = what we were created to do from before the foundation of the world.

PRACTICE = The fruit of our lives.

"Our identity must come first—to motivate us to practice. Our practice can never create role, identity or provision" (Lee Bennett—IBC 4/91).

"Because you are sons, God sent the Spirit of His Son into our hearts, the Spirit who calls out, 'Abba, Father'. So you are no longer a slave, but a son; and since you are a son, God has made you also an heir" (Gal. 4:6-7).

11. Listen expectantly for God to speak to you. Let Jesus become your chief counselor. Leanne Payne suggests:

   a. prayerful meditation on sacred texts of Scripture

   b. responsive speech to God's Word born within

   c. listening for the word that God speaks back to us

      (1) guidance

      (2) exhortation

      (3) words of wisdom and knowledge

12. Persist.

13. Pray with passion (Jer. 29:12-13).

H. LEARN TO TRUST AND USE GOD'S WORD.

"Your Word is a lamp to my feet and a light for my path" (Ps. 119:105).

1. Archaeological evidence is irrefutable. There are over 5,300 whole or partial manuscripts of New Testament books that date as far back as 60 A.D.

2. Proven by fulfilled prophecies

3. Proves itself in your own experience

4. Attested to by significant people

   a. Paul calls it "God-breathed" (2 Tim. 3:16), and the Word of God, rather than that of men (1 Thes. 2:13).

   b. Peter says it was spoken from God through the Holy Spirit (2 Pet. 1:20-21).

   c. Peter refers to Paul's writings as "scripture" (2 Pet. 3:15-16).

   d. Jesus refers to the writings of King David as coming from the Holy Spirit (Mark 12:35-36).

   e. Jesus refers to the Scriptures as significant down to the smallest points of lettering (Mt. 5:18).

I. LEARN TO FORGIVE.

1. God will judge others. That is not for you to do.

   "God is just: He will pay back trouble to those who trouble you and give relief to you who are troubled…This will happen when the Lord Jesus is revealed from heaven in blazing fire with His powerful angels. He will punish those who do not know God and do not obey the gospel of our Lord Jesus. They will be punished with everlasting destruction and shut out from the presence of the Lord and from the majesty of His power" (2 Thes. 1:6-9).

2. Jesus forgave you.

3. Believe God's Promise to Forgive Anyone who Repents of Their Sin and Receives Him as Savior and Lord.

   "…sinful desires war against your soul" (1 Pet. 2:11).

   "…he who sins sexually sins against his own body" (1 Cor. 6:18).

4. Decide to Believe in the Sinless Perfection of God.

   Be honest about your feelings toward God, and then once they have been vented or expressed, repent of them, for God can do no wrong. Anger directed toward God is risky business, but if your motivation is an honest venting of deep feelings, and a desire to be informed of the *fact* of God's faultlessness in the matter rather than revenge or disrespect, then God will honor your feelings.

"A man's own folly ruins his life, yet his heart rages against the Lord" (Prov. 19:3).

J. **MAKE HUMILITY A PRIORITY.**

"Pride is the armor of darkness itself" (*Frangipane*).

1. See others as more important than yourself.

"Do nothing out of selfish ambition or vain conceit, but *in humility consider others better than yourselves.* Each of you should look not only to your own interests, but also to the interests of others. *Your attitude should be the same as that of Christ Jesus: Who* being in very nature God, did not consider equality with God something to be grasped, but *made Himself nothing, taking the very nature of a servant,* being made in human likeness. And being found in appearance as a man, *He humbled Himself and became obedient to death*—even death on a cross" (Phil. 2:3-8)!

2. A byproduct of humility is servanthood.

3. Knowing Christ more and more creates humility.

4. Always recognize that it is God's glory and power at work in your life that bears the fruit of righteousness, not your own.

5. Always be willing to be known for who you really are.

K. **DISCERN GOD'S VOICE.**

1. God's voice is positive, affirming, encouraging, unrushed, gently relentless (like soft waves on a seashore) and brings you closer to Him.

2. Satan's voice is negative, condemning, discouraging, impulsive, puts distance between you and God, and puts in doubt what God has said.

L. **MAKE THE PURSUIT OF GOD, YOUR LIFE'S OBSESSION.**

1. This goes against the controlled system of a dysfunctional back-

ground, but *your* destiny, as a child of God, a new creation, is to become conformed to the image of Jesus Christ (Rom. 8:29).

2. "Know Him"—everything that we need for life and godliness (the will, the power, etc.), is found in knowing Him (2 Cor. 1:21; Jude 1, 24).

"His divine power has given us everything we need for life and *godliness through our knowledge of Him* who called us by His own glory and goodness. Through these He has given us His very great and precious promises, *so that through them you may* participate in the divine nature and *escape the corruption in the world caused by evil desires"* (2 Pet. 1:3-4).

3. Seek and Serve the Lord your God With All Your Heart, Mind, Soul and Strength (Deut. 10:12).

"Acknowledge the God of your father, and serve Him with wholehearted devotion and with a willing mind, for the Lord searches every heart and understands every motive behind the thoughts. If you seek Him, He will be found by you" (1 Chron. 28:9; see also Deut. 4:29; Ps. 105:4; Jer. 29:13)

"For the eyes of the Lord range throughout the earth to strengthen those whose hearts are fully committed to Him" (2 Chron. 16:9).

4. In this relationship with God, walk out your healing day to day by seeking and appropriating God's grace and power each moment.

"For this very reason, make every effort to add to your faith goodness; and to goodness, knowledge; and to knowledge, self-control; and to self-control, perseverance; and to perseverance, godliness; and to godliness, brotherly kindness; and to brotherly kindness, love. For if you possess these qualities in increasing measure, they will keep you from being ineffective and unproductive in your knowledge of our Lord Jesus Christ. But if anyone does not have them, he is nearsighted and blind, and has forgotten that he has been cleansed from his past sins" (2 Pet. 1:5-9).

5. Cultivate "The Tree of Life"—your spiritual man.

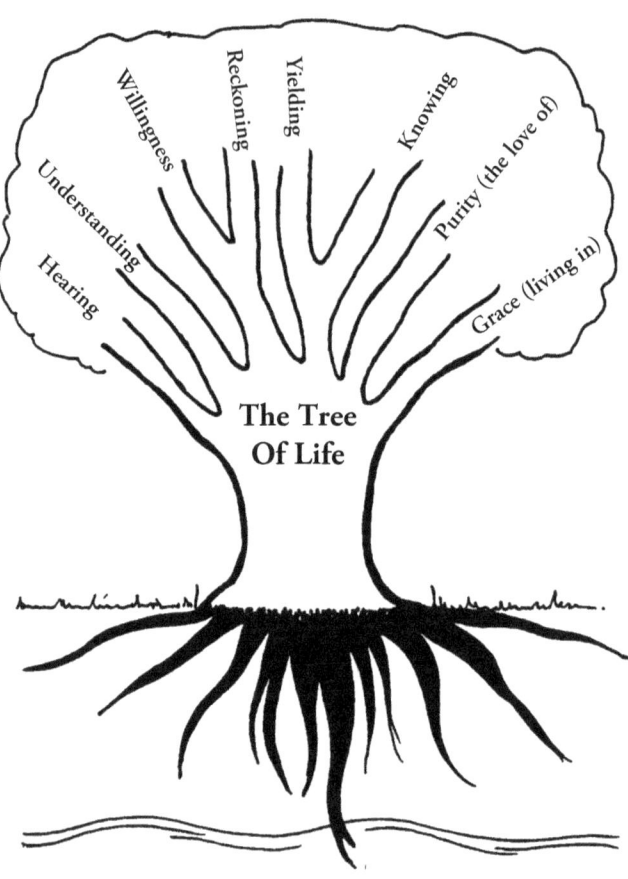

The Father

M. **LIVE BY FAITH, NOT FEELING.**

1. Our society is enslaved to its feelings.

2. Feeling and experience must not rule over us. They are not infallible guarantors of truth.

3. Experience must always be subservient to Scripture.

4. Faith's object is God, and what He has revealed to us.

5. Faith is a gift (Eph. 2:8).

6. Faith comes by hearing or "understanding" the Word of God (Rom. 10:17) (e.g., "Do you hear me?").

7. Living by faith often means living without answers to some very difficult questions.

   "The secret things belong to the Lord our God, but the things revealed belong to us and to our children forever, that we may follow all the words of this law" (Deut. 29:29).

   ** Remember, a world where humans can truly *love* requires freedom of choice.

   - That limits both God and Satan (as to their influence over mankind) to those actions that man "calls for," by prayer or by action.

   - When supernatural interference is called for out of free will choices, God or Satan is then "released" to act. Such actions do not affect the established free order of love and hate because they were initiated by the actions of the free agent (man).

   - Prayer releases God to bless and heal in ways He already wants. Other factors (such as unforgiveness, sin, etc.) can also affect the situation.

   - Invitations for blessing by God also come through actions that are in obedience to God's revealed will.

   - Invitations to Satan also come through actions which release him to act (e.g., idolatry, occultism, sexual sin, rebellion, disobedience, etc.).

   - Apparent injustices are the result of man's actions and choices, which are invitations for demonic influences to act.

- It takes repentance and/or prayers to God to rectify or counterbalance what man's free choices have brought about. God is then released to help.
- It is always God's desire to help in situations, if man will only call out in faith, in perseverance, in repentance, in dependence, without conditions (e.g., time, type of action/answer, etc.).

8. Believe the sacrifice of Jesus on the Cross and the declarations of Scripture concerning God's character, rather than the ignorance of your limited experience.

   "The Lord is righteous in all His ways and loving toward all He has made. The Lord is near to all who call on Him, to all who call on Him in truth. He fulfills the desires of those who fear Him; He hears their cry and saves them. The Lord watches over all who love Him" (Ps. 145:17-20).

N. LEARN THAT LOVE IS A COMMITMENT, NOT A FEELING OR REWARD OR EMOTION.

1. "If you love Me, you will obey My commandments" (Jn. 14:15).

2. Love is an unconditional action.

3. Stop all attempts to earn God's love and approval.

4. Accept God's love as a gift, just as you accepted His salvation as a gift.

5. Give God's love away to others.

O. YOUR CALL TO MINISTRY.

1. Sell out to the purposes of God and His kingdom.

   "(Jesus) died for all, that *those who live should no longer live for themselves but for Him who died for them* and was raised again" (2 Cor. 5:15).

   "*Christ* loved the Church and *gave Himself up for her to make her holy*...and to present her to Himself as a radiant church without stain or wrinkle or any other blemish, but holy and blameless" (Eph. 5:25-27).

2. You were born for a purpose (Jer. 29:11).

   There is fullness of meaning in everything that is, because it has been made by omniscience. It is impossible that there can be anything that doesn't reflect the full and rich mind of the perfect God who made it. Even the lowly gnat!

3. Lean not on your own understanding (Prov. 3:5-8).

4. In the midst of your dependency and intimacy with Him, God will direct your path.

   "It's time to get alone until you're not alone anymore."

   —From Rod Parsley, World Harvest Church

P. **A FINAL WORD FROM THE LORD.**

   "When you and your children return to the Lord your God and obey Him with all your heart and with all your soul according to everything I command you today, then the Lord your God will restore your fortunes and have compassion on you…The Lord your God will gather you and bring you back. He will bring you to the land that belonged to your fathers, and you will take possession of it…The Lord your God will circumcise your hearts and the hearts of your descendants, so that you may love Him with all your heart and with all your soul, and live…See, *I set before you today life and prosperity, death and destruction.* For I command you today to love the Lord your God, to walk in His ways, and to keep His commands, decrees and laws; then you will live and increase, and the Lord your God will bless you in the land you are entering to possess… *Now choose life, so that you and your children may live and that you may love the Lord your God, listen to His voice, and hold fast to Him. For the Lord is your life*" (Deut. 30:2-3, 4-6, 15-16, 19-20).

Exercises—
Comprehensive Game Plan

1. If you haven't already, express your sorrow over the sins that you have committed and tell the Lord of your willingness to change. Ask Jesus to come into your life and be your Lord and Savior. Ask Him to fill you with the power of the Holy Spirit so that you can live a godly life in this present age.

2. Write down a list of the damage and suffering that your sin has caused you and others. Allow the realization of all that it has done birth in you a holy anger against it and a firm determination never to return to it, by God's keeping power. Look at this list when you are tempted.

3. Write a letter to God, honestly laying out your true thoughts and feelings. Tell Him about your hopes and dreams, your disappointments and defeats, and your hope for the future. End the letter by declaring that by an act of your will, you are going to put your trust in Him to work all things out for the good.

4. Seek out the relationships in your life that are broken and unresolved and ask God to give you the wisdom and the courage to be reconciled with those people in all things. Sometimes it is good to write a letter to those who have hurt you, expressing your heart, how you have been changed, and your new willingness to understand, to forgive, and to be reconciled. Express love and concern for them. Don't forget to mention that it is Jesus Christ who has changed you. Break the old patterns of reaction and response to hurt by beginning a practice of "responding in the opposite spirit" when tempted to be drawn into old conflict patterns.

5. Ask God to give you His heart for the lost and hurting so that you can become other-centered. Keep asking until He changes you completely with the answer to your prayer.

6. When old memories of hurt and rejection from certain people come to tempt you, immediately replace them with memories of the good things about those people or by images of how God sees

them. (They are so precious in His eyes that He died for them, too.)

7. When Satan floods your mind with old pictures of yourself, take those old self-images and give them to Jesus. In your mind's eye, reach up and take the old image and hand it to Jesus. He will destroy it for you. Cultivate an image of son or daughter.

8. Regularly pray for God to instill in you a healthy sense of being— a sense of God having a divine love and purpose for having created you, a sense of it being good that you exist. Ask Him to fix in your spirit a strong and healthy sense of being male (or female) so that you can feel the goodness and security of it. Ask Him to strengthen your abilities to initiate and to do good, to be bold and single-minded in doing what is right and good in God's eyes.

9. Focus you eyes on Jesus. Practice knowing that He is with you at all times. Ask Him to reveal Himself in people and in circumstances. Sing love songs to Him. Thank Him. Praise Him.

10. Ask the Lord to instill in your daily awareness an eternal perspective, a sense of being an ambassador of the Kingdom of God.

Study Section— You As Minister

A. **YOU DO NOT HAVE TO BECOME PERFECT BEFORE GOD CAN USE YOU.**

"The foundation of all progress is the capacity to admit the pride that refuses to accept ourselves as fallen and imperfect."
—Leanne Payne

1. Self-acceptance is crucial.

    a. Accept the way God made you.

    b. Agree to live with the limitations set out for you by God.

    c. Jesus is, and always will be, your righteousness.

    "To walk in the Spirit is to celebrate your weakness and accept Christ's strength."   —Leanne Payne

    "Your true self will come when you are looking to Jesus."
    —C.S. Lewis

2. Model openness and respect in all that you do.

    —From *The Father Heart of God* by Floyd McClung

    "By creating room for those around us to be honest, we can lead them into a deeper relationship with God."

    "Delight yourself in the Lord and He will give you the desires of your heart" (Psalm 37:4, NASB).

    —From *Changing on the Inside* by John White (regarding the woman caught in adultery)

    "We are told little about her reactions. In the face of Jesus' calm acceptance, her own conscience must have been flayed raw, her shame and guilt unbearable. I have seen what happens to many people in parallel circumstances. Faced with kindness and acceptance, they repent.

This brings us to an important psychological reality. Although repentance may indeed be painful, it does not come about as a response to severity. Stern accusation and recrimination may exacerbate our feelings of guilt and shame, but they never give rise to true repentance.

Inevitably, it is the wonder of kindness that awakens repentance. Repentance is a concomitant of gratitude and thanksgiving. The relief of knowing we might be loved and accepted is what brings true change. Paul makes clear as he upbraids his unrepentant readers: 'Or do you show contempt for the riches of His kindness, tolerance and patience, not realizing that God's *kindness* leads you toward repentance'" (Rom. 2:4)?

B. YOUR CALLING IS A PIECE OF GOD'S VERY HEART.

"The Spirit of the Sovereign Lord is on me, because the Lord has anointed me to preach good news to the poor. He has sent me to bind up the brokenhearted, to proclaim freedom for the captives and release for the prisoners, to proclaim the year of the Lord's favor…to comfort all who mourn…to bestow on them…the oil of gladness instead of mourning, and a garment of praise instead of a spirit of despair" (Is. 61:1-3).

"He heals the brokenhearted and binds up their wounds" (Ps. 147:3, NASB).

"Christ's love compels us…(He) gave us the ministry of reconciliation…and He has committed to us the message of reconciliation. We are therefore Christ's ambassadors, as though God were making His appeal through us" (2 Cor. 5:14, 18b, 19b, 20a).

C. YOUR GOAL IS TO LEAD THEM INTO AN INTIMATE RELATIONSHIP WITH GOD, FROM WHOM ALL HEALING AND WHOLENESS COMES.

"The desire to minister the *life* of God must be stronger than your desire to minister the *truth* of God."
—Ron Smith

1. Worship must become foundational to their lifestyle.

2. Within that relationship, God will reveal the hidden "keys" to their healing.

3. You will serve as a better facilitator and mediator if you also are engaged in this fervent pursuit of relationship with God. Always be seeking the filling of the Holy Spirit for power, wisdom and discernment in ministry.

   In his book, *Passion for Jesus*, Mike Bickle says:

   "Ministry at its most basic definition is 'the manifestation of the knowledge of God through our lives'...

   Our most vital ministry is revealing the beauty and splendor of God's personality to others...

   There is a certain quality of ministry that comes only as you and I touch God in reality in our secret lives.

   To be mature Christians, each one of us must have a secret life in God hidden from the eyes of others...

   The most powerful witness you and I can give sinners is a radiant life demonstrating that the will of God is good, acceptable and perfect. Nonbelievers are looking for a contented, fulfilled people who aren't trying to cast off God's restraints—a people who are joyfully abandoned and totally committed to His cause...

   First we are drawn to Him in intimacy, then we run with Him in ministry...

   As we are drawn to greater intimacy with God, we have a greater spiritual depth and touch other people's spirits more effectively."

4. Assiduously avoid the trap of trusting in your own wisdom and intuition.

D. LISTEN BOTH TO THE COUNSELEE AND TO GOD.

The presenting problem is usually not really the problem. God will reveal the truth to you. Part of God's revelation to you will be knowing when to refer someone.

E. **LOOK FOR THE ROOT CAUSE.**

This often involves inner vows that were made in judgment against God, parents, etc., which must be renounced and broken. The vow "not to become like...." often becomes prophetic in its opposite, when someone has self-hatred, because they punish themselves by becoming the very thing they hate.

F. **BE AGGRESSIVE AGAINST DEMONIC FORCES (WHEN PRESENT) BY USING YOUR KINGDOM PRIVILEGES AND AUTHORITY.**

G. **ACCORDING TO LEANNE PAYNE, HEALING WILL INVARIABLY NEED TO TAKE PLACE IN SEVERAL AREAS:**

1. the mind, with its concepts

2. the feelings and emotions

3. the perceptions and evaluations

4. relationships

5. memories

H. **TYPICAL MINISTRY FOR SOMEONE OVER A PERIOD OF ONE OR MORE SESSIONS MAY INCLUDE:**

1. Ascertaining whether or not the person seriously wants to be healed and is willing to do whatever it takes to achieve that goal. The Lord may give you discernment quickly here or you may have to engage the person in conversation for a while in order to gain this knowledge.

    Ask: *"What do you want God to do for you?"* (seek specifics)

    "Are you willing to do whatever God indicates is necessary for your healing?"

2. Invoke the presence of God.

3. Ask the person if they were happy as a child, and when did any

unhappiness start.

   a. Help them express their feelings.

   b. Supply them with the words for what they are feeling by using leading statements.

   c. Normalize their pain by letting them know that experiencing pain when surrounded by painful things is valid.

4. Ask God to bring up the root memory.

5. Be on the lookout for the problem of introspection, narcissism—an obsessive looking inward.

6. Be careful not to practice the presence of the "old man," with misplaced empathy or sympathy.

7. Never let the counselee develop emotional dependency on you. Your are trying to lead them into dependence on God.

8. Ask the Lord to reveal His presence at the time of the memory and thereby heal the debilitating response and consequent neurosis that has grown up around it.

9. Take the counselee through a prayer of relinquishment of "rights," where they repent of their sinful responses to the memory, and offer forgiveness for the people who were involved.

10. Ask the Holy Spirit to reveal any demonic strongholds, and break them in the name of Jesus.

11. Ask the Holy Spirit to fill in the empty places left by the departing spirits.

12. Address any evident patterns of broken relationships in the person's life and lead them into resolution.

13. Discuss spiritual principles that bear on the subject to help prevent a recurrence of the problem.

14. Ask the Holy Spirit if there is anything else that He would like to do at that time.

15. Discuss practical matters of spiritual growth (e.g., church-going,

Bible reading, prayer, etc.).

16. Expect that God will heal quickly, powerfully and simply—at each point of hurt or trauma. There is often no need for more than one or two sessions when this is the case. Extended counseling usually serves one of two purposes: getting the person to the place of wanting to be made whole, with all their heart; or helping the counselee who has been seriously dysfunctional for a long period of time learn healthy response patterns to life's problems.

17. In Summary:
    - Discover Satan's ground and recover it.
        - Discover weakness in the personality.
            - Ask God to come heal that weakness and replace it with His strength in that area.
                - Teach mature thinking and walking.
                    - Encourage them.
                        - Keep them accountable.

Exercises— You As Minister

1. Ask the Lord to show you anything in your own life that might hinder the work that He wants to do through you in helping others. Respond by doing whatever He says to do.

2. Ask the Lord to reveal the pride that lies hidden within you so that you can minister on an equal level with those who have been engaged in depraved activities. Show them love and respect.

3. Ask the Lord to give you the servant heart of Christ. Keep asking until you are changed by having truly received that heart.

4. Deepen your own intimacy with the Lord so that He shines out of you, bringing hope to those you minister to.

5. Increase, through practice, your facility to hear the voice of God. Read Peter Lord's, *Hearing God,* Joyce Huggett's, *The Joy of Listening to God* and/or Leanne Payne's *Listening Prayer* and respond to what you read.

6. Ask God for a passion for Jesus and for the things that He is passionate about. Ask the Father to cause you to feel toward Jesus the way He does.

7. Ask the Lord to prevent you from ministering from a co-dependent heart—one that seeks to meet its own dysfunctional need through ministry to others, depending on their neediness to feel secure. If God shows you that you have co-dependent tendencies, seek good Christian counseling for that problem so that you can minister aright.

8. When ministering, depend on God for revelation and power. Do not lean on your own understanding. Ask God to show you when you are depending on yourself.

9. Learn spiritual warfare and use it. Read the books on this subject by authors like Dean Sherman and Dr. Timothy Warner.

10. Specialize in communicating "hope" and "certainty of transformation." Spend time talking about who they are in Christ, the purpose of life, the Kingdom of God, and the goodness and mercy of God. Keep pointing them back to the Father and the fact that their healing will only come through a diligent pursuit of an intimate relationship with Him.

Miscellaneous Issues

Psychology

God gives wisdom to all men. Therefore we should expect to (and do) find wisdom among unbelievers and all manner of sinners. Therefore, just as in other learning disciplines, it is legitimate to avail ourselves of the wisdom that God has given to unbelievers in the fields of behavioral science as well as in the fields of medicine, biology, astronomy—or any other that hasn't been expressly forbidden by God.

As with other fields of science, psychology can be a good thing or a bad thing, depending on the perspective of the therapist and the one being counseled.

The field of psychology was birthed in a virulently anti-Christian atmosphere that still exists today in many quarters. Faith is allowed only if it is important to the client but even then is ignored as the primary focus of therapy. Such practitioners usually see it as naive, simplistic or as a primitive delusion.

It should also be noted that Carl Jung, (a giant in the field), received many revelations near the end of his career from spirit guides, (and wrote about it), so caution is in order for the believer.

For the client who does not believe in or want God involved, or who is not willing to pursue God's help with their issue, their feelings should be respected. For such people, secular therapy can be life saving, especially when they are a danger to themselves and/or others. Ditto for those who have suffered from extreme trauma or disorders such as multiple personality/dissociative disorders, schizophrenia, ritual abuse, pedophilia, rape or other serious events or conditions. In such cases, an expert secular therapist is better than no therapist at all.

Surprisingly, Christian psychology can sometimes be counterproductive to a client's growth. When a therapist gets so enthralled with the latest (admittedly fascinating) discovery or intellectual approach to therapy, he or she can fall into "intellectual idolatry" and thereby lose God's help. This form of "rationalism" is a conscious or unconscious belief that the intellect rather than God's supernatural revelation is sufficient for the problem.

In such cases and to the extent that the therapeutic approach relieves the immediate issue, both parties may become convinced that they have no need for God's help and thus any need to pursue Him. They have unwittingly circumvented His plan for bringing permanent, interior and supernatural "transformation" and replaced it with a human-wisdom-centered "maintenance program." Consequently, it may only be a matter of time before the problem resurfaces.

Therefore, we must ask God for the gift of discernment, so that when we seek to appropriate the wisdom that He has given to unbelievers, we are not lured into the worldly system or philosophical view that surrounds it, nor fooled by a hidden foolishness lurking within them that masquerades as wisdom.

The field of psychology is a particular mine field because the mind is so little understood and appears to have a metaphysical dimension to it. Consequently, the search to understand it has sometimes led in occultic and other anti-biblical directions, especially with topics such as homosexual confusion, transgenderism, pornography, etc. We must be very cautious before seeking help from those who approve of what God has forbidden.

Conclusion: With few exceptions, if we seek out professional counsel, we should seek out Christian counselors rather than non-Christian. Dr. Sandra Brown defines Christian counseling as: "private lessons in applied theology." And that is what it should be. Even among Christian counselors, however, we must ask God to lead us to those who truly put the wisdom of God above the wisdom of men, who have an active dependence on God as their source of wisdom, and whose primary goal is to guide us into dependence on the Holy Spirit as our primary counselor.

Inner Healing

When inner healing first became popular many years ago, there was a naiveté and lack of discernment among many of the practitioners regarding some of the techniques and processes that were being used, making it potentially dangerous. Techniques with occultic roots and underpinnings were often blithely employed—much to the detriment of the patient and practitioner. Modern versions of this danger include "Mindfulness", "Centering Prayer", "Contemplative Prayer", "Yoga", "Reiki" and "Enneagram" practices.

Since the early days of inner healing, godly wisdom and discernment has entered the field in some quarters—seeking to take what is of God and leave what is of Satan. These teachers and ministers have sought to distance themselves from the carelessness and error of the past and so, often refer to their ministry as the "healing of memories."

Occultic inner healing springs from a belief in past lives, in spirit guides, in subconscious configurations of the personality that are independent and autonomous and have the potential to control the conscious life, in hidden knowledge (Gnosticism), in man having a divine nature, or in some inherent generative power within man's own nature that can heal and transform. They seek hidden wisdom and revelation from these sources rather than from God. Their looking inward or looking back is a search for power and control distinct from dependence on the God of the Bible, even though it may be cloaked in Christianese.

Fortunately, Christian "inner healing" or "healing of memories" has evolved into something that can be very helpful now that we have gotten discernment and wisdom from God in this area. There has also been a similar maturing in the field of deliverance, which can be a vital part of any transformation process.

However, when an occult-based therapist or minister leads someone into inner healing, they often employ hypnotic techniques—describing serene imaginary settings to lead the client into a disconnected, suggestive state. They lead them into encounters with spirit guides or images which then take over and lead the person into dependence on the newfound tutor. These images, although purported to be imaginary figures, or the spirits of dead relatives or even Jesus Himself, are demonic "angels of light" that have come to take God's place as Lord. The benefit they bring is temporary—just enough to deceive and enslave.

I had such an experience in my early Christian life. With eyes closed, I was led (by a Christian counselor) through an imaginary grassy field to a river where I encountered a being who looked like Jesus—the robe, the beard, the whole bit! It was like being in a movie—the figure was very much alive and real to me. He looked at me and said, "Follow me and I will show you how to beat the devil." That certainly sounded like something Jesus would say, but just as I turned (in my imagination) to follow him, a strong check came into my spirit and held me back. For days I was puzzled about that and finally God showed me the element that should have alerted me to the deception that I'd almost fallen for (and from which the Holy Spirit had held me back). The Jesus figure was attempting to create a relationship of dependence—one where I would be persuaded to return to him again and again for more guidance. It was a spirit trying to get me to follow after its image. If I had fallen into that, I would no longer have felt the need to seek God in other ways, feeling that I already had a great connection with Him through this new means. It had been an "angel of light" masquerading as Jesus Himself, and it would have seduced me into more and more occult activities and beliefs.

Interestingly enough, I have also had a true vision of the Lord during inner healing prayer. That vision, however, was different in many aspects. First, it was not a clear, detailed image of Jesus. Rather, it was a form enshrouded in light who I simply knew to be Jesus. There was no clear image upon which to later dwell or revisit.

Second, this Jesus did not draw me into repeatedly seeking His image, as the occult one had. He simply healed something very negative in my past. As I was remembering (in prayer) the time when I committed the worst sin of my life—pushing my father down some stairs (a sin for which I did not believe there could be any forgiveness)—the being of light entered into the memory and held both my father and myself in a healing embrace of love. In that embrace, He healed me from my inability to believe that God had forgiven me. His acceptance of me at the point of my worst sin destroyed forever Satan's power to cause me to doubt God's forgiveness and favor. It was a moment of inestimable healing power which did not leave me seeking after an image. Rather, it left me weeping and more in love with Jesus than ever. Whereas the occult vision, described earlier, only promised aid if I followed after it, the godly vision actually brought healing, and did not leave me with a need to keep seeking after it for more.

Third, the godly vision was not brought about through an emptying of the mind, as occult visions are. It was brought about through prayer, a specific focusing of the mind on a particular event, and asking God to come present to heal.

Many Christians do not like to bring up issues of the past because they do not want to fall into the trap of blaming someone else for their sinful predilections. This sounds good on the surface, and to be sure, much of secular counseling engages in the examination of past hurts in order to justify present behavior through blaming others. However, when a biblically balanced Christian minister or therapist takes you on a tour of your past, (such as in prayer for the healing of memories), they are doing so, not to fix blame on those who have hurt you, but so that you can release such people from the blame that you already fixed on them years ago, and which you may have forgotten or denied over the years. You see, when you were hurt as a child or adolescent, you reacted from a very simplistic, black and white world-view, with judgments and vows against those who hurt or neglected you. Now that you are an adult, it is important to go back to those moments of pain in order to rescind the previously made judgments, to offer forgiveness and to seek resolution.

Does the Bible teach that there is a subconscious where forgotten or denied things lie hidden? Christian psychologist, John Smeltzer has given us an excellent commentary on the entire issue (paraphrased):

In First Corinthians 4:3-5, Paul says, "I do not even examine myself. I am conscious of nothing against myself, yet I am not by this acquitted... (the Lord) will both bring to light the things hidden in the darkness and disclose the motives of men's hearts" (NASB).

And David prays, "Search me, O God, and know my heart; Try me and know my anxious thoughts; and see if there be any hurtful way in me" (Ps. 139:23-24, NASB).

Hebrews 12:2 tells us to "fix our eyes upon Jesus." Ephesians 1:18 is a prayer asking that "the eyes of our heart be enlightened." This is not forced visualization (as occultists do). It is faith that Jesus (the Alpha and the Omega) is there in the past event as well as in present and future events, that He wants to be there for us and that He wants to help us change the way we reacted to various hurts from our past. It's asking Jesus to be there in the memory, to believe that He was there, using God-given imagination to move into faith, because when we move in faith, God heals.

We are very used to going back in prayer to make right the sins that we committed against others in the past. Just so, we should also go back to sins committed against us in the past, to invite Jesus to heal the hurt and to correct our sinful reactions to the wounds (e.g., the vows, judgments, condemnations, roots of bitterness, lies believed, etc.).

Healing of memories is not a fishing expedition. We do not independently seek after revelation. Instead, we respond to the leading of the Holy Spirit. God resurrects the places of wounding for us so our reactions to them can be repented of and healed—so we can gain strength and faith from the realization of His presence there. It is Jesus entering into the past with us to facilitate the healing—we in our memory, He in reality. We cannot travel back in time, but He is there.

The Bible teaches that past sins affect us in three ways:

1. Adam's sin is imputed to us (Rom. 5:12-14).
2. The sins of the fathers are passed down to the third and fourth generation (Ex 20:5-6, 34:7b; Lev 26:39b; Num 14:18b).
3. The character of the mother is found in the daughter (Prov. 31:28-29).

Inner healing releases suppressed and denied wounds and our sinful reactions to them. It is a powerful gift from God that has brought significant and multiple healings to the many areas of unhealed trauma in my life.

But if a picture of Jesus comes into your mind and presents itself as the real Jesus, beware. If some power within the unconscious mind itself is stirred up to heal, beware.

Hypnosis

Hypnosis is the seeking for hidden (i.e., occult) knowledge beyond the channels that God has provided for us and it achieves that through a yielding and/or emptying of the mind. It takes us into a forbidden realm, in fact (see Dt. 18:10-13). The proof for this can be found in the experiences of many who have been hypnotized—experiences such as being engaged by spirit guides, false memories or the emergence of imagined past lives, etc. Hypnotism opens us up to the deceptions that lie in the metaphysical pursuits, which is certainly one of the reasons that God has forbidden it.

The fact that there are people who seem to receive some benefit from hypnotism is not a proper criterion for its sanction. It is one of the tricks of the demonic realm to lure people into sin by providing them with a temporary benefit.

The demonic realm has been around longer than we have. They live in the dimensions in which we blindly stumble when we employ hypnosis or other occult pursuits. And when we walk into their territory, they have great power to seduce and deceive by virtue of the sin of our disobedience to God, if by no other reason.

If you have been helped through hypnosis, you got lucky. Now repent for your participation in it, renounce it and ask God to take back the ground that you have given to the realm of fallen spirits. God will graciously respond to your prayer with forgiveness.

12 Step Groups

Many people have been involved in a sin for so long that it seems to them to be an integral part of their personality and emotional fabric. The specter of the removal of the sinful behavior is similar to the specter of having one of their dearest loved ones ripped away, in terms of how they perceive their ability to function once it has been permanently removed.

These people live in great fear of having nothing to replace what needs to be removed. They are highly dependent on the behavior as a coping mechanism and are very dependent on the relationships surrounding the behavior for emotional survival—at least so they believe.

Some of these people can be greatly helped by a structured program that integrates supportive relationships and accountability into the healing and transformation process. Support groups often fill this bill nicely.

They are also helpful for the person who is coming out of a behavior and who feels isolated and alone—who isn't aware of just how many people suffer from the same problem. A support group can help this person achieve a sense of belonging and acceptability in community (particularly if their sin was socially unacceptable). It can also be a storehouse of wisdom and information for the healing process.

Lastly, a support group can be vital to the person who has been out-of-control. The accountability and regular hands-on support, as well as the structured environment is important to their sobriety until they have grown in spiritual and emotional maturity.

Support groups, however, are usually only as healthy as the person who supervises them, so their track record must be carefully examined before choosing one. They can become pity parties or blame games or excuse factories for continued sinful behavior. They can also degenerate into covens of self-focused introverts. This is very unhealthy.

If they are non-Christian, they are often counterproductive altogether, although God has been known to use them for good in the midst of the bad.

Taking all of this into account, it would seem that a Christian-based twelve step or other support group, such as "Celebrate Recovery" or "Everyman's Battle", can be very beneficial in the early stages of the healing process, particularly for those who need the regular support of others to keep from falling. However, they can become counterproductive if used over a long period of time. Long-term dependency on a "sin specific" support group often indicates that the person is not being led into dependency on the Lord as the source for their healing and that they may have developed unhealthy dependent relationships within the group. Some simply need to be pushed out of the nest.

The best plan for someone who enters a support group is for them to plan to move into normal church groups (home fellowships, men's or women's groups, etc.), as soon as possible. Most people, in fact, needn't ever go to a "sin specific" support group, but can be integrated into the regular life of the church immediately upon repentance. (This assumes, of course, that their church is not legalistic and judgmental toward people like them). It is in these settings that the love and affirmation that the person needs finally comes. And so, they must become integrated into normal, healthy social relationships. A good support group leader will already be actively working toward that goal.

Support groups then, if run properly, can be useful in the early stages of healing and transformation for those coming out of sins that tie into deep emotional issues. They aren't necessary for everyone. The person who goes to one should be weaned off of the group in as short a period of time as is healthy. (This time will vary widely according to the willingness of the person to do whatever it takes to be made whole, but will generally range from one week to six months, although there are "live-in" programs for extreme cases that last as long as a year).

Drug Therapy

In recent years, it has become the practice of many psychiatrists (Christian and secular) to prescribe mood altering drugs (such as Prozac) as part of therapy for those with a chemical imbalance in the brain. These drugs are often very successful in ending suicidal feelings or other manifestations of severe depression. They help correct physiological problems having to do with synaptic patterns and chemical neuro-transmitters in the brain.

There has been a great deal of opposition to drug therapy in a certain segment of the Christian community, which believes that at worse, it is tantamount to the practice of sorcery, and at best, it is a failure to believe in the power of God to heal.

Oddly enough, most of those same Christians would find no problem in taking an aspirin for a headache—another drug which chemically alters brain structures that are out of whack. I cannot see where psychoactive drugs are any different. Both the aspirin and the Prozac do things that God *could* do without them, but in so many cases He doesn't and not because they lack the right amount of faith!

However, I would recommend first seeking a healing intervention from God. The bonding and enrichment of the God-man relationship that comes in the midst of His personal healing touch is of inestimable value not only in the physical life, but in the spiritual life as well.

I am one who has suffered from severe depressive states but have always sought the intervention of the Lord before doing anything else.

And so, I cannot condemn someone who goes the drug therapy route. Not everyone has the same experiences with God. Not everyone has the same amount of drive to engage Him in every aspect of life. We are all at different stages in our experience and understanding of Him.

It is wrong for seasoned believers to *demand* from others the same level of faith in God that they have. To exhort, yes; to demand or to manipulate through guilt tripping, no. Such attitudes can snuff out the delicate embers of a fire that is just beginning to glow in some new believers.

All things being equal, drug therapy is not the better way, but it is not a sin. If after a client has been encouraged to seek God's intervention and finally decides to try drug therapy, I do not believe that they have sinned. Neither do I believe that the therapist has sinned who first tries to exhort the client to find healing through a renewed mind, but who then accedes to their subsequent need for medication. Every case stands or falls on its own merits and we must constantly seek the wisdom of the Holy Spirit as we minister to one another.

Sex Trafficking

This is one of the most incomprehensible scourges in our world today. It includes kidnapping, murder, brainwashing, and possibly the "Stockholm Syndrome" (where victims develop a psychological alliance with their captors as a survival strategy - also known as "trauma bonding") and the "Helsinki Syndrome" (where a person being held captive begins to identify with and grow sympathetic to his or her captor, simultaneously becoming unsympathetic towards the police or other authorities).

One major problem is that corrupt judges, policing authorities and politicians have turned the punishment for what should be a capital crime into a slap on the wrist.

Another problem is the legalization of the most violent and perverse forms of pornography known to man, which emboldens both the sex criminal and the abuser alike. Such pornography is available to any child who can run a computer or operate a tablet or smart device and so we are grooming a generation of kids who are used to seeing exploitive sex and who have no regard for healthy, holy sexual behavior.

The increase and approval of adultery, promiscuity, homosexual and transgender behavior (and the blasphemy of so-called "gay marriage") has produced a mockery of God's design for human sexuality. As the Bible prophesied, we have been given over to the idols that we have worshipped and it is they who are punishing us (see Jer 2:19; Ez 16:39; 23:49; Eph 5:5; Col 3:5).

In addition, the destruction of children in their mother's womb through abortion has resulted in an epidemic of seared consciences (1 Tim. 4:2) and the proliferation of a spirit of murder (Matt. 15:19). It is as Jesus prophesied: "Because of the increase of wickedness, the love of most will grow cold" (Matt. 24:12).

For the victims of sex trafficking, there is wholesale drug addiction and alcoholism. Suicide rates are extremely high. Most who survive will never find freedom from the profound and debilitating damage done to them. Adolescent victims in particular experience neurological damage as a result of being trafficked. Chronic fear damages cognitive processing and decision making. The ability to trust is completely destroyed.

Such victims need help from professionals who specialize in this kind of trauma as well as deep inner healing.

They need safe homes and other practical resources and they need to be kept safe from their victimizers.

They need help to be freed from various substance abuse habits.

They also need sources of genuine love and affirmation.

They need God but understandably don't trust Him. Kind and patient counselors and friends are crucial.

Many harbor a deep hatred of God for not rescuing them sooner, so that will need to be addressed in its proper time.

They may have dissociative disorders due to the relentless and brutal treatment that they have suffered from both trafficker and customer.

Creative arts are known to be useful for many victims, especially in the early stages of treatment. They can help them work through various traumatic experiences without having to reenact them as themselves.

Most of all, they need to be led into a saving relationship with Jesus Christ and to slowly get acquainted with God the Father, so that they can discover that He is nothing like they have imagined.

Programs such as Agape International, Street Grace, Wellspring Living and other programs work hard to help such survivors.

Transgender Conditions

Transsexuals

As noted in the chapter on transgender, a transsexual is someone who suffers from a psychiatric disturbance known as "Gender Identity Disorder" (now called "Gender Dysphoria"), where a person identifies so strongly with the opposite sex that they seek to adopt their behavior and sometimes even their physiology to fit this desired identity rather than the gender they were given at birth.

In some cases there is a hormonal or other physical malformity involved, but for the most part, this desire to be the opposite sex is an emotional problem that stems from a profound disassociation from one's own gender group. This often occurs in childhood when the child is unable to bond with their same-sex parent or parent figure and they instead chose to take on the behavior and mannerisms of the opposite sex. In one way or another, they have gotten the message that they are unacceptable or incapable of operating as the gender that they were born and so have failed to achieve an integrated identity. Some go as far as seeking a sex change operation, although Johns Hopkins University (which began the sex change operation phenomena in the U.S.) stopped doing the surgeries in 1979 when studies showed that they did not solve the problem.

Dr. Elizabeth Moberly, in her book, *Homosexuality: A New Christian Ethic*, states that transsexuals generally operate out of a defensive detachment from their same-sex parent or gender group. They cross over emotionally and identify with the opposite sex parent or gender group in reaction to rejection or disaffirmation from the same-sex parent. Former transsexual Sy Rogers states that: "Outright rejection of gender identity occurs for many transsexuals in adolescence when they have been shamed and rejected by peers and society due to a failure to perform in or conform to the expected gender role. Transsexuals usually view their true gender identity as 'the enemy' and cause of their often intense suffering."

How does one help the transsexual? First, search out local Christian counselors who have experience in this area. Become educated about the nature of transsexualism. Not all transsexuals are homosexual. Not all have had or want a sex change operation. They will need loving compassion and patient long-suffering as they deal in counseling with issues such as rejection, self-obsession, anger, bitterness, unforgiveness, self-hatred, inadequacy, their view of God, their view of sexuality and gender in light of God's creative intent, etc. Some who have undergone a sex change operation may even choose to have it surgically reversed, which is possible to some extent. These will need a great deal of additional support in working through the issues involved.

Transvestites

A transvestite is someone who likes to cross dress (dress in the clothes of the opposite sex) but who is not necessarily unhappy with being the gender that they are. They are not necessarily homosexual either. Often, their obsession with wearing opposite-sex clothing stems from some eroticized comfort they received from it during childhood or adolescence. It is fetishistic in nature—focusing on certain items and associated body parts. It has to do with the creation of a secret world, with erotic ritual objects and masturbation, a desire to escape into fantasy and the need for instant gratification. Deep inside, it is a passive-aggressive protest against one's own gender, though without the outright rejection of it that one sees in the transsexual.

A young boy who is raised in an emotionally frightening, male-dominated environment will sometimes seek comfort, in secret, by running to the softer, more loving and accepting female world through the act of feeling and wearing his mother's clothing—thereby temporarily escaping through fantasy into her relatively safe existence. "Symbolic confusion" fuels this aberrant pursuit—this flight from reality into erotic safety. It soon becomes an idolatrous pursuit and one that is compulsive and addictive.

Another example: a young boy who has to watch his mother get beaten regularly by his father will sometimes retreat into his mother's closet in order to avoid a similar beating. In that secret world, he may comfort himself by feeling his mother's clothing. She is the safe one and his father is the enemy. He doesn't want anything to do with being male because his primary male role model is repulsive and there is no one to draw him into healthy masculinity. He may then go on to associate female clothing with safety and eventually develop an erotic connection to it as he moves into puberty.

Former transvestite Rev. Jerry Leach offered six suggestions for ministry and intervention for the transvestite:

1. Lead them into realizing their new identity in Christ (Rom. 6-8).
2. Help them remain accountable to individuals in the church and through group therapy.
3. Train them in the biblical model for intimacy and transparency with the opposite sex.
4. Expose them to a variety of same-sex events.
5. Work with them on issues of forgiveness.
6. Teach them the scriptural mandates and processes for dying to self and becoming "alive unto Christ."

God Can Redeem Our Mistakes

Whether it be Pharaoh, or hypnosis or anything else, God can take the wrong choices that we make or the evil that someone has done to us and turn it to good. In Genesis 50:50, Joseph alluded to this phenomenon when he referred to the fact that God had used the evil of his brothers selling him into slavery for good—making him the second highest leader in all of Egypt.

A good outcome does not mean that what we or someone else has done is right—only that God *turned it* to good. Never judge according to outcome alone. Jesus said:

> *Stop judging by mere appearances, and make a right judgment.*
> (John 7:24)

Consequently, *we must distinguish between something that God has used for good and the goodness of what He has used.* We must be careful not to recommend that people turn to something for help simply because it has worked for others, but we must also recognize that God has given wisdom to nonbelievers. Biblical discernment is always critical.

The Person Who Doesn't Want To Be Helped

Your primary weapon here is "believing prayer"—regularly assaulting the throne of grace for their salvation and/or deliverance. Be aware, however, that although He will exert great influence in a loved one's life in response to your prayers, God will not interfere with that person's free will and force them to change. Many people will not change until they have hit rock bottom. Also, there are those who, even though saved, are finally taken home (to heaven) by God because of their unrepentant sin (see 1 Cor. 5:1-5).

Your other weapon against the deception that has captured the heart of the friend or loved one who doesn't want to be helped is the witness of your own life. If they can see a transformed person in you, if they can regularly hear personal testimonies of God's powerful work in your own life, and if they can experience His loving heart through your actions and attitudes toward them, then they just might be intrigued enough to approach Him and be set free.

Part Four:
Appendices

Appendix I
Recommended Reading List

❖❖ = books that simply *must* be read   ❖ = books that *should* be read

Communicating With God

❖❖ *Bridal Intercession* by Gary Wiens

❖❖ *Experiencing God* by Henry Blackaby and Claude King

❖❖ *Experiencing the Depths of Jesus Christ* by Mme. Jeanne Guyon

❖ *The Father Heart of God* by Floyd McClung, Jr.

❖ *Final Steps in Christian Maturity* by Mme. Jeanne Guyon

❖❖ *He Touched Me* by John Powell

❖❖ *Hearing God* by Peter Lord

❖❖ *Holiness, Truth and the Presence of God* by Francis Frangipane

❖❖ *Hungry for More of God* by Rob Currie

❖❖ *I Will Be Found by You* by Francis Frangipane

❖❖ *Into Abba's Arms* by Dr. Sandra Wilson

❖❖ *The Joy of Listening to God* by Joyce Huggett

❖ *The Knowledge of the Holy* by A.W. Tozer

❖❖ *Listening Prayer* by Leanne Payne

❖ *Transformed Into His Image* by David Kyle Foster

❖❖ *Passion for Jesus* by Mike Bickle

❖ *Practicing His Presence* by Brother Lawrence

❖ *The Cross of Christ* by Dr. John R.W. Stott

❖❖ *The Pursuit of God* by A.W. Tozer

Mental and Emotional Freedom

❖❖ *The Bondage Breaker* by Neil T. Anderson

❖ *Freedom from Addiction* by Neil T. Anderson

❖❖ *Free Indeed* by Tom Marshall

❖❖ *Freedom Tools* by Andy Reese

❖❖ *Grace Works* by Dudley Hall

❖ *Healing of Memories* by David A. Seamands

❖ *Healing for Damaged Emotions* by David A. Seamands

❖ *The Healing Presence* by Leanne Payne

❖ *Healing the Masculine Soul* by Gordon Dalbey

❖❖ *Healing Through Deliverance* by Peter Horrobin

❖❖ *Living in the Freedom of the Spirit* by Tom Marshall

❖❖ *Ministering Freedom to the Sexually Broken* by Doris Wagner

❖❖ *Redeeming the Feminie Soul* by Julie Roys

❖❖ *Spiritual Warfare* by Timothy Warner

❖❖ *Spiritual Warfare for Every Christian* by Dean Sherman

❖❖ *The Three Battlegrounds* by Francis Frangipane

APPENDIX I—RECOMMENDED READING LIST   489

Sexual Addiction

- ❖❖ *A Way of Escape* by Neil T. Anderson
- ❖❖ *An Affair of the Mind* by Laurie Hall
- ❖❖ *Breaking Free* by Russell Willingham
- ❖ *Don't Call it Love: Recovery from Sexual Addiction* by Patrick Carnes
- ❖❖ *False Intimacy* by Dr. Harry Schaumburg
- ❖❖ *Every Man's Battle* by Stephen Arterburn
- ❖❖ *Every Woman's Battle* by Shannon Ethridge
- ❖❖ *Experiencing the Father's Embrace* by Jack Frost
- ❖❖ *Finding Freedom in a Sex-Obsessed World* by Neil T. Anderson
- ❖❖ *Porn Nation* by Michael Leahy
- ❖❖ *Pure Desire* by Ted Roberts
- ❖❖ *Unwanted* by Jay Stringer
- ❖❖ *Winning the Battle Within* by Neil T. Anderson
- ❖❖ *Wired for Intimacy* by William Struthers

Sexual Child Abuse

- ❖ *Abuse in the Family* by Karen Mains
- ❖ *Child Sexual Abuse* by Maxine Hancock and Karen Mains
- ❖ *Challenging the Darkness: Child Sexual Abuse and the Church* by D. Mitchell Whitman
- ❖ *Door of Hope* by Jan Frank
- ❖ *Healing Victims of Sexual Abuse* by Paula Sandford

- ❖❖ *Helping Victims of Sexual Abuse* by Lynn Heitritter and Jeannette Vought
- ❖❖ *How to Rise Above Abuse* by June Hunt
- ❖❖ *Hush* by Nicole Bromley
- ❖❖ *On the Threshold of Hope* by Diane Langberg
- ❖❖ *Unclaimed Baggage* by Don and Jan Frank
- ❖❖ *When a Man You Love was Abused* by Cecil Murphey
- ❖❖ *When a Woman You Love was Abused* by Cecil Murphey
- ❖❖ *The Wounded Heart* by Dr. Dan B. Allender
- ❖ *Your Wife Was Sexually Abused* written by John Courtright and Dr. Sid Rogers

Sexual Identity Confusion Homosexuality and Bisexuality

- ❖❖ *A Queer Thing Happened to America* by Dr. Michael Brown
- ❖❖ *The Battle for Normality* by Gerard van den Aardweg
- ❖❖ *The Bible and Homosexual Practice* by Dr. Robert Gagnon
- ❖❖ *The Broken Image* by Leanne Payne
- ❖❖ *Crisis in Masculinity* by Leanne Payne
- ❖❖ *Desires in Conflict* by Joe Dallas
- ❖❖ *Love Hunger* by David Kyle Foster
- ❖❖ *Freedom Realized* by Stephen Black
- ❖❖ *Homosexuality and the Politics of Truth* by Dr. Jeffrey Satinover

- ❖ *Love Hunger* by David Kyle Foster
- ❖❖ *My Genes Made Me Do It* by Briar Whitehead
- ❖ *Out of Egypt* by Jeanette Howard
- ❖❖ *Pursuing Sexual Wholeness* by Andrew Comiskey
- ❖❖ *Restoring Sexual Identity* by Anne Paulk
- ❖❖ *Setting Love in Order* by Mario Bergner
- ❖ *Someone I Love is Gay* by Anita Worthen and Bob Davies
- ❖❖ *What Does the Bible Really Teach About Homosexuality?* by Kevin DeYoung
- ❖❖ *When Homosexuality Hits Home* by Joe Dallas

Sexuality in General

- ❖ *Eros Redeemed* by Dr. John White
- ❖❖ *Good News About Sex and Marriage* by Christopher West
- ❖❖ *Rethinking Sexuality* by Dr. Juli Slattery
- ❖❖ *Sex, Jesus and the Conversations the Church Forgot* by Mo Isom
- ❖❖ *The Truth About Sex* by Kay Arthur

Transgender Confusion

- ❖ *Gender, Lies and Suicide* by Walter Heyer
- ❖❖ *Transgender* by Vaughan Roberts
- ❖ *Transgender Confusion* by Denise Shick

Appendix II
A Brief Worship Guide

The Dennis Jernigan Collection–Volume 1
(HeartCry, 1995)

The Best Loved Worship and Praise Songs from the Vineyard
(Vineyard Music Group, 1994)
Volume 2 also available.

Vineyard Psalms
(Vineyard Ministries International, 1992)
Volume 2 and 3 also available.

Live Worship With Bob Fitts
(Maranatha Music, 1991)

Hosanna Music Classics
(Hosanna Music, 1994)

Vineyard Collection—Volume 1
(Frontline Music Group, 1988)
Volumes 2 and 3 also available.

The Highest Place with Bob Fitts
(Hosanna Music, 1991)

Appendix III
Resource Directory

The presence of a ministry or organization in this directory does *not* mean that "Mastering Life Ministries" recommends that organization for you. This directory is for informational purposes only. You should check out the organization for yourself before seeking counsel from them. All organizations are "professing Christian" ones.

Child Sexual Abuse

Elijah House
www.elijahhouse.org

Ellel Ministries International
www.ellel.org

Grace
www.netgrace.org

Hope For The Heart
www.hopefortheheart.org

Jenna Quinn
www.jennaquinn.org

Mending the Soul
www.mendingthesoul.org

One Voice
www.iamonevoice.org

The Place of Refuge
www.placeofrefuge.net

Restoring the Foundations
www.restoringthefoundations.org

Treasures Ministries
www.iamatreasure.com

Voice Today
angelakwilliams.com

Homosexuality

Core Issues Trust (England)
www.core-issues.org

Courage (Roman Catholic)
www.couragerc.net

Desert Stream Ministries
www.desertstream.org

Equipped to Love
www.equippedtolove.com

Exodus Global Alliance
www.exodusglobalalliance.org

First Stone Ministries
www.firststone.org

Genesis Counseling
www.genesiscounseling.org

His Wonderful Works
www.hiswonderfulworks.com

Hope for Wholeness
(A Network of Ministries to Homosexuals and Their Loved Ones)
www.hopeforwholeness.org

Living Hope Ministries
www.livehope.org

Overcomers Network
(A Network of Ministries to Homosexuals and Their Loved Ones)
www.overcomersnetwork.org

PFOX (Parents and Friends of Ex-Gays and Gays)
www.pfox.org

Restored Hope Network
(A Network of Ministries to Homosexuals and Their Loved Ones)
www.RestoredHopeNetwork.org

The Portland Fellowship
www.portlandfellowship.com

Voice of the Voiceless
www.voiceofthevoiceless.info

Porn/Sex Addiction

Be Broken Ministries
www.bebroken.com

Bethesda Workshops
www.bethesdaworkshops.org

Conquer Series
www.conquerseries.com

Covenant Eyes
www.covenanteyes.com

Free Indeed Ministries
www.freeindeedne.com

New Creation Ministries
www.ncmfresno.org

New Life Ministries
www.NewLife.com

Prodigals International
www.prodigalsonline.org

Pure Community Ministries
www.purecommunity.org

Pure Desire Ministries
www.puredesire.org

Pure Life Ministries
www.purelifeministries.org

Transgender

Help 4 Families
www.help4families.com

Sex Change Regret
www.sexchangeregret.com

About the Author

Dr. David Kyle Foster

Dr. David Kyle Foster (M-Div - Trinity Evangelical Divinity School; D-Min - Trinity School for Ministry) is also the author of ***Love Hunger: A Harrowing Journey from Sexual Addiction to True Fulfillment*** and ***Transformed Into His Image: Hidden Steps on the Journey to Christlikeness***.

He has served as adjunct professor at Asbury Theological Seminary, Bible Institute of Hawaii, Trinity School for Ministry, Logos Christian College and Graduate School, and Wagner Leadership Institute.

Dr. Foster founded Mastering Life Ministries (aka Pure Passion Media) in 1987 and produced and/or directed the award-winning "Pure Passion" TV program. He is also the producer and/or director of the award-winning documentaries, "Such Were Some of You", "How Do You Like Me Now?", "Tranzformed", and "Broken and Poured Out".

David loves hanging out with Jesus during the Autumn in a quiet mountain cabin and being in the company of people who can't stop talking about how much they love God.

www.ingramcontent.com/pod-product-compliance
Lightning Source LLC
Chambersburg PA
CBHW050424240426
43661CB00055B/2263